PROVIDING HEALTH CARE:
THE ECONOMICS OF
ALTERNATIVE SYSTEMS OF
FINANCE AND DELIVERY

Providing Health Care: the Economics of Alternative Systems of Finance and Delivery

Edited by

ALISTAIR McGUIRE, PAUL FENN,
and KEN MAYHEW

OXFORD UNIVERSITY PRESS

1991

Oxford University Press, Walton Street, Oxford OX2 6DP

Oxford New York Toronto
Delhi Bombay Calcutta Madras Karachi
Petaling Jaya Singapore Hong Kong Tokyo
Nairobi Dar es Salaam Cape Town
Melbourne Auckland
and associated companies in
Berlin Ibadan

Oxford is a trade mark of Oxford University Press

Published in the United States
by Oxford University Press, New York

British Library Cataloguing in Publication Data
Providing health care: the economics of alternative systems
of finance and delivery.—(OREP special issue).
1. Health services. Economic aspects
I. McGuire, Alistair II. Fenn, Paul III. Mayhew, Ken
IV. Series
338.473621
ISBN 0–19–828322–9

Library of Congress Cataloging-in-Publication Data
Providing health care: the economics of alternative systems of
finance and delivery/edited by Alistair McGuire, Paul Fenn, and
Ken Mayhew.
p.   cm.
Consists of papers based on a seminar held at Wolfson College.
Includes bibliographical references and index.
1. Medical care, Cost of—Great Britain.   2. Medical care, Cost
of—United States.   3. Medical care, Cost of—Europe, Western.
I. McGuire, Alistair.   II. Fenn, Paul.   III. Mayhew, Ken.
IV. Wolfson College (University of Oxford)
RA410.55.G7P76   1990   338.4'33621—dc20   90-23968
ISBN 0–19–828322–9

Typeset by Oxford Review of Economic Policy 1991
Printed in Great Britain by
Biddles Ltd,
Guildford and King's Lynn

Preface

This volume grew out of the Spring 1989 issue of the *Oxford Review of Economic Policy*. It benefited from the discussion arising from a one-day seminar on the reform of the UK National Health Service held at Wolfson College and we take this opportunity to thank the many participants for their comments on the papers presented, some of which, suitably amended, appear within these covers. Colleagues at the Centre for Socio-Legal Studies have also provided stimulating comment on various thoughts, ideas, and drafts.

Contents

Introduction

ALISTAIR McGUIRE, PAUL FENN, AND KEN MAYHEW

This volume is an attempt to assess the contribution of economic analysis to our understanding of the health care sector. It comes at a particularly appropriate time. A number of European countries, including the Netherlands, Spain, Sweden, and the UK, are reforming or considering reforming their health care sector with the aim of containing costs and, they hope, improving efficiency. Others, including the USA, are becoming increasingly concerned about the share of GDP devoted to health care.

Since its inception the British National Health Service (NHS) has been subject to critical scrutiny. Concern with rising costs prompted a governmental enquiry in the early 1950s, chaired by the Cambridge economist Guillebaud. Critics of the newly formed NHS had argued that the integrated structure of health care and the fact that consumption was free at the point of delivery was leading to demand-pull pressures on funding. However, the Committee found that although costs had been increasing rapidly in nominal terms, in real terms the cost rises were no higher than had been anticipated. Moreover, while the committee did not fully endorse the presumed benefits of the integrated structure of delivery, it certainly did not recommend radical changes to this structure.

The arguments found in the Guillebaud Committee's report have uncanny echoes in today's debate. First, there remains controversy over the cost of the NHS. The arguments are now more elaborate. It is recognized that there is room for disagreement over the importance of demographic and technical change as contributory factors to cost escalation, while changes in activity levels (essentially patient throughput) now provide an additional dimension to the debate. Secondly, the structure of the NHS has been increasingly drawn to the centre of the debate. In particular, focus has been on the administration and management of the system and the perceived lack of incentives to ensure value for money. Following a period of considerable restructuring during the 1970s and 1980s, when the health sector witnessed increased centralization in management and control of expenditure, the latest proposals introduce changes which, it is hoped, will increase competition for resources, thereby ensuring the delivery of low cost and high quality health care.

The fundamental problem has not changed—what is the appropriate level of health care expenditure for a country? There is of course no simple answer to this question. A major reason for this is that we have no unique and readily measurable definition of output. Health itself is multidimensional and difficult to compare across individuals, and in any case health care may be more concerned with respite from ill health than the delivery of improved health *per se*. Even if we could measure output adequately, we would still be faced with questions of what was the efficient level of health care to be delivered. Given that resources are scare this inevitably means that all demands on health care resources cannot be met. This raises further questions of who should and who should not receive health care. Such questions of equity are bound quickly to enter the arena.

If it is accepted that the delivery of health care cannot be left to market provision—and such an assumption is itself contended by some—then the choice of institution to provide it also becomes important. If health care were similar to the majority of commodities, individuals would simply purchase, on the market, the amount they required as and when their demands became apparent. However, health care has certain characteristics which makes such a simple interaction of supply and demand inadequate analytically and operationally. The uncertainty of the timing and level of consumption leads to the demand for insurance and consequently a third party enters the analysis. This means that we have to choose between private or public health care insurance, as well as between private or public health care provision.

Even the present UK reforms, which advocate increased competition as a means of providing more cost-effective health care, appear to endorse the benefits of public health insurance. Indeed some argue that it is because the UK has integrated public insurance with provision that its expenditure on health care has been contained. But one consequence of this system has been that little information on resource flows has been gathered—another criticism raised by the Guillebaud Committee—since there is no billing. It ought also to be recognized that public insurers have their own objectives which need not match the objectives of providers or consumers. Public insurance normally embodies some aspect of redistribution and this will inevitably be one determinant of health care expenditure. Moreover the involvement of public insurers will influence the incentives faced by the other agents in the health care sector.

In the UK, for example, competition will be constrained in at least two ways. First, overall expenditure, in that it remains largely in the public sector, will be dictated by the public finance objectives of the government. The reforms, while a reaction to under-funding, may not be a solution to this perceived problem. Secondly, competition relies on the existence of appropriate incentives, which it is hoped that the reformed structure of the NHS will provide, and on appropriate information. The extent of competition is in fact a function of the information generated by the system. In a perfect market, prices act as costless transmitters of information on marginal values. In a system of third-party, public insurers such information may not emerge. In other words, given the institutional constraints within which competition must operate it is not necessarily the case that efficiency will prevail.

Thus the choice of institutional delivery of either insurance or provision will have both costs and benefits attached. Which form of health care system is chosen will be dependent on these costs and benefits and the objectives to be met. Both the means and the ends will determine the level of expenditure ultimately achieved.

This volume attempts to provide an analytical perspective within which the choice of the means, if not the objective, can be evaluated. The first chapter, by McGuire, Fenn, and Mayhew, discusses the various institutional means of providing health insurance and health care in the context of efficiency and equity. This sets a framework within which the current reforms of the NHS may be judged.

The other chapters in this book explore a wide range of the themes raised above. Besley discusses health insurance, contrasting, for example, re-imbursement in kind (as in the NHS system) with insurance payments based on expenditure. The latter, it is argued, carries the inherent danger of leading to over-spending, and Besley asks how this might be minimized. Culyer considers output measures within what he terms an extra-welfarist approach to health economics. This takes into account wider considerations than the narrower welfarist tradition founded purely on 'willingness to pay'. He argues that the nature of the output, which he defines as health, is so fundamental to our enjoyment and pursuit of other activities that it is only within such a wider context that the policy concerns raised above may be evaluated—even though the difficulties then raised are considerable. Drummond also analyses the measurement of output in the health care sector, arguing for refined QALY (quality-adjusted life-year) measures rather than other cruder measures of both output and throughput. Mooney and Olsen take this issue further forward by arguing that QALYs have attempted to be all-encompassing. Their focus however should be limited to extending output measures by quality weights. They argue that QALYs cannot take account of other arguments in utility functions—such as those concerned with altruism—let alone be used to dictate policy, as they are merely concerned with efficiency and do not impart knowledge about equity.

Four further articles discuss the conceptual and practical problems arising from international comparisons of health care systems. Parkin discusses the empirical and theoretical problems involved in making consistent comparisons of input, throughput, and output. Wagstaff et al. are concerned with how to compare equity across countries both in the delivery and financing of health care, concentrating in particular on the USA, the UK, the Netherlands, and Italy. Quam evaluates the US experience with one particular · institutional phenomenon—the health maintenance organization (HMO). Scheffler and Nauenberg continue the American focus by questioning whether or not the UK can learn anything from the increased competition witnessed in the US amongst health care providers.

Finally, Gray gives an account of the UK's health service before the Second World War and contrasts the present NHS and the proposed reforms with this historical record.

The papers in this volume do not give any answer to the question, 'What is the correct level of health care expenditure?'. Indeed there is no simple answer. However, the papers explain why this is so, and warn against believing that institutional reforms are an easy panacea.

The Economics of Health Care

ALISTAIR McGUIRE,* PAUL FENN,** AND KEN MAYHEW***

1. Introduction

(a) *Background*

In some countries there is concern about excess spending on medical services, whilst in others under-funding is a major political issue. Certainly the proportion of GDP devoted to health care varies significantly from nation to nation, as do the institutional arrangements for its provision both with regard to who delivers it and to whether the consumer pays according to use or indirectly through taxation. At one extreme it is delivered by the public sector and financed as part of general taxation. At the other, it is privately delivered and charged for much like any other good and service. In between there are a variety of systems, both of delivery and financing.

From the British viewpoint this diversity highlights a number of policy considerations. Most important is the debate about the relative roles of the public and private sectors. Should there be a move in the UK to private insurance, or indeed to the private provision of health care itself ? At a more specific level, concern has been expressed about the appropriate reward structures for doctors, nurses, and other staff; the efficiency of insurance markets; strategies for cost containment; the reasons for the observed variations in medical practice; and the 'internalization' of markets—the creation of competing internal units within the NHS.

An analysis of the economics underlying these issues is particularly pertinent at a time when there is such intense debate about the UK's existing health care system. General practitioners are under scrutiny with regard to performance audit and payment. The nursing profession is being subjected to restructuring

  * Centre for Socio-Legal Studies and Pembroke College, Oxford.
 ** Centre for Socio-Legal Studies and Wolfson College, Oxford.
*** Pembroke College, Oxford, and National Economic Development Office.
The views expressed in this chapter are the personal views of the authors and are not to be attributed to the organizations to which they belong.

after years of disquiet about recruitment, retention, and relative pay. Those aspects of the NHS which have historically been charged for, dental and optical care and prescriptions, have seen substantial increases in charges. The hospital sector has been the object of performance review in an attempt to increase efficiency. The Social Services Committee has reported on the future of the NHS, and the Government's reforms of the NHS are currently being discussed extensively. It is generally anticipated that some form of increased competition in the delivery of health care will be encouraged. Most of the debate has focused relatively narrowly on issues of financing and delivery. As yet there has been little discussion of the impact that different institutional structures have on the health of populations—perhaps not surprisingly given the difficulties in measuring the latter.

(b) *Health, Health Care, and Health Insurance*

It is important to begin with a clear idea of the relationships between the various commodities provided within the health sector. First let us note that people's preferences are fundamentally defined over the state of health itself; GP visits and hospital treatment are valued purely as a means to secure improvements to that end. The demand for health *per se* can be divided into the demand for health as a consumption good, from which utility is derived directly as well as through the enhancement of consumption of other activities, and the demand for health as an investment good, which increases the time available for market activity and improves productivity with consequent benefits in terms of potential earnings. However, given that we cannot buy or sell health in the market-place (it is non-marketable) and given that health care inputs must be allocated between individuals, a case can be made for focusing on the demand for health care as a derived demand (Grossman, 1972b). It is because of such separability that focus can be placed on the provision of health care as distinct from the provision of the wider class of social services and other commodities that contribute to 'good health'. Moreover, because both health status and the derived call on medical inputs are subject to considerable uncertainty, there are associated demands for insurance policies against the consequences of ill health. Insurance contracts exist which pay out benefits in relation to the severity of disability, the extent of wage loss, and the costs of care.

In this introductory chapter, we discuss the difficulties that both private markets and state organizations have in coping with health care provision and insurance, in terms of both efficiency and equity. We then consider the policy implications of our analysis, especially in the light of current debates. Section 2 analyses the extent of market failure in provision, whilst section 3 covers issues of market failure in insurance. Section 4 introduces the major conceptual issues arising from equity considerations. Following these discussions of market failure, section 5 is concerned with the institutional responses to such failure. Section 6 considers the role of equity objectives and section 7 then outlines the problems of measuring performance in the health care sector. Section 8 draws on this analysis to assess the proposed reforms of the National Health Service.

2. Market Failure in the Health Care Sector

The issue of the most appropriate institutional form for the delivery of health care embraces both efficiency and social justice criteria (Barr,1987). In instrumental terms, it is usual for economists to evaluate policy at the microeconomic level by reference to a particular idealized model for the allocation and distribution of goods and services. This model—the perfectly competitive market—is only one amongst several structural means by which an optimal allocation of resources may be obtained, but it serves as a useful reference point against which alternatives can be measured (Helm,1986).

In spelling out the conditions under which the idealized market system will achieve a just and efficient outcome, the economist is laying down a framework for assessing alternative institutional forms. Such institutional responses to market failure may themselves fail so that the policy-maker's problem becomes one of choosing between a number of second-best options. What are the conditions which must be met for the market to succeed? Clearly it may fail simply because there are insufficient numbers of buyers or sellers (for example, because of barriers to entry) for a competitive market to exist. However, even where all the participants are 'price-takers', there may still be obstacles preventing the achievement of allocative efficiency. These obstacles may be placed into three broad categories:

(1)   *Property rights may not be clearly defined or legally enforced.* In this case market participants find it difficult to trade. This can be a particular problem where external effects in production or consumption exist and cannot be traded away.

(2)   *Individuals may not have full information about the nature of those property rights which are defined and legally enforced.* If this is the case, the trading may take place at 'incorrect' prices.

(3)   *There may not exist a unique, market-clearing price for each commodity over which property rights are defined and legally enforced.*[1] This may occur as a result of irregularities in demand and supply relationships. If, for example, consumer preferences or production technologies are de-

---

[1] Such irregularities may take the form of discontinuities or non-convexities in utility or production functions.

fined such that 'more' always means 'better', then a competitive equilibrium will not be sustainable.

Each of these obstacles may be present, singly or together, in relation to any particular commodity. Defence, for example, or law and order—so called 'public goods'—are typically characterized by all three problems, which is why they are almost never provided by the market. Health care is similarly confronted by serious problems of this kind, and the following sections describe their importance.

(a) *Informational Asymmetry*

It is a basic tenet of normative economic analysis that the consumer is the best judge of his own welfare.[2] It is not obviously true, however, that the consumer is the best judge of the appropriate means of achieving it. In the context of health care, the derived nature of the consumer's demand implies that he must obtain information about the production relationships which govern the effectiveness of all available treatments. In addition, information relating to the likely future effect on well-being of failing to intervene with medical treatment now is essential given the diversity of disease pathologies (Weisbrod,1978). It is widely acknowledged that consumers lack information about the timing of consumption needs, about the level and form of treatment required, and about its effectiveness. The fact that the consumer does not readily possess all this information does not in itself necessarily lead to market failure, provided that its efficient acquisition is possible. However the complexity of the technical data, the multiplicity of choices, and the distressed state of mind of many who discover that they are ill, result in the consumer relying on the supplier for the provision of information. Such reliance relates to both the definition of the potential choices available and the utility gains associated with the treatment.

These informational asymmetries are a fundamental source of market failure: as Evans (1981) points out, they 'leave open the possibility (or certainty) of severe exploitation of buyers by sellers in an arms-length, *caveat emptor* market environment'. Thus even if it were possible to trade such information on the open market the fundamental asymmetry would remain, giving the medical profession a secure monopoly position. As a contractual response to this, an agency relationship may be formed between the producer and consumer (the doctor and the patient). That is, the consumer/patient relies on an agent to act on his behalf to accumulate information and be willing to make choices with regard to

---

[2] There are however circumstances where this basic assumption may fail. The concept of merit goods, for example, is difficult to reconcile with the axioms of rationality and consumer sovereignty in welfare economics. One defence of the notion is that there are areas of choice in which preference failure occurs and therefore the state must intervene in the decision-making process. Compulsory health care insurance provides an example.

consumption. The degree of a consumer's reliance on an agent will depend on both the uncertainty and the complexity surrounding the decisions to be taken. In this respect it is worth emphasizing the heterogeneous nature of health care. As the uncertainty and complexity increase, the cost of gaining information also increases. Moreover the potentially high anxiety costs to the patient associated with the decision-making process itself, including those of making wrong decisions, lead to a heavy reliance on the agent. Indeed such costs may become so high that the consumer is willing to default completely on the decision-making process. In any case the consumer may give up some sovereignty over choice, or as Evans and Wolfson (1980) state, property rights in the consumer's utility function will not be as well-defined (with respect to the consumer and the producer) as market efficiency requirements dictate. The allocation of property rights does not lead to problems of common ownership, but rather the specification of preferences and, consequently, demand are no longer clearly in the domain of choice over which the consumer has fundamental control.

(b) *Complexity and Uncertainty*

Information failings are not confined to the consumer. Health care is difficult to store. It is also poorly substitutable across broad categories of consumer since it is an intermediate commodity relating to the production of health status: different patients require different treatments. Production therefore varies across diagnostic categories and even across individuals with common diagnostic characteristics. As Harris (1977) remarks, as the complexity of treatment increases the commodity becomes increasingly customized. This has a fundamental impact on the delivery of health care.

Because every case is potentially different from every other and may also develop in a different way from previous cases, there are problems with exchange. The supply of health care represents 'a complicated sequence of adaptive responses in the face of uncertainty' (Harris, 1977). The intermediate nature of health care means that production must be organized in such a manner that what is produced (diagnosis, information, and treatment) is quickly responsive to changed requirements.

The market is unable to cope efficiently with these problems. Pure market solutions would rely wholly on re-contracting as a means of alleviating uncertainty. However, even assuming that the consumer/patient is physically able to renegotiate the contractual agreement with the supplier (i.e. the doctor), information on the effectiveness of health care and the expected outcome (i.e. prognosis) remains difficult for the patient to obtain. In other words, the acquisition of such information is not costless for the patient and therefore re-contracting will not lead to an efficient solution. Furthermore these contractual difficulties are exacerbated by the transaction problems associated with small numbers exchange. These mean that considerable resources are liable to be expended in attempting to agree on a market clearing price, the problem being that competitive pressures simply are not operative (Arrow,1969).

The agency relationship between the producer/doctor and the consumer/patient may be viewed as an example of vertical integration which attempts to internalize the transaction costs associated with the decision-making process and the associated implicit contractual agreements (Evans, 1981). Vertical integration is, of course, also important to ensure ready access to the appropriate type of care. The intermediate nature of health care and the heterogeneity of treatment mean that consumers must have ready access to all levels of production. Moreover, as an intermediate commodity, any particular aspect of it should be viewed as complementary to other inputs in the production of health and seen as part of a flow process rather than one in which separate component production exists. In other words the consumption/production process exhibits a considerable degree of technological interdependency. Thus economies of integration are important to this sector.

Not only is depth of production important, scale considerations are also fundamental. Given the uncertainty surrounding treatment requirements, with regard to both timing and form, it is necessary to hold reserve 'excess' capacity at any point in time if production is to be readily responsive to demands. However, since it is difficult to define the efficient level of such capacity it is difficult to define the efficient scale of production.

(c) Indivisibilities and Externalities

Inefficiencies associated with increasing returns also play some role. As medical care becomes more and more complex there will be an increasing need for specialist advice and possibly specialist medical equipment, but such aspects of production are subject to indivisibilities and therefore increasing returns and consequently non-market clearing. Thus the importance of the depth of production in guaranteeing access to treatment, of scale of production in guaranteeing the use of production resources as and when necessary, and of the indivisibilities and increasing costs of some forms of health care, all combine to increase the probability of monopoly supply emerging. However, it would be wrong to devote too much attention to indivisibilities in health care as monopoly supply is problematic only in the case of highly specialized technology.

While property rights are not well assigned between the consumer and the producer, as witnessed in the agency relationship, neither are they well defined across different consumption patterns. This occurs because, as noted above, individuals appear to care about other people's health. If such 'caring externalities' do exist then there appears to be a philanthropic case for at least some charitable (i.e. public in the widest sense) provision of health care. Individuals care about the health status of others and will therefore seek to provide care for them as an altruistic act. It may be argued that such interpersonal utility considerations could be satisfied through the payment of income subsidies—essentially increasing ability to pay via income maintenance. However, this neglects the fact that the subsidized individual could spend the subsidy on other goods (or even inefficiently with regards to health care) and still require treatment to be provided at a later date. For this reason, it is potentially more efficient to provide the health care directly.

The familiar free-rider problems also occur in the provision of charity. Namely certain individuals, while experiencing the externalities associated with other people's health status, will rely on others to provide the appropriate resources. This will of course lead to an underprovision of charity.

Other arguments for the philanthropic provision of health care have stressed the importance of 'specific egalitarianism' (Tobin, 1970). Lindsay (1969), for example, argues that an egalitarian argument enters into the individual utility function with the result that philanthropic concerns are seen to affect behaviour directly. However, not only is this open to the free-rider concerns outlined above, but neither is it explained why this egalitarian concern does not apply to other commodities.

3. Market Failure in Health Care Insurance

The lack of information over the form, amount, and cost of their future health care requirements leads to a further derived demand arising from the individual's primary demand for good health—the demand for insurance. Arrow's (1963) pioneering article remains the most influential analysis. The basic welfare arguments for insurance are elucidated, and these are contrasted with the clear failure of the market to offer individuals insurance against many illnesses. The reasons for this failure are principally concerned with informational requirements faced by insurance providers, and Arrow suggests that a wide range of public and private institutional provisions in the health care sector can be seen as responses to this failure, substituting for the missing competitive market. The advantages of Arrow's analysis of the insurance decision is that it shows how a legally enforceable claim against an insurance company is just another commodity, which has been bought in the market-place and which is therefore subject to the standard results of neoclassical price theory as discussed in detail in Besley's chapter. We have seen above that these results imply, *inter alia*, that the efficient allocation of commodities in the free market-place requires well-defined property rights (no externalities), well-informed consumers and producers, and well-behaved demand and supply functions. These conditions are not satisfied.

(a) *High-Risk Groups*.

For insurance to be appropriate the probability of the occurrence of the insurable event must be less than one—i.e. the event must not be a certainty. Just as it would not be possible to insure your house if you knew it would certainly be burgled or set on fire, so it is not possible to gain insurance coverage if you are certain to demand health care. The only way insurers could make a profit in such a situation would be to relate premiums to the cost of care itself rather than to the risk of needing it. Then, of course, it would not be worthwhile insuring. This immediately raises problems for those people with chronic illnesses or congenital problems and for the older segments of society. Ali such groups have a very high probability of requiring treatment (a probability close to or equal to one). Note also that these groups represent a substantial proportion of the users of medical services.

(b) *Interdependent Risks*

A primary requirement for efficient insurance is that the risks to be covered are independent. If insurance is appropriate it obviously requires independence in order to cover losses; the losers are compensated by the pooling of risks and these risks must be independent. Thus an obvious insurance failure occurs in the coverage of contagious diseases. This is really an externality problem where the risk associated with one individual's use of health care is dependent on others' risks.

(c) *Adverse Selection*

A further related problem is adverse selection. This arises when there is an asymmetry of information between the parties involved in the insurance contract. Insurance requires the maximum possible discrimination of risks for the attainment of full welfare benefit. However, individuals may have more information on their expected health status than the seller of insurance. Those who recognize that they face a high level of risk may deceive the insurance company and reap a financial reward in a lower than actuarially fair premium. This of course imposes costs on the insurance company and, if it can, it transmits these on to other individuals seeking insurance.

   In other words, the problem stems from the fact that the aggregate benefits of insurance are dependent on the ability to discriminate among different classes of risk, the result being that those groups who face a higher risk of illness should, *ceteris paribus*, pay higher premiums. However, given the insurer's uncertainty over which individuals are in which risk categories, there is a tendency towards equalized premiums. In which case wealth is redistributed *ex ante* from low-risk to high-risk individuals, with the associated costs passed on to the consumer in the form of higher than actuarially fair premiums for low-risk cover. This may lead to further welfare losses in the form of gaps in coverage if loading on low-risk individuals becomes, to their mind, unacceptably high (Arrow, op. cit.).

Thus adverse selection results in high-risk individuals paying a subsidized premium, the subsidy being paid by the rest of the covered population. Consequently low-risk individuals may opt out, thereby diminishing the insurance pool. In the extreme this could render the market unprofitable. This is likely to be a significant problem in the health care sector. Akerlof (1970) points out that, as the price of insurance (the premium) rises, individuals who insure will be those who are increasingly certain that they will require insurance and are liable to have a better assessment of the risks faced than the insurance company. The result is that the average health status of individuals seeking insurance falls as the price rises. This will lead to gaps in coverage as insurers try to identify (which is in itself costly) and ultimately exclude high-risk individuals from coverage.

One common means of circumventing such problems is to relate insurance to non-health characteristics. For example, insurance may be sold to private companies who pass it on as a benefit to employees; coverage is thus linked to employment. Thus the risks to the insurer associated with adverse selection are minimized. However, this solution is not efficient: the premiums do not normally reflect health risks.[3]

(d) *Increasing Returns*

Another source of market failure relates to the fact that the operating costs of an insurance company may exhibit increasing returns to scale. Obviously as insurance involves the spreading of risks there are inherent characteristics which lend themselves to economies of scale—especially where discrimination between risk categories is difficult. Such economies of scale may be large enough for monopoly provision of health care insurance to develop. If monopoly power becomes excessive, premiums may be pushed to higher than actuarially fair ones.

One of the reasons for such increasing returns to scale is the existence of high transaction costs associated with the costs of processing applications for insurance and claims for payment and of maintaining records. The transaction cost per client will diminish as the number of insured increases and monopoly insurance provision will tend to minimize these costs. From this point of view, monopoly provision may be efficient.

---

[3] Neither does it overcome the problem of moral hazard, discussed below, except to the extent that the working population tends to be healthier than the non-working population, and also that they have an incentive (i.e. in the form of a return to work and income) towards quick recovery.

(e) *Moral Hazard*

A further source of failure is associated with moral hazard, which occurs when individuals have little incentive to restrict their consumption levels to those that would prevail if they faced the full cost of their consumption. If health care insurance covers all costs, health care is effectively a 'free' good at the point of consumption, and cost (or price) becomes an ineffective constraint.

There are, then, fundamental failures in the private provision of health care which result in individuals being unable to convert desired demands into effective demands. The degree of such failure is reflected in the evidence cited by Pauly (1986), reporting over 11 per cent of the US population to be without any health care insurance cover. Note that this figure does not include those simply with inadequate cover. While a partial explanation might relate to tax distortions (see Pauly, op. cit.), the major one is market failure. Because of this, substantial regulation is called for. Yet such regulation cannot completely overcome the inherent difficulties involved in insurance; i.e. exclusion from the market of the chronically ill, adverse selection, and moral hazard.

4. Equity Considerations

Markets evidently may fail to secure an efficient allocation of health care and health care insurance. Even if this were not the case, concern might still be expressed about the distributional outcome achieved by market solutions. If these equity concerns are manifested in individual utility functions, they leave open the prospect of voluntary exchange to achieve Pareto-improvements (Hochman and Rogers, 1969). To the extent that the resulting redistribution of health care between individuals is non-coercive, then the efficiency and equity goals are consistent.

But equity concerns are typically held to be wider than this. At some societal level, there may be a perception that the distribution of health care which results after voluntary transfer in cash or kind remains unsatisfactory. The expression of such societal concern is referred to as a social welfare function. Providing that such a function can be defined, then it is possible to shift the distribution of outcomes to a more or less egalitarian level, by means of redistribution through institutional responses such as the tax/transfer mechanism. However, because these mechanisms tend to distort relative prices, they carry with them some loss in efficiency: the goals are no longer consistent.

In the context of health care or health care insurance, such equity considerations tend to take the form of merit good arguments. These suggest that certain minimum levels of consumption are desirable from society's point of view, and consequently individuals should be coerced into complying with these in their own best (but unrecognized) interest as perceived by others. Presumably such societal values can be transmitted to those who take policy decisions through the voting mechanism (Mueller, 1979).

An alternative class of equity concerns relies on deontological arguments concerning duties and absolute rights. It is argued that there are certain rights which are fundamental and non-tradeable (inalienable in the terminology of Calabresi and Melamed, 1972). Clearly this is inconsistent with the social welfare philosophy which, while designating health as a 'special' kind of good, nevertheless incorporates it within society's aggregate welfare function in such a way that improvements in specific health-related egalitarianism can be traded against improvements in other goods (Lindsay, 1969; Tobin, 1970; Wietzman, 1977). Such approaches have been labelled as 'welfarist' (Sen, 1979; Dasgupta, 1986).

Culyer's contribution to this volume contrasts this welfarist approach with what he terms 'extra-welfarist' approaches. Here health is seen as fundamental commodity, indistinguishable from utility itself, and as such the impact of health care on it has to take account of this characteristic. There is currently considerable debate about such alternative normative stances. Dasgupta (1986), for example, has introduced the concept of positive rights goods and has made the point that it is perfectly feasible for such goods (in contrast to public goods) to be provided within a market system. However the market mechanism

can never be guaranteed to distribute [resources] in a way which ensures the protection of positive freedom for all members of society. An efficient allocation is consistent with a fraction of the population disenfranchised from economic activities and left cold and hungry and diseased. And the competitive market mechanism—even when fully functioning—can under a large class of circumstances be guaranteed to bring about precisely that. (Dasgupta, 1986, p. 29)

The most explicitly duty-based analysis of health is the extension of Titmuss's work on voluntary blood donations in defence of the NHS as a social institution (Titmuss, 1970). This is based on what Collard (1978) has termed the contagion thesis—i.e. altruism in one individual is a positive function of the amount of altruism around him—and a Kantian moral imperative. In this light Titmuss characterizes the establishment of the NHS as 'the most unsordid act of British social policy in the twentieth century [which] has allowed and encouraged sentiments of altruism, reciprocity and social duty to express themselves' (1970). Titmuss thus saw the NHS as promoting not just health (or health care provision) but also altruism.

There is of course a sense in which duty and responsibility are a means of opting out of choices. Indeed, Collard (1978) has argued that Kantian behaviour is only one element in the utility function and that it can be tradeable in the sense that as the costs of expressing altruism increase, the sense of duty may be reduced. In this context the value of an institution such as the NHS lies not so much in its conformity with an absolutist moral standard but in the worth of the institution as a means of facilitating altruism in order to maximize social welfare. This is a rather corrupted form of moral imperative—although it may provide a rationale for government intervention in the area of social insurance as a means of promoting duty by making it costly to opt out (free ride). Further, this normative justification does not appear to be supported by the pursuit of access to care which has long remained, at least in principle, the foundation of policy.

5. Responses to Market Failure

(a) *Health Care Provision*

The inherent informational asymmetries in the provision of health care, and the agency relationships which arise in response, blur the distinction between demand and supply. As Arrow (1963) pointed out, the recognition of the existence of fundamental informational asymmetries by both parties colours the relationship between the producer and the consumer. The consumer is well aware of the possibility of the exploitation of the monopoly power that accompanies the informational asymmetries which relate not only to production technologies, but also to the utility consequences associated with consumption. Therefore it is necessary to maintain an environment which supports the agency relationship if complete failure in resource allocation is to be avoided. A competitive environment where suppliers pursue profit maximization is unlikely to serve this function. Although individual doctors may choose to invest in reputational capital in order to signal quality, the consumer is not necessarily capable of acting upon this additional information. The response has been the development of self-regulated standards of professional conduct by the medical profession (Dingwall and Fenn, 1987).

In other words, to secure the agency relationship the medical profession has recognized that certain expectations are imposed on their behaviour. The response is self-regulation of entry to the profession and the imposition of ethical standards of behaviour after entry. The first response does of course mean that the net return to be gained by the medical profession is higher than would prevail under competitive conditions. Entry barriers restrict supply and therefore increase the price of health care. It should be noted that these barriers are also supplemented by heavy subsidization of training costs, which may be defended in so far as they attract highly qualified individuals into the profession. Both forces are thus presumed to maintain product quality and, given the lack of information about product characteristics available at low cost to the consumer, are seen to be fundamental forms of regulation.

One obvious danger is that such barriers restrict the emergence of substitutes, for example less medically qualified staff providing particular services. If there is a large variance around product quality characteristics, competitive pressures usually ensure that a range of quality is available at appropriate prices, to match individual preferences. Socially subsidized entry barriers have curtailed the availability of alternatives. This may mean that the medical profession is easily able to appropriate monopoly rent.

This therefore places an even greater emphasis on the importance of ethical behaviour. The primary importance of ethical behaviour is that it replaces demand as a constraint on supply. It is an internalized check on suppliers. Normally consumers can acquire information at low cost on product quality and will also have an indication of the expected utility to be gained from consumption. Such information formulates individual demands, and supply responds, via price signals, to these demands. With health care the individual is unable to formulate demands on both counts. Moreover, not only are there prohibitive costs in gaining such information but the consumer may also wish to default on the decision-making process completely. As we saw, this is why the consumer willingly engages an agent. *Ex ante* because of his lack of information the consumer cannot evaluate the performance of his agent or verify the expected utility content of consumption. Medically ethical conduct, as regulated by the profession, serves to sustain the agency relationship providing reassurance that the supplier (doctor) is acting in the consumer's (patient's) best interest.

Note that ethical conduct is defined with regards to medical rather than economic objectives. Indeed these professional codes serve to affirm to the consumer (patient) that there is a separation of medical from economic considerations; one characteristic that underlies the agency relationship. In turn this separation is enhanced by the peculiar pricing practices pursued by the medical profession. Price discrimination by income is common in private heath care systems, bounded at the extreme by charity. But in all systems there has historically been a marked tendency away from pre-payment schemes with domination by fee-for-service or salary. Harris (1977) explicitly states that in the US health care sector one function of the fee-for-service payments is to seal the ethical bond between doctor and patient. At first glance this may seem somewhat odd, but given the structure of the sector where the doctor is hired directly by the patient, it does make sense.[4] The separation of doctors' fees from those of the hospital is a means of keeping the doctor apart from the full consequences of the resource allocation implications of specifying treatment. Under a salaried regime the doctor is of course ostensibly much more directly under the scrutiny

---

[4] The contractual arrangements in the USA between doctors and patients is witnessing substantial change as a consequence of the introduction of new institutional forms of provision (e.g. HMOs). It remains far from clear how such changes will affect the ethical relationship between these parties.

of the employer—e.g. the hospital or regional health board. If the clinician was using too much of the revenue budget the employer could attempt to clamp down. However it is here that the rights to self-regulation enjoyed by the medical profession are so important. In effect the employer has foregone his rights to dictate conduct to a group of employees. Once again there is a blurring of property rights in the sector with the result that self-regulation, most notably in the guise of the defence of clinical freedom, is seen to be supportive of the agency relationship.

The consequence is that medical conduct, which dictates the nature of the health care production process, has little concern with the resource cost implications of that process. Thus the agency relationship between the doctor and the patient, which is a direct response to informational failings, may lead to a disparity between private and social cost. Medical objectives, pursued in an environment of entry restrictions to the profession and a high level of importance attached to professional conduct, are most unlikely to coincide with technical and allocative efficiency. This is not to say that the agency relationship is not an efficiency response to market failure, but rather to note that such responses are liable to have their own accompanying inefficiencies.

(b) *Health Care Insurance*

A number of institutional and regulatory responses have evolved with regard to the market failures associated with health care insurance. Arguments for its public provision relate largely to issues of exclusion and adverse selection—i.e. the fact that at prevailing premiums individuals who have a desired demand for insurance cannot transmute that demand into an effective demand. Even private provision of health care insurance is subject to considerable regulation arising from problems associated with moral hazard.

Moral hazard, as we have seen, may occur when insured individuals have little incentive to restrict their consumption levels to those that would prevail if they faced the full cost of consumption. It also restricts the incentive to shop around. Thus the expected loss to be insured against is increased. It may be argued that the relationship between the doctor and the patient limits the extent of moral hazard, in that the professional conduct of the doctor means that he acts, to some degree, as an agent for the insurer. However if the doctor is acting as a true agent of the patient—providing information and treatment demanded by the patient—the potential for moral hazard remains. Alternatively, if the doctor is less than a perfect agent and exploits his monopoly position then moral hazard remains, although stemming from the supplier's modified behaviour.[5] To the extent that moral hazard exists, a minimal form of regulation is cost-sharing which attempts

---

[5] The literature refers to the realization of such monopoly potential as supplier-induced demand. Supplier-induced demand arises from both consumers lacking information over choice and the existence of conditions which allow for moral hazard.

to limit overconsumption by shifting some of the costs incurred at the point of consumption back to the individual.[6] This is, of course, only a partial remedy in that, given the high cost of a significant amount of health care, this may again lead to problems of exclusion.

There are three main types of cost-sharing schemes: a 'deductible', which is a fixed amount to be paid by the insured individual before any insurance benefit occurs; a 'co-payment' which is a fixed amount paid by both parties of the insurance contract; and 'co-insurance' which is a payment of a set proportion of the cost of each service. All represent significant amendments to the price of insurance cover and indeed the empirical evidence confirms that utilization is affected by these amendments. It is however difficult to define precisely the price of health care *per se*. The insurance premium paid by the individual is a common proxy used in empirical analysis but this of course relates to insurance not health care itself. It is difficult, therefore, to distinguish price effects associated with the latter as opposed to the distortions introduced by insurance coverage, third-party payment, and related tax distortions. None the less the consensus is that price rationing does reduce consumption. Manning *et al.* (1987) report results from the extensive RAND Health Insurance Experiment[7] which clearly show that health care utilization is affected by out-of-pocket expenses. They argue that price elasticities are in the range of –0.1 and –0.2. What is less clear is how this response is formulated. One interpretation would rely on the consumer ultimately being sovereign over choice—after being informed by his agent, he defines his preference schedule and matches this to his budget constraint as defined by his insurance cover. But a fuller recognition of the supplier's role in defining consumption, and the consequent possibility of moral hazard arising from his behaviour, raises issues of regulating such behaviour. In other words, attempts to regulate the health care insurance sector may not be easily divorced from issues of regulating the health care sector itself once the importance of provider behaviour is recognized.

Even so there are arguments for the specific regulation of the insurance market. At the very least minimal intervention is justified if adverse selection occurs, in order to ensure the extension of coverage to those high-risk individuals who have an effective demand, as well as ensuring that premiums reflect the risks involved. Even here high-risk individuals may not be able to afford the actuarially fair premiums. This provides a justifiable argument, if interpersonal utility considerations and other externality arguments are accepted, for the public provision of insurance (Pauly, 1970; Culyer, 1971a; Lindsay, 1969). If

[6] See Van de Ven (1983) for a discussion of alternative cost-sharing mechanisms.

[7] This experiment ran from 1974 to 1982 with the participation of 2,005 families in six population centres across the USA. Families were randomly assigned to 14 experimental insurance plans. These plans can be grouped into four categories, one providing free care and the other three requiring different forms of cost-sharing. Some sections of the population were excluded, such as those over the age of 61 and those on supplementary security income.

individuals feel that inability to pay for health care insurance should not be a criterion for exclusion, then this leads to an acceptance of its public provision, at least for certain low-income and/or high-risk groups. However, a direct income subsidy would not necessarily be efficient since the subsidy could be spent inefficiently or on non-health-enhancing goods.

(c) *Integrating Provision and Insurance*

A more radical form of regulation is to integrate insurance and provision, primarily as a means of overcoming moral hazard. As Barr (1987) points out, third-party payment schemes create an externality by causing a divergence between private and social costs—i.e. moral hazard is defined as an external cost arising from insurance. In accepting that it is doctors (the suppliers) who specify consumption levels and who are therefore responsible for the existence of moral hazard the possibility of regulating their behaviour arises. This obviously entails costs and one means to minimize such costs is to integrate. Pre-payment schemes are essentially forms of such integration. As Arrow (1963) argues, such schemes are an alternative to insurance where the insurance is in effect paid in kind and thus push the financial risk-bearing function on to the doctor. Of course it may be that the doctor is unwilling to carry such risks, but even if he is, other problems present themselves. Pre-payment locks the consumer to a particular provider for some pre-specified time period. It involves pooling of risks and therefore the exercising of control over prices and benefits. As such it may serve to undermine the agency relationship. This relationship rests on the separation of medical from economic concerns, whereas pre-payment schemes operate to integrate them.

Pre-payment schemes have become a common means of regulating insurance in the USA where there has been considerable concern over the escalating costs of health care provision, with a considerable emphasis placed on moral hazard as an explanation (Feldstein,1980). There are various types of scheme, with health maintenance organizations (HMOs) being the most publicized. These organizations give comprehensive medical coverage by providing primary services and contracting out for secondary services for a fixed periodic *per capita* payment. This payment being set in advance is not linked to the quantity of services consumed.

The HMOs are meant to compete for members in terms of quality and cost. However there are a number of complications: moral hazard may still exist at the secondary level; they do not overcome the problems of exclusion or adverse selection; and there are obvious pressures towards cartelization. HMOs could be regulated to include high-risk groups. They could also in principle implement differential payment schemes to discriminate amongst risks. But in practice this may be costly given that adverse selection occurs from asymmetric informational problems. Alternatively payment may be compulsorily fixed across the potential population such that low-risk individuals will be subsidizing high-risk individuals; if it were not compulsory, low-risk individuals could opt out.

Another pre-payment institution that has emerged recently in the USA is the preferred provider organization (PPO). This institution involves the insurer contracting with the provider (e.g. a doctor, group practice, or hospital) at a pre-agreed fixed rate to provide certain levels of service. The provider is then locked into the contract. Integration is thus not as complete as in the HMO. Consumers are given incentives to choose the contracted provider, but can choose others if they want, any extra cost being borne by themselves.

Neither institution overcomes the problem of adverse selection. This was so extensive in the USA that two further institutions were set up in the 1960s—Medicaid and Medicare—to provide insurance cover and health care for high-risk population groups. Pre-payment has affected these institutions to the extent that Medicare is now regulated by the prospective payment system for in-patient hospital cases. This will result in Medicaid hospitals being paid a fixed pre-determined rate per case with cases being defined across a number of diagnostic categories (diagnosis-related groups—DRGs). This will hopefully contain costs as well as utilization.[8]

All such institutions represent attempts to integrate forward from the health care insurance sector into health care itself, largely in an attempt directly to monitor the economic consequences of medical behaviour. To some extent this occurs because self-regulation has focused on medical rather than economic behaviour, with the not unsurprising consequence of cost escalation. Forward integration gives the potential for greater control over costs by bringing together economic and medical information and allowing for direct intervention in the forward planning of utilization levels.

As an alternative to such private financing arrangements, some countries, most notably Canada, have dismissed the effectiveness of private health care insurance, but retain private health care provision. The former has been replaced by public finance which is not founded on actuarial insurance principles but rather enforces compulsory membership, the benefits of which are universal coverage of the risks attached to financing treatment. Thus because the cover is not defined by insurance risk the problem of adverse selection disappears and administrative costs are lowered. Moreover there is some tendency towards counteracting moral hazard in a publicly funded system. This is because the controls over public expenditure are normally prospective and thus a ceiling is imposed on total spending which does of course restrict output levels. Evans (1987) goes further by arguing that public financing provides a collective purchasing role, and as a monopsonist, the state is able to monitor the mix of services, as well as their overall level, more efficiently.

---

[8] Although as Enthoven points out the pre-payment only operates on rising costs and not on out-patients either (see Enthoven, 1987, p. 245).

This provides an argument for the integration of public financing with public provision. Under such a system we have similar insurance advantages as those maintained above. However, by full integration into provision the public financier is no longer a monopsonistic bargainer but the actual provider of the funds for provision. There is a much more direct control over any moral hazard in the system. It is subject to the overall financial constraints imposed by the prevailing public finance allocation mechanism, and any specific treatment is subject to the publicly administered regulation of service-mix. Whereas the private insurer reacts to moral hazard by offering a range of different priced insurance contracts, a public funded body reacts with a variety of non-price rationing devices. If the insurance principle has already failed, due say to adverse selection as well as the lack of cover for high-risk groups, then it may be possible for a monopsonist to dictate various prices for various treatments, but he will not be in a strong position because of the information monopoly which remains held by the supplier—i.e. the doctor. It may be better, therefore, to integrate into provision and enforce output constraints directly, particularly if the medical profession is salaried and thus operates within the resource limits determined by public policy. This will not entirely remove moral hazard, but should be more effective in controlling overprovision. This is the system currently operated by the NHS.

The difficulty faced by all systems that fully integrate the financing and provision of health care is that the enforcement of utilization and output constraints operates at an aggregate level. The integrated system is able to contain costs through avoiding many of the administration and billing costs associated with insurance and containing the incomes of providers. However, the medical profession retains its monopoly over information and continues to respond to the basic diagnostic and prognostic uncertainties which dominate the production process through the highly individualistic agency relationship, and to pursue medically dictated objectives. Behaviour, and associated resource allocation, is therefore constrained by aggregate measures, but there are no incentives to ensure that such allocation is efficient. In other words, while the governance structures that accompany integration temper any tendency to over-supply and constrain the monopoly potential of the medical profession to be realized in the form of income, they do not necessarily provide incentives to ensure that resources are put to efficient use. Moreover, if public financing is dictated by macroeconomic concerns and there is a lack of detailed information about the demands being placed on the sector, it is likely that resource allocation will not be paired to highest valued use. Finally, generation of the public finances to fund public provision will lead to the distortion of economic behaviour in other sectors—the commonly cited example being that higher income taxes lead to changes in the trade-off between work and leisure.

Thus it is not only markets which may be inefficient, the institutional structures that replace them may be too. In any case, there will be transactions costs incurred by these institutional replacements associated with the monitoring and policing of resource flows. What must be ascertained is whether or not these costs outweigh the benefits associated with the non-market-based institutional provision. A major problem is that, whatever the institutional form of delivery selected, the individual doctors retain their monopoly over information. However, by moving away from a fee-for-service remuneration package to a salaried one, the medical profession cannot over-price and there is less incentive to over-supply. But monitoring and policing resource use remain difficult even in a fully integrated system, and therefore self-regulation continues to be important.

Self-regulation is as important as administrative rules in governing the mix of services provided. The medical profession, as well as the individual doctor, is ultimately concerned with resource inputs. However it is the usage of such inputs rather than their cost which forms the basis of this concern. Thus the rights to self-government held by the medical profession may be seen as reinforcing the agency role of the individual doctor, in as much as they serve to separate medical conduct and performance from resource allocation decisions at an aggregate level. In this sense the doctor is acting as the agent of the collective demanders—society itself—and this forms part of the mechanics of the planning process, by formulating the demands to be placed on the system. If used properly, self-regulation is an efficient means of ensuring quality control within a supply-constrained environment rather than a means of maintaining monopoly power. But, because it is concerned with medical rather than economic conduct, it will not provide incentives to ensure that resource allocation is efficient.

6. Equity Considerations in Practice

Of course pure market solutions have little concern with equity given that such solutions are based on the current distribution of purchasing power. Although government intervention may be justified on equity grounds alone, it must be recognized that it is normally difficult to reconcile equity and efficiency. If public finance and provision is accepted on efficiency grounds, it becomes possible to incorporate equity objectives directly into the health care programme. Yet the pursuit of distributional motives is dogged by complications. We must first be able meaningfully and precisely to define equity. In practice, equality rather than equity has often dominated UK discussion. Yet it is possible to have equitable inequalities and inequitable equalities. Equity within the context of the NHS has long been defined with regard to equal access for equal need (HMSO, 1979).[9]

[9] It is in fact the case that various definitions and objectives for equality in the NHS have been proposed (see Mooney, 1986). Most are difficult, if not impossible, to reconcile with any other. For policy purposes the objective that is commonly emphasized is 'equal access for equal need', yet in practice even this becomes 'equal inputs for equal need'.

The NHS has always aimed to react to local needs while being financed from largely central taxation. Economies of scale are achieved through the centralized tax and financial system, while local knowledge underlies the definition of need. The latter, while difficult to make operational (Culyer, 1976), does reflect the fact that, because of the presence of informational asymmetries, it is the medical profession which formalizes the demands being placed on the system. Moreover, constraints can be better recognized at the local level. It is therefore efficient, because of informational requirements and the fact that there may be locational economies of scale, that decision-making and the organization of provision are undertaken locally.

Need is assessed with respect to standardized mortality ratios (SMRs) to determine the expected level of demand at a regional level. At a lower level (the district), priorities are drawn up through a complex bargaining process. The importance of the clinician in the determination of resource allocation should not be underestimated. Particularly within the hospital sector, the clinician implements decisions which have large and often far-reaching implications. Thus it is through a complex mix of planning and bargaining that the financial allocation process attempts to match resources to needs.

There are, however, definitional problems relating to the meaning of inequality of access, and therefore use, within geographical areas. While the use of SMRs helps to define local needs, they are aggregate measures and do not impart information on specific individual requirements. The small amount of empirical work that has been undertaken on such issues suggests that, both in terms of health status itself and the utilization of health care services, substantial inequalities exist. The Black Report (HMSO, 1980) highlights the differential in health status to be found across socio-economic groups. Using a variety of morbidity and mortality measures, it concludes that the higher socio-economic groups are healthier and have greater longevity than lower groupings and that the NHS has failed significantly to affect this disparity. Le Grand (1978) also found that, in terms of utilization, the top socio-economic group was receiving 40 per cent more NHS expenditure per person reporting illness than the bottom one. However the progressivity or otherwise of the NHS cannot be judged on the basis of expenditure or utilization rates alone; the financial aspect must also be considered. The chapter by Wagstaff et al. in this volume highlights the importance of using both income and expenditure measures in attempts to analyse the redistributional impact of health care services.

7. Performance Measurement

Health care services may then be delivered and financed through a variety of institutional mechanisms. This raises the question of how output should be measured in this sector to permit performance comparisons, both with regard to efficiency and equity. The first step in answering this question might be to determine some acceptable manner for the measurement of improvements in health status. The second stage might require individuals to place a value on such improvements relative to other goods and services.

Associated with these aims are alternative concepts of efficiency. *Technical efficiency* in the production of health implies that the maximum improvement in health status is obtained from a given set of inputs. *Productive efficiency* requires that a given improvement in health status is obtained at least cost (i.e. taking into account input prices). *Allocative efficiency* requires further that the social value of improvements in health is maximized. These three kinds of efficiency correspond to three possible types of evaluation within the health sector. *Randomized controlled trials* can be used to compare the effectiveness of different treatments using available medical resources; *cost-effectiveness analyses* can be carried out which measure effectiveness against input cost; *cost–benefit analyses* can be performed to determine whether particular medical interventions are socially beneficial.

Output measurement in the health sector consequently varies in relation to the kind of evaluation being performed. Drummond's chapter describes both disease-specific and global measures of health output, where the latter comprise suitably weighted functions of recognized components of good health. The way in which the weights are determined is of critical importance, and is central to much of the current debate over the use of quality-of-life measures for health service planning. Various attempts have been made to identify utility weights which reflect the preferences of a representative panel of individuals. The result is a consensual 'quality-of-life' measure which can be used in conjunction with life tables in order to produce a 'quality-adjusted life-year' (QALY) (Weinstein and Stason, 1976; Williams, 1985). Comparisons of costs-per-QALY in the delivery of health services may therefore be seen as a way of monitoring economic efficiency. Culyer's chapter suggests that this approach can be characterized as 'extra-welfarist' (Sen, 1979), in that it avoids the need to question the relative value of health as an end compared to other competing goods and services. The chapter by Mooney and Olsen raises further questions by suggesting that QALYs impart only limited information on health care in any case. An attempt to place a monetary value on health, such as by estimating consumers' willingness to pay for different health states, would be integral to the use of cost–benefit analysis as a means by which allocative efficiency could be pursued. The rarity of such exercises is testimony to the methodological difficulties involved, as well as to the notion that health is a fundamental commodity which ought not to be tradeable in the way implied by willingness-to-pay estimates.

Whichever concept of efficiency is used, monitoring performance presupposes that inputs are measurable and that hospital treatment technologies are well defined. Given the complexity of agency decision-making and informational difficulties involved, it is not clear that this is the case (McGuire,1986). Setting aside this reservation, and granted that there are ways of monitoring efficiency, how does this relate to actual policy? Clearly there are several tiers of evaluation which are possible. Performance can be measured at the level of the individual treatment decision, the production unit, or the global provider. The intention in so doing is to introduce an appropriate set of property right assignments amongst decision-takers. The incentive structure within non-market institutions providing health care is important in determining the extent of any institutional failure by comparison with the market failures described earlier.

Finally, the measurement of health output is also important for monitoring the achievement of equity objectives. The chapter by Wagstaff *et al.* suggests that there exist several ways of measuring 'improvements' in equity: on the basis of the distribution of access to health, the consumption of health care services, or health itself. The need in the UK for a grant distribution formula is in itself an acknowledgement of the historically unequal provision of facilities throughout the country. But clearly the way in which the grant is distributed may distort the health production process if output measures are inadequate.

8. The Proposed Reforms of the UK Health Care Sector

We have so far outlined the enormous difficulties involved in evaluating the different means of financing and delivering health care. The NHS celebrated its fortieth birthday in 1988, and throughout its history there has been debate about whether or not it provides value for money. The last fifteen years have witnessed a major restructuring of its organization and its management. The recently published White Paper—Working for Patients (HMSO, 1989)—heralds further reorganization. Given the difficulties involved in defining efficient institutional forms of delivery and financing, as well as the added complications introduced by equity concerns, this continual reappraisal is hardly surprising.

At present there is advocacy of increased competition in the delivery of health care and the search for viable alternative means of financing. Both reflect a strong belief in the superiority of the private sector with regards to efficiency; that an efficient allocation of health care resources will be delivered by incentive rather than by administrative structures. We have suggested above that there are no necessary *a priori* grounds for this belief when considering health care. How then should the current policy options be assessed? Obviously the costs and benefits of the proposed reforms should be compared to the costs and benefits associated with the present system.

(a) *The Present Structure.*

The UK health sector is currently dominated by the NHS. With some small exceptions such as NHS private pay-beds, the NHS is a public funded body which provides public health care. As such there is public financing, from general taxation, and public provision. Public provision has been based on an administrative regulation of the sector as presented schematically in Figure 1.1. This structure allows direct central government administrative control over the allocation of capital and revenue resources to regional health authorities (RHAs). The health care sector is allocated a budget from general taxation as part of the annual round of public expenditure plans. An annual White Paper outlines these plans and contains pronouncements on general economic policy and may also outline priority areas for future funding. Planned public expenditure on health care is related to the priorities as outlined in policy documents issued by the Department of Health and approved by the UK Treasury. Once allocated, this public expenditure is passed forward through the Department of Health to the RHAs. The RHAs then further allocate revenue resources to district health authorities (DHAs).

These regional budget allocations are determined by a resource allocation formula taken from the Resources Allocation Working Party Report (the RAWP Report: DHSS, 1976). The RAWP recommendations were that allocations should be based on the relative health needs of the individual regions as approximated by calculations relating to standardized mortality ratios and age-

Figure 1.1
Public Provision of Health Care in the UK (pre-White Paper)

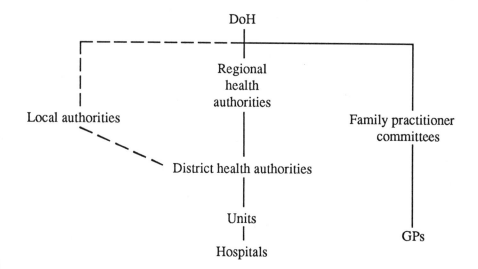

and sex-adjusted national utilization rates, with some adjustment made for the costs associated with treating patients from outside the region. Thus while revenue resource allocation is based on local health needs, the means by which such needs were met was governed by a centralized administrative structure. The allocation process to date has been largely budget-oriented. Administrative regulation has concentrated on the control of NHS expenditure as advocated by central government and in line with the tightening of control over public expenditure generally. Thus the expenditure process in the NHS has become increasingly formalized by, for example, the introduction of cash limits in the hospital sector setting an upper limit on the budget to be allocated to the hospital sector. Accompanying the evolution of tighter controls over public expenditure there has been an increasing formalization of the resource allocation process itself. The government, through the Public Accounts Committee has carefully monitored the administration of budgetary control (Public Accounts Committee, 1980–1; 1983–4).

Monitoring and control have also advanced on other fronts. Until the early 1980s there had, for example, been little monitoring of regional health authority resource allocation plans. Following the 1982 reorganization of the management of the health service, a process of ministerial review has been set up, whereby annual meetings between regional chairmen and the Minister for Health, both supported by appropriate staff, are held. These reviews are concerned with ensuring that the RHAs are meeting their statutory requirements in the provision of health care and are implementing government policies. The development of performance indicators is another move towards increased monitoring of resource allocation in the NHS. At a lower level of aggregation, and in recognition that expenditure on health services is mainly determined by the decisions taken by medical consultants, the DHSS has also piloted the development of clinical budgeting in a few acute hospitals.

However, any portrayal of expenditure determination, control, and monitoring as being wholly dictated from the top down is misleading. While financial control is undoubtedly important, control of resource use as related to outcome is still more fundamental. The relationship of resource use to outcome has remained firmly within the control of the clinical profession. It must be recognized that expenditure on, for example, hospital services is mainly determined by the decisions taken by medical consultants. The importance of the clinicians in the overall process should not be underestimated. At the clinical level of management the pattern of resource allocation breaks down into a large array of confusing signals. What is clear is that individual clinicians have considerable power in interpreting local need and therefore determining resource usage. What is less clear is the extent to which monitoring and control is exercised, through the existing administrative allocation process, over this interpretation of need.

The medical profession has considerable rights to self-regulation. This emphasizes medical rather than economic conduct with the result that accountability is normally defined in terms of clinical practice. While the doctor does have a concern with treatment inputs, it is in relation to their usage rather than to their cost. And the doctor's conduct is regulated by the profession accordingly. This of course creates the conditions for opportunistic behaviour by the profession over its claims for resources which may conflict with the overall strategy advocated by the central government departments. Certainly, while making audit difficult, the rights to self-regulation enjoyed by the medical profession also impose a constraint upon the separation of strategic from operational behaviour. Indeed it is interesting to note that, in discussing the management of resource allocation and the regulation of medical behaviour, the Royal Commission on the NHS (1979) was emphatic in its criticism of the inadequate state of medical organization and management and the need for reform of the medical advisory committee structure.

Thus the difficulty appears to be that, while there has been an emergent process of control and monitoring associated with the budgetary process, there have not seemed to exist complementary mechanisms to control and monitor clinical practice and hence resource use. The rights to self-regulation that stem from clinical autonomy are, by definition, an internal mechanism and the degree of control and monitoring exercised is not readily apparent. At the extreme there are powers of litigation which may be used to control medical conduct, but the inherent uncertainties involved in diagnosis and prognosis and the individualistic nature of the production process (i.e. treatments) make both the choice and the efficacy of treatments open to significant variation. Recourse to litigation under such circumstances is probably a less than efficient means of regulation. However, the self-enforcing commitments that accompany self-regulation by the clinical profession do not readily lend themselves to control, while the inherent uncertainties associated with clinical practice render monitoring difficult.

As noted above, regulation of the health care sector and the health insurance sector must be mutually supportive. What has happened in the recent past is that there has been an increasing tendency towards further regulation in the health insurance sector (i.e. regulation of the public finances that fund the health care sector) while regulation in the health care sector has lagged behind. Increased regulation of the health insurance sector inevitably means increased control and monitoring of the health care sector itself. And, indeed, the proposed White Paper reforms extend the control and monitoring process into health care provision.

(b) *The Proposed Reforms*

In considering the proposed reforms of the NHS it is worth recalling that there is a wide variety of means of ensuring that consumers are able to meet both the demands for and the costs of treatment once (if) such events arise, including: private financing of consumption plus private production of health care; private financing and public production; public financing and private production; public financing and public production. The new proposals intend that all such mixes should be available, with choice a function of cost and quality of service as perceived by the individual patient or their newly created agents, the budget holders. The underlying rationale of the reforms appears to be one which emphasizes the possibility of improving the conduct and performance of the sector by means of changing its structure. We can examine the proposals within this framework.

While most of the reforms address issues concerned with provision, there is one financing reform. Tax relief is to be given to purchasers of private insurance who are aged 60 and over. This may be to aid the adverse selection problems currently faced by this age group. However it is unlikely that price subsidies will have a great impact. The probability of utilization is too close to one, and the expected costs too high for this class of consumer. Price subsidies may help the insurer cover cost, but even here the subsidy would have to be substantial. They do not affect the probability of take-up.

On the provision side the reforms appear to have three main objectives: to increase consumer choice; to strengthen managerial control; and to increase competition amongst providers. We consider each in turn.

Consumer choice

It should be obvious that the current interest in increased consumerism in health care is potentially misleading. Individuals do not have adequate knowledge to make informed choices about their treatment. Consequently the health sector is always likely to be subject to some form of regulation. Reflection on the arguments outlined above should convince readers that the health care sector is supply dominated and that consumer choice has little meaning in this sector. This may also be true of other sectors, but it remains the case that wrong choices in this sector have potentially more disastrous outcomes attached.

Managerial control

The strengthening of managerial control merely extends the recent moves within the NHS to shift property rights over resource allocation towards managers and away from clinicians. The past emphasis on reforming management structure will continue, although there is also an attempt to increase managerial control through fuller specification of consultant contracts, for example. One interpretation is that the managers are to become more active in their role of agent for the citizen, in ensuring that health care resources are efficiently allocated. While previous managerial initiatives focused on budgetary allocations, it is hoped that these reforms will allow managers to exert greater control over resource allocation, although the medical profession will of course retain monopoly control over treatment specification.

The future degree of vertical integration of the NHS will rely on the extension of line management. Overall responsibility will lie with a newly created NHS management executive, which will oversee the activities of the hospital and community services as at present, but will also extend its responsibilities to cover family practitioner services. The objectives of this executive will be set by an NHS policy board, chaired by the Secretary of State for Health. Such developments are in line with the Griffiths proposals to centralize management within the NHS, while delegating as much responsibility as possible to the local level (HMSO, 1983). It remains an open question as to whether devolved responsibility can be maintained within a management system that relies on centralized accountability.

One of the objectives behind this extension of line management is to encourage a more 'business-like' approach to management within the NHS. One potential problem is that with centralized management there is a conflict, at various levels within organizations, between operational management functions and strategic management functions (see Chandler, 1962; Williamson, 1975). To the extent that the new managerial framework will allow greater separation of strategic from operational responsibilities it is to be welcomed. The extension of line management and the desire to devolve more day-to-day decision-making may improve the managerial efficiency. The presumed objective is to reinforce central accountability but simultaneously devolve local responsibility. To the extent that both RHAs and DHAs remain unclear as to their exact roles and function within the reorganized NHS, as they appear to, there is concern over the implementation of these new management functions.

Competition

At present the NHS is a vertically integrated structure in as much as the administrative organization, outlined above, integrates both financing and provision. The White Paper does not substantially alter this degree of vertical integration, since the NHS will remain largely financed through taxation. However, in as much as budget holders will have control over their expenditure patterns there is a weakening of the direct monitoring that accompanies full vertical integration. The aim is to introduce greater competition for this finance through encouraging providers to compete for funds mainly through increasing their patient flows and giving them greater ability to bargain with other providers over costs. The new system may be characterized as one of partial vertical integration accompanied by horizontal competition.

It should be recognized that, while the White Paper was a response to a review of funding and perceived shortage in the NHS, there is no suggested change in the overall allocation of finance to the sector. The NHS budget will remain determined by the annual expenditure process controlled by Whitehall and the Treasury. Thus the degree of horizontal competition will be constrained by the budgetary allocations given to the central government health departments, and subsequently to the RHAs and DHAs. The allocations to RHAs and DHAs are to be based on weighted capitation, the weights relating to the resident population's age and morbidity structure—in other words, this formula will be similar to the RAWP formula which it replaces. So the aggregate expenditure determination and the subsequent allocations to RHAs and DHAs will not be much different.

However, RHAs and DHAs will no longer be compensated for those patients who are treated outside their administrative boundaries. These patients were financed through a cross-boundary flow element in the RAWP financing formulae, but now costs of care will have to be negotiated with competing providers. This is not a small matter—for example, in central Birmingham 78.6 per cent of the non-maternity/non-psychiatric cases treated were from residences outside the DHA in 1986. For teaching DHAs generally, the mean percentage of cases treated who were outside residents was approximately 50 per cent.

The mechanics of future financial operation of the NHS may be gleaned from Figure 1.2. Increased competition is meant to arise from individual providers competing for funds. This can happen in two basic ways. First, as funds will be linked to capitation, providers will compete for patients. The greater the number of patients attracted, the greater the allocated funds. Second, individual providers will have the opportunity to become budget holders. In this case funds will be allocated directly to these providers, rather than being administered through RHAs and DHAs. These funds will be based on the level of services that are contracted for by DHAs, or other providers of health care, and payment will be gained from purchasers.

General practitioners, for example, will compete with each other for patients. The proposals to increase the proportion of GP income from capitation will act as the incentive here. GPs will also have the opportunity to become budget holders, competing with other GPs and even hospitals for contracts from DHAs. If any savings are achieved, then these may be used to improve their services, making them stronger for future competition.

The GP budget allocation mechanism will be primarily prospective payment estimated from past utilization. However it is difficult to see how such a prospective payment scheme would operate if focused on primary care. If such care is to continue to react to local needs, it may be difficult to predict in advance

Figure 1.2
Proposed Reforms of Financing and Provision of UK Health Care

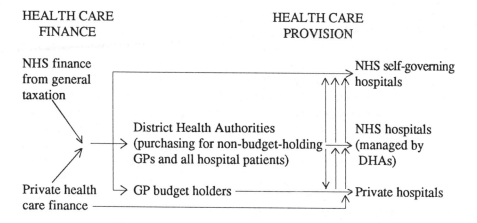

HEALTH CARE
FINANCE

HEALTH CARE
PROVISION

what form resource utilization will take, particularly given the output measurement problems discussed above. Basing this year's budget on last year's utilization may not be justified. Basing the hospital referral component of the GP's budget on the difference between last year's referral patterns and the district's average, as proposed by the White Paper, seems much less so.

GPs act as gatekeepers to other parts of the health sector. If they are to act as budget holders for patients then they become the risk bearers, at least to the extent that any consequences of over-spending their budget cannot be passed on to their patients. Assuming that they are willing to accept this risk-bearing role, to operate efficiently they will need information on both the prospective cases for the remaining budget period and on the cost and quality of the available range of services for any particular diagnosis. Moreover, a significant proportion of patients are referred for further diagnostic information—that is a proportion of GP referrals are open-ended contracts with secondary providers.

The contingencies associated with any given contract will therefore be substantial. In other words, the formalization of the agency relationship, such that the GP acts as the agent for the consumer/patient in bargaining with other providers of health care resources, does not overcome the fundamental diagnostic and prognostic uncertainties and complexities faced by both consumers and producers. Cash-limiting such budgets might increase rather than reduce resource allocation problems, as GPs attempt continually to reconcile unpredicted resource commitments with their budget constraints. Yet if such budgets were not effectively limited there would be little difference from the prevailing system where the incentive structures relating to resource use are far from clear.

Moreover, the fundamental uncertainties and complexities which govern transactions may also lead to costs associated with continual re-contracting in all internal market solutions.

One perverse incentive is that it will pay GPs who do opt for budgets to select 'healthy' patients. Healthy patients will not place heavy demands on budgets and therefore become attractive to the budget holders. Scheffler (1989) used HMO utilization data and the average budgeting figures given in the White Paper to simulate the impact of changes in utilization on a GP practice of 11,000 patients (the minimum size specified for budget holding). He shows that only 1.5 per cent of the total patients on the list would have to increase their utilization (i.e. take up services having previously had zero consumption) for an average budget to be exceeded, assuming these 1.5 per cent of new users were high utilization patients (defined as part of the top 7.5 per cent of the population that uses 25 per cent of the GP's services). Clearly the finances of GP budget holders are sensitive to changed patterns of utilization. As such there may be strong incentives to limit utilization by skewing the practice towards healthy sections of the population—e.g. the younger population.

The problem is one of adverse selection. By passing the financial, essentially the insurance, costs on to the budget holding GPs, the White Paper is making them bear all risk. This risk can be shared across the patient pool—a lower budget and therefore access to care for other patients—or can be minimized through selecting patients with lower than average expected utilization. The government recognizes that such possibilities exists. The White Paper states that by weighting the capitation system by age this will mitigate any tendency towards younger patient lists, which would be an obvious response to adverse selection. It also suggests that patients costing any GP budget holder more than £5,000 per annum will become the responsibility of the DHAs. Such tools are useful in limiting adverse selection, but they do not remove the problem.

In the hospital sector the government is encouraging hospitals to become self-governing. Such hospitals, referred to as NHS Hospital Trusts, will receive funding to the extent that they successfully win contracts with DHAs, GPs, private insurers, and patients to provide care. DHAs are thus seen to become purchasing agents who, on behalf of the patient, will purchase high quality, low cost health care from various providers. GP budget holders are also to act as purchasing agents on behalf of the patient. As such the agency relationship between doctor and patient will be mediated in as much as the doctor, as provider, will also have explicitly to consider the role of the patient's new agent, the purchaser. In the case of the budget-holding GP these two agency roles will be merged and there will no longer be a clear separation of medical and economic conduct. It is uncertain what effect this will have on the patient/doctor relationship.

The White Paper, in emphasizing the new purchasing agency role of the DHA or GP, has attempted to replace the administration of financing with internal markets for care. The major difficulty with this contracting perspective is that, given the sequential nature of the production process as discussed above, it is unclear how contracts will cover all the evolving contingencies that accompany episodes of illness. The contracts are envisaged to be one of three basic types: block contracts which will form pre-payment schemes for access to a defined range of services; cost and volume contracts which are prospective payment schemes for a given number of treatments or cases; and finally cost per case contracts. In all forms of contract the financial risk is moved to the provider, as such costs, and therefore the provision of services, will have to be maintained within the agreed contractual price. To aid this cost-containment, budget holders will be free to negotiate the pay and conditions of staff.

Of particular importance in this respect are the proposed changed arrangements for negotiating consultants' contracts. Consultants are presently employees of RHAs and have fairly ill-defined remits, largely acknowledging the clinical freedom that is enjoyed by the profession in their role as agents for patients. The consultant may now be employed by an RHA or a self-governing hospital. More importantly there will be a tightening up of the consultants' job description. The District General Manager will take a more active role in the appointments procedure, which to date has been seen to be controlled by the medical profession, and the job tenure enjoyed by consultants will be replaced by negotiated contract arrangements. Such changes in contractual arrangements draw the consultants more into line with management objectives, but at the possible cost of undermining the clinical freedom and agency role of the clinician.

(c) *Structure, Conduct, and Performance under the New Regime*

The government's proposed reform of the health service has, as we have seen, been based on the belief that structural change in the industry will have beneficial effects on efficiency. The NHS represents a considerable degree of both vertical and horizontal integration, and the proposed reforms attempt to break up this structure in several ways. The vertical link between primary and secondary providers is broken through the establishment of budget-holding GPs with the discretion to 'shop around' for hospital care. The vertical link between insurer and provider is broken through the provision that self-governing hospitals can compete for both privately and publicly insured patients. Moreover, at each level of the industry, horizontal competition has been encouraged. Private insurers are to be subsidized to the extent that tax relief is extended for the elderly. Self-governing hospitals are to compete with both private and public alternatives. Budget-holding GPs are to compete with each other and with non-budget-holding practices for patients. This whole process of 'disintegration' necessitates the introduction of explicit contracts governing transactions between the newly independent organizations. This, of course, is the opposite process to the more familiar organizational tendency of integration in order to minimize contracting costs.

The justification for this deliberate and costly restructuring of the industry lies with the presumption that competitive pressures provide incentives for efficiency, the benefits from which outweigh the transaction costs involved. This persuasive argument is derived from the paradigm of the competitive marketplace, in which profit-maximizing producers must minimize costs or else go out of business, because there will exist a single market-clearing price which equals the cost of production. Moreover, in addition to being productively efficient in this sense, the industry will also produce the right amount of output because consumers will buy up to the point at which their marginal valuation equals the cost of production. Hence it is argued that competition will lead to improved industrial performance, as judged by the twin criteria of cost and price.

In the NHS, of course, prices do not exist in any formal sense because transactions are internalized. Attempts to link costs to treatment categories are nevertheless useful for resource planning purposes, and the resource management initiative (RMI) introduced in 1986 was justified on this basis. The White Paper has recommended an acceleration in the RMI with a view to producing diagnosis-related costings which could be used as a basis for contractual negotiation over prices between hospitals and budget-holding GPs or district health authorities. Given the rather special characteristics of this market, the presumption of allocative efficiency requires that the purchasers of secondary health care are acting as agents for patients, reflecting the latters' valuation of the likely outcome from treatment. By introducing competition between hospitals, and by simultaneously confronting GPs with practice budget constraints, the White Paper intends that what was previously implicit—that is, the opportunity cost of treatment—will now be made explicit, with consequent improvements in efficiency throughout the health care market.

Clearly there are a number of difficulties with this view. To begin with, productive efficiency requires that there is a competitive market for all inputs, so that prices reflect marginal productivity. While this might be the case for some inputs, the NHS is for many categories of medical personnel a monopsonistic employer, and the medical profession has by its nature power over entry, which implies a degree of bilateral monopoly in the medical labour market. It has been suggested that the reduction in NHS monopsony power following the introduction of self-governing hospitals will lead to an upward pressure on salaries throughout the industry. It is argued that competition among private, self-governing, and/or NHS hospitals may be in the form of wage increases and/or working conditions and facilities provided. In this respect, a part of the expense incurred for expansion of inputs (i.e. facilities, technology, etc.) may be regarded as an implicit payment to clinicians—a fee paid to attract clinicians. In other words, the introduction of market contracting may in fact have the impact of increasing costs in the hospital sector. To attract medical staff, who will retain their monopoly over clinical information, increased competition may force hospitals to offer higher salaries and higher quality working conditions. The sector may become prone to pressures of what may be termed conspicuous production (Lee, 1971). There may thus be strong upward pressures on costs that have little to do with demand for increased facilities on the part of consumers. Because the consumer and the insurer have less knowledge over what character- izes quality of care than the medical profession, there is pressure to maintain high standards with regards to staffing levels, equipment, and technology. These proxies for high quality care impart inflationary pressures upon the system. Moreover, if local labour markets are tight it is likely that further wage inflation may be experienced.

With a system of cost-related prospective prices in place, such additional costs can be passed on—not to the patient directly, but to his agent, the budget-holding GP or the DHA. In principle, those hospitals which are most successful in controlling costs will attract most business. However, this is where the crucial problems begin to occur with the government's position. Contractually negoti- ated prices will relate to particular DRGs or packages of care. If, as is inevitable, the precise details of care are less than fully specified in the contract, then the option of substitution between price and quality of care arises. The hospitals which survive could therefore be the low cost, low quality end of the market. Clearly there is a need for contracts of this nature to be appropriately governed—the market by itself is inadequate for this purpose because of inherent informational problems. Consumers of health care cannot easily discriminate between differ- ent providers on the basis of quality. Even where consumers are represented by purchasing agents such as budget-holding GPs, informational asymmetry will remain between GP and hospital.

Moreover, the agents' incentive structure may conflict with the consumers' objectives: for example, GPs may have an incentive to choose the least costly treatment where patients are unable to observe variations in quality, or to exclude potentially high-cost patients from the register. If patients are able to observe some dimensions of quality, there may be competition between GPs to provide those dimensions, but there is no guarantee that what is observable is necessarily the most important. Measures directed at improving and disseminating informa- tion about quality of care can help, but are by themselves unlikely to remove the informational asymmetry.

Furthermore, extensive regulation would have to be introduced in the hospital sector to ensure that individual hospitals were not selecting particular patient groups or discharging patients back into other parts of the public sector to minimize their own costs. Such behaviour would result in extensive cross-subsidization across institutions and defeat the presumed competitive advantages to be gained from clearly defining budget holders. The proposed reforms do not explicitly outline the regulatory controls which would operate in such circumstances, but there are clearly going to be costs associated with any accompanying monitoring, policing, and enforcing of regulation. Such transaction costs arising from regulation of the new structure are liable to be substantive given the complex inter-relationships between providers in this sector and will themselves have an impact on the incentives of individuals in the sector. Quam's chapter clearly exposes the potential costs of such regulation.

Internal markets and the move towards competition may in fact perversely create greater tendencies to use monopoly power. Certain monopoly pressures exist in health care; in particular, local or teaching hospitals may exhibit a degree of monopoly power and the medical profession will retain its monopoly over medical practice. If competition is introduced it is liable to drive individual providers to use their monopoly power in order to protect their market position rather than relinquish it. It remains unclear how the reformed health care sector is going to regulate the monopolies that currently exist. For example, with the medical profession it is clear that exercising greater management control will increase the managerial, and even financial, accountability of individual clinicians. It is less clear that this will have an impact on the efficiency in use of resources with regard to medical practice. This will remain under the remit of the medical profession and covered by the operation of medical audit. It is not at all clear from the reforms how medical audit will be undertaken or what incentives will exist to alter any ineffective, let alone inefficient, behaviour.

All such structural changes emphasize altering incentives rather than attempting to increase the monitoring of provision. The normal advantages are seen to be a more efficient use of capacity, with a resultant reduction in both costs and waiting lists and an increase in the average quality of service. However, it is often not recognized that the creation of an internal market carries transactions costs and that the present situation, where informal trading takes place on a wide scale in the NHS, may economize on such costs in a production process characterized by extreme uncertainty and complexity. Not only are informal agreements reached on cross-boundary flows between districts (although there may be nominal compensation based on average treatment costs associated with such flows), there is also substantial informal trading between individual consultants. While the benefits and costs of these informal arrangements remain largely unquantified, they are a rational response to the delivery of a commodity under conditions of uncertainty when faced with binding resource constraints. As such, the proposals to formalize this trading need to be properly considered against the existing benefits of the present system.

There is little doubt that such reforms are going to alter the conduct of the providers of health care. What is less than clear is that conduct is going to be altered in a way that will improve productive efficiency. First, the NHS has been relatively successful in tempering the potential conflict between medical objectives (i.e. unlimited demands on resources) and economic objectives. By maintaining resource restrictions at fairly high levels of aggregation it is true that short-term requirements have dominated long-term ones. Thus we see the acute sector being maintained at the expense of the long-term care sector. However, there is some fluidity in the system; the acute sector accepts a sizeable proportion of long-term chronic patients and if crisis looms in the long-term sector, resources are shifted out of acute medicine into chronic care. Given the integrated nature of the system, the RHAs and DHAs are able to exercise some control over the identification of priority areas. Under the proposed contractual arrangements it is likely that the incentives to consider long-term care will be reduced, since it will be in each budget holder's interest to shift the costs of care on to others. This shifting of costs will be difficult to exercise with single, episodic treatments, but less so in the case of long-term care.

(d) *Governance in the Quasi-Market*

Given the difficulties in defining performance under the proposed reforms and the constrained nature of competition, it is widely recognized that the sector will continue to be heavily regulated. However the precise form of regulation to be imposed remains vague.

There are various non-market mechanisms by which the performance of health care contracts may be governed. Essentially these fall into three categories: self-regulation, civil litigation, and statutory regulation. Each has merits and costs.

(1)   Self-regulation, for example through the use of ethical codes of conduct, has long been recognized in the health care sector. If consumers, or their agents, are able to observe quality of care only imperfectly, producers may prefer to compete by introducing improvements in quality control, which are relatively transparent. Complaints procedures and patient satisfaction surveys are examples of this approach. Further, the use of medical audit through peer review has been endorsed by the medical profession itself, and explicitly encouraged in the White Paper (HMSO, 1989, Working Paper No. 6). It has been suggested that

audit arrangements are one of the factors health authorities will wish to take into account when taking decisions about the allocation of contracts between self-governing hospitals, the independent sector and directly managed units' (WP no. 6, para. 4.8).

However, what precisely is meant by the term 'medical audit' is not always clear. The White Paper defines it as the systematic, critical analysis of the quality of medical care including the procedures used for diagnosis and treatment, the use of resources, and the resulting outcome and quality of life for the patient.

To an economist this seems very close to being a working definition of cost-effectiveness—providing the best outcome from available resources. As such it is not immediately obvious that the medical profession itself is the most appropriate body to implement these proposals. It would surely be better to restrict the application of *medical* audit to assessing the efficacy and appropriateness of treatment and diagnosis. Determining cost-effectiveness could be seen as a parallel exercise undertaken by management, bringing together information on both costs (e.g. from the RMI) and quality (from medical audit). Crucial to both exercises is the development of acceptable indicators of outcome, in terms of both mortality and morbidity. The more generalizable these indicators (or 'quality-of-life' measures) the more useful they are, enabling comparisons to be made over a wider range of options for available resources. Of course, medical audit should not be seen as supplanting the existing procedures for professional discipline through the clinical complaints procedure and the GMC.

The difficulty with self-regulation is that monitoring, policing, and enforcement remain the preserve of the producers. If the producers retain monopoly control, as in the health care sector, there is no guarantee that self-regulation will not be used to strengthen monopoly positions rather than operating to protect consumers' interests. This is particularly true if the sector becomes more competitive and the medical profession perceives health care managers as a threat to their own position within the sector.

(2)   Civil litigation, or recourse to private law, as a means of governing performance relies on remedy. Although consumers, or their agents, may be uninformed about quality *ex ante*, they may have a clearer picture following an episode of medical care. Consequently, the prospect arises of civil actions by patients, GPs, or health authorities who are dissatisfied with the quality of care. These actions could either be over breach of contract or over negligence. In both cases, the assessment as to what should be an appropriate quality of care rests with the courts, who will determine what standard of care would have been specified by the parties involved (in the case of contract), or what duty of care is owed to the patient (in the case of negligence). Whether the courts by themselves have sufficient information to determine the socially appropriate quality of care is a moot point. As a mechanism for monitoring the quality of care, the private law has the advantage of providing patients with a financial incentive to bring information about inferior quality into the public domain. However, it does so at no little cost in terms of legal and other expenses, and hard evidence to support the notion that it has a significant incentive effect on quality is rare.

Quality control by means of private law to date has typically implied litigation against a particular (insured) clinician. With the advent of competitive contracts, and the recent adoption of crown indemnity—by which the NHS has undertaken to indemnify all its staff against the costs of medical negligence actions—the focus will now shift towards the provider organization as a target for litigation. However, it seems that the breach of a new-style 'contract' between, say, a budget-holding GP and a hospital will not be enforceable through the courts in the usual way, but rather by means of a system of mandatory conciliation and arbitration. Again, it is not clear to what extent arbitrators will be in a position to assess what the appropriate contractual performance should have been without taking into account consumer preferences.

(3)   The White Paper envisages recourse to statutory regulation as the major means of governing contractual relations and performance generally in the reformed health care sector. The system of cost and quality control through medical audit together with internal costing systems described above will be supplemented by some form of external audit. The White Paper suggests that the audit of the NHS should remain with the National Audit Office (NAO) and that the audit of health authorities, FPCs, and other NHS bodies should be the responsibility of the Audit Commission rather than the Department of Health as at present. Both the NAO and the Audit Commission are committed to a 'value-for-money' approach in addition to a purely financial audit. This means that both bodies attach considerable importance to the development of outcome measures. The Social Services Committee's recent report on the government's plans expressed a hope that 'the Audit Commission in conjunction with the relevant professional bodies and Royal Colleges will succeed in developing a methodology for assessing outcomes in health care'. Drummond's chapter reviews the contributions which economists and others have made in this direction.

A combination of internal and external audit along the lines suggested is clearly desirable whatever the structure of the health care industry. However, it is arguable whether such a limited regulatory framework will generate sufficient information about quality to enable purchasers to make satisfactory choices between competing providers. The establishment of a quality assurance inspectorate of some kind has been suggested, but rejected by the government who consider it to be bureaucratic and unnecessary. The alternative of developing a system of health facility accreditation seems to be gaining ground, although any system of *voluntary* certification relies on the ability of purchasers to distinguish between certified and uncertified providers, as well as to judge the importance of grading systems.

As noted above, increased governance has focused to date on the financial aspects of health care and it is only with the proposed White Paper reforms that attention has moved to the governance of health care provision itself. One of the features of public financing, at least in the UK, is that there has been little reconciliation of expenditure with clinical activity. This has undoubtedly led to savings in terms of administration costs, but it has also meant that appropriate information necessary for efficient planning has not been available. However, even if such information is acquired and monitoring is improved, it is less simple to implement accountability and enforcement procedures. This after all strikes at the heart of the self-regulatory role that has been enjoyed by the medical profession to date and raises awkward questions about the type of incentives to which this profession responds.

There has been little consideration of the impact that different remuneration schemes or peer review schemes may have on incentives and resource alloca-tion. Given the importance of clinical decisions for resource usage, this is surprising. There has been some experimentation with clinical budgeting which has served to highlight further our ignorance about the basis of clinical decision-making and the lack of appropriate data, both medical and economic, to monitor such behaviour. For example, there are still no routinely collected data on the hours worked by clinicians, let alone on what use is made of these hours. It would seem wise to remind ourselves that the Guillebaud Committee (HMSO, 1956) recommended that better information on costs, resource usage, performance, and effectiveness be collected as a matter of urgency. It remains an unanswered question as to whether the recent interest in monitoring performance, and recently initiated improvements in the collection of costing data within the sector, are going to have any impact on behaviour and resource use, particularly since the data collection exercises have been implemented without consideration of improved means of regulating clinical resource usage. Clinicians' traditional autonomy will have to be reconciled with a movement towards the monitoring of performance and effectiveness in medical interventions. The attention which has recently been given to output measurement (see contributions by Culyer, Drummond, and Mooney and Olsen in this volume) could usefully contribute to such a reconciliation by increasing awareness of the importance of evaluation.

Related to the above issues of performance governance are the current intense policy discussions of medical labour markets. These have been little examined by economists. Crude arguments are forwarded to suggest that doctors are monopoly suppliers. As a result the number of doctors is below its socially optimum level, and their pay is correspondingly 'too high'. There are counter-vailing arguments. The profession's own imposition of standards of entry, of competence, and of behaviour can be interpreted as a means of developing an agency relationship with inadequately informed consumers, in an attempt to mitigate the imperfections of decision-making that would otherwise result from this and other market failures. Nor is the restriction on numbers at the discretion of the medical profession. Rather it is a consequence of the funding of medical schools which is, of course, a matter for the government of the day. Certainly it is not obvious how a change in system, say to a more market-orientated one where individual provider organizations could negotiate over pay-scales as suggested by the White Paper, would alter this.

Besides, other labour market issues are of more immediate importance. The first is the distribution of pay and effort *within* the profession. The traditional progression up the hospital hierarchy—from junior doctor to senior consultant—has come under some questioning both inside and outside medical circles. Junior doctors have long felt underpaid and over-worked. Perhaps this resentment was moderated by the knowledge that some day the rewards of seniority would be theirs. Recently, career and promotion blockages have removed this source of consolation. The problem, however, is not just one of the morale of one part of the profession, but involves the efficient use of resources within the system as a whole. The whole issue of substitution across and between different types of labour within the health service remains to be resolved, as witnessed by the recent dispute over the nurses' regrading exercise and the ambulancemen's strike. It is not clear that recent and likely policy changes properly address this issue of optimal labour mix. Indeed, little analysis of the substitutability of factors of production has been undertaken (see Gray and McGuire, 1989).

9. Conclusions

It is undoubtedly true that there are problems associated with allocating resources within the NHS. However, it is also the case that many of the proposed reforms to improve performance could have been implemented within the current structure. There appear to be substantial benefits associated with policing and monitoring the system through vertical integration. Indeed, progress on improved collection, collation, and use of information on resource allocations is already underway through schemes such as the resource management initiative, the Department of Health experiments with clinical budgeting, and the various clinical experiments with medical audit. Therefore, to the extent that the proposed structure will entail costs and benefits over and above those that exist at present, it remains to be seen whether the reforms will be justified. A competitive system will certainly impose costs—not least those associated with explicit contracting and the collection of information on costs, throughput, and outcomes. It may be that such costs will be greater in a competitive environment than an administrative one; in a competitive situation there are advantages to be gained from retaining rather than sharing information. The change in the financial incentives towards prospective payment or relating fees to service provision seems likely to encourage cost escalation, as providers attempt to minimize financial losses. Regulation to minimize the adverse incentives, which are openly acknowledged to accompany the proposed reforms, will suffer the drawback that quality is not transparent in this sector. The reforms do not overcome the fundamental informational asymmetries that characterize the health care sector. As such it is not obvious that increased horizontal competition amongst providers will cut costs while simultaneously improving quality. Given the evidence from the USA, it seems likely that market initiatives increase the costs of providing any given quality of care. It remains an open empirical question as to how costs and quality will react to the changed structure and incentives. The lack of precision that has accompanied the proposed reforms does not encourage the view that the new regulatory framework will be able to constrain the cost pressures that will be introduced with these reforms.

Thus the impact of the reforms on the delivery of health care remains debatable. There is a dearth of evidence relating to the efficiency of different forms of delivery. There may be some *a priori* arguments that full integration of financing and delivery allows better monitoring and policing of the sector, at least at an aggregate level, and as such tempers the pressures associated with moral hazard. However, this is not to ignore the very real difficulties associated with both productive and allocative efficiency, which stem largely from a lack of incentive structures relating the utilization of health care services to their resource implications.

We can only suggest, given the lack of evidence, that the existing institutional financing and delivery of health care in the UK does appear to have a number of *a priori* benefits. In particular, it overcomes the major problems associated with insurance, and by integrating forward into provision provides a strong organizational means of monitoring resource use at the aggregate level. Certainly problems of allocation within the sector remain, and the proposals in the White Paper to collect better information on resource flows are to be commended, but to restructure the NHS because of these problems is likely to create a number of new and far-reaching difficulties which policy-makers may not have fully anticipated.

The White Paper implies that a more efficient allocation of health care resources can be achieved through maintaining public financing, but extending private production. The benefits, it is suggested, are to be achieved through the introduction of cost-based incentive schemes. Given that it remains undetermined how the budget holders themselves will gain from such schemes, it is debatable how appropriate such incentive schemes are. An obvious gain might be that high quality providers will receive a higher return for their services than low quality providers. But, given that it remains difficult to define quality, it is uncertain that variation in provider payments will necessarily produce this result. Moreover, given the fundamental uncertainties surrounding the production process it is unclear why private providers would willingly hold responsibility for all the contingencies associated with any contract. Certainly the presumed net benefits to be gained by replacing the existing governance structure, with its recognized faults, by a structure of budget-based incentive schemes, with its uncertain implications, remain unclear.

2

The Demand for Health Care and Health Insurance

TIMOTHY BESLEY*

1. Introduction

This chapter reviews the economic theory of the demand for health, health care, and health insurance, the main object being to exhibit explicitly the links between the three.

The analysis of demand plays a central role in modern economic analysis. It is central since it embodies some key tenets of the 'neoclassical' approach to microeconomics. Rational agents maximize a utility function, defined upon goods and services subject to a budget constraint. For many purposes, this conception is found to be satisfactory and as such, has been widely applied.[1]

An area in which the basic framework seems immediately less appropriate is in the realm of *health* (as, for example, Culyer, 1971c, has argued). None the less, there have been notable attempts at examining the demand for health as a good among others in an agent's utility function. This approach is associated most of all with the work of Grossman (1972a).[2] From the demand for health is derived the demand for health care. If health is regarded to be what yields utility directly (i.e. health care has no independent effect on utility) then the demand for health care is purely derived. But an agent's health state is subject to random shocks (such as the contraction of a disease), and to this end insurance is an issue. In many systems (and for reasons which we shall attempt to explain below), insurance is paid as a function of health expenditures, tying together the demand for health insurance and health care. It is with these demands and in particular their interdependencies that much of this chapter is concerned since they have important implications for the incentives to which health insurance gives rise. In the realm of policy, a proper understanding of them must precede measures designed to improve efficiency in health care provision and its finance.

* Princeton University. I am grateful to Paul Fenn and Alistair McGuire for their comments on an earlier version. However, they should not be held responsible for the contents of this chapter.

[1] For a comprehensive account of the modern theory see Deaton and Muellbauer (1980).

[2] For a simplified presentation, see McGuire, Henderson, and Mooney (1988).

Prior to addressing the main issues, I shall discuss a possible objection to proceeding via using conventional demand analysis at all. This is the view that health is such an important good that it cannot be traded off against other goods which we consume. How should we make sense of this claim? One reason why this may arise is because preferences between health and other goods are lexicographic[3] which, if true, prevents the construction of a utility function in the conventional way. However, assuming this degree of centrality for health seems too strong and quite contrary to any (albeit casual) evidence. People regularly undertake activities which worsen their health both now and in the future (e.g. smoking) yet presumably do so because they are prepared to trade a certain kind of pleasure against health. Most activities in which we engage have some implications for aspects of our health either now or in the future yet this aspect is rarely uppermost when we engage in them. Hence it does not seem so reasonable after all to claim that preferences for health are lexicographic. This does not deny that health may have a high value as compared with other goods, but this can be captured by the consumer's preferences and hence in the demand for health. In view of this, we will use some elements of standard demand theory as the cornerstone of an analysis of the demand for health, health care, and health insurance.

There are a number of policy issues of interest in studying these themes and we shall take many of these up again towards the end of this chapter. In most economic analyses, three types of motivation for state intervention can be found: arguments from the fact that the free market allocation is inefficient, arguments that it is inequitable, and arguments that individuals are not the best judges of their own interests. All three of these can be found in discussions of health and health care. This chapter reviews a particular framework for considering and weighing up these issues. Whilst in many ways simplistic, it has the virtue of putting them in sharp relief. Theoretical reasoning provides a tool for clear thinking about complex issues.

The parameters of interest for policy-makers are diverse and no amount of theorizing can provide a panacea for the problem of policy design. In much discussion in health economics, the focus has been upon the question of whether state provision of health care is desirable. Asking the question does not sit happily with the framework for analysis which much economics adopts and sits uncomfortably with the trichotomy of reasons for state intervention suggested in the last paragraph. While economists are interested in the state versus non-state provision question, perhaps because this has often been central to the political agenda, we shall proceed here in terms of a more traditional economic analysis.

---

[3] A preference for a good x is said to be lexicographically prior to that for a good y when more x is preferred *whatever* value of y is chosen. Hence states are evaluated in terms of the amount of x before the amount of y is brought into consideration. The term 'lexicographical' draws the analogy with words in a dictionary—all those beginning with a are ordered before any of those beginning with b.

Questions about the role of state provision are deliberately kept in the background. The framework of demand theory which we use here usefully permits these questions to be relegated.

The structure of this chapter is as follows. In the next section we examine the demand for health. In section three we look at the demand for health care, whilst section four considers insurance questions. Section five uses some of the earlier insights to reflect upon alternative systems of health care provision.

2. The Demand for Health

The demand for health is modelled much as the demand for any other commodity. Each individual maximizes utility subject to a budget constraint. Contrary to the simplest model of demand, health is not a good which can be bought and sold directly. Rather, health is produced using inputs in the form of health care. Hence a further constraint on individual utility maximization is imposed in the form of a technology for the production of health. Typically this technology will depend upon a whole set of a particular individual's characteristics. The model we are proposing here is not special to health demand. These models are generally known as 'household production models' and these have been examined by Becker (1965) and Gorman (1959/80) among others. In this more general case a household is thought of as caring about goods such as 'meals' into which food, energy, and time are inputs.

In the context of health, viewing the demand for health as being constrained by a technology is useful since it enables one, schematically, to divide the influences upon demand into those due to tastes and technologies. The latter we have already discussed. By the former we simply mean an individual's preferences. This kind of model was analysed in the context of the demand for health and health care by Grossman (1972). His analysis considers the dynamics of health care demand, i.e. how one invests in goods which improve one's health at different points in one's life cycle. He emphasizes that the gain from investing in one's health has two components. The first component is the consumption gain, i.e. the fact that being healthy enhances most things that one does. The second is an investment gain which constitutes a gain in one's lifetime earnings. This model has also been applied empirically, most notably by Grossman (1972) and by Wagstaff (1986).

3. The Demand for Health Care

As a first approximation, health care is often divided into two categories: preventative and curative. Whilst the categories undoubtedly overlap in some respects, there are pure cases. For example, taking an aspirin for a headache is a purely curative type of treatment, while a purely preventative treatment is something like a vaccine. Both of these can be set in the context of a demand for health. Curative medicine contributes directly to one's health state and hence can be seen as being motivated by the demand for health. On the other hand, preventative medicine is protection against future possible illnesses. By purchasing it, one affects the probability of becoming ill in the future and hence it is the *future* demand for health from which a demand for preventative medicine is derived.

In the purest case, a demand for curative health care arises when an agent wishes to demand more health immediately. Most often this arises in the face of a 'shock' to one's health state, i.e. if it is diminished for some reason (for example by contracting an illness). A central constraint faced by an agent in obtaining more health is the health technology described in the previous section.

After one's health state has fallen there are two possible effects to be accounted for. First, it may not be technologically possible to restore one's health to previous levels since the required technological means are unavailable. This arises for example if one has a limb amputated. However, in many instances one's day-to-day functioning might be restored despite certain injuries having been experienced. Hence, whilst one's state of health is in a strict sense irreversible it does not follow that one's functionings are permanently impaired. Second, even if this were not the case, the individual concerned may not choose to gain utility via an increase in health but rather chooses to substitute towards other goods and services because of the change in relative prices. Hence, we can think of experiencing ill health as analogous to a change in the relative prices of health and other goods. Health has become more expensive and agents may choose to switch from consuming it towards the consumption of other goods.

In many health care systems, the role of tastes is muted by the fact that insurance schemes are in force. These alter the price of health care to the consumer and in some cases provide health care free of charge. We postpone full consideration of insurance and its impact upon the demand for health care until later in the chapter. Whilst possibly diluting the role of tastes, it would be a mistake to think that it filters them out of the picture entirely. Even if health care itself is provided free of charge, the concomitant costs in consuming it might be substantial. For example, time off work and spent queuing may be substantial, or there may be travel costs involved in visiting a health facility. Furthermore, consumers have different degrees of aversion to submitting themselves for medical treatments. Hence, even if direct costs of purchasing health care are met by a third party, tastes may still play an important role in determining an agent's course of action in the face of ill health.

A third essential determinant of a consumer's reaction to an illness is his or her information. Better informed people may be inclined to treat themselves rather than seeking specialist advice. Alternatively, it may be those who are best informed who are inclined to seek specialist advice since they harbour less suspicion about putting themselves into the hands of health professionals. In many instances tastes and information are hard to disentangle. Knowing more may change my evaluation of an object, thereby changing my tastes.[4]

A further important factor determining the interaction between the demand for health and health care arises from introducing physicians into the picture. They play an important role in providing information and prescribing treatments. In doing so, however, they are constrained by technologies and to some degree by tastes. Patients have some say in what types of medical treatment they are prepared to submit to. Furthermore, individuals may choose whether or not to visit a health facility in the first place. Modelling the interactions between the tastes, technologies, and professional judgements which result in health care choices is a challenge for economic theory at a number of levels.[5] First, it seems implausible to model physicians as if they were entirely self-interested, yet one does not wish to model them with no self-interest either.[6] One wishes to model altruists not angels. Secondly, one has to recognize the 'power' available to physicians from the extreme asymmetric information which characterizes their dealings with most patients. Thirdly, one wishes to find some role for a patient's tastes. Neither a bargaining approach nor one based upon a principal–agent[7] relationship seems to capture all of the relevant subtleties of the physician/patient interaction, although either might cast some light upon the problem. Nevertheless, understanding the effects of medical insurance depends crucially upon obtaining some understanding of such interactions. Furthermore, as we suggest below, introducing insurance means that the interactions are complicated further since the insurance company becomes another actor whose behaviour influences the demand for health care.

There are a number of studies of the demand for health care which do not use the demand for health model of Grossman (1972). These studies are reviewed in detail by McGuire *et al.* (1988, Table 9.1, reproduced here as Table 2.1). The variable explained varies from patient-days, to admissions, to simply medical treatments. The way in which the price of health care is measured also varies somewhat. Once insurance is brought into the picture the price of health care

---

[4] Some of the issues concerning the role of information and evaluation in the provision for ill health are taken up in Besley (1989).

[5] A challenge first elucidated in Arrow (1963).

[6] For an interesting discussion on the morality and reality of the issues, see Gorovitz (1982).

[7] A principal–agent model is one in which a leader (a principal) sets an incentive scheme for a follower (the agent) subject to the actions of the follower being unobservable to the leader. For a detailed analysis of this problem, see Holmstron (1979). Some, for example Evans (1985), have remarked that the framework needs modification in the context of the demand for health care, since to some degree the principal and the agent do not have conflicting objectives. Whilst this is correct as a point of detail, it would be a mistake to attach too much importance to it unless one believed that the principal and agent had perfectly consonant interests. The principal–agent framework remains of interest as long as there is some difference in the interests of physicians and patients.

Table 2.1
Selected Own-price Elasticities of Demand: Hospital and Ambulatory Services

Study	Elasticities	Service	Price measurement	Data	Notes
Rosenthal (1970)	−0.24 to −0.70	Patient-days (length of stay) in medical categories	Cash payment as proportion of total hospital charge	Cross-section	Price criticized by Fuchs (1970) as not measuring price of service to consumer Variation in estimates due to estimation being based on various specialities
	−0.11 to −0.65	Patient-days (length of stay) in surgical categories	As above	As above	As above
Feldstein (1971)	−0.626	Hospital admissions	Net price calculated as insurance multiplied by gross price of service (proxied by average-cost deflated by RPI)	Pooled cross-section and time-series	Estimates relate to basic equation.
	−0.49	Mean length of stay			
	−1.12	Bed-days			
Davies and Russell (1972)	−0.19 to −0.46	Admissions	Variation in estimates reflects various price definitions	Cross-sectional	
Newhouse and Phelps (1974)	−0.29 to −0.13	Patient-days	Net price as proxied by gross price of bed multiplied by co-insurance rate	Cross-sectional	Variation in estimates reflects estimation procedure OLS or 2SLS
	−0.04 to −0.03	Hospital room and board	Co-insurance rate	Cross-sectional	As above
Newhouse and Phelps (1976)	−0.062	Patient-days	Net price as proxied by gross price of bed multiplied by co-insurance	Cross-sectional	Variation reflects different estimation procedures. 2SLS produced positive signed

Table 2.1, continued

Study	Elasticities	Service	Price measurement	Data	Notes
Newhouse and Phelps (1976)	−0.22 to −0.005 −0.24	Room and board Admissions	Co-insurance rate Co-insurance rate	Cross-sectional	
Feldstein (1977)	−0.13 (long-run) −0.01 (short-run)	Bed-days Bed-days	Net price proxied by average cost of service multiplied by insurance rate deflated by RPI	Pooled time-series and cross-sectional	Estimates relate to basic equations
Newhouse and Marquis (1978)	−0.05 −1.00	Hospital day Physician office visits	Co-insurance	Cross-sectional	Estimates relate to 1970 data
Carrin and van Dael (1984)	−0.22	Medical treatments	Reimbursed insurance cost as proxy for price	Time-series	Medical treatment is limited to certain technical treatments
Colle and Grossman (1978)	−0.106	Physician visits	Adjusted co-insurance rate	Cross-sectional	
Davis and Russell (1972)	−0.98 to −1.03	Out-patient services	Revenue from out-patient visits	Cross-sectional	
Fuchs and Kramer (1972)	−0.15 to −0.20	Physician visits	Average price of insurance	Cross-sectional	
Rossett and Huang (1973)	−0.35 to −1.15	Physician visits and hospitalization		Cross-sectional	
Newhouse and Phelps (1974)	−0.15 to −0.20	Physician visits	Co-insurance rate	Cross-sectional	
Manning et al.	−0.20	Total medical treatment	Co-insurance rate	Cross-sectional	Medical treatment includes all in-patient and out-patient care plus services provided by non-physicians, e.g. pharmacists

Source: The editors are grateful to Routledge and Kegan Paul for permission to use this table from *The Economics of Health Care*, by McGuire, Henderson, and Mooney (1988).

faced at the margin may become a function of the amount of care consumed. For example, this is true if there is a deductible, i.e. initially patients must pay their entire medical costs. Despite great differences in technique, data, and explanatory variables, most studies arrive at the intuitively agreeable result that the demand for health care is inelastic. However, there does seem to be some responsiveness by individuals to price. Hence individuals do seem to be prepared to trade off health care against other goods given some possibility. Recently, the evidence of Manning *et al.*(1987) from the Rand health insurance experiment has reinforced this conclusion. Confronting individuals with different co-insurance rates, they found that agents did seem to respond to co-payments in the way which demand theory predicts. They conclude that their 'results leave little doubt that demand elasticities are nonzero and indeed that the response to cost sharing is nontrivial' (Manning *et al.*, 1987).

Our discussion so far makes it clear that the demand for health care is not like the demand for many other commodities. On the other hand, one does not wish to divorce it too far from conventional analysis. Demanding other professional services, such as accountancy or legal advice, has many similar characteristics. There is no reason at all to believe that the conception of the process as a demand is inappropriate. It is more a question of extending demand analysis than of abandoning it. There is room for the economist's value theory, if it is desired, in the realm of health care demand. In view of this, we proceed to an investigation of health insurance.

4. The Demand for Health Insurance

The main function of an insurance contract is to reduce the risk faced by the person who buys it. Such contracts typically operate in terms of an agreement by the insurance company to pay something to the insured in the event of a particular outcome, in exchange for the payment of an insurance premium. An essential feature of a workable insurance contract is that the outcome which triggers the payment be observable to both parties to the contract. In the case of health insurance, the two parties to a contract are the patient and the insurance company, and there are two conditions upon which insurance payments can be made to depend: one is the state of health and the other is expenditure upon health care. Many insurance contracts also require there to be a third party whose role it is to assess whether a particular insurance claim seems reasonable, in the light of the state upon which insurance is paid out. In the case of health this would involve an insurance claim being assessed by a medically qualified individual with knowledge of the claimant's medical condition. For insurance based upon the latter, the role of the insurance assessor may be very important.

If insurance is written upon an agent's state of health, then an insurance contract typically pays a certain amount to the insured if a particular disease is experienced. In effect, the British NHS operates on such a basis. There is a payment in kind, in the form of health care which is determined as a function of one's health state. For example, if one needs a hip replacement the NHS 'pays out' in the form of a hip replacement operation tailored to the needs and particular circumstances of the patient in question. Similar contracts are also observed in the USA. The Medicare programme has recently instituted a system of diagnosis-related groups (DRGs) under which a hospital is paid a lump sum depending upon the disease in question and the treatment which it requires. Health maintenance organizations (HMOs), although forms of private insurance, operate in a fashion analogous to the NHS. We shall discuss these and DRGs further below.

At this point, it is essential to indicate that the question of what type of insurance system should be operated, is quite separate from the question of whether the state should be responsible for running the system. In fact, there are two distinct areas in which the role of the state can be important. The state may take on the role of insurer or the role of provider of medical care or both. However, there is no necessary connection between public provision of health care and insurance. It is better to organize the discussion around the structure of insurance contracts rather than around public versus private provision.

Whilst *in theory* disease-contingent contracts may be first-best[8] in the economic sense, in practice they may fall well short. A major problem is that in practice such contracts cannot practically be tailored to meet all individual needs. This has, indeed, been the major source of criticism of the DRG system which fails to discriminate between more or less complicated forms of disease. An NHS-style system, in which payment is in kind, can be more flexible, yet again does constrain some aspects of patients' choice. For example, food and other aspects of the environment in which one is treated are predetermined.

A second type of health insurance contract to which we give consideration bases insurance upon reimbursement of health expenditures. Instead of looking behind expenditures to the underlying condition for which treatment was received, such contracts reimburse the insured for expenditures incurred in the course of receiving treatment. This makes use of the fact that health expenditures are generally cheaply and easily observable to the patient and to the insurance company. This type of contract is often observed in practice: it is still

---

[8] In a world of diversified 'individual risks', optimal insurance, in the absence of any incentive problems, is that which sets the insured's marginal utility of expenditures equal to a constant no matter what his health state. Intuitively the optimality of this is seen by realizing that if it did not hold, then an agent could raise his utility overall by transferring resources from states where his marginal utility was at present high to those where it is low (assuming that marginal utility is decreasing in expenditure: the assumption of risk aversion).

Figure 2.1

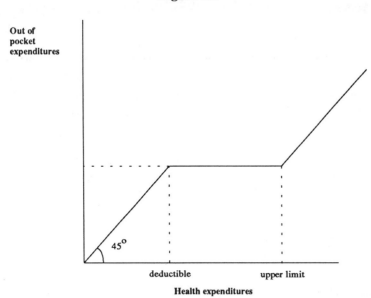

the dominant variety of insurance in the USA and in the private sector in the UK. In view of our discussions of sections two and three, these contracts are particularly interesting since they tie health insurance directly to the demand for health care and hence to the demand for health.

In practice such contracts have a simple structure.[9] The insured first of all faces a deductible, i.e. the first part of any claim is disallowed. After expenditures have exceeded this level there is reimbursement at a fixed rate (possibly 100 per cent), up to some upper limit, beyond which no coverage is given. A schedule of this form is given in Figure 2.1. Economic theory suggests that there is no reason why the best contract should be of this form, and there has been much discussion of optimal non-linear insurance schedules.[10] In practice the costs of calculating such schedules and the paucity of the information upon which such calculations could be based mean that economic agents are often most content with a simpler structure.

The deductible health insurance contract can be explained in a number of ways. Arrow (1963) has shown that without moral hazard, an optimal insurance contract has an agent completely insured above a deductible limit. However, deductibles may also serve a role in limiting the demand for health care if it is

[9] For a full discussion of the shape of such schedules and some of their implications see Keeler *et al.* (1977).
[10] See, for example, Holmstrom (1979). The key paper in the field, however, is by Mirrlees (1971).

deemed to be excessive, since it discourages repeated visits to a physician. The Rand Corporation's health insurance experiment has presented important evidence on this issue which is reported in Manning *et al.* (1987).[11] Deductibles in insurance contracts may also be explained by the presence of administrative costs[12] in processing insurance claims. Each claim has a fixed cost of processing and verifying the claim, i.e. a cost which is independent of the magnitude of the claim. Hence very small claims could not profitably be processed by an insurance company. With a deductible the size of claims is restricted to a level where all claims exceed their fixed administrative cost.

Both types of insurance scheme which we have considered, i.e. reimbursement insurance and disease-contingent insurance, are lacking in an important sense when viewed as means of compensation for those who are unhealthy. Both are structured around providing support for the cost of medical care. Neither, in practice, provides compensation for the fact that illnesses are unpleasant and impose psychic costs. In this sense most forms of health insurance that we observe are incomplete contracts. Further aspects of incompleteness derive from the fact that other costs of ill health, such as lost earnings, time spent queuing for treatment, and travel costs, are not covered. In some cases, separate insurances cover these contingencies, for example insurance against lost earnings in the event of sickness. However, one's overall impression of observed systems of health insurance, whether one looks at public or private insurance schemes, is of incomplete coverage against the effects of ill health. In this chapter we shall hereafter concentrate upon insurance focused upon coverage of medical expenses. We turn shortly to a discussion of the incentives which result from having an insurance scheme based upon reimbursing health care expenditures. Prior to this some more general issues, which form an essential backcloth, will be introduced.

(a) *Efficient and Equitable Allocations of Health Resources*

In most economic contexts normative questions about the allocation of resources are *neutral* with respect to the type of resource which is being considered. Normative questions are typically of two kinds: is the allocation efficient (normally in the sense of Pareto), and is the allocation equitable? These questions are normally raised with respect to allocations of all goods rather than with respect to health care in particular. Where health care is at issue, this neutrality is often rejected since some attach special significance to egalitarian distributions of health. As a general notion, this was introduced by Tobin (1970) as *specific egalitarianism*. Principally this view rejects the application of the

---

[11] Co-insurance rather than deductibles may be a more effective means of containing 'excessive' health expenditures. They are also compared in Manning *et al.* (1987).

[12] See Shavell (1977) for a development of a formal argument.

principle of consumers' sovereignty to health allocations.[13] If this is done, both
equity and efficiency characterizations must be modified.

Another reason for wishing to treat health differently has also emerged in the
influential work of Sen on welfare economics.[14] He has emphasized the poverty
of the traditional economists' approach to evaluation based upon utilitarian
accounts of value. The all-encompassing utility function in terms of which
outcomes are typically evaluated merges together different concepts. For
instance, while the statements that 'I desire x', 'I would be happy with x', and 'I
value x' are quite distinct (at least their meanings seem broadly different), the
framework for evaluation used in economics fails to make them distinct. Sen
advocates an approach to evaluating outcomes based on 'basic capabilities'.
Here is not, however, the place to expound this view. The interested reader is
referred to Sen (1986). None the less, the demand for health framework tends
to go hand-in-glove with the view that individual utility is the appropriate metric
for evaluating health outcomes. The reader should bear in mind that this way of
proceeding is not without its critics.

In our analysis, we will, however, proceed, for the time being, under the
assumption that individual choices over health *vis-à-vis* other goods provides a
sovereign criterion for evaluating the worth of these outcomes for normative
purposes.

We shall focus here primarily upon efficient rather than equitable allocations
of health care, although much of what we have to say has a bearing upon issues
of equity. To say that an allocation of resources is Pareto efficient implies that
nobody in the economy could be made better off without some other individual
being made worse off. One of the central theorems in microeconomic theory
says that all perfectly competitive equilibria with complete markets are Pareto
efficient. However, this theorem assumes that there are no externalities and that
the market structure is complete. It was Arrow (1964) and Debreu (1959) who
furnished us with the insight that the creation of markets for each 'state of the
world' could preserve the efficiency of competitive markets in the face of
uncertainty.[15]

In practice, markets *are* incomplete and hence competitive equilibria are in
general not efficient in theory. Economists have found it useful to refine the
notion of Pareto efficiency to that of *constrained* Pareto efficiency. This looks
at allocations which are Pareto efficient *given* the market structure in force (the
constraint being the markets in being). (See, for example, Diamond, 1967, and
Stiglitz, 1982, who discuss stock markets in this context.) Demands for health

[13] Musgrave (1959) refers to goods where we do not accept individual valuations as sovereign
as 'merit goods'. The idea is developed formally in Besley (1988a).

[14] See, for example, Sen (1986).

[15] Malinvaud (1972) refines this model to the case of 'individual risks' which is more appropriate
for the analysis of health care.

will none the less arise in each state of nature. Unless the equilibrium is constrained Pareto efficient then the demands will diverge from their efficient levels. Hence an increase or reduction (equally, a tax on or a subsidy to) in the demand for health care could be associated with a Pareto improvement.[16]

The importance of this tale emerges in trying to establish a benchmark for what one means by the efficient level of health care provision. It is often argued, as we observed above, that the demand for health care is increased by private or public insurance which leads to a socially excessive use of health inputs. While being unable to provide a cast-iron refutation of this one should at least be cautious in accepting it. Consider, for example, the case in which there is no insurance at all, then almost nobody would be able to afford to have certain kinds of expensive surgery, because of credit market failures. The advent of health insurance might greatly increase the demand for surgery. However, there is no *a priori* reason to regard the latter situation as necessarily less efficient. Indeed, compared with the initial position, it could yield a more efficient allocation of resources, if the economy were to progress towards the constrained Pareto optimal allocation of resources.

Once we are in the second best, one cannot maintain that anything which increases the demand for health care from its pre-insurance level results in 'excessive' demand for health care. Judgements of this variety require a more cautious approach.

A problem to which health insurance is subject, arising if individuals who are purchasing insurance are different in a way which affects the manner in which they demand health care, yet is unobservable to those from whom they purchase insurance, is that of adverse selection. This has been much analysed in the literature (see, for example, Pauly, 1974). In practice such problems are diminished when health insurance schemes operate for large groups of randomly selected individuals. This is likely to be true of schemes which operate in large firms, for example. Many health insurance schemes operate on this basis. Whilst conceding that the consequences of adverse selection in health insurance may be of importance, we shall not make this a focus of this paper. Instead, we shall concentrate on the problem of moral hazard to which we shall now turn.

(b) *Health Insurance and the Demand for Health Care: Moral Hazard*

Under reimbursement insurance there may be incentives to increase consumption of health care. These arise under three main headings, which tend to have been grouped under the single title of 'moral hazard' problems. We prefer to keep them separate.

---

[16] See Greenwald and Stiglitz (1986) for an extensive discussion of constrained Pareto efficiency and its theoretical implications for government intervention.

Insurance and Preventative Care

This variety of moral hazard problem arises when an insured individual alters his behaviour so as to affect the probability of incurring a particular level of health expenditures. For example, having health insurance may incline agents away from preventative medicine towards the now (relatively cheaper) curative medicine. Alternatively, in the knowledge that one is insured, one may pursue more dangerous sports (such as hang-gliding) or increase health damaging pursuits (such as smoking).

Whether these effects are likely to be observed in practice is uncertain and it seems unlikely that one might regard this as in any way the Achilles' heel of health insurance schemes. After all, given the intrinsic unpleasantness of illness, it seems unlikely that anyone would be inclined to trade cure for prevention to any great extent because insurance is available. None the less, as the direct analogue of the moral hazard problem discussed in the context of fire insurance—that once insured I may be less inclined to guard against a fire occurring—it is important to mention this potential moral hazard problem.

Physicians and Insurance

When patients are insured, then physicians may be inclined to change their behaviour also. They may prescribe more expensive and complex treatments than they would otherwise, since patients are to some degree insulated from the financial consequences of this. It seems unlikely that, but for having insurance, many patients would have the means to have a brain scan or to receive certain kinds of operation: a fact which would greatly constrain physicians' prescriptions.

It is for this reason that insurance companies often play an important role in the diffusion of new medical techniques. Physicians' behaviour is typically constrained by what forms of treatment are permissible for insurance purposes since otherwise they may be too expensive for many patients to undertake. The advent of new medical technologies therefore presents a problem for physicians. Until they are legitimized as objects of insurance coverage, they cannot be regularly prescribed.

Beyond the direct sphere of physicians' choice, there are other tendencies towards the inflation of costs due to health insurance as the 'non-health care' costs of seeking treatment are inflated. There is a tendency towards provision of more luxurious surroundings which is passed on into costs and is ultimately reflected in insurance premia.[17]

[17] For example, there may be a move towards more treatment in private rooms with luxuries such as televisions and telephones. These are not 'health care costs' as we commonly understand them. More borderline cases are things such as the installation of computerized record keeping—costs of which may be recouped from patients (and which may thereby be insurance financed) but which may or may not improve their medical conditions.

Arrow (1963, 1968) has emphasized the importance of trustworthy behaviour in ameliorating this problem: 'One of the characteristics of a successful economic system is that relations of trust and confidence between principal and agent are sufficiently strong so that the agent will not cheat even though it may be "rational economic behaviour" to do so.' This accords with our discussion of the role of physicians in the demand for health care.

Insurance and the Price of Health

As we mentioned above, reimbursement insurance works by designating a particular rate of coverage at the margin.[18] This *rate of insurance* determines a subsidy to health care. The insured's cost of health care is reduced by an amount proportional to the rate of insurance. This subsidy in turn induces an increased consumption of health care and, in accordance with the demand for health model, health. To see this, we can return to the model laid out in section 2 above.

When insurance is available at a rate α then health care with a cost of q per unit before insurance now costs $(1-\alpha)q$ per unit. Hence, the price of health care is lower at the margin under reimbursement insurance.

Referring to Figure 2.2, we can examine some consequences of this.[19] First, a fall in the price of health care from q to $(1-\alpha)q$ induces a rise in the demand for health from h to h'. The triangle ABC then represents the 'deadweight loss' resulting from such a move, i.e. loss in consumers' surplus. It arises since in otherwise competitive markets a subsidy on one good means that allocative efficiency is impaired (i.e. resources are no longer allocated in a Pareto efficient way).

The size of the triangle ABC is inversely related to the price elasticity of demand for health care (see Feldstein, 1973). This can be seen by noting that, for a given subsidy, the triangle analogous to ABC is larger, the flatter the demand curve, i.e. the more elastic is the demand for health care. Hence the 'deadweight loss' of having reimbursement health insurance increases as the elasticity of demand for health care increases.[20]

Against the loss implied by losing the conditions for allocative efficiency[21] one must weigh the gains from improved risk sharing. Consumers of health care gain since they are to some degree insulated in their health expenditures.

Note that the effect discussed here is quite different from that discussed in the previous sub-section on physicians and insurance. Physicians need play no part

---

[18] This has been recognized and discussed in Pauly (1968) and Feldstein (1973).

[19] Our presentation follows that of Feldstein (1973).

[20] This argument is generalized in Besley (1988b) to allow for cross elasticities and for different goods having different risk profiles.

[21] We are assuming here that the economy is otherwise first-best. This argument needs modifying if there are other distortions.

Figure 2.2

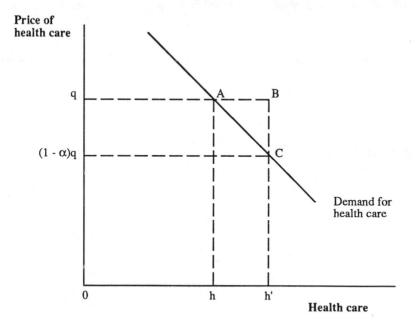

in the effects discussed in this section. They would occur *no matter who* was choosing health care provision.

(c) *Risk Sharing vs. Incentives in Health Insurance*

The previous discussions make it clear that insurance conditioned upon expenditures on health care may result in increases in demand for health and health care. Note, however, that one cannot say *a priori* that such increases are detrimental. As we argued in section 4(a), in the absence of insurance we are not in a 'first-best' world. Indeed it might seem reasonable to suppose that the demand for health care would be heavily constrained were there no insurance at all.

In part, this might be overcome if credit markets worked efficiently since then it might be possible for agents to borrow to finance medical treatments.[22] However, credit markets also tend to work imperfectly: lenders cannot distinguish between borrowers who are honest and dishonest, and are unable to monitor what their borrowers do with borrowed funds, which may be invested in a risky activity making repayment less likely.[23] The existence of imperfect credit markets therefore enhances the value of insurance.

[22] See Grossman and Weiss (1984) for a precise version of this argument.

[23] These are the adverse selection and moral hazard problems respectively.

The main issue in the provision of health resources therefore becomes that of trading risk-sharing possibilities against some possibly adverse incentives to consume increased amounts of health care. In much recent economics it is fashionable to appeal to asymmetries of information, i.e. one party in a contract knowing more than another, as the main constraint upon overcoming the incentive problems that we discussed in the previous section.

If an insurance company could monitor an agent's risk-taking behaviour (e.g. his propensity to go hang-gliding), then it would be possible to write an insurance contract which stipulated a maximum number of hang-gliding hours, for example. Similarly, if the insurance company could monitor in detail the activities of providers of medical care then it could stipulate precise modes of treatment which counteracted the incentives under insurance.

There are two main constraints upon this. First, monitoring and information acquisition is itself very costly, sometimes prohibitively so. Second, it ignores the ethical and social framework surrounding medical care. The nature of the relationship between physicians and patients is intrinsically confidential and one based on trust. It is unthinkable that any third party should be allowed to play a very detailed monitoring role. Mandates from insurance companies concerning modes of treatment could not be regarded as acceptable for ethical reasons.

Altogether, informational asymmetries and the social framework of control prevent the problems of incentives to consume excessive medical care from being solved directly. Instead, indirect solutions must be entertained. One such has recently emerged in the USA amidst some measure of controversy. This is the diagnosis-related group as mentioned above. Introduced for Medicare, this method of control pays out an amount for treatment which depends upon what illness a patient is suffering from. However, the categories are broad and neglect finer details. Such a scheme represents, in some ways, a break with the notion of reimbursement insurance, and a move towards disease contingent insurance. It can be viewed in the main as a response to the tendency of medical expenditures to increase under conventional reimbursement schemes. It fights against the tendency of physicians to prescribe expensive drugs and technologies. Moreover, it limits the inflation of medical costs resulting from the subsidy to medical care which health insurance grants. It therefore limits the increase in the demand for health and health care in the face of insurance.

However, this innovation has proved controversial, in the main because of the perceived encroachment upon the autonomy of physicians. For many, it presents an unacceptable intrusion into the ability of physicians to prescribe the correct treatment for a particular patient, rather than being constrained to prescribing what would be right for the patient on average.[24]

---

[24] The trend of medical-malpractice litigation in the USA may by itself have enforced a trend towards uniformity of treatment for certain diseases. For a survey of these issues see Danzon (1985).

In the next section we turn to the question of regulation of health insurance and its consequences for equity and efficiency.

5. Health Care Provision and Regulation

A number of implications for health care provision and regulation follow from the above. Most obviously there is the possibility that insurance based upon reimbursement of medical care may induce incentives towards increased consumption of medical care. Policy to counteract these incentives without subverting the whole institution of reimbursement insurance might be envisaged. First, the government might offer subsidized preventative care to help counteract any incentives away from this. Second, it might regulate the behaviour of health care providers directly in a broad way, i.e. regulating charges for medical treatment and to some extent the prescription of advanced and experimental treatments. A third solution might involve discouraging people from taking out high rates of coverage. A tax on health insurance which was negatively related to the degree of co-insurance might have such an effect. More crudely, a straight tax on health insurance or at least a removal of its tax advantage might help in controlling some of the incentives since individuals would choose less coverage.[25]

Arrow (1963, 1968) has emphasized the role of non-economic relations of 'trust' in combating unfavourable incentives and has doubted the efficiency of relying on purely economic incentives. For example, he mentions reliance upon 'the professional ethics of physicians not to prescribe frivolously expensive cost of treatment, at least where the gain is primarily in comfort and luxury rather than in health improvement proper'. This internalization of moral principles might go some way towards meeting the incentive problems which attend reimbursement insurance, but it seems unlikely that they could completely obviate the need for external intervention. This is especially true if one has reasons to doubt that physicians are the best judges of restraint in providing medical care, with the incentives which the Hippocratic oath entails.

Other solutions involve movements away from *reimbursement* insurance as an institution. Among these, we have discussed diagnosis-related groups which make insurance payments a function of the medical condition. An alternative is to move to a system of payment in kind. In a certain sense the health maintenance organizations (HMOs) which have grown up in the USA are such an example. This breaks with the third party structure which normally characterizes health insurance market and merges the provider of care with the insurer. The NHS is effectively such an institution which despite early prognostications[26] has not

[25] This issue of tax policy towards health insurance and health care in the USA has recently been analysed in Pauly (1986).

[26] See, for example, Buchanan (1964).

been subject to the large inflation in medical expenditures witnessed by the predominantly reimbursement system in the USA. These systems can be thought of as anathema to the demand for health conception, which emphasizes sovereignty of consumers and their demands. Breaking this link provides the central philosophical difference between reimbursement systems and those which focus on more direct controls of treatment and prescription.

What then can be said about the optimal provision of health care or the optimal design of health systems in the light of our discussion? First we must establish whether we regard individual valuations of health as sovereign. In terms of the above discussion, this pertains to whether or not we attach normative significance to the contracts reached in private health care markets between physicians and patients. This is an important first step.

For the sake of argument, suppose that this step in is complete and that we conclude that we accept private valuations. The second step involves considerations of equity and efficiency. The efficiency loss with private insurance may arise because of the problems of adverse selection and moral hazard referred to above. The equity issues are a little more complex. Individuals may lose from having to pay higher insurance premia. Moreover, these premia may increase to a point at which some consumers cannot afford to purchase insurance at all. Under plausible assumptions, these will be consumers with low incomes.

State systems of health care provision typically do not respect the demand for health directly. Most systems operate by providing a fixed quality of care in a particular way. This also entails an efficiency loss (see Besley and Coate, 1989, for the development of a particular model of this) since individuals are not finding the levels and types of health care which maximize their utility. This represents the efficiency loss in many public health care systems. It also rationalizes the two-tier system which tends to emerge with higher-income individuals opting out to buy care (and possibly insure) in the private sector. On the other hand, health care provision becomes a benefit targeted towards the poor and equity objectives may be served.

Since both public and private systems entail effects on equity and efficiency, one cannot say *a priori* which should be chosen. None the less, it is comforting that economic theory provides no grindstone for political axes. State versus non-state provision for health care is a second-order question. It is questions of efficiency and equity and one's acceptance or rejection of principles of consumer sovereignty in health care demand which are the desiderata of economic analyses.

3

The Normative Economics of Health Care
Finance and Provision

A.J. CULYER*

1. Introduction

Whereas in many countries the 'crisis' in medical care has been seen in terms of 'excess' spending on health services, in the UK it has been seen (at least by most of those who manage and work in the NHS) as a crisis of 'underfunding'. This has come about as the result of the government's successful attempts to restrain the rate of growth of real spending on the NHS, which in turn reflects the government's belief that its principal effective weapon against what it perceives to be inefficiency in the NHS is to challenge management (itself reformed and to some extent liberated) by systematic financial squeezes. The same concern has given rise to a host of proposals for reform of the NHS most of which involve a much greater role for private insurance, private finance of other kinds (such as out-of-pocket payments), and private provision of health care itself.

Few of these contributions have been informed by the work of health economists, particularly their normative work. There have been several reviews of the empirical literature (e.g. Culyer *et al.*, 1988; Culyer *et al.*, 1988). This essay is a review of the main contributions of a more conceptual kind.

I have adopted the rather general term 'normative' in my title, rather than 'welfare economics' for a reason. This is that much of the modern systematic approach to policy questions in the health territory is based on an approach that transcends (and may come to supersede in part) the 'welfarist' tradition of normative economics.

A key concept underlying the current discussion is 'efficiency'. This is, however, far from being an unambiguous notion and, because it is also so central a concept (one indeed that pervades the entire debate) it is the one that preoccupies me in this paper. The practical context in which the concept can

* University of York. I am grateful for the helpful comments of Richard Arnould, Gwyn Bevan, Paul Fenn, Alastair McGuire, Gavin Mooney, John Posnett, and Alan Williams. The usual disclaimer applies.

illuminate is, evidently, scarcely less important. For the purposes of this paper, the practical context is taken to relate to broad policy questions about the 'efficiency' (somehow defined) of ways of financing health care (e.g. through private, competitive insurance or via compulsory public insurance), and of the user-prices that it should carry (e.g. whether 'free', partially subsidized, not at all subsidized, differentially subsidized according to particular categories of user).

These are the principal 'demand-side' contextual questions whose discussion forms the bulk of the paper. There is, of course, a host of related questions that arises in specific policy formulation and a whole raft of supply-side 'efficiency' questions. These may from time to time be alluded to here, or cross-references made to other papers in this volume. They are not, however, the main focus.

The conventional ways in which economists use the term 'efficiency' (which at this level of generality are illuminating and ideologically innocuous) are the following:

technical efficiency: obtaining when for a given output the amount of inputs used is minimized, or (what is the same thing) when for a given combination of inputs, the output is maximized. This is a supply-side concept that is a necessary condition embodied in the subsequent concepts of efficiency. In economic jargon it means 'being on an isoquant'. Since there is usually more (many more) than one way of producing an output that meets this condition, the implied balance of resource use even for a given target output is not unique.

cost-effectiveness: obtaining when for a given output the cost is minimized, or (what is the same thing) when for a given cost the output is maximized. This is also a supply-side concept. It embodies technical efficiency (clearly if one were using more inputs than were technically necessary to produce an output, that cannot be cost-effective) and the cost-effectiveness version of efficiency is also embodied in the next concept of efficiency. Being cost-effective necessarily eliminates as 'inefficient' some technically efficient combinations of inputs, but it leaves unsettled the question of the efficient rate of production. In economic jargon, cost-effectiveness means 'being where an isocost line is tangential to an isoquant'.

ideal output: obtaining when cost-effective outputs are produced at a rate that is 'socially' optimal and allocated to individual members of society in a 'socially' optimal fashion. This is 'top-level' efficiency and arises from combining supply-side and the demand-side considerations. In a society with limited resources it entails establishing rates and allocations of outputs that are such that no alternative rates of reallocations can be perceived that are 'better'. In economic jargon it entails setting marginal rates of transformation on the production side equal to marginal rates of substitution in consumption.

While this trio is an extremely useful sorting device in discussions of efficiency, the main focus in this paper is on the third, though (as will be seen) ambiguities about the concept of 'output' will force us also to look to some extent at the other two notions of efficiency as well. Of the various tricky things embodied in 'ideal output' as a concept of efficiency, one that has come to the fore in health economics in a distinctive way concerns the meaning of 'socially' and 'better' (or 'optimal').

(a) *Welfarism and Extra Welfarism*

One approach in health economics, which has become the traditional one in economics as a whole, is what Sen (1977) calls 'welfarist'. This is very much in accord with liberal political opinion and asserts that social welfare (any increase in which is 'better' than none) is a function only of individual welfare (or utility) and judgements about the superiority of one state of the world (defined by reference to these utilities) over another are made irrespective of the non-utility aspects of each state. Moreover, the individual welfares (or utilities) are a function only of goods and services consumed.

The other approach, which might be termed 'extra-welfarist', relaxes what its adherents see as an undue information restriction in welfarism so that other aspects of each social state are also embodied in the judgement. Since, in the welfarist approach, the basis of social welfare—or diswelfare—is only the utility got from goods and services (including labour services), an important class of 'extra' welfare sources is the non-goods characteristics of individuals (like whether they are happy, out of pain, free to choose, physically mobile, honest). Extra-welfarism thus transcends traditional welfare: it does not exclude individual welfares from the judgement about the social state, but it does supplement them with other aspects of individuals (including even the quality of the relationships between individuals, groups, and social classes).

This distinction is actually quite old in the history of (the so-called 'new') welfare economics. In Bergson's (1938) classic theoretical article, for example, his social welfare function included unspecified terms that could be interpreted as extra-welfarist elements of the sort just described. But he dropped them in favour of an explicit 'partial' analysis after a page.

Another famous extra-welfarist strand in the wider literature is the notion of merit goods (Musgrave, 1959)—goods whose consumption is considered so meritorious (by government) that they are made available on terms that are more generous than in the market-place. Despite (unsuccessful) attempts to bring merit goods into the welfarist scheme of things (e.g. Culyer, 1971a), it seems altogether more preferable to adjust the scheme of things so as to incorporate such considerations fully rather than leaving them as a kind of *ad hoc* 'escape clause' (Margolis, 1982) lying outside traditional theory; not fitting into it but necessary in order to prevent theoretical emasculation (inability to explain why some common phenomena are observed, inability to discuss in a consistent normative framework some matters that are of evident normative importance). This plainly involves the possibility of overruling individual judgements of value and raises the question not only of the weights to be attached to individual utilities in a social welfare function but of who should be assigning those weights. Should the values of some members of society count for more than those of others?

More recently an explicit departure from welfarism was advocated by Williams (1972) and discussed further by Sugden and Williams (1978) in the context of cost–benefit analysis. This is the 'decision-making' approach which is contrasted with the 'Paretian' approach. The latter is one example of welfarist analysis in that social welfare is a function only of the utilities to individuals of goods and services. The former allows that governments (and other 'decision-makers') may have other objectives than the making of (actual or potential) Pareto improvements, which may involve not only imposing their own values on the consumption of individuals (rather than those of the individuals in question) as with merit goods, and their own view of the appropriate intertemporal discount rate, but also takes into account some extra-welfarist elements of choices that pure welfarism excludes. In this context the answer to the question 'who decides what entities with what weights go into the social welfare function?' is 'decision-makers'.

The bulk of the health economics literature is decidedly welfarist in orientation—and Paretian to boot. This is discussed in section 2. Section 3 addresses the more recent extra-welfarist tendencies of health economists, and also (since the approach lends itself so readily to this) looks at the ways in which extra-welfarism has infiltrated the supply-side notions of efficiency.

Although the discussion is of a normative literature, it should be pointed out that in neoclassical economics it is easy to slip between positive and normative (welfarist-style) according as to whether one treats utilities as behaviour-generating indices or ascribes direct normative value to them. Thus, some of the literature on the NHS (e.g. Lindsay, 1969; Culyer, 1971b) was ostensibly *explanatory*: the authors sought to provide empirically falsifiable accounts of some of the institutional features of the NHS by postulating the presence of particular arguments in individual utility functions. Under welfarism, it is quite easy to re-interpret these theories as claims for the Pareto-efficiency of the NHS. In the positive interpretation, the institutional features are phenomena shown (or so it is claimed) to be the predicted results of utility-maximizing individuals' behaviour in particular environments; in the normative interpretation, the institutional features are seen as desirable attributes rather than merely explained phenomena: the theory *justifies* what is or implies what *ought to be*, prescribing rather than predicting.

As a final prefatory remark it is worth pointing out that health economics (in common with many other fields of application within economics) has by and large addressed only a *part* of the agenda of the 'political economy' of health care, to do with finance, public or private. There is very little on the normative implications of different forms of ownership or organization on the provider side. Indeed, the aforementioned positive theories of the NHS (Lindsay, 1969; Culyer, 1971b) are typical in that they are concerned entirely with the *terms of access* to health care. Although it may have frequently been thought in the past that arguments for 'free' or subsidized or publicly financed health care were *ipso facto* arguments for publicly provided care, that is not so. Public finance can in principle be combined with public *or* private provision, just as privately financed consumption can be combined with public or private provision. That is why it is possible for people who support the general idea of free health care available at the time it is needed also to support private provision, or a public/private mix in provision, or competitive 'internal markets' within the public system. However, the focus here is on the demand side, and so no further development of these possibilities is attempted.

2. The Welfarist Approach to Health Care Finance and Provision

It was (and is) common for these issues to be addressed by considering a set of factors that make health care 'different' from other goods or services and which therefore may constitute a reason for wanting to allocate it differently from these 'other' goods or services (and to evaluate the efficiency of different allocations differently) (Culyer, 1971a). Implicit in this approach is the presumption that goods and services are in principle best allocated by market mechanisms and that departures from that mechanism require special warrants. This seems to be the product of a particular bit of cultural conditioning to which most (Western) economists are prone but, since it is my purpose more to outline an approach than to make sociological comments on its culture-contingency, I shall say no more on that here. The following sections embrace the usual 'list' of factors that make health care 'different' and I shall indicate the kind of reasoning that relates to each.

(a) *The Competence of the Consumer*

The welfarist approach requires that choices made by or for consumers be rational in the particular sense of that term used by economists. Should choices *not* be founded on axioms that include, for example, an ability to compare alternatives and to rank them consistently (transitively, if weakly) in order of preference, the entire edifice tumbles because it no longer becomes possible to infer from actual behaviour that the choices made were (subject to resource constraints) those most preferred. Even if consumers were better informed than they typically are about the pros and cons of alternative actions (for example, choices between alternative strategies of personal medical treatment) there are occasions when even mentally healthy people prove incapable of choosing (especially between alternatives that involve horrid consequences). Mentally ill and mentally handicapped people may more frequently be found to be 'irrational' in this sense. There are also occasions, of course, in which they are incapable of making any choices at all (for example, when they are the traumatic and unconscious victims of accidents).

It is common for the consumer, who is almost invariably incompetent in some degree, to defer some of the judgements involved in clinical choices to professionals, especially medical doctors, who act as *agents* on his or her behalf: ideally choosing in the way the individual would, had he or she been possessed of the same informational advantages as the professional, in a system characterized by what Evans (1981) has termed 'incomplete vertical integration' between consumers and producers.

The particular technical skill possessed by the professional that is relevant here is a better knowledge of the effect that health care will have on health. If one supposes that it is health which generates utility for individuals, both directly via a sense of well-being and indirectly in the sources of welfare of which better health enables one to take advantage, then health care is itself only instrumental: a means to an end. Even if the consumer is able rationally to value health, he or she will usually have much less information about the *process* of medicine and the *risks* that different processes imply. Contrary to the usual welfarist assumption, the buyer is not the best judge of his or her interests but must rely on the seller's advice. It is quite easy to imagine circumstances in which the selfish interest of the professional can conflict with the best interests of the patient. Health itself is not a traded commodity, yet that is what the rational consumer may be expected to seek. The traded commodities are information and health care, which the consumer unaided cannot normally be expected to evaluate, and neither of which are valued for themselves.

The technical expert is thus required to be more than 'merely' a technical expert. In acting as agent, the expert as it were 'enters the skin' of the patient. This is what seems to endow a *professional* relationship with its most important—but elusive and delicate—characteristic (Trebilcock *et al.*, 1979). Being delicate, it is vulnerable. It is vulnerable to cultural assumptions not shared by agent and client (the male-dominated specialty of obstetrics is often charged with sexist disregard of the interests of its wholly female clientele). It is vulnerable to misplaced technological zeal, in which the expert subjects the patient to painful diagnostic testing that yields little usable additional information, or makes presumptions about a patient's trade-offs between short-term risks and long-run benefits. It is vulnerable to class bias, in which the professional, as a member of a higher class than at least some patients, is incapable of 'entering their skins'. It is also vulnerable to financial distortions, whereby some systems of medical remuneration encourage the supply of services whose principal justification is the income they bring the expert rather than the benefit they bring the patient. This is sometimes referred to as *supplier-induced demand* (Evans, 1974, 1976). These 'vulnerabilities' are forms of market failure and are widely regarded as justifications for regulatory measures to protect both consumers and doctors; the former from quacks and the exploitation of a professional monopoly, the latter also from quacks (unfair competition) and the unreasonable demands of dissatisfied (and possibly litigious) customers. They also provide the basis for universally observed systems by which medical education is determined and entry to the profession regulated, and for subsidized in-service training systems and other professional activities. The existence of such market failures means that there are inevitably nice balances to be struck here between, for example, the self-regulating monopoly awarded to doctors in medical practice and its possible abuse by inhibiting innovation (e.g. alleged but not actual quackery, inefficiency in doing whatever is done, and the earning of monopoly rents). While economics is helpful in identifying the risks, and in predicting the consequences of policies designed to mitigate them, its role is mainly qualitative: much judgement is required in making assessments of the pros and cons, and their respective strengths, of alternative possible arrangements in what is effectively a second-best, or third-best, world.

(b) *Supplier-Induced Demand (SID)*

Evans' idea that physicians have a target income and adjust workload (under a fee-for-service system of paying doctors) in response to changes in the environment, seems to have grown out of the empirical observation that regional utilization of health care is positively associated with the regional stock of doctors, holding price and other variables constant (Fuchs, 1978; Cromwell and Mitchell, 1986; Phelps, 1986). The thesis is that physicians will induce patients to use more services in order to maintain income. A positive association has also sometimes been found between physician stock and prices, though this result is even more disputed than the fundamental utilization effect (Sloan and Feldman, 1978; Auster and Oaxaca, 1981; Green, 1978). There are, of course, huge econometric and empirical problems in testing for SID—only one study for example (Pauly, 1980) controlled (approximately) for patient health status—but Rice's claim (Rice, 1983, 1987) that experimental rather than routine data strongly support an inverse relationship between reimbursement rates and use of services seems persuasive.

SID is an area in health economics where we suffer an *embarras de richesses*. The target-income hypothesis is one possible explanation. But there are others too that have never been rigorously compared and tested: increasing the numbers of doctors increases their availability (less distance to travel, less time to wait) and hence reduces the 'time price' to patients; there may be 'excess'[1] demands at the existing stock and a non-market-clearing price, so that increasing utilization following increases in the stock is simply the meeting of previously unmet 'excess' demand. Doctors may be less vulnerable to the effects of consumer detection of SID in communities with a low doctor/population ratio since, given extensive consumer ignorance, new patients can always be found to replace any who leave because of the SID they detect—if so, cross-sectional analysis will produce the observed correlation between physician stock and utilization. It is unfortunate that this unsatisfactory state of the art persists—and is compounded by empirical uncertainty (at least in some minds) about the very existence of SID at all—given the huge potential threat that SID constitutes to the welfarist approach and especially to the pro-market camp within the welfarist school. If demand curves really do reflect the health-irrelevant preference of suppliers then, depending on the depth of this contamination, the use of willingness to pay as an indicator of consumer welfare is more or less illegitimate. Hence the considerable amount of passion found in the literature on this subject.

(c) *Where Does this Get Us?*

The chief lesson for health care finance to be drawn from this catalogue is not that the 'market' is inherently more flawed than the 'state' in the way in which medical care is financed (or *vice versa*) but that there are no simple lessons to be drawn. Market systems and their (usual) fee-for-service methods of paying doctors are prone to violate the underpinnings of welfarism in one way. State systems and their (usual) salary or capitation sytems are prone to violate the underpinnings in another. If fee-for-service may encourage an excess of interventionist zeal then salaries and capitation fees may do the opposite. Under either system it is common to see a lot of inter-regional variation (McPherson *et al.*, 1981; Vayda *et al.*, 1982).

The agency relationship must inherently be incomplete. The professional may know best about the instrumentality of health care and, if working in a system that encourages a concern for the *whole* patient (as is usually the case in general practitioner services in those medical care systems like the UK's that still have GPs), may also come to know a good deal of relevant information about the patient's values, financial circumstances, working life, and family context. In such circumstances the agency relationship is likely to be as perfect as it probably can be. But even in this situation, the agent too has his or her own

---

[1] I put the term in quotation marks as I do not wish to imply that the demands are necessarily in excess of a second-best rate of use, merely that they are excess in the (positive economics) sense of demand exceeding price at the going full user-price.

values, financial interests, working relationships, family, and social characteristics which need not be congruent to those of the patient (Evans, 1984). In both market and non-market systems of health-care finance and provision, the medical monopoly is strong which seems to produce higher monopoly rents in the more market-orientated systems (but see Lindsay, 1973).

As regards the terms of access for consumers, much of this discussion casts doubt on the usefulness of marginal willingness to pay as an adequate representation of the marginal benefit to consumers, but it is not clear what the notion of welfarism requires to be put in its place, nor is it clear whether 'free' care under the NHS or under first-pound zero-deductible health insurance encourages inefficient rates of use relative to a second-best optimum. On this issue, as will be seen, the extra-welfarists are able to be more forthright.

(d) Caring and Sharing

In the early days of the welfarist literature, the idea that health care was 'different' because the medical care consumption of others, or the health of others, may be a direct influence on the welfare of oneself, was given short shrift. There was early recognition (e.g. Weisbrod, 1961) that a direct physical externality might exist in cases of communicable disease (via infection or contagion): an individual in choosing or rejecting vaccination may fail to take account of the benefits accruing externally (viz. to others) in the form of a reduced probability of the others contracting a disease. This was conceded to provide a case (abstracting from the problems arising from consumer incompetence) for subsidized prices for such services and, in some cases, for making them compulsory (e.g. for immigrants). But the scope for interference with the market on this ground alone was evidently highly limited and the marginal externality probably falls quite fast as the proportion of immunized individuals rises.

The subtler kind of externality, direct interdependence of the form that makes one person's welfare directly dependent on the consumption of others, was not taken very seriously (e.g. Lees, 1960, 1962; Jewkes et al., 1963; Klarman, 1963, 1965; Buchanan, 1965). The view is well-encapsulated by Lees (1967):

It is argued that there is another relevant externality, namely, the disutility felt by an individual at the thought that others are not getting adequate medical care. This is no doubt so and is the basis of philanthropic support for health services. But the important point here is that there is nothing special about health services in this regard. Similar disutility is felt at the thought of others not getting adequate food, clothing, housing, and other goods commonly regarded as necessities. Apart from philanthropy, the community approach to this problem has typically been public subsidies to those in need. Externalities of this kind do not establish even a *prime facie* [sic] case for the abolition of markets and the substitution of collective arrangements.

Even where externalities exist, recent studies have shown that the scope for government spending to correct market imperfections and raise the general level of economic efficiency is less than conventional analysis had led us to believe. The implications of these studies may be summarized thus:

(a)   many externalities are irrelevant to human action and the achievement of optimal solutions;

(b)   many relevant externalities can be, and are, dealt with voluntarily;

(c)   the costs of governmental intervention, even when it is 'perfect', may outweigh the benefits;

(d)   the imperfections of government as a decision-making and choice-making process may make an 'imperfect' market situation more imperfect.

Such was the dominant idea at that time: the 'nothing special' about health argument; the distinction between philanthropy approved at one level of collectivity (private charity) but not at a higher (governmental) level; the reference to studies showing the scope for corrective government action to be limited; the mention of things which 'may be' (but which are not) measured to find out what actually is.

One of the ironies of the period was that these remarks and others in the same genre were being made in societies that had substantially altered the terms of financial access to health care, possibly for reasons (in part) of externality. At least, such a view would imply the possibility that the subsidy arrangements were a rational response to a real situation rather than the irrational constructions of ideologues unversed in the eternal truths of neoclassical economics. It might be thought that the reasons for this intervention were like those for similar interventions in education and housing. Since even crude policies might have gone sufficiently far to eliminate most Pareto-relevant marginal externalities, casual observation could not have revealed massive failures to internalize at efficient rates of utilization: one needed both observation of what was and what otherwise *would probably have been* to make an assessment of the significance of externalities; at the very least one needed the imagination to envisage what a counterfactual 'uninternalized' world might look like.

What sort of evidence might settle this issue of the existence and size of what some have called 'caring' externalities (e.g. Culyer, 1980)? One is introspective. Are sufficient numbers of introspectors prepared to sacrifice some of their own consumption so that others may have more? If so, they care in the externality sense. In particular, invite introspectors to try to imagine a society in which health care was supplied entirely by commercial organizations without public subsidy or by private charities. Ask each, given that they had imagined themselves into such a society, whether they would be willing to sacrifice some of what each has so that others would receive more. If each would (and they may want to add the side condition that each would sacrifice only if others similarly placed also made sacrifices) then they would be providing evidence for the existence of caring externalities of this sort.

One of the issues that arises in this context is the question of whether subsidies should be specific (e.g. in-kind or directly tied to purchases of specific goods and services as with voucher schemes) or general (essentially income support). The basic line of argument has tended to be that it seems that generalized support may be appropriate for goods and services that are highly income elastic at low levels of household income, where there will be a strong presumption that income supplements will be spent by most families on basic necessities like food (so there is no need for a 'National Food Service'), but that where this is not the case, or where people are held to be poor judges of their own welfare, specific subsidies are a more cost-effective means of promoting consumption of particular goods since they utilize substitution effects as well as income effects. It should be clear that the potential superiority of specific subsidies arises from the welfare gain to the subsidy-provider: in any comparison of alternatives, provided that the subsidy-receiver is not worse off under one than the other, that yielding the largest benefit to the subsidy-provider is Pareto-preferred.

There has been some speculation about the way in which inequality in health care consumption enters welfarist utility functions. This seems mostly to have arisen in the context of positive rather than normative economics: to provide *explanations* of the patterns of subsidy actually observed in various societies. From the late 1960s into the early 1970s, focus continued to be upon the *consumption of health services* as the principal source of external 'concern' (rather than, say, the effect of such consumption on health), though for some the focus was on absolute rates of consumption while for others it was relative.

Pauly (1971) argued that the (negatively sloped) external demand (marginal valuation) for a person's care was invariate with respect to the identity of the person of concern and that the demand for health care was, in general, income elastic. Detailed micro empirical studies (all North American) on this latter question yield little unambiguous evidence about direct income elasticities (though they seem to be positive) because of income-related upper limits on out-of-pocket expenses under health care insurance (see, e.g., Manning *et al.*, 1987), though aggregate studies show income elasticities of between 1.18 and 1.36, so that a 10 per cent increase in (aggregate) income can be expected to lead on average to a roughly 12.5 per cent increase in health-care spending (for a review see Culyer *et al.*, 1988 and, for a critique, Parkin *et al.*, 1987).

There seems little doubt about the overall negative slope of demand curves. The econometric evidence is not easily interpreted, partly because in those systems which have been most studied—North American—fee-for-service and the possibility of supplier-induced demand can cause supply-side contamination of the 'pure' substitution effects of changing user-prices. Beck (1974) estimated that the reduction in use following the introduction of charges of $1.50 per surgery visit and $2.00 per house call in Saskatchewan in 1968 was about 7 per cent for the whole population but 18 per cent for the poor. Early studies of price-elasticity found values in the range –0.4 to –1.0. Subsequent work by Phelps and Newhouse (1974), Newhouse and Phelps (1976), and, most recently and most authoritatively, the Rand study reported in Manning *et al.* (1987), found price-elasticities for all health care in the –0.2 to –0.1 range (i.e. a 10 per cent increase in user-price causes demand to fall by one to two per cent). The effects in the Rand study were, however, much stronger for the poor, for children's demand, and especially for the children of the poor (see Lohr *et al.*, 1986). These results have tremendous significance: the handicapping effects of, say, untreated otitis media in children far outweigh the short-term functional impairment, as further socializing and educational handicaps will almost inevitably become added for children already disadvantaged from birth.

The implications of the Pauly model are quite explicit: given a similar cost of care per person in a particular diagnostic group, efficient internalizing of the external effect requires a variable subsidy: varying from 100 per cent in the case of the lowest income group to 0 per cent at a sufficiently high level. This is archetypical 'selectivity' in social policy.

The argument can be seen quite simply in terms of Figure 3.1. In this figure the three marginal willingness-to-pay curves (marginal valuation curves or real income constant demand curves) of individuals A, B, and C are shown. Each is supposed to have a common 'taste' for health care and the difference between is postulated to arise from income differences (ability-to-pay). The curve *EMV* is the external marginal valuation curve reflecting the value that members of society other than these three place upon their consumption. It is assumed to be the same for all (anonymous) individuals. At a market price P_A, A consumes x_A, B consumes x_B, and C consumes no X at all (when a particular event strikes, such as a specific illness). The socially optimal amounts (assuming price represents marginal social cost accurately) are, however, x_C, x_B, and x_A, determined by the condition $MSC = MV_i + EMV$ for all i. This implies a variable subsidy such that C faces a marginal price of P_C, B faces P_B, and A pays the full price: the subsidy varies inversely with ability-to-pay. In practice, of course, fine distinctions between individuals will not be possible and general approximations will have to be made—but on this rationale they should clearly have the selective character shown.

Culyer (1971a; for a simple version see Cullis and West, 1979) attempted a model (again assuming conventional signs on the income and price elasticities) that implied zero prices, as in the NHS, and showed, using a triangular Edge-worth Box, that in a two-person world free care will be preferred by both the subsidized and the subsidizing parties over cash transfers, provided that the preference functions of the two individuals produced an appropriate configuration of offer curves.

Figure 3.1
Consumption Externalities and Selective Subsidies

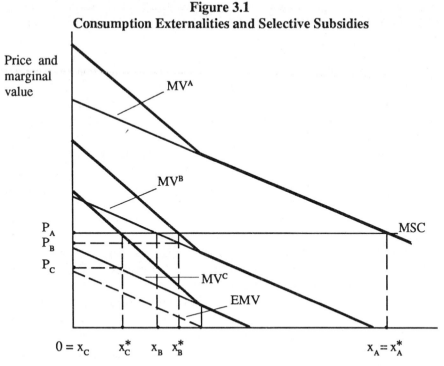

In contrast to these 'absolutist' externality models of 'caring', Lindsay (1969; see also Cullis and West, 1979) offered a 'relative' model of 'sharing' in which equal treatment for equal (medical) need was implied. He showed that the most cost-effective method of achieving a given level of equality is by a combination of standard subsidy (but not in general to reduce price to zero) and enforced denial of access via non-price rationing ('abstention' in his terminology) to the better off.

One set of problems arising from this set of externality models is that, while each provides an account of some of the features of health-care subsidy (e.g. *some* selectivity, some 'free' care, some degree of reduced inequality in access), their practical implementation (assuming that any one of them underlies the actual practice of democratic societies seeking to implement institutional arrangements that promote Pareto optimality more closely than would the market unaided) means that the apparently sharp distinctions between their implications at the theoretical level become blurred in practice. It is consequently hard to discriminate between them on empirical grounds.

There are also more deep-seated difficulties. One arises from the characteristic that the externality is in each case *public* so that its internalization is of benefit to all whether or not one contributes. It is in everyone's interest to 'free ride'. While, on the one hand, the 'club' view of government as a mechanism by which individuals voluntarily agree to be coerced to provide more optimal levels of public goods can be seen as a collective solution to the free-rider problem, it is quite clear that there are several types of activity (most notably private charitable giving) that are *not* collectivized and that are fully exposed to the problem of free-riding. Strictly, the free-rider problem implies that no one (save one whose marginal value of the external benefit most exceeds its marginal cost) has an incentive to contribute. Consequently, charities will have either no supporters or only one. Since this is plainly not so, there seems to be something wrong with the theory. And if each is therefore a wrong theory, none can be used to justify the kinds of public subsidy often seen in health care. The free-rider theorem is an example of 'overkill': its implications are too strong. The problem is further compounded by the well-known puzzle that a democratic collectivist solution requires individuals to vote. Yet the same welfarist free-riding argument predicts that no one will ever vote!

One solution to this sort of problem has been offered, by Collard (1978) among others, which appeals to the rationality rather than the public-spiritedness of individuals. This is the Kantian principle: 'if the interest of the action can without self-contradiction be universalized it is morally possible' (Kant, 1930). A non-Kantian altruist will consider only his own (usually) negligible contribution to the financing of public good and free ride. If all are non-Kantian, all free ride and the classic prisoners' dilemma result ensues. The Kantian altruist, *per contra*, reckons with the behaviour of others: if all do as he does and he free rides he knows (rationally) that the worst outcome will result, so he (and all other Kantians) behaves morally and pays up. While it is in many ways attractive to suppose that rules of morality actually may affect behaviour, it is plain that this approach is, in the welfarist context, *ad hoc*. It is, in fact, extra-welfarist.

Another, rather different, attempt to find a solution is to posit that individuals attach utility not only (possibly not at all) to changing the consumption of goods and services by others, but to the *act of contributing* itself: utility is derived from what one gives away rather than that what it is used for. This would get one quite neatly out of the free-rider problem, for the source of utility is no longer public: if *B* gives to the charity rather than *A*, *A* derives no utility. However, this seems to lead nowhere if one wishes to build a welfarist model of collective health care subsidies, for it is the very publicness of the external effect that generates the public subsidy argument. Perhaps a *mixture* of what Margolis (1982) calls 'goods altruism' and 'participation altruism' might be developed that helped to account for the simultaneous existence of collective and private acts of altruism.

Another problem has been pinpointed by Sugden (1980, 1982) again attacking the roots of the theory of welfarist altruism. Reverting once more to the private charity case, suppose you have decided to donate £100 to a charity. Under welfarism, you have selected this as your 'best' choice given your income, what you know about the charity, etc. You are on the point of writing out your cheque when you discover that your neighbour has just posted a cheque for £100 to the same charity. Since the charity is now as well off as you thought it would be with your own contribution, but you can now be £100 better off, your welfare is undoubtedly higher if you no longer write the cheque. In fact, since you are a bit richer than before, and charitable giving has a positive income elasticity, you may want to revise your initial view about how much to give slightly upwards, but even if you gave £10 instead of nothing, 10 per cent is a very large proportion of extra income (£100 in this case) for anyone to give away (see Collard, 1978 for a survey).

Put it even more dramatically. Suppose the charity's annual income is £10,000 and you are contributing £100 each year out of personal income of £1,000 (you are unusually generous). Now suppose, entirely by coincidence, that your income falls by £1 at the same time as everyone else's contributions rise from £9,900 to £9,901. With your preferences and the terms of trade constant, your initially preferred combination (£10,000 for the charity and £900 for yourself) is still available and will therefore still be preferred so you give £99: a fall in an altruist's income that is exactly matched by an increase in everyone else's contributions means that an altruist, as welfarists see him or her, will choose to reduce his or her contribution by the full amount by which personal income has fallen!

Once again, a theory that has such counter-intuitive (and counter-factual) empirical implications has to be regarded as an unusually weak foundation upon which to build normative propositions. Yet this is the same theory that underpins all these externality arguments for public subsidy (of one form or another, depending on which of the rival externality theories one is using).

Sugden suggests that it is preferable to invoke another (extra-welfarist) theory (specifically, of 'duty'). Unfortunately, he does not develop this in the context of individual charitable behaviour, let alone use it to mount any arguments (welfarist or other) for the welfare state or 'free' or subsidized health care, etc. It is worth noting, however, that it was precisely in the language of duty (as well as altruism and reciprocity) that Titmuss couched his defence of the NHS (Titmuss, 1970). This may not be the welfarist way—but it may be (*pace* all the economists who attacked Titmuss) the right way! Thus we reach a rather destructive end of a chain of welfarist attempts to build rationales based on altruism or philanthropy.

One interesting possibility that may yet rescue welfarism has been developed by Margolis (1982). He postulates that individuals have a split preference system in which one set of preferences relates to group-interests and another relates to selfish ones. This develops hints dropped by, for example, Harsanyi (1955), Pattanaik (1968), Meade (1973), and Rawls (1972), in which the ancient distinction of Plato between man as citizen and man as individual is developed in various ways, but each having the characteristic that one (higher) set of 'preferences', or morals, constrains or interacts with another (lower) set.

Let, then, a representative individual derive utility from s, expenditures on self, which are subject to the usual diminishing marginal valuation and from g, expenditure by the individual on the group (participation altruism). Since the individual's contribution is small relative to the group's as a whole, the marginal utility of g can be taken as constant. Thus, as g increases (and s correspondingly falls) the 'participation ratio' g/s rises, and the G'/S', the marginal rate of substitution (marginal utility of g-spending to that of s-spending) falls. What determines the individual's preferred balance of g and s? Margolis suggests that the higher is g/s the greater the weight given to s and the higher the ratio G'/S' the greater the weight given to g. This he terms the fair shares principle (FS). If the weight given to g relative to s is W, then a stable equilibrium occurs at E in Figure 3.2, with the consequent equilibrium of g occurring at g^*.

As a model of altruistic behaviour, this has several attractive welfarist features. Since it does not appeal to externality arguments, it is not flawed by free-rider problems, nor does it have any of the Sugden anomalies. It does not require that the individual be indifferent to the uses to which g is put (which are determined by the individual's preference over the set of possibilities that exist in the usual utility-maximizing way once the size of g has been decided). It does not elevate g-preferences to a higher status than s-preferences (they are *both* preferences—one is not a set of 'moral rules') so it is amenable to the usual welfarist interpretations. The W function, while *possible* to derive from some form of 'super' welfare function, is not required so to be derived (and Margolis advances some attractive reasons for *not* deriving it in this way). It gives rise to the possibility of private charities (since gains from trade are implied by the g-preference function) and, via scale economies and the saving of transaction costs, to governmental social spending and 'coercive' taxation.

The implications of the model have not been developed specifically for the health care sector (for a beginning, see Mooney, 1986) but, given the weakness of other welfarist models, it may be that it holds out the most promise for a satisfactory such model (Margolis himself developed it in a positive context, a positive–normative flip is thus required as was noted before in connection with Lindsay, 1969, and Culyer, 1971b).

(e) . . . and Where Does this Get Us?

Since the literature on externalities and 'caring' is largely *a priori* in nature, its value is primarily as an aid to introspection and judgement. One needs first to form a view about the existence of the general events that may fall into this class by imagining a state of the world devoid of attempts to optimize via subsidy and regulation, and to determine whether externalities are Pareto-relevant in total or at the margin (Buchanan and Stubblebine, 1962) or whether g-orientation is

Figure 3.2

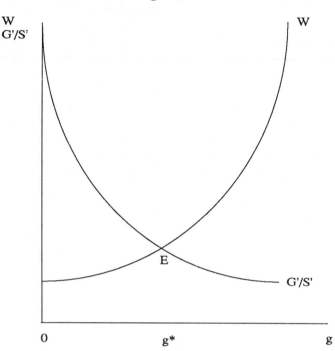

likely to be pervasive. Beyond this there are questions as to whether group concerns are better conceived as relating to absolute or relative levels of consumption and whether they are better seen as questions of *preference* (arguments of utility functions) or of morals (constraints on selfish welfare maximization). These rather useful sorting devices are further supplemented by the enrichment the literature affords of the concepts of 'altruism', 'selfishness', and 'caring'. As an aid to clarity of thought, the welfarist literature is valuable; it cannot be claimed, however, that it has yielded settled conclusions on those issues I have identified as requiring judgement. The view that the externality or group concern is derived not from health care consumption but from 'health' itself is not directly addressed in this literature but occurs in what I shall discuss later in the extra-welfarist section.

(f) *Uncertainty*

The stochastic nature of disease and ill-health has been held to be another respect in which health care is 'different' from at least some other goods and services. The standard welfarist economics of health insurance (e.g. Arrow, 1963; Culyer, 1979; Evans, 1983, 1984) is based on the expected utility maximizing model of risk-aversion (for a survey see Schoemaker, 1982). The aspect of health-affecting events that is insured against is the financial cost only of medical care (loss of employment income is not considered here). In this analysis, the welfare gain to the insured risk-averse individual arises from the implication that the welfare loss from paying a *certain* premium is less than the welfare loss of the expected financial loss (having the same actuarial value as the premium) of the uncertain prospect if the individual 'self-insures' by retaining net income in health and by paying medical expenses out-of-pocket if sickness strikes. This in turn arises because the marginal welfare loss from having to pay an uncertain but large sum is greater than that from having to pay a certain but smaller sum, due to the assumption of a diminishing marginal utility of income or wealth. It is usually assumed that the utility of income is independent of the stochastic states 'healthy' or 'sick'. If it is not, it is not clear what the optimal level of insurance is (Shavell, 1977).

Thus Figure 3.3 shows an individual's welfare as a function of income (diminishing marginal welfare). Let the individual's income be I_o, yielding a welfare level $W(I_o)$ on the vertical axis, and consider a choice between insuring against an uncertain event (illness), which will require an expenditure of H, or not insuring (self-insurance). If the event occurs, expenditure will be H, income net of expenditure I_o-H and the associated level of welfare is $W(I_o-H)$. Suppose the probability of the event occurring is known to the individual and insurance companies and is p. With self-insurance, income net of expected health expenditure is I_o-pH. The expected welfare of this option is $pW(I_o-H)$ +

Figure 3.3

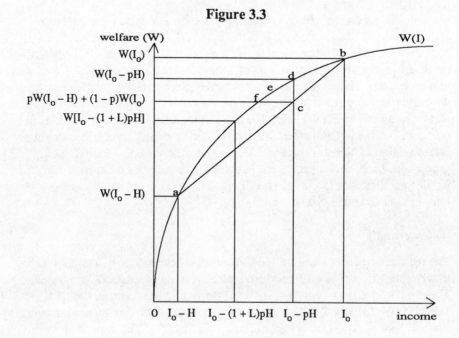

$(1-p)W(I_o)$: the sum of the expected welfare if sickness occurs plus the expected welfare if it does not. The point c on the chord ab is located proportionately to p. If p is, say, 0.4, then $bc/ac = 0.4$.

If an insurance firm offers insurance at an actuarially fair premium pH (the cost of the event times its probability), the welfare of the individual paying the premium is $W(I_o-pH)$. The choice confronting the individual is thus to self-insure or to purchase insurance, with payoffs as in Figure 3.4.

It is clear that, with diminishing marginal welfare from income (risk-aversion), welfare is higher with insurance, at d, than without it, at c. The certain monetary loss pH is preferable to the uncertain loss of H with the same probability. Fair insurance thus increases welfare.

The important question for health care financing is, of course, whether a voluntary competitive health insurance market is better able to maximize these welfare gains than a compulsory system of social insurance or tax finance.

(g) *Loading*

The analysis so far assumes that there is a competitive insurance market in which many insurers compete for trade (or potential entrance deters oligopoly premium-setting) and premiums are set at actuarially fair rates: the product of the probability and the estimated expense. In practice the genuine opportunity costs of insurance provision, together with any X-inefficiency and monopoly rent, will

Figure 3.4
Choice between Sure Thing and Uncertain Prospect

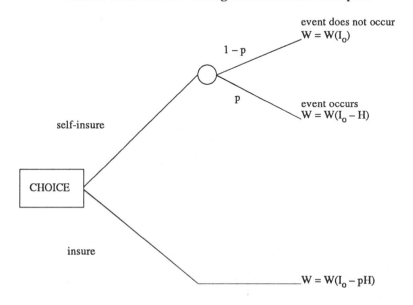

also be 'loaded' on to premiums which consequently rise above their actuarially fair level. In large group plans in the USA the loading is about 10 per cent (Pauly, 1986). This implies that the welfare gains for consumers of insurance will fall as premiums rise and some risk-averse individuals will no longer insure.

Let loading charges, L, be proportional to the premium pH. The premium now becomes $(1 + L)pH$ and the insurance outcome (in this case) now has a lower welfare for the individual, $W[I_o-(1 + L)pH]$, than self-insurance. Any loading large enough to bring the individual on to the section of the welfare function below f on the horizontal through c will reduce welfare relative to the self-insurance option. Any loading less than cf will not.

To the extent that the loading represents costs in excess of opportunity costs, this will thus cause deadweight welfare losses. To the extent that opportunity costs themselves can be lowered by scale economies and other measures that might be taken to reduce costs, the competitive insurance system itself may thus cause unnecessary welfare losses (in a first-best world).

Loading also leads to a preference for deductibles (Arrow, 1963). Suppose, as seems realistic, that the loading is not simply proportional to the size of the premium but is a relatively high proportion of small claims (say, checking for fraud etc. is equally costly for probable and less probable events). Then, as the limit of acceptable (to the consumer) loading is less than fc in Figure 3.3, as b is approached and as the cost of the event falls (point a is closer to b on the utility function) the probability of the loading exceeding the welfare gain rises: very probable events (e.g. routine dental care) will be more self-insured via deductibles and very expensive events (e.g. cancer-care treatment) will be more likely to be fully insured (no deductibles).

(h) *Adverse Selection*

Another problem that arises has its roots in another kind of informational asymmetry—this time, however, the informational advantage lies with the consumer rather than the supplier of the service (financial in this case). Premiums are set according to the calculated risks for groups in the community. In the simplest case of 'pure' community rating, the premium is set according to the population-wide probability of consuming health care. The typical consumer will, however, usually know better his or her own probability. Those whose probability times expected expenses is greater than the premium will gain welfare in excess of that expected in the model (viz. $> cd$ in Figure 3.3) and may gain even if they are not risk averse! Those whose true probability times expected expenses is less than the premium will tend (depending on their risk aversion) to self-insure. This phenomenon is known as *adverse selection*. It leads to a progressive upward pressure on premiums (as low potential users are driven out), with insurance cover increasingly restricted to the very worst risks. The upshot is a pool of uninsured people, many of whom are risk averse, in addition of course to those who are uninsurable by virtue of chronic disease or other disqualifying features, and a heavy financial burden on the sickest members of society who remain insured. In the United States, estimates vary of the numbers who are uninsured or inadequately insured, but seem to indicate a total of around 50 million (Farley, 1985; Mundinger, 1985). In any event, adverse selection, unless checked, is likely to cause massive externalities of the sort described earlier and become a major affront to most principles of equity.

Left to itself, adverse selection would destroy the market entirely. In practice this does not happen, partly because insurance plans are often based on employee groups in which a condition of employment may be that each joins the company plan; so opting out is not possible unless the gains from doing so would outweigh the losses from changing one's employment. Partly it does not happen because the presence of adverse selection itself affords gains from trade between self-insurers and profit-seeking insurance agencies (and non-profit-seeking too).

It pays insurers to offer policies with premiums that better approximate the true expected expenses of those driven out by adverse selection, even though the acquisition of this information is not costless. This erodes the principle of community-rating which becomes replaced by experience-rating and by packages of cover that fall short of fully comprehensive (e.g. 'major medical' only). In this fashion 'good risks' are creamed off. While there will remain some inefficiency in that some very low risk groups may still fail to find a suitable package at an actuarially appropriate premium, experience-rating is more efficient than community-rating. It differs also from community-rating in that, whereas under community-rating wealth is redistributed from low- to high-risk individuals and families in advance of any health care consumption, under experience-rating, there is an in-kind redistribution *ex post* from those (insured) who are well to those who are sick (as in all insurance).

Though more efficient from a welfarist perspective (Arrow, 1963), experience-rating is likely to violate the usual distributional criteria of equity: those with a history of sickness will face the highest premiums, have the less comprehensive cover, be most likely to pay deductibles (both of these latter options have the effect of reducing premiums as they reduce probable pay-outs by the insurer)—and, since ill health and income are correlated, will on average be the poorer members of the community. Many, moreover, can be expected to find their risk-aversion insufficient to warrant insurance of any kind.

(i) *Moral Hazard*

Another difficulty with insurance systems is known as *moral hazard*. One form of this has already been met in the shape of supplier-induced demand, which is a kind of producer's moral hazard, whereby producers (on a fee-for-service system of reimbursement) have an incentive to adjust the client's demand in pursuit of their personal income objectives. This is easier done (or at least is less likely to offend the doctor–patient relationship) if the cost of supplier-induced demand can be passed on to the insurer.

More commonly discussed in the literature, however, is consumer's moral hazard: in which the fact of being insured encourages the individual to take less care in ensuring that the undesired state (illness) does not occur (*ex ante* moral hazard) and, when sickness occurs, encourages the consumer to maximize the consumption of services beyond the point at which marginal cost (assuming that services are priced at marginal cost) equals marginal value (*ex post* moral hazard). In health insurance, *ex post* moral hazard seems to be the principal problem on the consumer side. Two caveats are worth noting here. One is that consumer demand is, as we have already seen, mostly interpreted by an agent, so the distinction between consumer's and producer's moral hazard is at best fuzzy. The other is that if hospital and other services are priced at *above* marginal cost, second-best considerations would dictate that the usual welfarist efficiency condition of $P = MV$ may no longer apply. Consumers may be receiving false signals about marginal cost from market prices and should probably be encouraged to consume beyond the rate at which $P = MV$, quite apart from any externality considerations, even if this implies even bigger rents for monopoly suppliers of health care, as income is redistributed from the insured to the suppliers via the insurers.

In any event, the effect on the insurance market is predictable: with moral hazard, consumption exceeds the rate on which premiums have been (historically) set, the (retrospective) reimbursement of suppliers rises to levels higher than predicted, and premiums rise. Higher premiums will drive out some risk-averse individuals from the insurance market (dead-weight losses) and may (but only 'may') cause an inefficiently large rate of consumption.

To retain their market, insurers offer packages that do not include 'first pound coverage' and the consumer has to pay deductibles (e.g. the first £x of any expense) or co-insurance (e.g. x per cent of the total bill). These out-of-pocket payments in the US currently amount to about 30 per cent of non-hospital expenses and 10 per cent of hospital expenses.

While the likely offence to equity principles is plain, the efficiency implications are less obvious in a welfarist context. With full 'first-pound' cover, and zero marginal (money) user price, the sick individual may be expected to consume OQ units of health care in Figure 3.5, given that he or she is sick, at which point $MV = 0$. This generates a welfare loss of abQ: the amount by which the cost of providing Q^*Q units exceeds their value to the individual ($Q^*abQ - Q^*aQ$). This analysis assumes that consumer marginal willingness to pay is adequately reflected in the demand curve and that OP is the marginal social opportunity cost.

The excess 'burden' can be reduced by co-insurance. Thus, if the consumer pays a proportion, p, of the daily cost P, and that is 50 per cent, user price becomes pP, consumption falls from Q to Q' (closer to the 'optimum' Q^*), the excess burden falls by more than half to acd, and total expenditure falls from $OPbQ$ to $OPcQ'$ implying a lower (future) premium.

In one of the few thorough empirical attempts to measure welfare effects in the literature, Feldstein (1973) estimated that the maximum reduction in the excess burden of health insurance in the US, by raising co-insurance from an average of 0.33 to 0.5, would have been $10 billion in 1969 prices after allowing for the loss of welfare to those who would no longer choose insurance. However, the implications of this analysis hinge crucially on the adequacy of prices as measures of marginal cost and on the absence of externalities. They also depend on the welfarist assumption that MV adequately represents the consumer's true estimate of the worth of medical care. (The actual calculation was also based on elasticity estimates that were almost certainly too high by a large factor.)

(j) . . . and Where Does this Get Us?

Insurance is shown plainly to have welfare-increasing properties though it seems clear also that optimal insurance may be less than complete insurance: some events should be uninsured and for others less than 100 per cent of the risk will be optimal. This analysis does not, however, take account of any contrary indications suggested by externality or equity factors and is entirely dependent

Figure 3.5
The Welfare Loss of 'Excess' Health Insurance

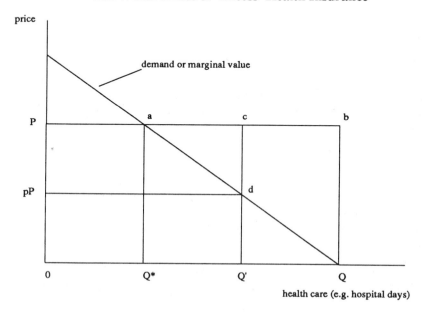

health care (e.g. hospital days)

on the strong assumption that consumer choices adequately reveal their preferences (viz. that the agency relationship is perfect).

Provided that it is not accompanied by compensating X-inefficiencies, a system of compulsory universal public insurance operated through the general tax system may have substantial cost advantages over competitive insurance: compulsion avoids adverse selection and enables scale economies to be gained (if they exist), reducing loading and increasing the welfare gains from comprehensive insurance cover. Universality and tax finance avoid the necessity of risk assessment and premium setting, billing, reimbursement, checking for fraud, and so on. These costs appear to vary substantially across different systems, being less than 3 per cent of total expenditure in countries with a tax-based social insurance system, like the UK and Canada, and in excess of 10 per cent in private insurance systems, or in systems with public finance but with complex systems of billing and reimbursement (e.g. USA and France) (OECD, 1977). It may be technically possible for a large country (like the USA) to operate a competitive system that would avoid monopoly exploitation and that would also realize scale economies (though this does not seem to have happened) but may be implausible in smaller countries like the UK. Moral hazard may be controlled in public or private insurance sytems by the adoption of (private or public) regulatory schemes defining the appropriateness of packages of care, and by prospective reimbursement acording to an agreed charge per case-type rather than retrospectively according to whatever the suppliers happen to have charged. Given a non-competitive health *care* industry (whether public or private), such regulation is commonly observed, and it is a question of judgement whether the regulation is better done by a publicly accountable agency or by the (insurance) industry itself.

(k) *The Welfarist Approach: an Overview*

The welfarist techniques of analysis have been the traditional way in which issues of health service finance have been addressed in the economics literature. Granted the acceptability of welfarism's value assumptions, its implications for policy hinge on judgements about the empirical significance of consumer rationality, the 'purity' of the agency relationship, the nature of any externalities (physical or utility interdependence or group-concern), the extent of adverse selection, moral hazard, supplier-induced demand, unnecessary premium loading under insurance, and the empirical validity of the neoclassical behavioural model that, in its normative version, is welfarism's centrepiece. Each will draw his or her own conclusions based on the (patchy) evidence and more casual experience.

3. The Extra-Welfarist Approach

Whereas welfarism holds that standards of living, the efficiency of social arrangements and the justice of distributions and redistributions are all to be evaluated in terms of individuals' utilities (or welfares), an extra-welfarist approach (Sen, 1979) admits non-utility information about individuals into the process of comparing social states. Using an illustration from Sen, consider three social states x, y, and z with the following (cardinal and even interpersonally comparable) utility numbers for persons 1 and 2.

	x	y	z
person 1's utility	4	7	7
person 2's utility	10	8	8

In x, person 1 is hungry while 2 eats amply. In y, 2 has been forced to surrender some food to 1 and 2's utility loss is less than 1's utility gain. Under welfarism, the fact of coercion is an irrelevance: the sum total of utility is higher in y than x so y is socially preferred. This is one example of the exclusion of non-utility information in the making of social comparisons. In z, person 1 is as hungry as in x and 2 is as amply fed but 1, who happens to be a sadist, is allowed to torture 2 (who is no masochist). It so happens that 1's utility gain and 2's utility loss are the same as under the food transfer programme. Under welfarism y is socially preferred to x but z is the same, utility-wise, as y, therefore z too is socially preferred to x. Again, the relevance of non-utility information (in this case the fact of torture and my disapproval of it) is denied.

Sen (1980) argues that a particularly important class of non-utility information about individuals is 'basic capabilities': a person being able to do certain things. It is, he suggests, because a cripple is unable to perform particular activities that he or she is seen as having special 'needs' that are independent of his or her total or marginal utility. Culyer (1989) advocates the more general notion of 'characteristics of people'—for example, their genetic endowment of health, their relative deprivation independently of the absolute consumption of commodities or the characteristics of commodities, their moral 'worth' and 'deservingness', whether or not they are in pain, or stigmatized by society. Characteristics may also relate to the character of relationships between people such as the quality of friendships, community support for the individual when in need, social isolation, or changes in them, such as becoming (as distinct from being) crippled.

Only some of the characteristics of people (which will include some of their capabilities) will be deemed relevant and the list of such relevant characteristics is likely to vary between cultures, climates, historical periods, and so on. It is, in short, contingent. It is related to a concept of need. If the characteristics of people are a way of describing deprivation, desired states, or significant changes in people's characteristics, then commodities and characteristics of commodities are what is often needed to remove the deprivation or to move towards the desired state, or to help people cope with change. They are the necessary means to a desired end. To compare the *ill-health* of different individuals or groups is not the same as to compare the health care they have received (they could receive the same amounts and still be unhealthy, or different amounts and be equally healthy).

(a) *Need and Extra-Welfarism*

Whereas the notion of 'need' has received a bad press from many welfarist economists, extra-welfarists have been able to use the term with some precision and confidence. In its most rudimentary form 'need' for health care would seem to imply that someone is better off with the 'needed' treatment than without it (Williams, 1974) and that the 'better offness' has to do with persons' health (Culyer *et al.*, 1971). Thus health services are needed (viz. are a necessary condition for achieving a particular outcome) only if the outcome is desired and there is no alternative (or more cost-effective) way of realizing it. Since inputs are nearly always substitutable, it will not normally make sense to say that a *specific* resource in a *specific* quantity is needed. Since there is no effective treatment for some conditions, it is nonsensical to say that persons suffering from such conditions need health services (they may need the fruits of research and they may need love and comfort, but they cannot need ineffective care, even though they may demand it, and such care may also damage health). Since health services are needed only for what they enable to be accomplished, in a world of scarcity judgements must be made about the value of what might be accomplished. *Some* services are bound not to be supplied in the light of such judgements and so it does not make much sense to require that all needs should be met. One of the first lessons of 'needology' is the lesson of the ethical acceptability of unmet need (Wiggins and Dirmen, 1987).

Since health services can be needed only if their outcomes are desired, the important question arises as to whose judgements ought to be decisive in assessing desirability of outcome. While the judgement of technicians (such as doctors) may be appropriate in evaluations of *effectiveness*, technical experts have no particular authority for making value judgements so it does not make much ethical sense to pretend that these essentially political decisions can be de-sanitized by being left to the experts. At the centre of this problem lies the issue of how one person's needs (viz. the potential improvement in his or her health attributable to health care) are to be weighed against another's, an issue taken up below.

In health economics, the extra-welfarist approach has taken 'health' as the proximate maximand. This does not imply the complete ousting of 'welfare' with its usual normative connotations, but the use of both sets of 'data' to evaluate alternatives. 'Health' is itself a descriptive characteristic of people, but in practice has been interpreted in the literature as a composite 'bundle' of other characteristics such as pain and restriction of activity (Culyer *et al.*, 1971).

The implications of the extra-welfarist approach for the finance of health care seem partly to take negative forms: insurance arrangements, user prices (money, time, etc.) should not act so as to discourage use of care that contributes to the objective of maximizing health. There are also implications for rationing care (equalizing marginal products in terms of health per unit of resource), selecting patients from waiting lists, conducting cost–benefit analyses in the health service.

At the core of the extra-welfarist approach is, of course, the issue of how the maximand is to be measured. This has proved to be an issue involving much cross-disciplinary collaboration between (for example) economists, physicians, psychologists, and political scientists which has exposed the complexities involved in defining 'health' and measuring it, and which has also developed a battery of experimental techniques designed to test theories and quantify the hitherto unquantified.

(b) *Measuring Health*

Extra-welfarists identify 'health' as the principal output of health services and its efficient production (technical efficiency, cost-effectiveness) as an issue upon which its insights can be particularly valuable, in contrast to welfarism, under which it is natural to take goods and services as the natural units of output. Much of the cost-effectiveness literature in health economics is implicitly extra-welfarist in seeking to identify the least-cost method of delivering a given health improvement (or prevention of deterioration) for a given patient group (or across patient groups). In many cases, extra-welfarist economists have joined hands with non-economists in the search for better measures of health and, of necessity, in identifying the production functions that underlie cost functions and cost–benefit relationships.

One approach to health measurement has been to use *ad hoc* numerical scales to quantify the bundle of characteristics (usually in the context of planning exercises or studies of the effectiveness of medical procedures). This approach involves the individual being assessed in several dimensions, with numbers being associated with each assessment and the resultant scores (sometimes weighted) being added up (e.g. Harris *et al.*, 1971; Grogono and Woodgate, 1971). The arbitrariness of such procedures has been spelled out several times (e.g. by Culyer, 1978a and b; see also Drummond, this volume):

(1)   criteria for selecting characteristics were usually unspecified;

(2)   the scaling systems often implied only order but were subsequently used to construct a cardinal index;

(3)   the possibility that combinations of characteristics may have higher or lower numbers than the sum of the separate scores was often excluded;

(4)   increasing marginal severity was rarely allowed;

(5)   criteria for selecting those making these (value) judgements were usually unspecified.

The approach that has most frequently been adopted by economists has become known as the quality-adjusted life-year or QALY, and has been mainly developed by Torrance in Canada (see Torrance, 1986 for a survey, and Drummond, this issue, for an extended discussion) and Williams in the UK (e.g. Williams, 1985, 1986). The QALY has two dimensions: life-expectancy (as a measure of the extra life-years that may be procured) and a quality-adjustment (as weights indicating the 'healthiness' of the expected life-years). In the context of the measurement of output of health services, productivity is thus to be seen as the difference over a period of time between expected QALYs with a particular procedure and without it (or with an alternative).

The ways in which the quality weights have been developed and interpersonal comparisons made are of particular analytical interest. A historical review of the health index literature (of which these quality weights form a part) is Rosser (1983) and a review of the techniques for measuring health indices is Torrance (1982).

There are three commonly-used methods of measuring scales of health (on this and other important distinctions see Culyer, 1986): the rating scale, the standard gamble, and the time trade-off (see Drummond *et al.*, 1987). These are defined in detail in Drummond (this issue).

However, such measures present a potential problem. The literature frequently characterizes measures of health as utility measures (e.g. Torrance, 1986). Here it is important to distinguish between the welfarist notion of utility as welfare and the extra-welfarist notion. Under Paretianism, for example, the notion of welfare relates to goods and services and is the utility of the individual affected by their consumption. Under extra-welfarism, while this notion of utility may still apply, there is the further idea that uses utility theory in order to derive measures of characteristics of individuals that are not goods, nor services, nor that necessarily have a value content that corresponds to the Paretian notion that 'the individual is the best judge of his/her own welfare'. Confusingly, however, these too are called 'utility' measures. The use of the standard gamble based on Neumann–Morgenstern assumptions described above is a good example. The possibility that one can have utility measures that are not welfarist is thus important to appreciate.

(c) *"Utility" is not 'Utility' is not Utility . . .*

A related puzzle that pervades some welfarist theory is the meaning to be attached to the word 'utility'. While it is commonplace to distinguish between utility as 'welfare' and utility as 'an index of choice' in normative and positive analyses respectively, some have difficulty in distinguishing (in a welfarist context) between utility-maximizing behaviour that is altruistic and that which is selfish: is not one who maximizes utility by giving, in some sense, selfish? In positive economics this poses little difficulty: altruism means simply that a person's allocation of wealth is influenced by the effects that the allocation has on others *and* that the person in question has benign intentions. Since both behaviour and motive are different from that of one for whom neither of these things is true, this is a distinction that needs to be made. It fails, however, to capture another distinction: that between fulfilling one's selfish preferences and acting contrary (at least in part) to those preferences by adopting a set of moral rules that may constrain. Such altruism, that is contrary to preference, is of a different kind and, perhaps, requires an appropriate term that differentiates it from purely 'welfarist altruism': it is, after all, extra-welfarist.

As a result, and given the difficulties in defining the relationship between health measures and utility measures discussed above, one of the normative issues that the extra-welfarist approach identifies (but does not resolve) concerns who shall decide the weights to be applied to different health states and to the components of health states. Who shall decide the categories of functioning, etc. to be considered? Who shall decide who shall decide?

The answers may well depend upon the nature of the problem under consideration: politicians, civil servants, managers, representatives of the public, persons at risk of particular disease, patients, doctors, nurses . . . all may have some claims by virtue of identity, skill, or position of trust. It does not, however, follow that those judged best able to exercise a judgement about, say, the effectiveness of a medical procedure are necessarily those best qualified to exercise a judgement about how pain and disability are to be traded off.

(d) *Extra-Welfarism and Distributional Weights*

The non-welfarist literature clearly sees information of the cost-per-QALY sort as a means of guiding resource allocation decisions in the NHS, whether on equity or efficiency grounds, and the literature is quite explicit in its departure from consumer-based willingness to pay as the basis for benefit valuation (Williams, 1988a).

The question that naturally arises next, of course, relates to *whose* willingness-to-pay is to be substituted for the consumer's. The most recent work has addressed this issue in the following way: '. . . is a particular improvement in health to be regarded as of equal value no matter who gets it; and, if not, what precisely is its relative value in accruing to one kind of person as opposed to another?' (Williams, 1988a). The current work has begun by seeking to find out what views are actually held by surveyed individuals on the matter. It would seem from the early results that there is a consensus that particular phases of the life-cycle are regarded as times when health is of greatest value. Two stood out of the ten phases used in Williams' survey: 'as infants' and 'when bringing up children'. The information available to date is only qualitative and a next phase of the work will address the issue of *how much* good health is worth at points in the life-cycle relative to others. It is also planned to unscramble the life-cycle phases into elements that are age-, role-, and sex-related.

If ethical authority is to be accorded these (or similar) results, a departure is implied from the distributive value-judgement normally (if only provisionally) embodied in measures of health such as QALYs: that a unit of 'health' is of equal value no matter who gets it. It thus seems possible that distributive judgements will be able to be built into outcome measures and, via cost-effectiveness analyses, into efficiency analysis (e.g. Culyer, 1988b). Indeed, if all of the features of distributional equity that are of (legitimate) concern are built into outcome data in this way, then a full integration of equity and efficiency will have been achieved in health policy: given routine information about population characteristics (disease incidence, etc.), medical technology (the possibilities for changing health states for the better), and cost information, it will be possible to make informed routine judgements about resource allocations to providers of health care.

(e) *Objections to QALYs*

There is, however, quite a long way before that dream becomes a reality—and some have seen it more as a nightmare possibility. One type of objection is represented by Smith (1987) who argues that the use of a quantitative algorithm obscures a process by which essentially arbitrary assessments of the values of people's lives are being made. To this Williams' (1987a) retort seems compelling: that far from obscuring the need for value judgement the procedure highlights the value-judgemental elements and offers techniques by which they could be made more explicitly; that far from imposing essentially arbitrary values, the process of quantification is, by virtue of its explicitness, open to criticism and change at every stage. Indeed, it is hard not to see Smith's objections as being much more aptly directed at present modes of making decisions (e.g. about health service cuts across the board).

Rather deeper is an objection of Broome (1985) that the measures ignore 'population': the outcome of health services may include not only the extra health for people who may also be having extra time, but also more people if an additional outcome includes children being born who would not otherwise have existed. In the welfarist tradition this poses a problem because although it might be possible to find out how extra QALYs are valued, it is not possible to find out how the unborn value being born. But this also poses a problem for the non-welfarists in so far as they too wish to ascribe a value to unborn lives—as well as the lives of the children of the unborn, and so on *ad infinitum*. Unfortunately, we have no basis at present for valuing population changes, therefore (says Broome) we have no basis for valuing life or QALYs.

Earlier Broome (1978) argued that the only appropriate value for a 'statistical' life was infinity on the grounds that, eventually, statistical probabilities of death (or of opportunities for life extensions not taken advantage of) translate into deaths of actual individuals who might reasonably be expected to exercise a veto. This clearly poses something of a challenge to Paretian welfarists though less of one, of course, to non-welfarists. A welfarist may find something of a defence in the reflection that he might himself agree to an option offering some benefit but with a very small prospect of its entailing his own death, so why should not a society of like-minded folk feel similarly? An extra-welfarist might take the view that she would be guided by the majority view on the value of (or differential values of) life.

It is worth, perhaps, reminding everyone (welfarist and extra-welfarist alike) that there is nothing to be gained in the context of resource allocation decision-making from taking an ontological view of QALYs, or life, or lives. One is not concerned with the inherent cherishable worth of people but rather with the value of resources that we might spend in order to gain better health or prevent (or postpone) death or change the prospects of either for the better. If we spend £2,000 per person to protect them from the consequences of some risk that is fatal for say one in five hundred, it is merely arithmetic that we shall spend, on average, £1 million per life saved: only in this sense is a life 'worth' £1 million.

Loomes (1988) mounts a far more powerful assault on both welfarist and non-welfarist traditions by attacking the usual behavioural axioms that are shared in both. He focuses on the systematic differences in measure that have been observed as between rating scales, standard gambles, and time trade-offs (e.g. Torrance, 1976; Bombardier *et al.*, 1982). His analysis hinges on a distinction between the utility gained as the result of one's own choice and 'choiceless' utility: viz. the utility 'experienced' as the consequence of a happening generated in any other way. The importance of the distinction lies in the fact that only in the former is there the possibility that, in an uncertain world, you may come to regret or rejoice over a decision you have made. The rating method does not involve choice; it requires the subject only to locate a state on a utility scale. The standard gamble, by contrast, does involve choice and so does the time trade-off method.

'Regret theory' is recommended as the *prima facie* better foundation for future work in the QALY territory. It seems clear that research should be expanded to incorporate regret theory into health status and QALY measurement experiments in order to compare results systematically with the other techniques. The potential from exploiting other substitutes for expected utility theory (such as prospect theory) remains to be explored.

(f) *Where does Extra-Welfarism Get Us?*

As far as the demand side is concerned, extra-welfarism in health economics may be seen to take 'health' output as the maximand. The emphasis is not in principle exclusive, as extra-welfarism is not exclusive, and it seems unlikely that any extra-welfarist would assign zero weights to such factors as consumer choice, privacy, speed of service, hospital hotel-services, and other factors that may be only remotely causally linked to health.

Extra-welfarism thus immediately implies another notion of efficiency, in which explicit (but not welfarist) value judgements are incorporated into the maximand which is a cardinal 'utility' index of health (the welfarist tradition, the Margolis model, and the insurance literature are also cardinal in the sense that 'utility' as used there is measurable up to a linear transformation). This index is extremely useful in supply-side efficiency studies. It is worth noting that it is not uniquely applicable under socialized systems of care and may, for example, be used in market systems where insurance companies seek to control producer moral hazard by reimbursing providers only for procedures that are demonstrably relatively cost-effective in restoring health and in any clinical research with a similar objective. In this territory, extra-welfarists have been more active empirically than welfarists typically have been.

As a matter of necessity, the literature has focused on the difficult issues of measuring health itself (or changes in it) in order to improve the ability of the system to produce health cost-effectively. It is quite possible for these efforts also to serve the cause of welfarism: after all, better information on outcomes can enhance the physician's ability to act as a good agent for the patient. But it is quite clear that other causes are served as well and that the implications of extra-welfarist health maximization are not the same as welfarist analysis.

Extra-welfarism resembles the welfarist externality arguments in implying free or subsidized terms of access to health care. Under welfarism, however, the reason for the subsidy lies in the optimal internalization of externalities. In extra-welfarism, the reason lies in more 'engineering' sorts of concern: optimal resource use is determined by equality of marginal health output per unit of resource in various activities and across various client groups. Willingness to pay is an irrelevance and may be directly counter to this objective if willingness to pay is positively associated with ability to pay, but ability to pay is inversely associated with 'potential for health improvement'. The extra-welfarist approach therefore attaches great importance to the identification of potential for benefit. Indeed, it is possible to see some traditional policy arguments cast in equity terms as possibly extra-welfarist health-maximization arguments. Assume, for example, that a (satisfactorily measured) QALY is judged to be equally valuable socially to whomsoever it may accrue. Now allow that the sickest in society are by and large those for whom the marginal product of health care in terms of QALYs is highest, that these are also the poorest, and that when (ceteris paribus) health service per capita rises, the marginal product in terms of health falls. It evidently follows that efforts to equalize the geographical distribution of resources, to channel more of them to the sick and more of them to the poor, might be seen not as distributional policies to be justified by equity arguments but efficient policies justified by heath maximization.

There is a danger in extra-welfarism of becoming too fixed on the 'bottom line'. The great advantage the approach can claim in issues like outcome measurement is rather like the claim made earlier on behalf of welfarism: it provides a conceptual framework for handling extremely complex issues in a systematic fashion and that exposes each aspect of an argument clearly. It is less important what the cost-per-QALY is, than that individuals with responsibility for resource allocation in health care have a means of working through the issues so that they can come to their own informed view about the pros and cons of different resource allocations. It is in this sense that it is important to emphasize that the method is intended (in an archetypical 'decision-makers' approach) as an aid to, rather than a substitute for, thought.

4. Conclusions

It will be clear from the foregoing that there is a paradigm clash in the normative economics of health, though it would be wrong to overdraw the differences. The extra-welfarist approach is, after all, inclusive of welfarism. There can be no question that the extra-welfarist approach is more tolerant of what may be seen as 'paternalism' and can be readily enlisted on behalf of the sorts of access terms and distributional issues that have lain at the heart of the ideology of the British NHS—and increasingly of policy towards it. Extra-welfarism is also providing a theoretical basis upon which usable output measures can be derived.

Ultimately, however, neither approach can yield final answers. They provide frameworks whose usefulness remains a matter for judgement. An earlier judgement by me upon the field, 'The heady atmosphere of grand designs has to be replaced by the mundane, but ultimately more fruitful, ground of systematically applied economics . . . In this scheme of things the role of welfare economics is to provide an appropriate theoretical base in which to build empirical studies and not to prejudge the facts' (Culyer, 1971) needs amendment in only one respect: add 'or extra-welfare' after 'welfare'.

4

Output Measurement for Resource-Allocation Decisions in Health Care

MICHAEL F. DRUMMOND*

1. Introduction

Because resources for the provision of health care are scarce, choices need to be made in their deployment. Although there are currently concerns about the level of funding of the National Health Service (NHS) and whether the United Kingdom devotes enough of its GNP to health care (Parkin, 1989), it should be recognized that scarcity confronts all medical systems in one way or another. Even the richest countries, such as the USA or Sweden, cannot meet all the possible requirements for medical interventions for all their population (Saltman and von Otter, 1987).

In many sectors of the economy, resource-allocation decisions are made through the market mechanism, but it is pointed out in other papers in this book that simple application of markets will not lead to efficient health care provision. It is also pointed out that there are other criteria, such as equity in health or health care, that are relevant to resource allocation decisions.

One consequence of the limited use of money prices in the exchange of health care goods and services is that there is very little information on individuals' willingness to pay and hence, in economic terms, few measures of the value of interventions and improvements in consumers' welfare. Indeed, most of the consumption decisions are made by doctors, acting as the agent of the patient. (The 'agency relationship' is discussed elsewhere in this volume.)

The absence of markets in health care has led economists to consider how the output of health services can be conceptualized. Feldstein (1967) states that health service output may be legitimately and usefully defined in any of four ways: by an index of the number of services provided, of the number of cases treated, of the number of successful treatments, or of various measures of the community's health. Each definition is progressively more difficult to imple-

* Centre for Health Economics, University of York

ment than the preceding one, but comes closer to what we want for welfare-oriented comparisons of output.

The commonly used measures of health service output are far from ideal. For example, the performance of health care systems at the national level is frequently measured in terms of changes in perinatal or infant mortality. The same approach is also used at the level of individual interventions, which may be assessed in terms of case fatality rates or five-year survival rates. Other clinical output measures are even more circumspect, such as changes in various bio-medical measures such as blood pressure or liver function. Occasionally measures of morbidity are used, such as complication rates from surgery, but little attention is paid to how these relate to restrictions in functioning or to the value individuals place on improvements in health.

Other types of routine measures, such as 'cases treated' or 'days of care provided' are equally unsatisfactory since they are more appropriately viewed as throughput measures, rather than true outputs. For example, the 'case' measure used in measuring hospital throughput in the United Kingdom does not distinguish between a death and a discharge (of a fully fit individual) from the hospital. Some attempts are being made to refine the throughput measures, through the use of diagnosis-related groups (DRGs) (Davis and Rhodes, 1988). This overcomes one problem, in that hospital cases differ greatly in their range and complexity, but does not bring us any closer to a measure of value.

The need for output measures in health care has been intensified because of the initiatives being taken to secure more value for money, or efficiency, in health care. Economists conceive of efficiency in terms of *technical efficiency*, ensuring that goods and services are produced at the lowest possible cost, and *allocative efficiency*, ensuring that goods and services are allocated so as to maximize the welfare of the community.

The initiatives being taken to improve efficiency are wide and varied. For example, in the United Kingdom health authorities have been required to make 'efficiency savings', where resource consumption is reduced in some activities in order to facilitate developments in others. (Some authorities that are close to their budgetary (cash) limit may require such reductions in resource consumption merely to avoid over-spending their budget.) Without good measures of output it is impossible to assess whether cuts in resource consumption have been achieved without reductions in benefits.

Similarly, experiments have been carried out in the field of clinical budgeting (Wickings and Coles, 1985). Here clinicians are encouraged to be more careful in the use of resources by being given freedom to redeploy a proportion of them to other activities. Without good measures of output it is hard to assess whether such experiments have led to an increase in efficiency. This will remain the case in the immediate future even though the most recent experiments incorporate a case-mix measure (DHSS, 1986).

The needs for output measures have also increased in other countries. For example, in the USA there has been a growth in prospective payment schemes for hospitals. Under this approach, the most famous example of which is the Medicare payment system based on DRGs, hospitals are rewarded prospectively according to an agreed set of fees, rather than retrospectively by the number of days of care provided. Prospective payment systems are supposed to encourage efficiency, but this depends on both benefits and costs. Without good measures of output it is hard to refute the claims of those who feel that such systems have had an adverse effect on the quality of care (Ginzberg, 1987).

The same concerns have been raised in the case of primary care in the USA, where competition among insurers, traditional suppliers, and new forms of service delivery, such as health maintenance organizations, has been encouraged in order to increase efficiency (Fuchs, 1987; Iglehart, 1988).

While governments and other third-party payers have intensified their search for more value for money in health care, there has been a proliferation of research in the field of output measurement. A number of disease-specific scales have been developed which are much broader in concept than the traditional clinical measures. In addition there are a number of general scales or health indices. Potentially, these can assess the impact of health-care interventions across a wide range of diseases. Typically they include assessments of physical mobility, activities of daily living, psycho-social state, and extent of social integration. Some indices are expressed as a profile of measures (Hunt *et al.*, 1986), others can be aggregated to give an overall score (Spitzer *et al.*, 1981).

Finally, the main output measure developed by economists is the quality-adjusted life-year (QALY). This combines data on the *utility* of health states, obtained from individuals, with data on life expectancy. The output of health-care interventions is thereby judged in terms of the contribution they make to the quality and quantity of life. This approach has the particular advantage that a single measure of output is produced, in contrast to the multiple measures embodied in most disease-specific or general health indices. This makes it easier to relate output to cost, as in the study by Williams (1985) comparing the cost per quality-adjusted life-year gained from a range of health-care interventions in the UK.

The development of output measures is not a costless activity and it is important that the research effort proceeds in an efficient manner. Therefore this paper reviews the contribution that existing output measures make, or could make, to resource allocation decisions in health care. In the next section of the paper three distinct types of resource allocation decision are specified. Then, in section 3, the essential features of the different output measures are outlined. In section 4 the ways in which the measures are, or could be, used are discussed and in the concluding section some priorities for further research are identified.

2. Resource-Allocation Decisions in Health Care

It is tempting to think of resource-allocation decisions in health care as being made by those managing the health care system at the central and local levels. Indeed, many key decisions are made in this forum, such as those concerning the total budget for health care, the location and size of hospitals, the balance of community and institutional care, and the relative priorities to be assigned to care groups such as the elderly, mentally ill, or mentally handicapped. These *health care policy decisions* are important in shaping the health care system and are most concerned with allocative efficiency. However, key resource-allocation decisions are made at other levels, too.

Many resource-allocation decisions are made at the level of the individual patient. That is, the clinical practitioner makes decisions about whether to admit the patient to hospital, which diagnostic tests to use, which treatment method to employ, and when to discharge the patient. These decisions have resource consequences, too; in the United Kingdom it was estimated that each hospital doctor made decisions which committed resources worth in excess of £140,000 annually (or more than £500,000 at today's prices) (Owen, 1976). These *clinical decisions* relate mainly to technical efficiency. Although they may be partially constrained by the facilities provided, in the main they are made without reference to those planning, managing, or funding the health care system.

The individual nature of clinical decisions is demonstrated by the wide variations in clinical practice that have been shown in many studies (Ham, 1988). However, on occasions *clinical policy decisions* may be made, affecting the care of a group of patients. For example, decisions may be made about the range of drugs to be stocked in the hospital pharmacy (Bloom and Jacobs, 1985), or about the appropriateness of routine X-rays for skull injury in patients admitted to accident and emergency departments (Royal College of Radiologists, 1981). These represent an intermediate group of resource-allocation decisions, broader than the individual patient, but narrower in scope than the health care policy decisions outlined earlier. They illustrate that a clear separation of clinical decisions and policy decisions is hard to achieve.

For output measures to bring about more efficiency they need to inform one or more of the types of resource-allocation decision discussed above. The next two sections of the paper describe the available measures and discuss their uses.

3. Output Measures in Health Care

(a) *Disease-specific Scales*

Disease-specific output measures have developed out of a recognition that traditional biomedical indicators of the presence or absence of disease do not fully capture the effects of disease on the patient. Indeed, they are a logical development of some clinical indicators such as 'complications', since these only have a meaning in so far as they result in pain, suffering, or restriction of activity for the patient. For example, in the arthritis field it is common to measure the number of tender joints, the number of swollen joints, time to walk 50 feet, duration of morning stiffness, and grip strength (Bombardier et al., 1986).

An example of a disease-specific measurement instrument is the chronic respiratory disease questionnaire developed by Guyatt et al., (1987). It was designed to measure the quality of life of patients in clinical trials of treatments for chronic lung disease and explores how shortness of breath affects the performance of everyday activities and the patient's overall psychological state.

Three main issues arise in the development of disease-specific measures: the *content* of the scale or scales, the *measurement* of improvement along each dimension, and the *weighting* of dimensions. A number of approaches have been used to determine the content of scales. Sometimes patients are asked to identify those aspects of their health or functioning which are most important, e.g. arthritis sufferers might point out the importance of everyday tasks such as tying of shoelaces. An alternative approach would be for clinical experts in the field concerned to specify the items that should be included. Usually the content of scales is assessed in terms of face validity; that is, does the scale appear to contain the items that are generally thought to be important?

The key issue in measurement is whether the methods used generate ordinal or cardinal measures, the latter being expressed on interval or ratio scales. Many measurements, such as level of distress expressed as mild, moderate, or severe, are merely ordinal, in that one can only state whether a particular position on the scale is better or worse than another, but not by how much. This greatly limits the amount of quantification that is possible. However, other measurements, such as time taken to walk 50 feet, are clearly on ratio scales. (That is, intervals on the scale are equal in importance and zero has a clear meaning.) The main debate is over the extent to which items typically measured on ordinal scales can be expressed on interval scales—e.g. can level of distress be quantified by asking the patient to mark a 10-centimetre line so that a change of one unit (centimetre) is the same at each point on the scale?

Although it may be possible to measure changes along each dimension or scale, overall quantification may require comparison of a number of dimensions. Simple addition of scores on different scales implies an equal weighting, unless explicit weights are used. Since health is a multi-dimensional concept all output measures have to address this issue in one way or another.

(b) *General Health Indices and Profiles*

A number of general output measures have been developed. These clearly acknowledge the multi-dimensional nature of health and encompass assess-

Table 4.1
Nottingham Health Profile: Dimensions, Statements, and Weights

Physical mobility

I find it hard to reach for things	9.30
I find it hard to bend	10.57
I have trouble getting up and down stairs or steps	10.79
I find it hard to stand for long	
(e.g. at the kitchen sink, waiting for a bus)	11.20
I can only walk about indoors	11.54
I find it hard to dress myself	12.61
I need help to walk about outside	
(e.g. a walking aid or someone to support me)	12.69
I am unable to walk at all	<u>21.30</u>
	100.00

Pain

I am in pain when going up and down stairs or steps	5.83
I am in pain when I am standing	8.96
I find it painful to change position	9.99
I am in pain when I am sitting	10.49
I am in pain when I walk	11.22
I have pain at night	12.91
I have unbearable pain	19.74
I am in constant pain	<u>20.86</u>
	100.00

Sleep

I am waking up in the early hours of the morning	12.57
It takes me a long time to get to sleep	16.10
I sleep badly at night	21.70
I take tablets to help me sleep	22.37
I lie awake for most of the night	<u>27.26</u>
	100.00

Energy

I soon run out of energy	24.00
Everything is an effort	36.80
I am tired all the time	<u>39.20</u>
	100.00

Social isolation

I am finding it hard to get on with people	15.97
I am finding it hard to make contact with people	19.36
I feel there is nobody I am close to	20.13
I feel lonely	22.01
I feel I am a burden to people	<u>22.53</u>
	100.00

Table 4.1, continued

Emotional reactions

The days seem to drag	7.08
I am feeling on edge	7.22
I have forgotten what it is like to enjoy myself	9.31
I lose my temper easily these days	9.76
Things are getting me down	10.47
I wake up feeling depressed	12.01
Worry is keeping me awake at night	13.95
I feel as if I am losing control	13.99
I feel that life is not worth living	<u>16.21</u>
	100.00

Derived from: Hunt *et al.* (1986)

ments of the patient's physical mobility, ability to perform activities of daily living, social functioning, and psycho-social status. The most well-known examples are the Karnofsky index (Karnofsky and Burchenal, 1949), the Sickness Impact Profile (Bergner *et al.*, 1976), the Spitzer QL Index (Spitzer *et al.*, 1981), the McMaster health index (Chambers *et al.*, 1976), the quality of well-being scale (Kaplan *et al.*, 1976) and the Nottingham health profile (Hunt *et al.*, 1986). Most of the above are reviewed in two recent publications (Walker and Rosser, 1988; Teeling Smith, 1988). The Nottingham health profile has six dimensions relating to physical mobility, pain, sleep, energy, social isolation, and emotional reactions and is administered by asking the respondent a series of 'yes/no' questions. The items are valued relative to one another within each of the six dimensions, based on the views of a sample of general population, but the dimensions are not then themselves weighted to give an overall composite score (see Table 4.1). This would be a limitation if comparing two health care interventions or programmes where one did not dominate the other in terms of its impact on all dimensions. Some general measures, such as the sickness impact profile, can be weighted to give an overall score.

Health indices and profiles have the advantage that they cover all aspects of health-related quality of life and do not therefore require assessments of what is important and what is not for a given disease or condition. Indeed, when they have been used alongside disease-specific scales, unanticipated effects of disease on quality of life have been identified. However, it is sometimes argued that the general measures, being all-embracing, may not be sensitive enough to pick up small improvements in the quality of life associated with some treatments (Ferguson *et al.*, 1987). Nevertheless, it is an advantage to measure the net effect of health interventions on quality of life. Paterson (1988) points out that traditional assessment of pharmaceuticals separates beneficial effects (efficacy) from adverse effects, and that in a clinical trial of a drug for a condition such as rheumatoid arthritis an overall quality of life assessment is required.

(c) *Utility Measurement*

Utility measurement yields a single value for states of health on an interval scale. Usually the scale is standardized so that 'dead' is equal to zero and 'perfect health' is equal to unity. Some states of health have been rated by respondents as being 'worse than death' and are represented by negative values (Boyle *et al.*, 1983). The utility approach is of particular interest to economists since the utility values, when combined with survival data, enable the calculation of the quality-adjusted life-years (QALYs) gained from health care interventions. The uses of this particular output measure will be discussed in section 4.

In North America three main measurement methods have emerged: the rating scale, the time trade-off approach, and the standard gamble. A typical *rating scale* consists of a line on a page with clearly defined end points. The most preferred health state is placed at one end of the line and the least preferred at the other end. The remaining health states lie between these two, such that the intervals or spacing between them correspond to the differences in preference as perceived by the person placing states on the line (the subject).

For example, the subject may be asked to select the best health state of a batch of descriptions concerning restrictions of activity, pain, and so on, and the worst, which may or may not be 'death'. He or she is then asked to locate the other states on the scale such that the distances between the locations are proportional to the subject's preference differences. The rating scale is measured between 0 and 1. If death is judged to be the worst state and placed at the 0 end of the rating scale, the preference value for each of the other states is simply the scale value of its location. If death is not judged to be the worst state but is placed at some intermediate point on the scale, say d, the preference values of the other states are given by the formula $(x-d)/(1-d)$, where x is the scale location of the health state. The resultant scale is a ratio scale akin to other measures of linear distance between points. In some studies more sophisticated 'props' are now being used to aid the respondent, such as 'health thermometers'.

Under the *time trade-off* approach the respondent is asked to consider the relative amounts of time he would be willing to spend in various health states. For example, in order to value a chronic health state, the respondent would be offered a choice of remaining in this state for the rest of his life *versus* returning to complete health for a shorter period. The amount of time that the individual is willing to 'trade' to return to perfect health can be used to obtain a preference value for the chronic health state. A similar approach can be used to calculate the relative values of temporary health states.

Figure 4.1
Time Trade-Off for a Temporary Health State

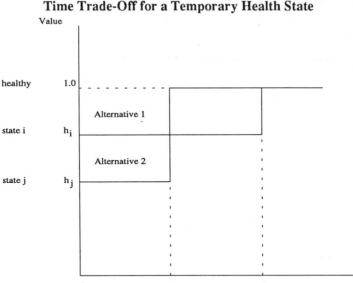

The time trade-off method was developed by Torrance *et al.* (1972) and yields an interval scale measure. Preferences for temporary health states can be measured as shown in Figure 4.1. As with the other scales, intermediate states *i* are measured relative to the best state (healthy) and the worst state (temporary state *j*). The subject is offered two alternatives:

1.   temporary state *i* for time *t* (the time duration specified for the temporary state), followed by healthy;

2.   temporary state *j* for time $x < t$, followed by healthy.

Time *x* is varied until the respondent is indifferent between the two alternatives, at which point $h_i = 1 - (1 - hj)x/t$. With $h_j = 0$, $h_i = 1 - x/t$.

The *standard gamble* is the classical method of measuring cardinal preferences, being based directly on the fundamental axioms of utility theory. In order to measure preferences for chronic states preferred to death the subject is offered two alternatives, either the gamble, a treatment with two possible outcomes (death or return to normal health for the remainder of his life), or the certain outcome of remaining in the chronic state for the rest of his life. The probability of a successful outcome to the gamble is varied until the respondent is indifferent between the gamble and the certainty. This probability can then be used to calculate the preference value for the health state. The method can be illustrated by the weights to be assigned to temporary health states where h is an index of health, as illustrated in Figure 4.2. Slightly different approaches are used to assess states worse than death and temporary health states.

The subject is offered two alternatives: alternative 1 is a procedure with two outcomes, normal health, h_h, with probability p or the worst state, h_j, with probability $1-p$; alternative 2 is some intermediate health state, h_i. Given initial arbitrary numbers assigned to h_h and h_j ($h_h > h_j$), the subject is offered alternative probabilities until he or she becomes indifferent between the two alternatives, at which point

$$h_i = p + (1-p)h_j.$$

Examples of utility values for a number of health states are given in Table 4.2. Many such measurements have now been made, by different methods, on different groups in the population and in different countries. Now that there is more experience with utility measurement a number of methodological issues have emerged (Mooney, 1988; Loomes and McKenzie, 1988).

First, it has been noted that different measurement methods yield different results (Buxton et al., 1986). Loomes (1988) has suggested that regret theory might explain many of the differences. That is, where the methods of utility

Figure 4.2
Standard Gamble for a Temporary Health State

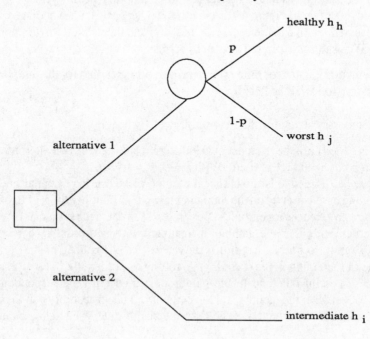

assessment involve the respondent making a choice, utility will be modified according to the level of decision regret or rejoicing associated with the choice. He explains this by reference to a choice between a 50–50 chance of £2 or £20 depending on whether a fair coin lands heads or tails, and a certainty of £10. An individual opting for the gamble would know that if the coin lands heads he will receive £2, but will also know that, as a result of his decision, he will have missed out on the £10 he would have received had he chosen differently. If this gives rise to a painful sensation—a decrement of utility—due to decision regret, we can anticipate that the individual's overall level of satisfaction with the outcome will be less than £2. On the other hand, if the individual opts for the gamble and the coin lands tails, the £20 will be augmented by an increment of utility due to rejoicing at having made the choice which turned out best.

Loomes argued that significant additional resources should not be invested in further refinement of estimation methods until the differences are better understood. Also, Drummond (1987) has argued that while utility estimates may differ according to method, it would be important to explore the significance of these differences for resource-allocation decisions. For example, the results of economic evaluations of alternative health care interventions may not always be highly sensitive to the utility values assumed.

Another explanation of why utility measurements may differ from study to study relates to the way in which health states are described to the respondent. For example, should the descriptions contain any mention of specific diseases or procedures (e.g. 'You are on dialysis') or should they be generic (e.g. 'You are restricted in taking holidays and experience spells of tiredness')? Also, should descriptions contain any prognostic information (e.g. 'There is a small probability that your cancer may return')? Opinions differ on both these points. On the one hand, if the ultimate use of utility measurements is in the calculation of QALYs to inform health care policy decisions, generic descriptions may be preferable. On the other hand, if utility assessments are required for the purpose of deciding on treatment for the individual patient, the method of describing the health states should be determined by what the patient and his/her doctor find relevant.

Secondly, it has been pointed out that individuals' valuations of the utility of health states may depend on their age (and hence number of quality-adjusted life-years remaining) and their current health. Table 4.2 illustrates a related point, that the valuation of health states is dependent on the length of time involved. More generally, analysts have debated the appropriateness of sources of the utility values: should they be those of current patients, past patients, doctors, or members of the general public? The answer to this depends partly on the purpose for which the values are being obtained. For individual clinical decisions the patient's values are most relevant. The position for various kinds of policy decisions is less clear. One might argue that the values of the general

Table 4.2
Mean Daily Health State Utilities in the General Population Sample

Duration	Health state	Observations		Mean daily health state utility	Standard error
		Total	Useable		
	Reference state: Perfect health			**1.00**	
3 months	home confinement for tuberculosis	246	239	0.68	0.020
3 months	home confinement for an unnamed contagious disease	246	240	0.65	0.022
3 months	hospital dialysis	246	243	0.62	0.023
3 months	hospital confinement for tuberculosis	246	241	0.60	0.022
3 months	hospital confinement for an unnamed contagious disease	246	242	0.56	0.023
3 months	depression	246	243	0.44	0.024
8 years	home dialysis	246	240	0.65	0.018
8 years	mastectomy for injury	60	56	0.63	0.038
8 years	kidney transplant	246	242	0.58	0.021
8 years	hospital dialysis	246	240	0.56	0.019
8 years	mastectomy for breast cancer	60	58	0.48	0.044
8 years	hospital confinement for an unnamed contagious disease	246	241	0.33	0.022
life	home dialysis	197	187	0.40	0.031
life	hospital dialysis	197	189	0.32	0.028
life	hospital confinement for an unnamed contagious disease	197	192	0.16	0.020
	Reference state: Dead			**0.00**	
	Total	3,171	3,093		

Source: Drummond *et al.* (1987).

public, who through taxes provide the majority of the funds for health care, are the most relevant. But those making decisions on behalf of the community as a whole may have an interest in knowing what those with experience of a particular health state think about it.

Thirdly, it has been argued that the methods of utility measurement do not encapsulate key elements of the 'real life' choices that individuals make about their medical treatment. For example, with the exception of the standard gamble, the choices are presented in terms of certainties of being in one health state or another. Therefore the values obtained do not reflect the respondent's attitude to risk. Also, the utility values obtained relate solely to the 'outcome' utility of the final state and do not consider that different medical treatments and resource allocation systems may have different 'process' utility associated with them. These issues would clearly need to be addressed if the utility values were to be used in making recommendations for the use of health care resources. Further discussion of these points can be found in Loomes (1988), Mooney (1988), and Dowie (1988).

4. Uses of Output Measures

In this section the potential usefulness of the three categories of output measure is reviewed in the context of the three levels of resource allocation decisions outlined in section 2.

(a) *Individual Clinical Decisions*

Disease-specific output measures would be relevant here since they focus the clinician's mind on the impact of therapy on the patient, rather than on obscure anatomical, physiological, or chemical variables. They may also be sensitive enough to show change, although it should be remembered that the clinician, in providing care, will typically be asking the patient whether he or she is feeling better or worse. Therefore the question is whether more extensive measurement of improvements is informative.

General health indices are unlikely to have much relevance to individual clinical decisions, apart from demonstrating that on occasions the removal or alleviation of one health problem may not improve a person's quality of life dramatically because of other functional limitations. However, Buxton (1987) argued that clinicians participating in an economic evaluation of heart transplants found the information generated by the Nottingham health profile useful for prognostic purposes.

Single output measurement scores, such as those generated by some of the general health indices or by utility measurement, are unlikely to be relevant to individual clinical decisions. For example, what does it mean clinically to change the patient's health status from 0.5 to 0.6? Indeed, in their study of oral gold therapy for rheumatoid arthritis, Thompson *et al.* (1988) explain an improvement in utility of 0.02 points in terms of 'all oral gold patients improving, identically, on the subscale of physical activity from moving one's own wheelchair without help to walking with physical limitations'. However, the trade-offs involved in utility measurement by the time trade-off or standard gamble do bear some relevance to the decisions patients and doctors have to take. Giving chemotherapy in the terminal stages of cancer is essentially the same as saying to the patient, 'Would you take a slight reduction in the quality of your life, owing to side effects, in order to have a slightly higher probability of living longer?' Therefore, the *processes* of utility measurement are relevant to clinical decisions for the individual patient. Whether utility values obtained from a group of patients participating in a clinical trial would be relevant to an individual patient discussing treatment options with his or her doctor is more open to question. The patient may require only data on the probability of various outcomes in order to make the trade-off.

(b) *Clinical Policy Decisions*

Here the objective is to make resource allocation decisions about the choice of treatment for a group of patients presenting with given symptoms, or to set priorities within a given clinical department, e.g. should day-case surgery be encouraged for hernias; what priority should be attached to the treatment of hernias as opposed to varicose veins? Disease-specific scales may help in answering the first category of question, providing the improvements on the scale are compared, in a cost-effectiveness analysis, with the costs. This would be an improvement over indices such as 'cost per case successfully treated', although there may be difficulties if one treatment is superior to another on some items but not others. Utility measurement would then be required.

General health indices may assist in answering the second category of question, dealing with priorities within a given specialty. However, as outlined above, if the scale concerned does not reduce to a single score it would be unsuitable unless one treatment or programme dominated the other on all dimensions. Again, utility measurement (or some kind of scoring) would be required, although it might be argued that clinicians and patients would find it easier to make the trade-offs using the disaggregated data.

(c) *Health Care Policy Decisions*

Economic analysis is most relevant in the case of health care policy decisions, since it is clear that decisions are being made for a group or community of individuals rather than for the individual patient. As such decisions are broad in scope, disease-specific output measures are likely to have little relevance over

Table 4.3
'League Table' of Costs and QALYS for Selected
Health Care Interventions (1983–4 prices)

Intervention	Present value of extra cost per QALY gained (£)
GP advice to stop smoking	170
Pacemaker implantation for heart block	700
Hip replacement	750
CABG for severe angina LMD	1040
GP control of total serum cholesterol	1700
CABG for severe angina with 2VD	2280
Kidney transplantation (cadaver)	3000
Breast cancer screening	3500
Heart transplantation	5000
CABG for mild angina 2VD	12600
Hospital haemodialysis	14000

Notes:	CABG	coronary artery bypass graft
	LMD	left main disease
	2VD	two vessel disease
Adapted from:	Williams (1985)	

and above giving a better assessment of the effectiveness of health care interventions and programmes. Therefore the discussion here centres on the use of general health indices and utility measures.

An example of the use of a general health index for health care policy decisions is the work of Buxton *et al.* (1985) on the economic evaluation of the heart transplant programme at Harefield and Papworth Hospitals in the United Kingdom. They compared the costs of transplantation with the benefits, measured in terms of increased survival and quality of life, using the Nottingham health profile. They were able to demonstrate, using a 'before and after' research design, that transplantation gave an increase in good quality life-years to many patients. This information, presented alongside the data on costs, was useful to the Department of Health and Social Security in deciding on the expansion of the programme to other centres (Buxton, 1987). It was not thought necessary to go to the next stage, of calculating the quality-adjusted life-years gained from treatment.

However, in this case transplant improved the quality of life on all dimensions of the Nottingham health profile. The situation would have been more complicated if, because of the adverse effects of therapy, the quality of life had been reduced on some dimensions. This is often the case with anti-hypertensive therapy and cancer chemotherapy, for example. Also the data presented by Buxton *et al.* would not greatly assist a policy-maker deciding between expansion in the transplant programme and another health programme competing for the same resources. A more generic measure of output, like the quality-adjusted life-year, would be required.

In principle, the general scales could be used to produce such a generic measure. O'Brien *et al.* (1986) examined alternative approaches to collapsing the Nottingham health profile to a single index. They found that the result did not appear to be very sensitive to the weighting system used. The sickness impact profile can also be scored to produce a summary index of quality of life. In addition, one general scale, the quality of well-being questionnaire, has a set of weights derived from a sample of the general population that can be used to calculate an overall utility value for health states. This was used in an economic evaluation of oral gold therapy for rheumatoid arthritis in the USA (Thompson *et al.*, 1988).

However, the recent economics literature has centred on the use of the quality-adjusted life-year as a generic output measure and the construction of 'league tables' of health care interventions in terms of their cost per QALY gained (see Table 4.3). Many economists, most notably Williams (1985), have argued that such league tables can assist policy-makers in assigning priorities for the allocation of resources. In the United Kingdom the most frequently used utility values have been those derived by Kind *et al.* (1982) from a sample of 70 respondents for a matrix of 32 combinations of disability and distress (see Table 4.4). These can be combined with prognostic data on the likely course of disease with or without treatment, from clinical trials or expert opinion, to derive the type of diagram shown in Figure 4.3. In North America effort has concentrated on obtaining direct measurements from individuals for a wide range of health states (Torrance, 1987).

The use of cost-per-QALY league tables has been a source of heated debate. First, it has been argued that the mortality and morbidity data upon which QALY calculations are based are not sufficiently precise. However, the supporters of QALYs argue that, notwithstanding their problems, these data are the best available for decision making and that their use in this way may stimulate epidemiologists and clinical researchers to improve upon them.

Secondly, it has been noted that the different utility methods yield different results. This issue merits further investigation. In the meantime it would be important to assess, through sensitivity analyses, whether health utility values *do* have a critical influence on study results. It may be that the results are just as sensitive to other estimates, such as those of costs. In situations where the utility values are critical, the analyst can only make this explicit and leave it up to the

Table 4.4
Valuation Matrix for Seventy Respondents

Disability rating	Distress rating			
	A no distress	B mild	C moderate	D severe
1. No disability	1.000	0.995	0.990	0.967
2. Slight social disability	0.990	0.986	0.973	0.932
3. Severe social disability and/or slight physical impairment	0.980	0.972	0.956	0.912
4. Physical ability severely limited (e.g. light housework only)	0.964	0.956	0.942	0.870
5. Unable to take paid employment or education, largely housebound	0.946	0.935	0.900	0.700
6. Confined to chair or wheelchair	0.875	0.845	0.680	0.000
7. Confined to bed	0.677	0.564	0.000	−1.486
8. Unconscious	−1.078	*	*	*

Notes: Healthy = 1.0, Dead = 0.0, * = not applicable
Source: Kind *et al.* (1982)

decision-maker to come to his or her own conclusions about the validity and reliability of the estimation methods used.

Thirdly, it has been noted that many of the cost-per-QALY values reported in the literature are average values, whereas the real choices are at the margins. For example, in considering Table 4.3 it can be seen that pacemaker implantation is near the top of the league and is therefore a strong candidate for expansion. However, the cost per QALY of the next stage in the expansion of use of pacemaker technology may not be the same as that reported in the table. For example, the pacemakers required for the extra patients may be more sophisticated in design and consequently more costly. Furthermore, it is likely that the patients who would be treated in the next expansion of pacemaker technology are less seriously ill than those who have already been implanted. Therefore the benefits of treatment would be slightly lower. However, Table 4.3 and some of

Figure 4.3
Quality-adjusted Life-years Added by Treatment

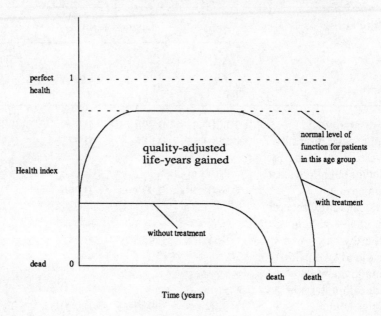

the others reported do embody margins to the extent that they consider the expansions in the indications for therapy (e.g. as here from severe angina with left main disease, to moderate angina with two vessel disease). Consideration of these margins, and the resulting costs and QALYs, would be relevant for the clinicians concerned to decide upon their treatment priorities, given limited resources.

Fourthly, it has been argued that the highly summarized presentation of data, in one cost-per-QALY estimate, is dangerous in that it suggests quick and easy solutions to the decision-maker. This is a very important point and to the extent that these league tables encourage *less* thought by decision-makers about the difficulty and complexity of health care choices, they may be counterproductive. For example, is the decision-maker happy to accept that a gain of one year of healthy life is equivalent to a gain of 0.1 in utility for each of ten years? Are gains in length of life and quality of life different attributes that should be presented separately? Because of these and other complexities, it is the responsibility of economic analysts to continue to stress that such estimates are only an *aid* to decision-making, not a substitute for thought.

Fifthly, some commentators have suggested that broad comparisons across widely different medical fields are unwise. Of course, these choices have to be made, indeed *are* made, through the policy process in health care. The question is therefore again one of whether such analysis helps those making the choices.

In addition, it should be noted that many of the cost-per-QALY league tables also address choices *within* given clinical fields, such as open heart surgery and chronic renal failure, as well as between different branches of medicine. Another way forward would be to consider the costs and QALYs of different interventions for a given care group, such as the elderly or children, on the grounds that the allocation of a budget for the care of the group concerned would have already been made through the political process and that the main question is that of how best to use the budget.

A sixth objection is that the strict application of the cost-per-QALY league table would imply that some groups in society, whose treatment has a high cost per QALY, would receive no care. Of course it is true that the decision rule that is being applied is one that would maximize the total amount of health (as measured by QALYs) given the resources available. That is, it is concerned with economic efficiency rather than with notions of equity or justice in the distribution of health care resources. Society may take the view that it wishes to give everyone an equal chance of receiving care no matter what condition they are suffering from. However, this view needs to be examined critically, since at the limit it would imply that two individuals, one suffering from an incurable condition and another suffering from one that is easily curable, should both receive equal treatment even though the chances of success are zero in one case and high in the other. Perhaps there are better ways in which society could exercise its moral duty, by giving access to palliative care and psychological help to those suffering from terminal illness, rather than engaging in heroic, unproven therapy. This does not deny the need for more medical research in such cases, however, providing this is carried out in accordance with a well-reasoned research protocol. Also it should be remembered that the cost-per-QALY league table does embody a kind of equality, in that a QALY is considered to be worth the same to every individual.

A seventh point, also linked to research, is that the cost-per-QALY estimates relate to treatment interventions at a particular stage in their development. Technological advances may make some of the interventions much more attractive in the future and these advances may never be realized if the treatments are discontinued. Certainly the cost-per-QALY estimates should be continually updated to take account of technological advances and research should continue to take place into all developing treatments. However, it is not wise to continue funding interventions that give poor value for money merely in the anticipation of future technological advances; equally, technological advances in other, competing, fields may make them even less worthwhile in the future. Nevertheless, the calculation of costs and QALYs helps indicate situations where technological advances would potentially generate large benefits.

Finally, economists have questioned whether the measurement methods do in fact measure utility in the strictest economic sense and have pointed out the difficulties of making interpersonal utility comparisons. Therefore it might be wise, as suggested by Dowie (1988), to view these measures merely as preferences for health states rather than true utilities and to regard the construction of QALYs not as a method of measuring the total utility gains from health care interventions, but as a way of making the difficult trade-offs of length and quality of life more explicit. Therefore the value of the approach rests on whether decision-makers make better resource-allocation decisions if given this information. For example, the appropriate use of the information in Table 4.3 is not necessarily to cease treatment for kidney dialysis patients. Rather it is to discourage health authorities from cutting back on high value for money treatments like hip replacement in the interests of short-run political expediency, and to stimulate a debate among the cardiovascular surgeons on the appropriate indications for coronary artery bypass grafting.

5. Concluding Remarks

Despite the methodological and practical difficulties of output measurement in health care, such measures are clearly required for resource-allocation decisions. The alternative, of relying on measures of mortality, or throughput measures such as 'cases treated', is far from satisfactory. Therefore policy-makers need to use the available measures intelligently, whilst simultaneously encouraging research into their refinement.

Considering the use of the available measures, the quality-adjusted life-year, despite its problems, has undoubted attractions. Therefore policy-makers should encourage the production of data on the costs and QALYs gained from health care interventions. However, care should be taken in interpreting the results, given the methodological differences between studies and the concerns over whether this approach fully reflects all the relevant dimensions of choice at the societal level, in particular the equity aspects. The production of cost and QALY values should be viewed as a way of asking questions about the resource consequences of interventions and their contribution to length and quality of life, not as the sole basis for decision-making. It will probably be of more use within individual clinical specialties than in making broad comparisons across a wide range of health care programmes.

In addition there are three areas in which further research is required. First, there needs to be more comparison of clinical measures, disease-specific scales, general scales, and utility measures within clinical trials. Since there is no 'gold standard' for the measurement of health-related quality of life, it is important to explore the convergent validity of the various measures. Clinical trials, which are now established as the major method of evaluating the 'success' of drugs and medical procedures, are an obvious vehicle for this research.

Secondly, there needs to be more exploration of the differences between the alternative approaches to utility measurement and the relative importance of the issues identified in section 3 above. In addition some of the estimation methods need to be applied to larger populations of patients, doctors, and members of the general public before firm conclusions can be reached about their validity and reliability. Whilst it is unlikely that one approach to utility measurement will become universally accepted, it may be possible to narrow down the area of disagreement and debate. Also, if 'league tables' of costs and QALYs are to be constructed, some degree of standardization of study methodology would be advisable for that purpose.

Finally, there needs to be more research into the nature of choice at the level of health care policy. Many commentators argue that costs and QALYs do not encapsulate all the relevant factors. Indeed, since economists are agreed on the difficulties of interpersonal comparisons of utility, it is surprising that the only methodology yet developed to assist health care policy decisions is based on the aggregation of individuals' preferences for health states. Perhaps there should be some exploration of choices presented to members of the general public in the aggregate, such as 'Should the health authority invest more money in cardiac surgery for children, or devote funds to ensure that infant immunization rates are improved?' It would be interesting to compare the results from these kinds of trade-offs with those derived from cost-per-QALY league tables.

5

QALYs: Where Next?

GAVIN MOONEY* and JAN ABEL OLSEN**

1. Introduction

Why QALYs (quality-adjusted life-years)? The answer is that QALYs represent one way of measuring multi-dimensional outputs and that this in turn allows cost utility analysis (CUA) to proceed as an economic evaluative tool in health programmes. So why CUA? Primarily because CUA overcomes a major deficiency in cost-effectiveness analysis (CEA), namely that CEA can only deal with output which is uni-dimensional, such as lives saved. However, health programmes are frequently multi-dimensional and often reflect not just quantity *or* quality of life but both. CUA allows economic evaluation to reflect this multi-dimensional nature of the outputs—provided these different dimensions of quantity of life and quality of life can be measured and brought together in a single index. This is what QALYs aim to do.

If QALYs can be measured they can be used at different levels of decision making in health care, for example by clinicians in comparing one form of treatment against another for a particular disease or condition; or by health service planners and policy-makers to help to decide on priorities for where to spend the next increment in resources. It is in this latter context that marginal cost-per-QALY 'league tables' have been developed (Williams, 1985).

As economists we are interested in the measurement of health in the context of decision making with respect to resource allocation. This has two facets to it. The first is efficiency and the second equity, social justice, or, to use a more neutral term, distribution.

* Institute of Social Medicine, University of Copenhagen.
** Department of Economics, University of Tromsø.
We would like to thank Tony Culyer, Jack Dowie, Paul Fenn, Jørgen Hilden, Ali McGuire, and Alan Williams for helpful comments on an earlier draft of this paper and Anne Haastrup for secretarial assistance.
Gavin Mooney is grateful to the Egmont Foundation for financial support, as is Jan Abel Olsen to the Norwegian Research Council for Science and the Humanities. The authors alone are responsible for any remaining errors and the opinions expressed.

This chapter concentrates primarily on two questions. To what extent in the context of efficiency do QALYs adequately reflect what health services are trying to produce? And to what extent in the context of health output do QALYs adequately measure changes in health?

In addressing these issues it will be immediately clear that this is not a comprehensive review of QALYs, nor does it attempt to examine specific alternatives to QALYs such as healthy year equivalents (HYEs) as recently proposed by Mehrez and Gafni (1989). It also restricts attention to 'formal' health services while it is clearly the case that QALYs have potential relevance to other health producing (or diminishing) activities such as road safety, environmental pollution, and diet.

One of the central difficulties we see in discussions surrounding QALYs in both principle and practice is how efficiency is to be defined and measured and thereafter pursued or implemented. This may seem an odd comment for economists to make but it lies at the heart of the whole QALY debate. What do we want from our doctors? What do we want from our health services?

Additionally, QALYs tend to assume that the only concern of health services is health maximization, consequently that other benefits are not relevant and that distributional questions are not of concern. It is also normally assumed that how health enters the *social* welfare function is as a simple aggregation of how health enters *individuals'* utility functions. Thus, implicitly and sometimes explicitly, the proposal to use marginal cost per QALY as a basis for a league table in priority setting involves the assumption that *all* that is relevant in answering the above two questions is encapsulated in QALYs and that QALYs adequately reflect somebody's valuation of the benefits of health status gains.

What we are attempting in this chapter is to further discussion about ways of improving and developing QALYs and at the same time to point to their limitations. We suggest adding to them other relevant outputs or characteristics of health care—such as information—and giving due consideration to equity concerns. We then indicate some avenues for dealing with some of the existing measurement problems.

2. What Are Health Services Trying To Do?

(a) *Health Care and Utility*

For economists, it is reasonable to assume that the objective of the clinical doctor, as the patients' agent, is to maximize the utility of her patients subject to some resource constraint; similarly for a health service, that it is trying to maximize the welfare of the citizenry in some aggregate form (usually referred to as 'the social welfare function'), again subject to some resource constraint. One interesting question which can be posed at each of these levels is then: how are the utility function and the social welfare function to be defined? What is it for the individual patient and for society that is to be maximized?

To try to address these questions, it is necessary to examine the nature of the demand for the commodity that we are dealing with, i.e. (primarily) health care. This has been summed up as follows:

The uncertainty generated by ignorance about health status, availability and effectiveness of treatment, etc. makes decision-making about the consumption of treatment difficult, especially as there may be substantial anxiety about making a wrong decision which could have serious adverse (ill-health) outcomes. Consequently, the consumption of health care—especially for life-threatening conditions—may also include the characteristic of being able to pass the burden of decision-making to the clinician. In other words, the demand for health care may include a demand to avoid having to make difficult decisions and bear the responsibility of such decision-making. These informational and decision-making features are central to the issue of the 'agency relationship' whereby the doctor acts as an agent on behalf of and in the interests of the patient. (McGuire *et al.*, 1988)

Given the characteristics of this commodity, the economists' standard approach to studying the market for goods and services (neoclassical economics) is not particularly helpful. Essentially this is because neoclassical economics assumes *inter alia* a degree of knowledge on the part of consumers which patients in health care simply do not have.

Thus the extent to which individuals can respond in an informed and rational way to health problems and thereafter demand health care in such a way as to maximize their expected utility (i.e. their future satisfaction) is severely limited. (It should be noted at the same time that it can be problematical to apply this 'expected utility theory' in other markets as well.) For a particularly good discussion of the problems in this context in health care, see Evans and Wolfson, 1980.

QALYs need to be viewed in the context of the nature of health care as a commodity. Rationality for the health care consumer is seriously 'bounded' as Simon (1961) described it, i.e. patients are 'intendedly rational, but only limitedly so'. There exists 'information impactedness' (Williamson, 1973) which results in patients simply being unable to cope with the complexities with which they are faced and thereby relying on the doctor for information.

One of the important emphases in expected utility theory is on consequentialism. The *only* considerations that are utility bearing in expected utility theory are the consequences (or outcomes) resulting from various choices. In utilitarian philosophy as Mill (1979) states 'actions are right in proportion as they tend to promote happiness; wrong as they tend to produce the reverse of happiness' or more crudely as it is often interpreted the goal is 'the greatest good of the greatest number'. It is the consequences or outcomes that count in judging the extent of happiness or of goodness. Further, the Mill view tends to assume that the social welfare function is simply an aggregation of individuals' utilities.

These factors rule out any good or utility associated with the 'process' or 'action', e.g. utility in choosing or indeed in not choosing, the latter perhaps being better expressed as not having to choose. It also says nothing about the desirability of different *distributions* of happiness. Further, it may, if interpreted too narrowly, rule out the inclusion of the utility of information. There is a need for care here.

Using the formulation of Hey (1979):

$$U(C_j) = \sum_{i=1}^{I} P_i U(A_{ij})$$

where $U(C_j)$ is the expected utility associated with the choice, C, for individual j; A_{ij} is the consequence if the individual chooses C_j and the state of the world, i, occurs; $U(A_{ij})$ is the utility associated with A_{ij}; P_i is the probability that the state of the world, i, occurs; I is the number of possible states of the world such that $i = 1, 2, \ldots I$. Here, then, the *only* source of utility is from the A_{ij}s, i.e. the consequences.

This assumption on consequences underlies much of the work on QALYs. It leads quickly to the view that

(1)   the only relevant arguments in the health care consumer's utility function are the consequences of that consumption, often reduced to health status changes *only* and thereby QALYs;

(2)   priorities in health care can be determined on the basis of marginal costs per QALY.

Additionally, when it comes to the question of considerations of the social welfare function, much of the QALY literature assumes that the only relevant arguments in that function relate to individuals' utility and only then from health and with no consideration of equity entering in. Consequently the social welfare function for health care for a society of n individuals is assumed to take the form

$$\sum_{j=1}^{n} U(C_j)$$

and where utility is derived solely from health status gains. In this context we want to consider three issues: information; decision making/autonomy; and equity/distribution.

Before turning to these considerations, it is relevant to comment briefly on the question of interpersonal comparisons of utility—for example, *can* we compare the satisfaction that different individuals get from health—and the related question of cardinal measurement of utility. We would make three basic points here. First, QALYs in no sense resolve the problems in principle which surround interpersonal comparisons of utility. Second, no claim is made that QALYs do 'solve' this problem. Third, it can be argued that, in practice, the issue of interpersonal comparisons of utility is addressed daily by both clinical decision-makers and health-service planners and in cardinal terms. Decisions are made in practice which involve comparisons of one person's cardinal utility from treatment (or quicker treatment) with another's and which involve allocating extra resources to benefit one group of individuals, say, pregnant women rather than another, say, diabetics. (Of course it can be argued that doctors do not attempt such comparisons but simply impose their value judgements without even attempting to judge individuals' relative utilities. We believe doctors make some effort to understand, judge, and compare different individuals' utilities.)

Certainly, the whole idea of interpersonal utility comparisons has been met with much resistance in economic theory since the seminal paper by Robbins (1938). However, although we cannot, on scientific grounds, compare the utility of one person with the utility of another, it is possible to frame comparisons in the form of imaginary choices, such as: 'Would you rather be person A or person B given the choice?' (see e.g. Harsanyi, 1955).

When measuring health state utilities (of which more in section 3, and see also Drummond in this volume), for example, using the time trade-off (TTO) method, utility comparisons are made by such imaginary choices. 'Would you rather have X years in perfect health than Y years in a described inferior state?' However, the problem of interpersonal comparison is not being resolved. Although two individuals might share the same X/Y and thus be assigned the same cardinal utility, the *strength* of the preference for *both* X and Y might well be higher for one of them. The reason is that while everyone might agree that being dead has a utility of 0, the utility from a year in a specified (less than perfect) health state might well differ between individuals.

By assigning the same finite end points, $0 - 1$, on the cardinal scale (as is normally done in QALYs—but see the discussion in 3(c) below), individual differences in their relative strength of preferences are being ignored. Hence, individual differences in the utility increment by moving from one inferior health state to an improved state are ignored in a QALY framework. These would *not* be ignored within a strict utilitarian framework where, *ceteris paribus*, the individual with the highest potential utility increment would be preferred. Thus, QALYs are normally at best and in practice 'quasi-utilitarian'.

It is thus in our view important to assert three things with respect to interpersonal comparisons of utility. First, the problems associated with such comparisons are not solved in QALYs and, in our view, cannot be solved. Second, this fact is not to be seen as an argument against QALYs but rather as a recognition that in the real world of health care interpersonal comparisons *are* made. Third, that in this real world, such comparisons are made only or, at least, very largely implicitly—and not explicitly as QALYs require.

(b) *Information and Decision-Making*

It is quite apparent from what has been said about the nature of the commodity health care, that the consumer is not informed to the extent that would commonly be assumed by expected utility (EU) theory. The normal formulation of EU theory requires knowledge regarding: (1) the choices available; (2) the states of the world that are the consequences of these choices; and (3) the probabilities that the states of the world will occur.

The consumer of health care is lacking information on all three fronts. She does not know what set of treatments/procedures is available, how effective these are, nor what the probabilities are that the various possible outcomes will occur. To assist in the process of choice, the consumer may want to reduce the extent of her imperfection of knowledge on any or all of these issues—or may seek to default on decision-making, passing that responsibility to the doctor.

If it is assumed, however, that it is only consequences that are relevant in terms of being utility bearing and, beyond that, that health status changes are the only consequences that are relevant, then information from the doctor/agent is not utility bearing in itself.

This seems problematical. Culyer, in this volume, suggests that neither health care nor information 'are valued for themselves'. (While it might be simply semantics, it would seem better to include information as a characteristic of health care and therefore reword this to say instead 'neither treatment nor information'.) While we would agree that (normally) treatment will not be valued *positively* for itself (but we can envisage it quite frequently as a 'bad'—many treatments involve pain, for example), there are situations where information will be of value for itself. For example, the majority of individuals screened do not have any health improvement; however, those screened as true negatives get information which is valued for itself. It is of course possible to include in QALYs such factors as anxiety or reductions therein as Feeny and Torrance (1989) propose in the context of pre-natal screening. Information can be incorporated at least partly here. But there are situations where QALYs have not embraced this element and situations where information can itself be an argument in the utility function.

There may even be situations where information which confirms the presence of disease carries positive utility. This would appear to be the case where women agree to a prenatal diagnosis, for example, for polycystic kidney disease, when they have already decided that they will *not* abort if the test is positive. The benefits associated with information were also revealed in the study by Berwick and Weinstein (1985) which indicated women's willingness to pay for information on various aspects of their pregnancy at least some of which had no bearing on changes or feasible changes in health status.

Certainly there will be other ways in which information will affect expected utility than simply as a consequence in the utility function. We do not want to dispute that. Rather, we simply want for our purposes to propose that health status improvements are *not* the only relevant states of the world.

A more detailed example may be helpful here. In a study in Denmark currently being undertaken by one of the authors, doctors were interviewed about various aspects regarding the decision to operate. One doctor stated clearly that in the end it was the patient's decision. However, when pressed on what he did when the patient persisted in wanting the operation when he thought this was not the best option, he stated: 'I then tell her about the possible adverse outcomes.' We believe this is an example of a situation where the disutility (as perceived by the doctor/agent) of information was such that full information was initially not disclosed and only when the 'wrong' decision was about to be made was the information forthcoming.

We do not recount this as an example of something necessarily being wrong in a moral sense with what this doctor said he would do. Rather, we believe it reflects a much wider consideration where at least some doctors do sometimes attempt to take account of the utility and disutility of informing patients. (They may not get it right in terms of utility maximization but that is something else!)

We would also want to distinguish between information and decision making. It is pertinent to suggest that perhaps because of the emphasis in EU theory on the presence of an informed, rational consumer, and the problems for many economists in rejecting this, the emphasis in health economics tends to remain too often on the same informed and rational idea, albeit via an agent. In other words, it is assumed that the perfect agent's task is to allow the patient/consumer to *end up* where she would have been if informed and rational.

In this context we want to quote from Williams (1988b) at some length.

The basic weakness of the idealized view of both [basically 'public' and 'private'] systems is the peculiar 'agency' role which doctors play in all health care systems. The essence of this problem is that the 'consumers' rely on doctors to act as their agents, in a system which ostensibly works on the principle that the doctor's role is to give the patient all the information the patient needs in order to enable the patient to make a decision, and the doctor should then implement that decision once the patient has made it. I am sure that the reader would find the above statement closer to his or her own experience if the postulated roles of patient and doctor were interchanged, so that the sentence would then read 'the *patient's* role is to give the *doctor* all the information the *doctor* needs in order to enable the *doctor* to make a decision, and the *patient* should then implement that decision once the *doctor* has made it.

Given the nature of health care, then the case has yet to be made that the role of the doctor/agent *is* necessarily idealized through giving the patient '*all* the information the patient needs' *or* through having the patient make the decision. This holds only if perfect information and consumer sovereignty are necessary ingredients of any theory with which we are operating—and, strictly, if the provision of information is costless. (Otherwise optimal information will be less than perfect information.)

But are they? It is certainly not certain that perfect or total information (even if costless to provide) will always be optimal to the patient's utility function. Being the decision-maker may not result in maximum utility to the patient—even where health status improvements (QALYs gained, if you like) are the same.

An alternative to consumer sovereignty (other than paternalism), and one to which many doctors subscribe, is autonomy. Defining autonomy is not un-problematical. We have adopted the (rather broad) definition of the principle of autonomy as stated by Beauchamp and Childress (1983): 'Autonomous actions and choices should not be constrained by others. ' They argue that this principle 'asserts a right of non-interference and correlatively an obligation not to constrain autonomous actions—nothing more but also nothing less.'

Our view of such autonomy in the current context is that, depending on the preferences of the patient and assuming that the patient is competent to form self-interested preferences, for some patients (1) autonomy will mean the same as consumer sovereignty with the informed patient choosing; for others (2) it will mean choosing to have someone else make the decisions regarding treatment; and for yet others (3) autonomy will lie somewhere in between. Note that in the case of (2) the position is not constrained by the level of information—the patient can choose to receive any level of information from zero to fully informed and then choose to have someone else make the decision.

We thus argue that the question of patient autonomy enters the patient's utility function in the form of a variable reflecting the patient's preferences for decision making. The job of the perfect agent is then not necessarily to inform *fully* to allow the patient to decide but rather to inform *optimally* and to allow *optimal* involvement in decision making—where optimal in both instances is defined according to the *patient's* preferences. (We would also endorse Beauchamp and Childress' view that the principle of autonomy 'does not apply to persons who are not in a position to act in a sufficiently autonomous manner'—but we will not pursue here how that is to be defined in practice.)

There are thus in our view three arguments in the patient's utility function: health, information, and decision making. The perfect agency relationship would allow the patient to maximize the utility associated with all of these arguments—and not just health. We are clear that for the patient there is more to health care than improved health status or QALYs gained. For those who doubt the possibility of the non-health variables being present in the patient's utility function, we would pose the following questions: Are there no circumstances in health care where your utility as a patient would be unaffected by who made the decision? Are there no circumstances where too little or too much information might not lead to a fall in your utility?

We find it difficult to see how the decision-making component (and perhaps even information *per se*) can be included in the *consequentialist* utility of expected utility theory (but see Dowie, 1989). We would suggest that, however one handles these other aspects, the crucial point is that they *are* additional to considerations of only health.

How information is incorporated is, however, a relevant issue. The answer is at least partly dependent on the decision environment. For example, if annual check-ups picked up, let us say, no health defects but increased individuals' utility by reducing their anxiety, is such utility to be counted in? More generally in the context of information, what is the role of information with regard to individuals' perceptions or misperceptions of probabilities?

In the proposal on prenatal screening by Feeny and Torrance (1989) mentioned earlier, they imply either that respondents' perceptions of the probabilities involved (e.g. of some problem in the foetus) are 'accurate' or that they are irrelevant. They state that the expected utility of diagnostic tests can be estimated by combining the utilities of the relevant health states 'with estimates drawn from the trial results on the frequency and duration of each state'.

QALYs need to be set more clearly in the decision-making frame of the clinical setting and health service planning, particularly with respect to information and patient autonomy. Just how these factors affect the patient's utility function is not clear. We have indicated that information and decision making seem to be important arguments in at least some instances. More research is needed to determine how to incorporate these—and any other factors that the patient wants included—into the patient's utility function.

(c) *Equity*

Most health services include, at least implicitly, but often explicitly, equity as a goal. Many of these express this goal in terms of equality of access (often with the qualification, 'for equal need'). One of us has argued elsewhere (Mooney, 1986) on the merits of the Margolis (1982) 'fair shares' approach in addressing the issue of equality in health care—at least in part because it endorses the most frequently found health service equity goal, i.e. it is access-related.

Margolis draws a distinction between 'selfish' and 'group' utility. The former is the 'normal' outcome or consequentialist utility. The latter is based on the idea that individuals derive utility from *doing* their 'fair share' (hence the name of Margolis' model) for some group, e.g. some community or society generally, of which they are themselves members.

According to this theory, if we examine it in the context of health care, the concept of 'fair sharing' would lead individuals to want to participate in the provision of health services which were available to all. Since in the Margolis model participation utility is derived not from the outcome for the group but from the participation *per se*, it follows that it is the provision of *access* to health care which is the basis of the utility here. The approach is discussed by Culyer at some length in this volume.

However, the essential point on equity in the context of QALYs is that it is very clear that for most (all?) health services, equity in the form of access is a consideration in the social welfare function for health care. This is not currently reflected in QALYS, which are primarily about individuals' utility from health rather than about the social welfare function *per se*.

What is particularly relevant here in the specific context of QALYs is that if the Margolis model were accepted and with it the notion of participation altruism then caring about access would enter the individual's utility function and through that could then be incorporated into the social welfare function.

The question of what is meant by caring in this context is important. Earlier Culyer (1980) wrote of the 'caring externality' to explain the way in which others' health entered an individual's utility function. Culyer's caring does not itself bear utility; nor in fact does being cared for bear utility.

Indeed there would seem at times to be some confusion about the notion of caring. Our view is summarized by Wright (1987):

When we speak of caring, often a subtle ambiguity creeps into our thinking, for caring can be quite good, in the technical sense of meeting physiological needs and correctly utilizing science and technology, and yet not be caring at all . . . If I am seeing to your every physiological need, I am certainly giving you care or *taking care* of you, but I may be doing this without *caring for* you at all. I may be seeing what I do simply as my job, something that must be done to guarantee my paycheck. Although such a view is appropriate for fixing cars or manufacturing spoons, it is not appropriate in dealing with other persons, because then the person is treated as an object.

We would want to put forward the view that caring (and being cared for) and equity, specifically with respect to access, are also possible arguments in the social welfare function regarding health care. We would also suggest that these are perhaps better accommodated in some utility function that more readily accepts participation or process utility in addition to consequentialist utility than does expected utility theory.

What this means, we believe, is not that QALYs should be abandoned. Rather, there is a need to examine first what, in addition to health, is in the patient's utility function, so that these can be added to the QALYs when using health care outputs, and second, what the nature of the relevant social welfare function is. Certainly if it is proposed, as Culyer (1988), does, that health services exist to promote health only or as he states 'given the resources available to the health services, the health of the community should be maximized' then any measure of health status—QALYs or whatever—potentially covers everything relevant to the individual's consumption of health care. But Culyer's subsequent comment that 'egalitarianism equals health maximisation' can only hold if the assumption is made (and others are also necessary) that health care is *only* about health and it can hold if we retain the assumption that the relevant social welfare function is simply a summation of individuals' utility functions (in which health is the only argument).

What are the implications of accepting a broader based social welfare function based not purely on the summation of individuals' utility functions in which only health enters? At a clinical level, this might mean accepting that doctors spend time listening to patients and trying to assess how much information they wish to have and how sovereign as consumers they wish to be. At a planning level it might mean that geographically remote areas might get higher priority in terms of resource allocation if equity considerations were included in health care priority setting than if they were not. And depending on such considerations as economies of scale this equity consideration could alter rankings of marginal cost per QALY, i.e. if the geographical location of the relevant technologies were determined not just on efficiency grounds but on equity grounds. (We would hazard the guess that the additional costs to meet some sort of geographical equity criterion would be relatively greater in the case of heart transplants than pacemakers.)

In terms of social class, too, the inclusion of some equity criterion is likely to affect the rankings of marginal costs per QALY. Thus if the costs considered include those falling on potential patients and not just health service costs, then in instances where the *only* difference in terms of marginal cost per QALY between choosing to treat a social class I patient and a social class V patient was the access cost to the patient, the patient with the higher access cost would have a higher marginal cost per QALY.

3. Measurement Issues

Even given the limitations of QALYs as indicated above, it is none the less important to consider, within their own lights, how adequate QALYs are as measurements of health. In this section of the chapter, beyond a brief description of the main methods for measuring QALYs, we consider five measurement issues that arise with QALYs that we would claim are both important and to date not satisfactorily resolved.

The most frequently used methods in the QALY literature are the standard gamble (SG), the time trade-off (TTO) and category scaling (CS). Only a brief explanation of the methods is given here. For a more complete exposition see Torrance (1986, 1987), Drummond *et al.*(1987), and Drummond in this volume.

SG is based on von Neumann and Morgenstern (1944). Respondents are faced with the choice between a certain prospect and a lottery with two possible outcomes, one of which is better than the certain prospect and the other is worse. The question is then to find the probability level, p, in the lottery, at which the respondent is indifferent between entering the lottery and accepting the certain prospect. In health status terms, the preference value of the certain health state, i, is then $h_i = p$.

A different version of the classic SG is the use of 'certainty equivalents' (McNeil *et al.*, 1978). Acknowledging the difficulties people have in understanding gambles other than the flip of a coin, respondents are asked to specify the period of certain survival that is considered to be equal to entering a gamble with a 50 per cent probability of dying and a 50 per cent probability of survival in a given period. If the certainty equivalent is lower than the expected utility of the gamble, this indicates risk aversion.

The practical problems with SG are, first, that it is difficult for untrained respondents to understand it and, second, that it is highly sensitive to the actual framing of the questions (Kahneman and Tversky, 1979). Further, it can be costly to apply and the revealed values may contain at least an element of people's attitudes to risks.

The TTO was developed by Torrance *et al.* (1972). The method aims at excluding the influence of respondents' attitudes to risk by presenting two alternative health outcomes which are to occur with certainty: either Y years in a described (inferior) state or X ($<Y$) years in perfect health. The respondent is asked to trade off some years in the inferior state for a shorter life in perfect health, so that Y years in the inferior state is equated to X years in perfect health.

Category scales are sometimes termed category rating or rating scales. A related method is magnitude estimation. In this approach, respondents are asked to assign relative values or utilities to describe health states in relation to fixed end-points where normally death is worst and assigned a value of 0, whereas the best imaginable state is assigned a value of 1. As Torrance (1987) describes it: 'The remaining health states are placed on the line between these two, in order of preference, such that the intervals between the placements correspond to the differences in preference as perceived by the subject.'

Using CS, respondents' utilities are derived *explicitly*. Using SG and TTO, the utilities—or health state values—are elicited *implicitly*, based on raters' responses to decision situations. In all instances the utilities are measured cardinally.

(a) Utility Evaluation Bias

There appear to be systematic disparities between the values obtained by the different approaches, what Loomes and McKenzie (1989) call the 'utility evaluation effect'. Torrance (1976) compared the values obtained from the three methods and found that CS values were lower that SG and TTO. A study by

Llewellyn-Thomas *et al.* (1984) comparing SG and CS, supported Torrance's findings that the CS values were lower than SG values.

Read *et al.* (1984) arrived at a different conclusion from Torrance. They found that the SG method gave significantly higher values than TTO and concluded that SG $\geq$ TTO $\geq$ CS.

A possible explanation for the relatively low CS values may be the choiceless context of the CS method as opposed to TTO and SG. In CS, subjects are asked merely to assign relative values to the quality of inferior health states. A respondent might well suggest that the quality of a given health state is 1/3 of perfect health, but not imply from this that she is willing to trade 3 such years with 1 perfectly healthy year. By its very nature, CS does not press for a 'tragic choice' between a long life in an inferior state and a short life in a perfect state. In CS the respondents do not have to 'pay', either by giving up life-years or by undertaking gambles which might involve losing.

In other words, we suggest that there is a likelihood of some strong 'preferences for living'—that life is considered very or even too precious in any trade-off with improved quality. Such an attitude was revealed in a study by Pliskin *et al.* (1980). Although acknowledging that angina was not a perfect health state, some of their respondents were not very ready to trade off life years to obtain perfect health. This observation might explain why TTO values are higher than CS values.

In TTO the two alternatives are presented with certainty, whereas SG involves gambling. It seems to be generally accepted that individuals are risk-averse with respect to choices involving health outcomes (see e.g. Hellinger, 1989), which is likely to serve as an explanation for the higher SG scores.

What, then, are the relative strengths and weaknesses of the different methods? The SG approach appears to have its strongest advocates among medical decision theorists. Llewellyn-Thomas *et al.* (1984) call it 'widely accepted and theoretically sound'. Mehrez and Gafni (1989) call it the 'gold standard' measure. At the same time, Loomes (1988) contends that measures of choiceless utility are not appropriate when decisions have to be made but adds 'neither are the values generated by the standard gambles, if they fail to take account of any regret and rejoicing that may be involved.'

The CS appears not to be posing the right questions at a planning level, where the health aim is to maximize health improvements measured by quality and length of lives within a given budget. The reason is that when revealing their preferences through CS, the respondents are not faced with the same trade-off considerations that decision-makers face when allocating scarce resources.

This choice issue is important in choosing between measurement techniques and on that basis alone it would seem that the TTO is the 'true' QALY method.

Whichever method is used, some interesting implications for resource allocation arise. For example, the low CS values will favour improving lives compared to extending lives, whereas the high SG values will favour extending *vis-à-vis* improving lives. What we would conclude is that, in many situations, the TTO poses the right QALY-question. Whether it gets reliable answers is another question!

(b) *Should Attitudes to Risk Be Taken Into Account?*

One of the potential problems about the measures is that the CS does not offer a choice, the TTO offers choice with certainty and the SG, while introducing risk, is based on von Neumann–Morgenstern which explicitly assumes risk neutrality. Yet individual decision-makers, whether they be patients, clinicians, or planners may well have non-neutral attitudes to risk.

However, if SG is applied in practice to derive the index values, what emerges will inevitably measure not only the utilities of living in the inferior conditions, but also any aversion to undertaking risky treatments that are likely to improve the states. Whether it is relevant, within a QALY health state utility framework at the planning level, to 'boost' the utility values to reflect individuals' risk aversion if they are offered improvement, is an issue of debate. We see no reason to exclude this factor.

However, the concept of risk aversion is more ambiguous than that which follows from conventional wisdom. An individual is normally classified as risk-averse if she prefers the certain outcome to a gamble with the same expected nominal value. By introducing the notion of strength of preferences, Dyer and Sarin (1982) offer a competing explanation to such behaviour, namely the diminishing marginal value placed on extra units of the goods being offered. Their illustrative example is where there is indifference between three oranges for certain and a gamble involving a 50 per cent chance of eight oranges and 50 per cent of none. An analogous example in health would be being indifferent between the certainty of three years in a given inferior state or a gamble involving a 50 per cent chance of eight years in the same state and a 50 per cent chance of dying. The conventional explanation of such behaviour would be risk aversion. However, within the Dyer and Sarin (1982) framework, this could be explained by the likelihood that the person assigns decreasing marginal values to each succeeding year in the particular state—an explanation that violates the assumption of constant health state utilities which is assumed in most of the QALY literature (and which we consider in the next section).

How to include risk attitudes in practice does not yet appear to have been satisfactorily resolved. What may be particularly problematical here is the question of *whose* attitudes to risk should be incorporated. It may seem obvious that, at least in a clinical setting, these should be those of the patient. However, given the earlier discussion (in section 2) about the utility to be derived by some patients in passing the burden of decision making and thereby at least some of the elements of risk taking to the clinician, it is not so clear that it *is* the patient's risk attitudes that are relevant. In principle, the answer might be for patients to choose clinicians who share their attitudes to risk; in practice a rather difficult solution to obtain!

On the question of the relevance at a planning level of individuals' attitudes to risk, as stated above we see no reason to omit these. It would only be if the goal of health service planning were health maximization with no concern about patients' attitudes to risk or if patients were risk-neutral that it would seem justified at a planning level to omit considerations of patients' attitudes to risk.

(c) *Constant Health State Utilities?*

In TTO, the question posed seeks an indifference point between Y years in a described inferior health state and X years in perfect health. When a respondent reveals her indifference point, the analyst assigns a cardinal utility equivalent to X/Y throughout the Y years, i.e. constant health state utility is assumed. The respondents' underlying considerations are, however, likely to be influenced by a whole range of 'time-related variables' that will give a more complicated utility scenario than the X/Y assumption does (see, for example, Nord, 1988).

The aim with the various health state measurement techniques is to assign a health state value to a described health state. Thus, the health state is intended to be an objective description of the state the individual is thought to remain in throughout the whole period. The health state value is an average (= X/Y when TTO is used) of the described health state.

This is open to question. First, there is the issue of different utilities depending on life stages. Although it seems generally accepted in the literature that we consider some life stages to be more important than others, there is scant empirical evidence. An exception is a preliminary attempt by Williams to examine the issue. Using data from a questionnaire survey, he elicited some 'entirely hypothetical' weights against an average index of 1.0 on the relative importance of different life stages. 'As infants' and 'when bringing up children' were life stages that were considered much more important than the average, respectively 2.75 and 3.31 (Williams, 1988a). While Williams stresses that the numbers are purely indicative, it does seem likely that if someone has a life stage of bringing up children in front of her, when responding to a TTO or SG question, that individual would be less willing, *ceteris paribus*, to trade off these life-years.

However, the question of the relative importance of different life stages is not directly relevant to the weighting of QALYs *per se* in cost utility analyses. Here the relevant consideration is the value attached to gains in quantity and/or quality of life. We are interested in marginal gains (and losses) and the fact that a life stage is judged to be more important than the average does not necessarily tell us anything about the relative valuation of some reduction or increment in health status at that life stage as compared with that at the 'average' life stage.

Secondly, there is the issue raised by many authors (for example, Nord, 1988) that the health state utility of inferior health states is likely to decrease because individuals will get weary and satiated after some time in a dysfunctional state. The explanation put forward for the diminished utility is that, after some time, people will have problems in coping mentally with their dysfunctional state. However, for some dysfunctional states, it is possible that the actual health state description will change. The physical disability may get worse as well as the distress.

Sutherland *et al.* (1982) introduced the concept of 'maximal endurable time' (MET), beyond which 'additional time spent in that state was regarded as a penalty and assigned a negative value relative to death'. The more dysfunctional the health state, the shorter was the MET.

When questioning the assumption of constant health state utilities, the literature seems to be concerned only with the possibility that they might decrease. However, it might be that when individuals learn to cope with their new situation, they adjust to and tolerate it, thereby increasing their health state utility as compared with the initial set-back.

While acknowledging the relevance of these non-constancy possibilities at the clinical level, a pragmatic counterargument to the validity of assuming constancy can be presented for the planning level. Given that the objective of QALYs is to serve as an aid for resource-allocation decisions at the planning level, and that this is a continual process, the average health state utilities revealed by individuals in any period would be a representative reflection of the utility at the group level.

In an interesting consideration of the treatment of utility over time, Richardson *et al.* (1989) presented respondents with three health states spread over a period of 16 years, the last year being particularly unpleasant. While their results can be interpreted in various ways, their preferred explanation is 'that future prognosis affects—contaminates—the assessment of previous health states in such a way that the holistic and composite approaches to measurement are incommensurable . . . the knowledge of future suffering and death casts a shadow over—it devalues—the enjoyment of earlier life years.'

The measurement problems here are not conceptual but purely empirical. We simply need more empirical evidence to be able to judge the validity of the constancy position.

(d) *Is There a Time Preference for Health?*

The observation that the utility in chronic dysfunctional states may decrease has led some authors to argue for positive time preferences for health. We would suggest that this has nothing to do with time preference *per se*. Sutherland *et al.* (1982) claimed that the existence of a 'maximal endurable time' (MET) means that the time preference rate for health in these dysfunctional states increases as one is approaching the MET, i.e. the time preference rate (TPR) is non-monotonic. The observation that an individual 'values less each succeeding year in a chronic dysfunctional state simply because he is getting weary or satiated with the situation' made Gafni and Torrance (1984) introduce the notion of a 'quantity effect' as an argument for increasing the discount rate for health.

However, accepting that the health state utilities are decreasing with succeeding years in a dysfunctional state implies that we are no longer comparing two identical utility levels taking place in two different time periods, which is the relevant consideration when assessing individuals' time preferences. Rather, we are comparing different utility levels in different time periods, or to put it in Böhm-Bawerk's (1888) original terminology: 'the true intensity of their future marginal utility' is *changing*. An important distinction should be made: the decreasing future utility in a chronic dysfunctional state may be due to a real decrease in utility as time goes by. It may not be due to the remoteness in time of the future utility, which essentially is the impatience argument for assigning lower utility levels to future consumption.

Although Gafni and Torrance (1984) explicitly separate the 'quantity effect' from pure time preference, the introduction of this effect contains two implicit assumptions. First, it is assumed that the utility-decrease from getting wearied and satiated follows a smooth monotonic pattern in the same way as the time preference rate. A study by Sutherland *et al.* (1982) does not support this view. Secondly, it is implied that the health state utility will always decrease over time. As discussed in 3(c) above, the utility might well *increase* as compared with the initial setback as the individual learns to cope. These sorts of problems would seem to support our suggestion for sticking to a narrow understanding of the time preference concept, and in addition for being explicit with respect to time-related utility changes which have no time preference element.

When a positive time preference rate for health is observed using gambling approaches (McNeil *et al.*,1978, 1981; Pauker and McNeil, 1981; Sutherland *et al.*, 1982), a competing explanation could be found in people's attitudes to risk. McNeil *et al.* (1978) found that 'life during the next few years is much more important than life many years later'. This might be due to a positive TPR. However, it might well be due to changing attitudes to risk because, according to Mehrez and Gafni (1987), risk aversion is more common for shorter periods while risk seeking increases with the length of the time period considered.

In a recent study by Hellinger (1989), fifty individuals were asked whether they valued each of the next thirty years, assuming good health, equally. Of the nineteen who did so, and thus revealed no time preference, eighteen were risk-averse.

While it might sound peculiar to use the concept of pure time preference for life *years* in a given health state, perfect or inferior, it is more meaningful to use the concept for temporary health gains or losses. Lipscomb (1989) observed positive time preference by varying the delay of onset of a temporary inferior health state and also the duration of the inferior state.

Llewellyn-Thomas *et al.* (1984) observed a non-monotonical time preference rate—increasing as the patient approached the time when pain set in. Fuchs (1982) refers to a study which indicated that the time preference rate was lower when assessing the relative preferences between two points both in the future than between the present versus the future. In other words, short-sightedness is a short-sighted phenomenon!

To date there are poor empirical estimates of any TPR for health. The claimed positive TPR may often be due to risk aversion or decreasing utility in an inferior health state due to satiation. Measures of TPR for health seem to be highly conditional on the specific situation. The revealed TPR in one situation might be irrelevant in another. An individual's short-term preference for immediate pain relief might indicate a very high TPR, while her healthy life-style might indicate a low TPR for health in the long run.

Not only is the revealed TPR situation specific, it might also be sensitive to the actual framing of the question. Say that an individual values her life-years equally in the next thirty years, the implication being that there is no time preference. The message to the QALY tool-kit is to leave QALYs undiscounted when ranking alternative programmes. However, say that two programmes, A and B, have identical net present costs and identical undiscounted numbers of QALYs, i.e. the cost per undiscounted QALY is the same. The only difference between the two programmes is that A saves QALYs in the present period, whereas B saves QALYs in ten years. Which of the two programmes would the individual vote for? Intuitively, we would expect that A is preferred.

Thus, although one might reveal an individual TPR for health equal to zero, the social TPR to use in QALY decisions at the planning level might still be positive. If society is not indifferent between the timing of its QALY gains, the social TPR for health would serve as the appropriate measure for the relative strength of its preferences for present versus future health gains. Note that it is not *a priori* given that this social TPR for health would be identical to that applied as the social TPR elsewhere in the economy—but clearly this creates some problems in allocating resources between health and other sectors.

Weinstein and Stason (1977) suggested that since health benefits are being valued relative to monetary units, then, for the sake of consistency, they have to be discounted at the same rate as costs. Keeler and Cretin (1983) elaborated on this point and showed that if health benefits were discounted at a lower rate, it would have a 'paralysing effect' on decision-makers, as it becomes better always to postpone any project. The point is clearly relevant for intertemporal budget allocations. However, this conventional wisdom does not, in our view, under-mine the idea of ranking health programmes according to net present costs per undiscounted QALY (or per discounted QALY using a lower rate than on the cost side) within the *current* budget.

(e) *Whose Values?*

A key measurement issue is quite simply whose values to elicit. There is little agreement in the literature on this point—but this may be all right as it is probably not for the analyst to decide. Analysts need, however, to accept that the answer to the question 'Whose values?' will tend to vary with the decision environment. Mulley (1989) in this context makes the following pleas for future research:

Utility theorists need to pay more attention to the departures from the normative model and the cognitive heuristics and biases that patients use in its stead if they are to help clinicians help patients make their best decision. The clinician needs to better understand the shared nature of both decision-making and decision-making responsibility so that patient autonomy can be realized while still offering protection from unnecessary anxiety and regret.

And he then poses two key questions: 'Whose utilities should be used to develop consensus values for appropriateness? To what extent can variability in utilities for health outcomes be used to distinguish between health care "needs" that reflect societal consensus and health care "wants" about which consensus may not be possible?'

As one possible way forward on this front we would suggest that a random sample of the population should be asked not only for their values but also what weight should be attached to their values (and perhaps also what weight should be attached to others' values). Thus in the context of screening women for breast cancer, we two males might be part of the random sample but might then choose to have zero or low weights attached to our responses and we might also want to have some say in proposing that women should have a higher weight than men, and women with breast cancer the highest weight of all.

4. *Que Faire?*

On measurement issues, we have tried to indicate some of the current difficulties in QALYs. None of these is in our view overwhelmingly problematical. But there is a need for greater empirical work in the area, especially, we believe, in respect of the choice of the basic measuring technique and of the question of time preference.

These problems of measurement are not surprising. Given the work by Kahneman and Tversky (1979) on the variations in responses as a result of different ways of framing questions, it is perhaps inevitably difficult not to get different answers emerging from different measurement methods.

Beyond that, perhaps the underlying theme for the future research agenda on QALYs should be the decision environment in health care at both the clinical and the planning/health policy level. There is too little understanding of the behaviour of the key actors in the system, what is in their utility functions, how they make their decisions and how different stimuli affect their decisions. Simply as examples of this lack of understanding, we still know little today about the nature of GPs' decision-making and the impact on that of different forms of remuneration (Donaldson and Gerard, 1989). In the hospital sector, most of the economic research adopts models that seem to show little appreciation of what goes on in hospitals (McGuire, 1987).

Much that is relevant to the peculiarities of health care relates to information, consequently information processing and decision making. More than a quarter of a century ago, Arrow (1963) argued that the medical profession specialized in information. What is clearer today is that the information processing of medical doctors and of patients and the decision-making procedures based on this are particularly complex phenomena that economists might usefully appraise more than they have to date. There is something missing at the very centre of health economics when we present models of supplier-induced demand and of the agency relationship and yet still argue that the only relevant output from health care is health and that the measuring processes for health should be based on expected utility theory. More research is needed by economists on decision making in health care, perhaps looking to the economics of institutions (Simon, 1961; Williamson, 1973; Langlois, 1986) where the extent of information and of rationality is recognized as being limited. What QALYs currently appear to lack—despite their strengths and despite the improvements they offer on what exists in health care today—is a better understanding of the decision-making milieu of health care and a wider view of the nature of the health care social welfare function.

Loomes and McKenzie (1989) have previously drawn attention to the potential merits of alternatives to expected utility (EU) theory in the form of either prospect theory or regret theory. Their proposals need to be seen against a background of considerable evidence that EU maximization appears not to be a general description of how individuals behave and that the axioms of EU theory as expressed earlier are frequently violated (Schoemaker, 1982). There do seem to be several attractive features of these alternative theories that merit examination. Prospect theory has in our view the decided advantages of giving much more consideration to the specific context of decisions; the framing of questions; and the certainty effect (which results in states of the world which occur with certainty looking disproportionately large as compared with uncertain states of the world). Perhaps most important, prospect theory echoes the view of Simon (1955) that gains and losses are better or more easily viewed in terms of some reference point, specifically emphasizing that the utility function is likely to be convex for losses and concave for gains.

In regret theory, allowance is made for the context of choice. Loomes and Sugden (1982) do not include the process utility of choosing per se but do attempt to incorporate the idea of regret or rejoicing associated with making a bad or good, respectively, decision. These approaches are worthy of closer examination especially as the context of health service decision making, particularly at the clinical level, is so far removed from the neoclassical paradigm.

There is more than health and therefore more than QALYs in the patient's utility function, whether this is seen through the patient's eyes directly or through the doctor's as the patient's agent. And there is more to the relevant social welfare function than the aggregation of individual patients' utilities from health improvements. Health economists currently may be falling into the medical trap of thinking that health services are about health only rather than some wider based notion of utility.

Emphasizing the decision-making frame, and thereby considering other avenues than expected utility theory and other arguments in the utility function than simply health, would seem to be the way to go with QALYs. Given the nature of health care for the consumer and the role of the doctor-agent, issues of information and decision making need to be considered more when defining the patient's utility function. And given the nature of health care for the citizen, issues of equity need to be reflected more in any health care social welfare function.

6

Equity in the Finance and Delivery of Health Care: Some Tentative Cross-Country Comparisons

ADAM WAGSTAFF,* EDDY VAN DOORSLAER,** AND PIERELLA PACI***

1. Introduction

Equity is widely acknowledged to be an important goal in the field of health care. Indeed, McLachlan and Maynard (1982) have gone so far as to suggest that 'the vast majority of the population would elect for equity to be the prime consideration'—a view endorsed by Mooney (1986, p. 145). Several researchers have investigated how successful their own country's delivery and/or financing system is in achieving its stated equity goals. In general the strategy of these studies is to compare the current situation with some ideal or 'target' situation. Le Grand (1978), for example, in what has become a classic study in the field, compares the distributions across socio-economic groups of illness and public expenditure on health care in Britain in 1972, and concludes that the National Health Service (NHS) has failed to achieve equity in the delivery of health care.[1]

Though studies such as Le Grand's are extremely valuable, an arguably more interesting strategy is to compare the current situation, not simply with some ideal distribution, but with a situation that prevailed before (for example: is the NHS becoming more or less equitable?) or with the situation prevailing in other

* School of Social Sciences, University of Sussex.
** Department of Health Economics, University of Limburg.
*** Department of Social Sciences, City University.

We are grateful to Frans Rutten for support throughout the research leading up to this chapter; to the Centro Europa Ricerche (CER) in Rome—and in particular to Stefania Gabriele—for providing data from the CER *Health Care Consumption Survey*; to Ugo Ercolani and George France for help in obtaining data on Italian health care expenditure; and to Jaap van den Berg of the Dutch Central Bureau of Statistics (CBS) for providing pre-release versions of recently published tables from the CBS *Health Interview Survey*.

[1] Le Grand finds that 'the top socioeconomic group (professionals, employers and managers) receives 40 per cent more NHS expenditure per person reporting illness than the bottom one (semi-skilled and manual workers)' (Le Grand, 1982).

types of health care system (for example: does the NHS fare better than the French health care system?). In other words, studies of a comparative nature may be more relevant for policy purposes than studies appraising a system only relative to some ideal (and possibly unattainable) state.

Under the auspices of the European Community (EC), researchers from ten countries have recently begun collaborating on a comparative study of this type.[2] The project's initial aim is to facilitate comparisons of the distributional consequences of alternative health care financing and delivery systems. Later it is planned to examine the distributional consequences of specific cost-containment measures. It is hoped that the project will allow participants to address issues such as: would country X's equity goals be better served if it moved closer to country Y's delivery system? If so, which particular facets of the delivery system should it try to emulate? Would adoption by country X of country Y's financing system be desirable given country X's equity objectives? What can country X learn about the distributional effects of co-payments from country Y's recent experience? And so on.

The idea of a comparative study of health care systems is, of course, not a new one. The EC study differs, however, from the majority of previous comparative studies in at least three respects. First, it has distributional themes as its prime concern. Though there are exceptions (for example, Le Grand and Rabin, 1986; Le Grand, 1987a), previous studies have tended to be directed at other issues (Culyer, 1987). The studies of Maynard (1975) and Maxwell (1981), for example, both compare health care systems, but are largely descriptive and seem to have been motivated mainly out of efficiency considerations (see Maynard, 1975). Studies along the lines of that of Newhouse (1977) and Parkin *et al.* (1987) also compare health care systems, but aim at explaining international variations in expenditure. The second difference is that the EC study employs micro-level data, whereas previous empirical studies of a comparative nature have almost all been based on aggregate data. This switch to the use of micro-level data in international comparisons has already occurred elsewhere in social policy analysis (Smeeding *et al.*, 1985; Atkinson, 1987). The third difference is that, in the EC study, the analysis for each country is being undertaken, for the most part, by citizens of the country in question. This contrasts with previous comparative studies in the health field where one researcher tends to perform the analysis for all the countries in the study (e.g. Abel-Smith, 1984).

This paper outlines some of the methods currently being used in the EC study and presents some tentative cross-country comparisons using data from Britain, Italy, the Netherlands, and the United States. It examines equity both in the finance of health care and in its delivery.

---

[2] The project forms one of several projects in the EC-COMAC Health Services Research Programme. The ten countries include eight EC countries and two non-EC countries.

In section 2 we explore the question 'What is equity?', summarizing various important distinctions that have been made in the health economics literature regarding this concept . Section 3 considers the problem of defining equity. Section 4 investigates the issue of measuring it. This is a topic that has received hardly any attention at all in the health economics literature but is clearly crucial if cross-country comparisons are to be performed. In section 5 we outline some measurement methods that might be employed. We then employ these measures in section 6 to analyse equity in the finance and delivery of health care in our four countries. The final section contains a summary and a discussion.

2. What is Equity?

Equity, like efficiency, is a goal that is pursued by policy-makers in all types of health care systems (McLachlan and Maynard, 1982). There is, however, much less agreement over what constitutes equity than there is over what constitutes efficiency: as McLachlan and Maynard note, 'equity, like beauty, is in the mind of the beholder'. Not all individuals subscribe to the same concept of equity: contrary to what is often suggested, for example, not everyone takes the view that equity is about equality. Moreover, distributional issues do not always concern equity: they may arise from feelings of compassion or altruism. This too is a distinction that is not generally appreciated: distributional goals and equity goals are typically viewed as one and the same. In this section we examine the principal concepts of equity and consider the extent to which support for each varies across countries. We begin, however, with the distinction between distributional goals that derive from equity considerations and those that do not.

(a) *Equity versus Altruism*

Distributional objectives in health care, and in social policy generally, can arise from two sources. First, they can arise from considerations of social justice and fairness (i.e. equity). In other words an equitable distribution of health care would be one that is considered to be fair or just. Alternatively, distributional objectives can arise from feelings of altruism or caring. The concepts of equity and altruism are often confused.[3] Equity and altruism are, however, as Culyer (1980) and Goodin and Le Grand (1987) emphasize, quite distinct and have quite different implications for health policy.[4]

[3] Mooney (1986), for example, asks whether one can rationalize the equity goals of the NHS in terms of altruism. To the extent that the NHS's equity goals are genuinely about equity and social justice rather than altruism, the question would seem somewhat misguided. Of course, it may be that what are passed off as equity objectives are really not equity objectives at all, but rather are redistributional objectives reflecting altruism. It is not obvious, however, that it makes sense to assume that this is the case *ex hypothesi*.

[4] This section draws heavily on Culyer (1980).

Caring and altruism are matters of *preference*. In the context of health care a caring individual might be one who derives utility—i.e. an external benefit—from seeing another person receiving health care (Culyer, 1980). In this case the caring individual *prefers* that the person in question receives health care and is prepared to sacrifice resources to ensure that the person actually obtains treatment. Quite how much he is prepared to sacrifice will depend on how much he cares (which will depend on *inter alia* his income) and on the cost of providing health care. Alternatively a caring individual might be one that derives utility from the *act* of providing health care for others (Mooney, 1986). Quite how much of his income the individual will be prepared to sacrifice to provide health care for others will depend on the utility he derives from the act of providing medical care (which again will depend on his income) and on the cost of providing health care. With caring preferences of either type, therefore, 'costs and benefits are balanced at the margin and . . . the level of provision is . . . determined by the wealth of the community' (Culyer, 1980). The language of caring is thus the language of efficiency. Hence the term 'Pareto optimal redistribution' (Hochman and Rodgers, 1969).

Social justice or equity, on the other hand, is not a matter of individual preference. In the words of Culyer (op. cit.):

the source of value for making judgements about equity lies outside, or is extrinsic to, preferences. . . . The whole point of making a judgement about justice is so to frame it that it is (and can be seen to be) a judgement made independently of the interests of the individual making it. (p. 60)

Social justice thus derives from a set of principles concerning what a person ought to have *as of right*. The different motivations behind equity and caring have at least two important implications for health care policy. First, decisions regarding health care provision prompted by considerations of social justice ought not to be influenced by cost: justice requires that an equitable pattern of provision be ensured, irrespective of the cost to the rest of society (Culyer, 1980). Second, there is scope for conflict between efficiency and equity: an efficient redistributional programme prompted by caring preferences need not be equitable, and vice versa (Culyer, 1980).

For some purposes it may not be important to be able to separate out considerations of equity from considerations of altruism. One might be content to analyse the extent to which society's stated distributional goals—however motivated—are being achieved. This strategy is explicitly adopted by Le Grand (1982) and Goodin and Le Grand (1987). In the light of the discussion above, though, this is not altogether satisfactory. Ideally, one would like to analyse equity objectives independently of distributional objectives that are motivated by altruism. That there is so much talk of equity objectives in the context of health care suggests either that a separate analysis of equity is held to be desirable, or that the distinction between altruism and equity is not widely appreciated.

(b) *Social Justice and Concepts of Equity*

There is another important but often overlooked distinction in the literature, namely the distinction between equity objectives that are couched in terms of *equality* and those that are couched in terms of *minimum standards* (Le Grand and Robinson, 1984).[5] Policies whose objectives are couched in terms of equality aim at eliminating inequalities; policies whose objectives are couched in terms of minimum standards aim merely at ensuring that nobody falls below some specified minimum level.

Equity goals couched in terms of *equality* may be viewed as coming from a theory of social justice built around the notion of *distribution according to need* (Culyer, 1980). This in turn is a key component of 20th-century egalitarianism (Sugden, 1983). Egalitarians view

access to health care [as] a citizen's right ..., which ought not to be influenced by income and wealth. (Maynard and Williams, 1984)

Egalitarians emphasize *fraternity*—a sense of brotherhood and collective citizenship between people (Sugden, op. cit.). They espouse an explicitly *collectivist* philosophy of social justice and view social unity as a good thing in its own right. This egalitarian view suggests that an NHS-type state sector should predominate in the health care sector, with health care being rationed according to 'need' (Maynard and Williams, op. cit.; Williams, 1988b).

To an egalitarian an equitable health care financing system is one in which payments for health care are positively related to ability to pay: he would regard it as right and proper that persons who are able to pay more towards health care should do so. On the delivery side this viewpoint gives rise to a set of equity objectives that are couched in terms of *equality*. One such goal is 'equal treatment for equal need'; another is 'equality of access' (see section 3 below). Both refer to equality rather than to minimum standards (Goodin and Le Grand, 1987). All—or nearly all—inequalities are inequitable. An egalitarian would, for example, argue that

it is wholly wrong that, when two people are in equal need of medical care ..., one should receive more than the other. (Sugden, 1983)

Sugden, in fact, goes further and argues that unequal treatment of persons in equal need would be viewed as inequitable, *even if the inequality arises out of the free choice of the individuals concerned*; even if, for example, one of the persons had voluntarily chosen not to take out health insurance. Thus:

---

[5] The distinction between equality and minimum standards is made in both the literature on caring *and* the literature on equity and social justice (Culyer, 1980). The rationale for each could therefore be sought either in terms of altruism or in terms of considerations of social justice. Here we focus on the latter.

Once it is accepted that social unity is a good thing in its own right, and a 'sense of separateness' is bad, it becomes natural to say that people in like circumstances ought to consume the same combinations of goods and services whether they would choose to do so or not. (Sugden, 1983)

This view is hotly disputed by Le Grand (1987b), who argues that, depending on circumstances, there may be instances where equal treatment for equal need would 'conflict with intuitive judgements' (Le Grand, 1984). He gives the example of a drunk driver crashing his car and injuring himself and a pedestrian in the process, and suggests that equity would require giving the victim preference. One cannot, Le Grand concludes,

simply observe inequality . . . and thereby judge, *on the basis of that inequality alone*, whether or not an allocation is equitable or inequitable. (Le Grand, 1984; emphasis in original)

Whether a true egalitarian would accept this or not is, perhaps, a moot point. In its emphasis on individual circumstances and its suggestion that some individuals are more deserving than others, Le Grand's ideas would seem to run counter to the egalitarian emphasis on fraternity and common citizenship. An egalitarian might argue that there is no space in his philosophy for what are essentially *individualistic* 'intuitive judgements'.

A second set of equity goals is defined in terms of *minimum standards* (Le Grand and Robinson, 1984). Culyer (1980) suggests that an emphasis on minimum standards might be viewed as the outcome of a Rawlsian conceptual experiment in which 'all would come to the same conclusion behind the "veil of ignorance" that certain minima . . . ought to be guaranteed each member of society' (Culyer, 1980). In the context of health care the emphasis on minimum standards is particularly prevalent amongst what Maynard and Williams (op. cit.) call the 'libertarian' school. This regards access to health care as part of society's reward system and maintains that people should, at the margin at least, 'be permitted to use their income and wealth to gain more or better health care (than their fellow citizens in otherwise identical circumstances) if they so desire' (Maynard and Williams, 1984). This reflects the fundamentally *individualistic* nature of the libertarian viewpoint:

To anyone whose values are individualistic, it is natural that social arrangements should reflect the diversity of people's interests and preferences. That different people should consume different bundles of goods and services is entirely right and proper. (Sugden, 1983)

The libertarian approach points, as Maynard and Williams note, towards a mainly private health care sector, with health care being rationed primarily according to willingness and ability to pay. It requires that state involvement be minimal and limited to providing a minimum standard of care for the poor.

According to this viewpoint, on the delivery side, considerations of social justice require that everybody be guaranteed a basic minimum level of health care. On the *finance* side, there should be income transfers from the non-poor to the poor, but these should be *in-kind* transfers in the form of free or subsidized health care. Nothing is indicated about how the burden of financing the transfers should be distributed across the non-poor.

(c) *Cross-Country Differences in Equity Goals*

The differences between countries in their health care systems probably reflect, at least to some extent, the differences in the type of equity goals pursued. [6] In the United States, equity goals tend to be defined in terms of minimum standards rather than in terms of equal treatment for equal need, or equality of access.[7] In several of the European countries, by contrast, policy statements on equity frequently have a distinctly egalitarian flavour (e.g. British Ministry of Health, 1944).

The fact that not all countries subscribe to the same equity goals means that a country's health care system can be appraised in either of two ways (Culyer *et al.*, 1981). One way would be to appraise it with reference to its own equity goals. This would be the relevant assessment if one were interested in answering the question: how successful is the country in question in achieving its own equity objectives? Alternatively, the country's system might be appraised with reference to another country's equity goals. This cross-cultural assessment would be relevant if one were interested in answering the question: does 'their' system do better than 'ours'?

3. How should Equity be Defined?

In the previous section we considered what are essentially *concepts* of equity. In this section we look at the various *definitions* of equity that have been proposed in the literature. In doing so we focus exclusively on *egalitarian* goals and ignore completely minimum standards goals. We also consider separately the finance of health care and its delivery.

[6] Such a conclusion may be unwarranted. As Maxwell (1981) notes, the mix between different sources of finance frequently seems to depend more on history than on principle. It may well be wrong, in other words, to assume that a particular mix represents the outcome of a deliberate and well-informed decision.

[7] Tobin (1970) is rather ambivalent about attitudes in the United States towards health care. He suggests that Americans are concerned about inequality in access to medical care and that equity in health care might be taken to mean that 'the treatment of an individual depends on his medical condition and symptoms, not on his ability or willingness to pay'. Later, however, he notes that in practice the American health care system aims at bringing the medical care received by the poor up to a minimum standard rather than at promoting equality of access.

(a) *Defining Equity in the Finance of Health Care*

Egalitarians typically define equity on the finance side in terms of a requirement that payments for health care be directly related to ability to pay. In effect, this is a statement about *vertical equity*—the requirement that unequals (defined here in terms of 'ability to pay') be treated unequally.[8] As a definition it is rather vague. How is 'ability to pay' to be measured? By pre-tax income? By pre-tax income plus imputed income from physical assets such as the individual's house? Should those with greater ability to pay be paying more in proportional terms? In other words, ought the relationship between ability to pay and payments to be progressive?[9] Or should they merely be paying more in absolute terms? In other words, can the relationship between ability to pay and payments be proportional or even regressive?[10] If the relationship is to be progressive, how progressive ought it to be? Typically policy statements fail to address questions such as these. It seems reasonable, however, to conclude that for an egalitarian, payments for health care ought not to be regressive and probably ought to be progressive.

The issue of *horizontal equity* on the finance side (the requirement that equals be treated equally) is rarely discussed by policy-makers and has received little attention in the health economics literature. The logic of the discussion above suggests that horizontal equity might be defined in terms of the extent to which those of equal ability to pay actually end up making equal payments, regardless of, for example, gender, marital status, trade union membership, place of residence, etc. Horizontal *inequity* might arise for a number of reasons. In a tax-funded system such as the British NHS it might arise through anomalies in the personal income tax system (e.g. tax reliefs such as mortgage interest tax relief). In a private insurance system low-risk groups (e.g. non-drinkers) may receive reduced premiums. A strict egalitarian might well consider this inequitable.[11] In a mixed system different occupational groups may be eligible for different health insurance schemes. Some examples of horizontal inequity in the Dutch health care financing system are provided by Rutten and Janssen (1987): they find, for example, that single persons on an income of Dfl 17,000 in 1981 could end up paying as little as 2 per cent of their income towards health care if they were over 65 but as much as 13 per cent if they were under 65 but self-employed.

---

[8] On the distinction between vertical and horizontal equity, see Cullis and West (1979) and West (1981).

[9] A finance system is progressive if the proportion of income paid out for health care rises as the level of income rises.

[10] A finance system is proportional if the proportion of income paid out for health care is the same at all income levels and regressive if the proportion of income paid out falls as income rises.

[11] Le Grand (1987b) would presumably argue otherwise. The argument would be that individuals who choose to drink, knowing the risks involved to themselves and others (e.g. through drunk driving), should, on equity grounds, be called on to pay towards the cost of any treatment they or others require as a result of their drinking.

(b) *Defining Equity in the Delivery of Health Care*

Common to all egalitarian definitions of equity in the delivery of health care is the emphasis on *equality*. The various possible definitions have been discussed by Le Grand (1982, 1987b) and Mooney (1983, 1986). The three most common definitions are: (1) equal treatment for equal need, (2) equality of access, and (3) equality of health. Another definition that is implicit in some of the empirical work is: (4) equality of final incomes. The idea here is that health care should be allocated in a way that favours the poor, so that inequalities in final incomes (i.e. income plus imputed benefits from health care) are reduced.[12]

There are various points that are worth noting before considering the relevance of each of these definitions. First, the concept of 'access' is often ill-defined in policy documents. Le Grand (1982) suggests that it might best be interpreted in terms of the time and money costs that individuals incur in using health care facilities. As Mooney (1983) emphasizes, this makes 'access' a supply-side phenomenon and contrasts with 'treatment', which is a function of both supply and demand: i.e. the latter depends not only on the costs facing an individual but also on his perception of the benefits of health care. Second, definitions (2) and (3) both view equity in terms of the attainment of equality *across the population as a whole*, whilst the first views equity in terms of the attainment of equality amongst *specific sub-groups in the population*, notably those in equal 'need' (Goodin and Le Grand, 1987). In the context of the latter it is important to note that the judgement about whether a person is in 'need' is to be made not by the individual but by a third party (usually the physician) (Williams, 1978, 1987c). Third, all three definitions are difficult to operationalize. How should treatment be measured? By utilization or by imputed resource costs? On what criteria is need to be assessed? How should access be measured? How far can one blame inequalities in health on the health care system?

With definition (1) it is natural to go one step further and make the distinction between horizontal equity and vertical equity. As it stands, definition (1) is a statement only about horizontal equity: it says nothing about how those in unequal need should be treated. Supplementing definition (1) with its vertical equity counterpart is, in principle, important, because horizontal equity does not guarantee vertical equity. In practice, however, operationalizing the concept of vertical equity is hampered by some major problems. These include determining what constitutes unequal need, determining the degree of inequality between those considered to be in different degrees of need, and deciding what form the unequal treatment of unequals should take (Le Grand, 1984; Mooney, 1986). With some exceptions (e.g. Cullis and West, 1979, pp. 237–39) the issue of

---

[12] Mooney (1983) adds another definition, namely 'equal access for equal need'. This definition seems, in fact, to be at the heart of the resource allocation formula of the English Resource Allocation Working Party (cf. DHSS, 1976).

vertical equity in the delivery of health care rarely gets discussed in the health economics literature.

In applied work it is definitions (1), (3), and (4) that are the most common. The extent to which the British NHS has been successful in achieving equal treatment for equal need has been analysed by Le Grand (1978), Collins and Klein (1980), and Hurst (1985).[13] Le Grand and Rabin (1986) and Illsley and Le Grand (1987) present evidence on trends in inequalities in health in Britain, while Le Grand (1987a) compares inequalities in health in Britain with inequalities in health elsewhere. The British Central Statistical Office (CSO) regularly presents analyses of the extent to which the NHS and other parts of the Welfare State redistribute income (e.g. CSO, 1987). Income redistribution studies in the field of health care are more popular, though, in the German-speaking countries: Leu and Frey (1985), for example, present the results of a budget incidence study assessing the extent to which the Swiss health care system as a whole results in income redistribution.

Mooney and McGuire (1987) have examined various policy statements in Britain and conclude that the equity objectives of the NHS are best captured by definitions (1) and (2). They note that, despite the extensive interest in inequalities in health in Britain (e.g. DHSS, 1980), there is no evidence whatsoever that equality of health is, or ever has been, an objective of government policy. The same might be said of countries such as Italy: though the Italian National Health Service Act talks about the *protection* of health, there is no indication that *equality* of health is a policy goal (Italian Ministry of Justice, 1978). Nor, it might be added, is there any evidence that the equity goals of Britain and Italy are couched in terms of income redistribution. This suggests that budget incidence studies such as that of Leu and Frey (op. cit.) are of little relevance in the health care sector. It also casts doubt on the assertion of Lambert and Pfahler (1988) to the effect that 'equitable ... distributions of ... expenditure benefits are not the ultimate objective of government policy; they are rather employed as means to achieve desired distributional equity of postfisc income'.

None of this is to say, of course, that the adoption by governments of definitions (1) and (2) is sensible or consistent. Several authors have, indeed, suggested otherwise (e.g. Le Grand, 1987b; Mooney, 1987; Culyer, this volume). It may well be that one day governments will respond to these criticisms by redefining their equity objectives in health care. If this happens, researchers will clearly need to devise new methods for monitoring the success of health care systems in achieving equity objectives. In the meantime, in the absence of consensus and new methods, it would seem to make sense to continue with the existing definitions.

---

[13] Collins and Klein (1980) claim to examine access. Their measure of access is whether or not the person in question contacted a primary care physician, which is clearly a measure of utilization rather than access.

4. How should Equity be Measured?

In order to be able to perform international comparisons it is clearly necessary to have some means of *measuring* equity. In the remainder of the paper we discuss ways in which this might be done, focusing on specific aspects and definitions. On the finance side we look only at vertical equity and ignore the issue of horizontal equity. On the delivery side we focus on the definition of equal treatment for equal need but ignore its vertical equity counterpart.

(a) *Measuring Equity in the Finance of Health Care*

In the absence of a clear statement on the desired relationship between ability to pay and payments, the obvious strategy to adopt in analysing vertical equity on the finance side is simply to *describe* the current relationship. Hurst (1985) does this in his comparison of the distribution of payments in Britain, Canada, and the United States: he presents tables indicating estimates of the average payment in each income group for each country and compares average payments with average incomes in the bottom and top income groups. He finds that the health care financing system is regressive in the USA, but progressive in Britain and Canada. Thus, for example, in Britain 'household income rises about 4.5 times between the second and ninth deciles whereas household tax contributions rose about seven-fold over this range' (Hurst, 1985).

A similar approach was adopted by Gottschalk *et al.* (1986) in their comparison of the health care financing systems of the Netherlands, the United Kingdom, and the United States in 1981. They compare the percentage of (post-tax) income received by each decile with the percentage of total health care payments it bears. Figure 6.1 presents their results for the American system. Again, the results imply that the financing system in the United States is regressive. Thus, for example, the bottom income decile received 1.4 per cent of post-tax income but made 3.9 per cent of health care payments. The Dutch system is found to be roughly proportional and the British system progressive.

Tabulation of average incomes and health care payments by income group does not in itself enable one to answer the question of how much more (or less) progressive one system is than another. At best it can indicate whether a system is progressive, regressive, or proportional. A way round this problem is to employ *progressivity indices*. A variety of indices have been proposed in the literature on tax progressivity (e.g. Lambert, 1985) and these might be used to perform cross-country comparisons of the progressivity of health care financing systems.

One popular index is the index proposed by Kakwani (1977). Kakwani's index is based on the extent to which a tax system departs from proportionality

Figure 6.1
Health Care Financing in the US: Relative Shares of Income Deciles

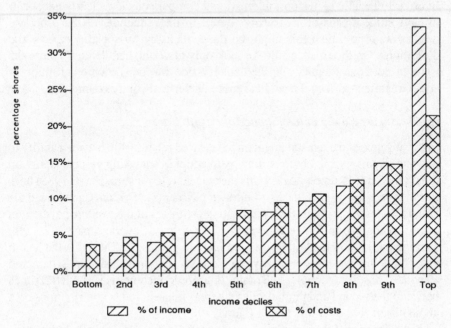

and can best be illustrated using Figure 6.2.[14] The curve labelled g^{inc} gives the Lorenz curve for pre-tax income.[15] The second curve—labelled g^{tax}—gives the *tax concentration curve*, which plots the cumulative proportions of the population (ranked according to pre-tax income as with g^{inc}) against the proportions of total tax payments. If taxes are levied strictly in proportion to income, the tax concentration curve and the Lorenz curve for pre-tax income would coincide. If the average tax rate rises with income (so that the tax system is progressive), the tax concentration curve lies outside the Lorenz curve for pre-tax income. The opposite is true if taxes are regressive. The degree of progressivity might therefore be assessed by looking at the size of the area between g^{inc} and g^{tax}. If G^{inc}

---

[14] Not all indices of progressivity are based on the extent to which the tax system departs from proportionality. Some—such as that of Reynolds and Smolensky (1977)—are based on the redistributive effect of taxation (cf. Lambert, 1985).

[15] The Lorenz curve plots cumulative proportions of the population (from the poorest to the richest) against the proportions of total income they receive. If incomes are distributed equally the Lorenz curve and the diagonal coincide. Otherwise it will be a bowed-out line as in Figure 6.2: thus, for example, the bottom 20 per cent of the population receive less than 20 per cent of the community's total income.

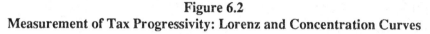

Figure 6.2
Measurement of Tax Progressivity: Lorenz and Concentration Curves

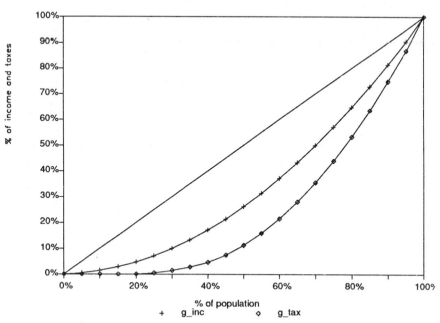

is the Gini co-efficient for pre-tax income[16] and C^{tax} is the concentration index for tax payments, Kakwani's index of progressivity, P^K, is defined as

$$P^K = C^{tax} - G^{inc} \qquad (1)$$

which is twice the area between g^{tax} and g^{inc}. If the system is regressive so that g^{tax} lies above g^{inc}, P^K is negative. The lowest value P^K can take is –2.0. This occurs when all pre-tax income is concentrated in the hands of the richest person (so that the Lorenz curve is ⌋ -shaped) and the entire tax burden falls on the poorest person (so that the tax concentration curve is ⌈-shaped). The highest value P^K can take is 1.0. This occurs when pre-tax income is distributed equally (so that the Lorenz curve coincides with the diagonal) and the entire tax burden falls on the richest person (so that the tax concentration curve is ⌋ -shaped).

---

[16] The Gini co-efficient is the ellipse-shaped area between the Lorenz curve as a proportion of the total area under the diagonal. It is therefore equal to one minus the area under the Lorenz curve and ranges from 0 (when there is complete equality and the Lorenz curve coincides with the diagonal) to 1 (when all income is concentrated in the hands of one person and the Lorenz curve is ⌋ -shaped). The concentration index is defined in exactly the same way except that the concentration curve is used instead of the Lorenz curve.

(b) *Measuring Equity in the Delivery of Health Care*

Under the definition given above (horizontal) equity in the delivery of health care requires that persons of equal need actually end up receiving equal treatment, irrespective of personal characteristics that are irrelevant to real need. The key 'third' variables here tend to be ability to pay, race, gender, and place of residence. We focus here on ability to pay.

In the British empirical literature 'ability to pay' is proxied either by income or by socio-economic status. 'Need' is proxied by self-reported health status and 'treatment' is measured either by utilization (e.g. whether the individual had seen a general practitioner in the previous two weeks) or by imputed expenditure. The extent of inequity is then determined by comparing the distributions of need and treatment across income deciles or socio-economic groups (SEGs).

Figure 6.3 presents the results for Le Grand's (1978) analysis of the 1972 *General Household Survey* data. The first pair of bars indicate that whilst 32 per cent of the 'ill' are to be found in SEGs V and VI (semi-skilled and unskilled manual workers), these SEGs together receive only 27 per cent of total expenditure. The final pair of bars indicates that whilst only 14 per cent of the 'ill' are to be found in SEGs I and II (professional, employers, and managers), these two groups receive 17 per cent of total expenditure. By 'ill' is meant persons reporting either acute sickness or limiting long-standing illness. Expenditure comprises the imputed resource costs of utilization of primary care facilities and hospital in-patient and out-patient facilities. Note that the gap narrows as one moves from the first to the second pair of bars and widens as one moves from the third to the fourth pair of bars. The implication of Figure 6.3 is that whilst the lower SEGs received a higher proportion of public expenditure on health care than the higher SEGs, their share was less than their share of reported sickness. Hurst (1985) has undertaken a similar analysis using the 1976 *General Household Survey* but based on income deciles. His results appear in Figure 6.4.[17] From the third decile upwards the results are similar to those of Le Grand.

Le Grand (1982) concludes from his results that the NHS has failed to achieve equal treatment for equal need (Le Grand, 1982). The argument is straightforward. Assume that all persons reporting ill are in equal need and that only persons who are ill receive health care. Then if horizontal equity is achieved—so that those in equal need receive the same amount of public expenditure—the share of NHS expenditure going to each SEG will be proportional to its share of persons reporting ill. If, as seems to be the case, the share of NHS expenditure received by the lower SEGs is *less* than their share of persons reporting ill, it must be concluded that the sick in the lower SEGs receive less NHS expenditure than the sick in the higher SEGs. Equals are not being treated equally and—contrary

---

[17] Expenditure figures are derived from Hurst's Figure 7.4 and are therefore subject to some error.

Figure 6.3
Distribution of Health Care by SEG, England and Wales, 1972

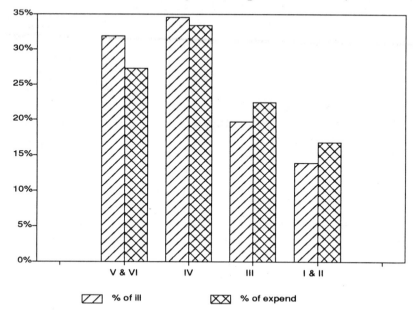

Figure 6.4
Distribution of Health Care: England and Wales, 1976

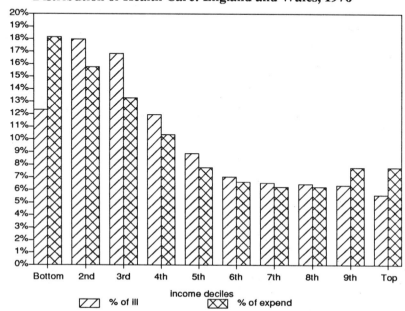

to the aims of the founding fathers of the NHS—this inequity is apparently related to income.

As already mentioned, this argument assumes that all persons who are classified as ill are in equal need and that those who are not classified as ill do not make any use of the health service. As Puffer (1986) notes, if a person is classified as ill if he reports chronic *or* acute conditions (as in Le Grand's analysis but not in Hurst's), the first assumption is clearly unwarranted: the two groups are most unlikely to be regarded as requiring the same amounts of health care resources. In this case the argument above concerning horizontal equity breaks down. Trying to get round this problem by classifying people as ill if they are, say, chronically sick (as Hurst does) exacerbates the second problem: the fewer people one classifies as ill, the more people one leaves as non-sick and the less likely it is that the distribution of expenditure reflects what is received by those classified as ill. A way round both problems would be to break the sample down into groups with similar needs and then analyse for each sub-sample the distributions of illness and expenditure. The expenditure shares here would be the shares not of the total expenditure received by the sample but of the total expenditure received by the group in question. This approach has been used by Collins and Klein (1980) and O'Donnell (1987). Though it is hoped to make some use of this alternative approach in future work, the present paper sticks to Le Grand's original approach.

Bearing these shortcomings in mind we turn now to the problem of measuring inequity. As they stand, Figures 6.3 and 6.4 do not enable one to perform comparisons of the degree of equity of different delivery systems. At best they can show whether inequity exists. The discussion does, however, suggest a method for performing such comparisons. Le Grand's strategy involves determining whether the shares of expenditure received by the various SEGs (or income deciles) are proportional to their share of total ill-health: inequity favouring the rich results in the higher SEGs receiving more than their 'fair' share and the lower SEGs receiving less than their 'fair' share.

The extent of such inequity might be measured as follows. First, rank individuals according to their 'ability to pay', beginning with the poorest. Then construct an *illness concentration curve*: this is the curve labelled g^{ill} in Figure 6.5 and plots the cumulative proportions of the population against the proportions of total ill-health. Note that because illness is concentrated amongst the lower income groups, the illness concentration curve lies above the diagonal: thus in Figure 6.5 persons in the bottom 40 per cent of the income distribution account for more than 40 per cent of all persons reporting ill health. It is important to appreciate that in constructing the curve labelled g^{ill} persons are ranked by their income. This distinguishes our concentration curve from the

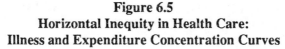

Figure 6.5
Horizontal Inequity in Health Care:
Illness and Expenditure Concentration Curves

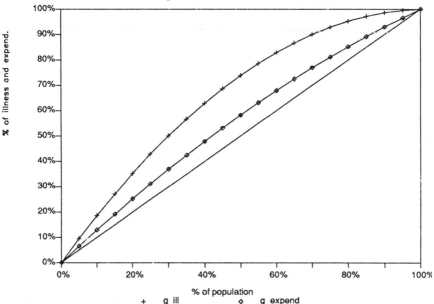

Lorenz curve used by *inter alia* Illsley and Le Grand (1987): in this latter approach persons are ranked by their health rather than by their income.[18]

Next plot an *expenditure concentration curve*: this is the curve labelled g^{exp} in Figure 6.5 and plots the cumulative proportions of the population against the proportions of total expenditure received.[19] Note that in so far as the lower income groups are more intensive users of health services than the higher income groups (as is the case in Britain), the expenditure concentration curve lies above the diagonal. Comparison of the two concentration curves provides an indication of the extent of inequity. If health care expenditures are allocated across income groups in proportion to their share of total ill-health, the two concentration curves would coincide. If those in lower income groups receive less than their 'fair' share and those in higher income groups receive more than their 'fair' share, the expenditure concentration curve will lie below the illness concentra-

[18] It is perhaps worth noting that the concentration curve would seem to be more suited to measuring inequalities in health than the Lorenz curve. The Lorenz curve is open to the objection that it measures inequalities *per se* rather than inequalities associated with income—a shortcoming acknowledged by Illsley and Le Grand (1987, p. 33). The same criticism cannot, of course, be levelled at the concentration curve.

[19] Morris and Preston (1986) use an expenditure concentration curve for social security benefits.

tion curve.[20] The extent of inequity might therefore be assessed by looking at the size of the area between the two concentration curves. Following the logic of Kakwani's tax progressivity index, one might measure the extent of inequity as twice the area between the two curves. If C^{ill} is the concentration co-efficient for illness and C^{exp} is the concentration index for expenditures, twice the area between the two concentration curves is equal to[21]

$$HI^{LG} = C^{exp} - C^{ill} \qquad (2)$$

The HI^{LG} index is positive if there is horizontal inequity favouring the rich and negative if there is horizontal inequity favouring the poor.[22]

5. Some Illustrative Cross-Country Comparisons

In this section we present some empirical illustrations of the equity measures proposed in the previous section.

(a) Equity in the Finance of Health Care

Most countries finance the bulk of their health care expenditures from one or more of four sources: (1) taxation, (2) social insurance contributions, (3) out-of-pocket payments, and (4) private insurance premiums. The mix of sources varies considerably from one country to the next (Maynard, 1975; Maxwell, 1981; Abel-Smith, 1984). Some idea of this variation can be gleaned from Table 6.1, though the data are rather old.

The United States stands out as the only country relying on out-of-pocket payments and private insurance premiums for the majority of its revenues: in 1975 these two sources together accounted for 57 per cent of total expenditures. In Europe the picture is markedly different, with taxation and social insurance contributions together typically accounting for around three-quarters of health care expenditures: the average for the European countries listed in Table 6.1 is 80 per cent. The relative importance of taxation and social insurance in Europe varies, however, from country to country. The Nordic countries, Britain, Ireland, and Portugal all rely heavily on taxation: in Britain, for example, social insurance contributions account for only about 5 per cent of health care revenues, whilst in

---

[20] The opposite will of course be true if the poor receive more than their fair share and the rich receive less than their fair share.

[21] Note that the concentration indices are negative if the concentration curve lies above the diagonal.

[22] It might be argued that whether inequity favours the rich or the poor is immaterial. If this is the view taken and the concentration curves do not cross, HI^{LG} might be defined instead as twice the absolute value of the difference between C^{exp} and C^{ill}. If, however, the concentration curves cross (as, for example, in the case of Hurst's results), the formula for HI^{LG} in equation (2) would be invalid.

Portugal the role of social insurance contributions was reduced over the period 1974–8 and was finally abolished in 1978 (Abel-Smith, 1984). The other European countries all rely heavily on (compulsory) social insurance contributions: this includes countries such as Germany and the Netherlands where contributions are paid to sickness funds, as well as countries such as Italy and Spain where contributions are paid to central government.

The distinction between the different sources of finance is important, because the distribution of contributions across income groups tends to vary from one source to another. As Maxwell (1981) notes, social insurance systems tend to be less progressive than tax-financed systems. The precise degree of progressivity depends, however, on the details of the scheme. The tax-financed systems operating in the Scandinavian countries, for example, rely heavily on local income tax (which tends to be proportional rather than progressive), whilst the British tax-financed NHS draws its funds from general tax revenues (which, on conventional assumptions about the incidence of indirect taxes, tend to be mildly progressive). The estimated progressivity of the social insurance schemes will depend *inter alia* on the split between employee and employer contributions, the assumptions one makes about who bears the employer contribution and on the progressivity of the two sets of contribution schedules.

Our empirical analysis in this section covers three countries: the United States, Britain, and the Netherlands. We selected these countries partly because the

Table 6.1
Health Care Expenditures by Source of Finance, 1975

Country	General tax %	Social insurance %	Direct payment %	Private insurance %
Australia	62.7	1.7	21.1	13.8
Canada	66.3	9.1	19.5	2.5
France	7.0	69.0	19.6	3.0
W. Germany	14.6	62.5	12.5	5.3
Italy	23.8	67.5	8.7	–
Netherlands	15.1	56.0	27.3	–
Sweden	78.5	13.1	8.4	0.0
Switzerland	41.7	24.8	33.5	–
UK	87.3	5.0	5.8	1.2
USA	31.0	11.7	27.1	25.6

Source: Maxwell (1981), Table 4-1.
Note: Figures for direct payment for Italy, the Netherlands, and Switzerland include insurance premiums.

necessary data were readily available in tabulated form. We begin with the case of the United States. This offers an interesting polar case, because of the importance of private health insurance and out-of-pocket payments. Of the ten countries listed in Table 6.1 the United States raised proportionally more revenue through private insurance premiums and out-of-pocket payments than any other. Public involvement in health care is limited and is mainly directed at the two programmes, Medicaid and Medicare.[23] The former is financed out of federal and state general tax revenues, whilst the latter is financed out of general tax revenues, payroll taxes, premiums, and direct payments.

Table 6.2, which is based on Gottschalk *et al* (1986), indicates *inter alia* the proportion of total expenditures from each source of finance borne by each income decile in 1981.[24] The first column indicates each decile's share of total pre-tax income. Columns 2–5 indicate the proportions of total payments borne by each decile: thus the first row of the table indicates that the bottom income decile contributed a total of 0.20 per cent of income tax revenues, 0.61 per cent of payroll tax revenues, 8.91 per cent of revenues from direct payments, and 2.61 per cent of revenues from insurance premiums. In the case of employer contributions to social insurance premiums (i.e. payroll taxes) and private insurance premiums it has been assumed that the burden is borne entirely by the employee in the form of lower wages. Also indicated in the table are the Gini co-efficient for pre-tax income, the concentration co-efficients for health care payments and the values of the Kakwani progressivity index.[25] The latter indicate that the income tax is progressive but that the other means of raising revenue are all regressive: out-of-pocket payments are particularly regressive. The overall result is a regressive health care financing system. This is reflected in the fact that the payment concentration curve lies inside the Lorenz curve for pre-tax income (see Figure 6.6 below).

In Britain, despite the growth of the private sector in the late 1970s, the NHS still accounts for well over 90 per cent of health care expenditure. As indicated

[23] Medicaid covers certain groups on low incomes. Medicare covers persons over 65, persons on renal dialysis, and the permanently disabled. There are other subsidy programmes (for example, for war veterans), but these are much smaller. There are also 'tax expenditures' in the form of exemptions for certain categories of private expenditure: health insurance is often a fringe benefit which is exempt from taxation and co-payments and co-insurance (above a certain minimum) are also tax-deductible. See Gottschalk *et al.* (1986) for details.

[24] It would seem from the description of the financing system in Gottschalk *et al.* (1986) that column 2 ought to be *general* taxation rather than *income* taxation. Because indirect taxes tend to be less progressive than income tax (indirect taxes are, in fact, often regressive), the progressivity of the financing system will be overstated.

[25] Throughout the chapter the Gini coefficients and concentration indices are computed from the grouped data in the tables and are obtained by building up Lorenz and concentration curves using line segments (cf. e.g. Fuller and Lury, 1977). This approach in effect assumes that there is no inequality within each income range and therefore provides only the lower limit of the index in question (cf. e.g. Kakwani and Podder, 1976, p. 145).

Table 6.2
Distribution of Health Care Payments in the US, 1981

Decile	(1) Income	(2)	(3)	(4)	(5)	(6)
	Pre-tax income %	Income tax %	Payroll tax %	Direct payments %	Insurance premiums %	Total payments %
				Health Care Payments		
Bottom	1.3	0.2	0.6	8.9	2.6	3.9
2nd	2.8	0.8	1.5	10.3	4.1	4.9
3rd	4.2	2.0	3.7	8.8	6.0	5.5
4th	5.5	3.0	6.1	9.6	8.0	7.0
5th	7.0	4.9	8.9	9.5	10.3	8.6
6th	8.4	6.5	10.7	9.2	12.2	9.7
7th	9.9	8.7	12.6	9.3	13.4	10.9
8th	12.0	12.1	14.7	10.7	14.9	12.8
9th	15.1	17.4	18.1	11.7	14.9	15.0
Top	33.8	44.5	23.0	11.9	13.6	21.7
% total revenue		23.6	15.2	32.8	28.4	
Gini	0.43					
Concentration		0.58	0.39	0.04	0.23	0.28
Kakwani		0.15	−0.04	−0.39	−0.19	−0.15

Sources: Column (1): Pechman (1985) Table 4–6;
Columns (2) to (6): Gottschalk *et al.* (1986), Table 3.

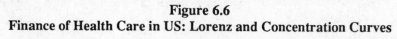

Figure 6.6
Finance of Health Care in US: Lorenz and Concentration Curves

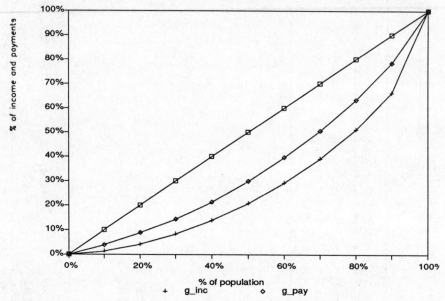

% of population
+   g_inc   ◇   g_pay

in Table 6.1, almost 90 per cent of its revenues are derived from general taxation and only a small proportion from social insurance contributions. Out-of-pocket payments account only about 5 per cent of NHS expenditures.

Table 6.3, which is also based on Gottschalk *et al.* (1986), indicates *inter alia* the proportion of each source of finance for the NHS borne by each income decile in 1981. The first column indicates each decile's share of total pre-tax income.[26] The assumptions underlying the incidence of taxes are those employed by CSO (e.g. CSO, 1987). As in the case of the United States, the burden of employer contributions to social insurance premiums (i.e. employer National Insurance contributions) has been assumed to fall entirely on the employee. Following Gottschalk *et al.*, the total payments column is based on a weighted average of columns (2) and (3), where the weights are equal to 0.9 and 0.1 respectively. Also indicated in the table are the Gini co-efficient for pre-tax income, the concentration co-efficients for health care payments, and the values of the Kakwani progressivity index. The latter indicate that taxation is mildly progressive and that the National Insurance system is also mildly progressive. The overall result for the NHS is a progressive health care financing system. This is reflected in the fact that the payment concentration curve lies outside the Lorenz curve for pre-tax income (see Figure 6.7 below).

[26] Households are ranked by pre-tax income in all columns in Table 6.3.

Table 6.3
Distribution of Health Care Payments in the UK, 1981

	(1)	(2)	(3)	(4)
	Income	Health care payments		
Decile	Pre-tax income %	Tax revenues %	Social insurance %	Total payments %
Bottom	2.3	1.7	1.3	1.7
2nd	3.4	2.6	1.9	2.5
3rd	4.7	4.1	3.4	4.0
4th	6.4	6.2	6.3	6.2
5th	8.0	7.9	8.5	7.9
6th	9.5	9.7	10.6	9.8
7th	11.2	11.4	12.5	11.5
8th	13.4	13.4	14.8	13.5
9th	16.2	17.0	17.6	17.1
Top	24.9	25.9	23.0	25.6
% total revenue		90.0	10.0	
Gini	0.35			
Concentration		0.38	0.38	0.38
Kakwani		0.02	0.03	0.03

Sources: Columns 1–3: CSO (1982), Table 7; Column 4: 90 per cent from col. 2, 10 per cent from col. 3.

Health care in the Netherlands is financed mainly out of social and private insurance contributions, and direct payments. Only 6 per cent is financed out of general taxation. Social insurance contributions are of two types. The first type of contribution—the AWBZ contribution—is compulsory for all persons below pensionable age and covers expenses incurred in respect of 'catastrophic illness' (illness requiring long-term institutional care), out-patient mental care, and home nursing. AWBZ contributions are a fixed proportion of 'premium income', up to a ceiling and are paid by the employer. The second type of social insurance contribution is paid to sick funds to cover short-term care. These contributions are compulsory only for those with an income below a certain level. Prior to 1986, non-wage earners with an income below a certain level could contribute to a sick fund on a voluntary basis. Sick fund contributions are

Figure 6.7
Health Care Finance in UK: Lorenz and Concentration Curves

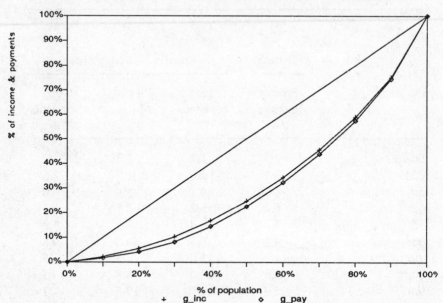

proportional to gross income up to a ceiling and are paid by employee and employer. Private insurance premiums are not income-related, but are instead often risk-related (for example, according to age). Persons with private insurance can often elect to be covered only for certain types of care and/or to bear some fixed amount of treatment costs via deductibles.

Table 6.4, which is based on tables from the *Household Expenditure Survey* of the Dutch Central Bureau of Statistics (CBS), indicates *inter alia* the proportion of total expenditures from each source of finance borne by each income decile in 1984.[27] Unfortunately we have been unable to break down insurance premiums—column (2)—into sick fund contributions and private insurance premiums. It should also be noted that the estimates of the AWBZ contributions in Table 6.4 are very approximate.[28] It is evident from the bottom line of the table

---

[27] Gottschalk *et al.* (1986), in their analysis of the Dutch financing system, use tables from the *Health Interview Survey*. We prefer the *Household Expenditure Survey* for three reasons: (1) it contains more reliable estimates of health care expenditures (direct payments, and sick fund and private insurance premiums combined); (2) it indicates average gross income for each decile of net income, whereas tables from the *Health Interview Survey* only indicate net income; (3) the *Household Expenditure Survey* does not treat all persons over 18 as a separate household, so that one does not run into the problem that the bottom decile (which includes a lot of student 'households') receives only a tiny proportion of income (cf. footnote to Table 7 of Gottschalk *et al.*, 1986).

[28] The AWBZ data in the table were estimated especially for us by the Department of Income Statistics of CBS.

Table 6.4
Distribution of Health Care Payments in the Netherlands, 1984

	(1)	(2)	(3)	(4)	(5)
	Income	Health Care Payments			
Income decile	Pre-tax income %	Insurance premiums %	AWBZ premiums %	Direct payments %	Total payments %
Bottom	3.3	3.8	1.5	1.8	3.0
2nd	4.9	6.0	3.7	2.4	5.1
3rd	6.2	8.0	5.9	4.3	7.2
4th	7.3	9.0	7.9	3.2	8.5
5th	8.3	9.6	9.5	7.0	9.5
6th	9.3	10.8	10.8	7.8	10.7
7th	10.7	11.4	12.3	12.5	11.7
8th	12.3	11.9	14.2	18.6	12.8
9th	14.9	14.2	16.0	18.8	14.9
Top	22.7	15.3	18.1	23.5	16.5
% total revenue		65.8	31.2	3.7	
Gini	0.29				
Concentration		0.19	0.29	0.41	0.23
Kakwani		−0.10	0.00	0.12	−0.06

Source: All except AWBZ premiums from *Household Expenditure Survey*, 1984. AWBZ premiums from CBS *Personal Income Distribution in 1983: Households*.

Notes: Premiums include Sick Fund and private health insurance premiums. AWBZ premiums: compulsory social insurance against catastrophic illness.

that the two biggest components of the health care financing system (the sick fund contributions and the private insurance premiums) are both regressive. Interestingly the direct payments component of the financing system is quite progressive: this presumably reflects the fact that persons in high-income groups relying on private insurance often elect to cover themselves only partially and/or to reduce their premiums by accepting deductibles. The overall effect, however, is a regressive health care financing system. This means that in the case of the Netherlands, as for the United States, the payment concentration curve lies inside the Lorenz curve for pre-tax income. A comparison of the Kakwani indices in Tables 6.2 and 6.4 reveals, however, that the American financing system is more regressive than the Dutch.

(b) *Equity in the Delivery of Health Care*

As is evident from the results of the previous section, the overall progressivity of any health care financing system depends on the mix of sources of finance and the rules relating contributions to income. On the delivery side the degree of inequity depends on the extent to which a person's income (or ability to pay) influences the probability of his seeking care when ill and the amount of care he receives once the initial contact has been made. The influence of income is likely to be greater the larger are the various pecuniary and non-pecuniary costs individuals incur in utilizing medical care. Examples include insurance premiums, out-of-pocket payments, transport costs, and the opportunity cost of time spent travelling and waiting (Le Grand, 1982). Since these costs will tend to vary from one delivery system to the next, one would expect the degree of inequity to vary accordingly.

In this section we present some evidence on the extent of inequity in the delivery of health care in three countries: Italy, the Netherlands, and Britain. Again, our choice of countries was influenced by considerations of data availability. We begin with Britain.

Table 6.5, which is based on the data of Hurst (1985), indicates *inter alia* the distributions of illness and public expenditure on health care across income deciles. The data were derived from the 1976 *General Household Survey*, conducted by CSO. Income here is the gross income of the person's household. Individuals are classified as ill if they report limiting long-standing (i.e. chronic) sickness. The expenditure figure is derived from information on (1) the number of general practitioner consultations, (2) the number of days in hospital, and (3) the number of visits to hospital as an out-patient. Each category of utilization is weighted by its unit cost.

The first row of Table 6.5 indicates that 12.3 per cent of persons reporting limiting long-standing illness are to be found in the bottom income decile, but the bottom income decile receives as much as 18.2 per cent of public expenditure on health care. The second row indicates that 18.0 per cent of persons reporting limiting long-standing illness are to be found in the second income decile, but that this decile receives only 15.8 per cent of public expenditure on health care. The table also indicates the values of the concentration indices for illness and expenditure, as well as the index of horizontal inequity (cf. equation (2) above). The concentration index for illness is negative indicating that persons in the lower income groups tend to be in poorer health than persons in the higher income groups. The concentration index for expenditure is also negative indicat-

Table 6.5
Distribution of Health Care Expenditure in England and Wales, 1976

Income decile	% persons with chronic illness	% of expenditure
Bottom	12.3	18.2
2nd	18.0	15.8
3rd	16.8	13.3
4th	12.0	10.4
5th	8.9	7.8
6th	7.0	6.6
7th	6.6	6.2
8th	6.5	6.2
9th	6.4	7.8
Top	5.6	7.8
Concentration index	−0.212	−0.198
Horizontal inequity	0.014	

Source: Hurst (1985).

ing that persons in the lower income groups tend to receive more health care than persons in the higher income groups. The index of inequity, however, is positive indicating that, on average, the expenditure concentration curve lies inside the illness concentration curve. The NHS is thus associated with horizontal inequity favouring the rich.

Table 6.6 presents similar data for the Netherlands. The data were derived from the *Health Interview Survey*, conducted by CBS. Income here is the net income of the individual's household. Two alternative health indicators were used: (1) the presence or absence of chronic conditions, and (2) whether the person viewed his health as being 'not so good' (*minder goed*). The expenditure figure is derived from information on (1) the number of general practitioner consultations, (2) the number of specialist consultations, and (3) the number of days in hospital. Again, each category is weighted by its unit cost.

The concentration index for chronic illness is negative as in Britain, indicating that inequalities in health exist in the Netherlands as well as in Britain. The absolute value of the index is, however, much smaller in the case of the Netherlands. Interpreted literally this means that there is less inequality in health in the Netherlands than in Britain. The bottom line of Table 6.6 indicates that though the index of horizontal inequity is positive in the case of the 'health not good' indicator, it is *negative* in the case of the chronic conditions indicator. Since it is the latter that comes closest to the indicator used by Hurst, the

Table 6.6
Distribution of Health Care Expenditure in the Netherlands, 1981–5

Income range (Dfl 000)	% of population	% of expenditure	% persons with chronic illness	% persons with health not good
<18	17.7	27.7	22.4	27.3
18–22	14.7	18.6	17.4	20.2
22–28	21.5	18.7	21.5	21.9
28–36	18.2	15.4	15.8	14.0
36–45	14.2	9.3	11.8	8.9
45+	13.7	10.3	11.0	7.7
Concentration index		–0.163	–0.095	–0.201
Horizontal inequity			–0.068	0.038

Source: Based on tabulations from *Health Interview Survey 1981–1985*.

implication is that whilst the delivery of health care in Britain is associated with inequity favouring the rich, the delivery of health care in the Netherlands is associated with inequity favouring the poor. Thus in the case of the Netherlands the expenditure concentration curve lies above the concentration curve for chronic illness (see Figure 6.8).

Table 6.7 presents the distributions of illness and health care expenditure for Italy. The data were derived from the 1985 *Health Care Consumption Survey*, conducted by the Centro Europa Ricerche. Income here is the *gross* income of the respondent's family. As in the case of the Netherlands we use two alternative health indicators: (1) the presence or absence of chronic conditions, and (2) whether the person viewed his health as being 'not good' (*non buono*). The expenditure figure is derived from information on (1) the number of physician consultations (general practitioners *and* specialists), and (2) the number of spells in hospital.[29] Again both categories were weighted by their unit costs.[30]

[29] Later we hope to produce more precise estimates of expenditure per person by distinguishing between visits to general practitioners and visits to specialists, and by using information on length of stay per hospital spell.

[30] For physician visits we have used a weighted average of the cost per GP visit and the cost per specialist visit, where the weights are the share of each type of visit in the total number of physician visits. Both costs are based on public sector costs. Our figure for cost per visit was Lire 31,077 (1985 prices). For hospitals we have used the cost per case for those private hospitals providing services to the state on a contractual basis (*ospedali convenzionati*): apparently it is impossible with the existing data collection system to compute cost per case for Italian state-owned hospitals. Our figure for cost per case was Lire 4,001,375 (1985 prices). Details of the calculations are available from the authors on request.

Figure 6.8
Illness and Expenditure Concentration Curves: the Netherlands, 1985

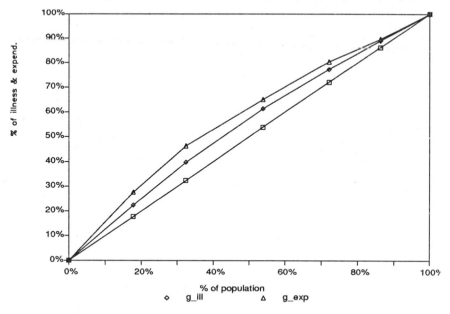

% of illness & expend.

% of population

◇   g_ill   △   g_exp

Table 6.7
Distribution of Health Care Expenditure in Italy, 1985

Income range (Lire m.)	% of population	% of expenditure	% persons with chronic illness	% persons with health not good
<12	18.1	23.1	22.6	31.3
12–18	15.4	13.6	16.0	15.6
18–25	21.8	22.3	19.1	19.0
25–50	23.3	20.1	22.6	17.9
50+	21.4	20.9	19.8	16.2
Concentration index		−0.047	−0.052	−0.165
Horizontal inequity			0.005	0.118

Source: Based on data from *Health Care Consumption Survey* conducted by Centro Europa Ricerche 1985.

From the penultimate line in Table 6.7 it is evident that inequalities in health between rich and poor exist in Italy as in our other two countries. However, comparing Tables 6.5, 6.6, and 6.7 reveals that inequalities in chronic ill health seem to be less pronounced in Italy than they are in both Britain and the Netherlands. The ranking of Italy and the Netherlands is unchanged if the 'health not good' indicator is used instead. The indices of inequity provide a rather different picture. The index is positive for Italy for *both* health indicators, though in the case of the chronic illness indicator the index is close to zero and is substantially smaller than that of Britain. Thus though there is apparently some inequity favouring the rich, the degree of inequity is small both in absolute terms and relative to the degree of inequity present in Britain. It is worth noting that the indices of inequity in Tables 6.6 and 6.7 present a fairly consistent picture: the two indices for Italy are both larger than their Dutch counterparts (suggesting greater inequity in Italy than in the Netherlands), and the 'not good health' indicator presents a less favourable picture in both countries.

6. Discussion

Before summarizing and discussing what we have done, it may be worth pointing out what we have not done. First, we have looked only at egalitarian definitions of equity: we have said nothing about minimum standards definitions. For countries which do not aspire to egalitarian goals (such as the United States), this is an important omission. Second, in the measurement part of the paper we have looked only at vertical equity on the finance side: the issue of how to measure horizontal equity on the finance side was not discussed. Finally, in the measurement part of the paper we have looked only at one definition of (horizontal) equity on the delivery side: we have not discussed how, for example, the concept of equality of access might be operationalized.

Our results may be summarized as follows. Of the three countries whose financing systems we examined—the Netherlands, Britain, and the United States—two were found to have regressive financing systems (the Netherlands and the United States) and one a mildly progressive financing system (Britain). According to the index of progressivity used (the Kakwani index), the Dutch system was marginally less regressive than the American. Out-of-pocket payments were found to be particularly regressive in the United States, whilst in the Netherlands sick fund contributions and private insurance premiums combined were found to be significantly regressive. Of the three countries whose health care delivery systems we looked at—Britain, Italy, and the Netherlands—two were found to exhibit inequity favouring the rich (Britain and Italy), though of the two Britain seemed less equitable. In the case of the Netherlands we discovered inequity favouring the rich only in the case of the 'health not good' health indicator: in the case of the chronic illness indicator the inequity favoured the poor. All three countries displayed inequalities in chronic ill-health. Of the three, Britain recorded the highest degree of inequality.

The implication of these results is that Britain tends to fare well in respect of equity in the finance of health care (at least in so far as progressivity is concerned) but badly in respect of equity in the delivery of health care. The opposite seems to be true of the Netherlands.

Our results ought, however, to be interpreted with some caution, particularly on the delivery side. One of the problems has already been touched on, namely the assumption implicit in our approach that it is only persons who are classified as ill who receive health care. There is, however, another difficulty that has not been mentioned. This is the possibility—discussed by Le Grand (1982)—that the results reported in Tables 6.5, 6.6, and 6.7 may be statistical artefacts. They may be caused simply by differences in the age and sex composition of the income deciles. It may well be the case, for example, that the expenditure concentration curve lies below the illness concentration curve in Italy and Britain because (1) age affects the amount of expenditure a person receives when they fall ill, and (2) age and income are correlated. Suppose, for example, that the over-65s receive less treatment when ill than the under-65s and that the over-65s are concentrated in the bottom income decile. Then even if there is no inequity associated with income, the system will still appear to be inequitable, since the concentration of over-65s in the bottom income decile will mean that the share of health care expenditures received by this decile will be less than their share of ill-health. As a result, the expenditure concentration curve will lie below the illness concentration curve. This suggests that in order to be able to measure equity properly one really needs to take into account inter-group differences in demographic structure.

7

Comparing Health Service Efficiency
Across Countries

DAVID PARKIN*

1. Introduction

A commonly made observation is that problems which health care systems face are similar, despite widespread variations between countries in their financing and organization (McLachlan and Maynard, 1982). Throughout the industrialized world, the main policy issue currently facing health care delivery systems appears to be their efficiency. In most countries, this has taken the form of a concern about cost inflation, arising from the presence in the 1970s of rising health care expenditures at a time of recession. A response in many countries was to look abroad, to see if this was simply a worldwide phenomenon or if there were factors peculiar to them.

That this concern about cost inflation was widespread is shown by the fact that cost-containment programmes, with similar features, were implemented in many countries (Abel-Smith, 1984), and these continue. This suggests that not only are problems similar across countries, so too are the solutions produced. For example, policy-makers must deal with the ever-present problem of how to reconcile health care supply with demand. Where these appear to be unbalanced, interest in alternative ways of financing and providing health care always increases. Changing the finance system is invariably suggested as a solution to problems of all sorts with health care delivery. Again, international comparisons are sought to explore this.

Consequently, international comparisons should be of interest not simply for curiosity's sake, but for insights that they give people about their own country. All countries can learn from elsewhere, and may be better able to assess their own ways of dealing with issues by observing how others do it.

* Division of Community Medicine, University of Newcastle-upon-Tyne. Much of this paper is based on work carried out jointly with Alistair McGuire and Brian Yule. Thanks also to Paul Fenn, Ken Mayhew, and Christopher Allsopp. Although all are implicated, none is responsible for the final contents.

However, such comparisons are notoriously difficult to carry out and interpret. Disadvantages include the inadequacies of available data, difficulties in matching research questions to appropriate data, and the temptation to draw sweeping conclusions. Numerical data are invariably poor and usually not comparable between countries. They rarely show anything conclusive, especially since there is always a let-out clause for those who dislike any apparent implications—'special factors (e.g. cultural) make it different here (or elsewhere)'.

In order to illustrate such problems, this paper concentrates on a particular issue. Most countries' worry about cost inflation is that too much is spent on health care. In the United Kingdom, by contrast, international comparisons have been widely used to assert that the National Health Service (NHS) is not adequately funded: in other words, too little is spent on health care. It is, of course, difficult to decide by any means what is the appropriate amount of public expenditure on anything (Beckerman, 1986). International comparisons can be particularly treacherous: apart from difficulties with the health expenditure data available, there are a large number of conceptual problems involved in analysing them.

Whether or not the UK spends too little is essentially a normative question. However, international comparisons have mainly attempted to answer this by means of positive economics. In particular, the question of what the UK is able to afford is seen as a crucial factor, and one line of enquiry has therefore been to analyse the relationship between national income and health expenditures. In looking at this, it is possible to discuss other issues that can in principle be illuminated by such analysis, but which in practice usually prove beyond its power. Unfortunately, this has not prevented many from using the results of simple analyses to make judgements on complex matters.

2. Health Sector Inputs and Outputs—Some Evidence

Before looking at the analysis of expenditures, it is instructive to set this in a context of the poor data which international comparisons must use, and (more importantly) the lack of an analytical framework with which to interpret them. We therefore begin by reviewing some of the statistical information available to assess the efficiency of health services at a macro level.

Recently there have been many international comparative studies of expenditures (Abel-Smith, 1967; Maxwell, 1974, 1981; Abel-Smith and Maynard, 1979), provision and financing systems (Maynard, 1975; Raffel, 1984; Yule and Parkin, 1986) and the mix of public and private financing and provision (McLachlan and Maynard, 1982; Culyer and Jönsson, 1986). The Organization of Economic Co-operation and Development has carried out extensive and intensive statistical studies, albeit only for its member states. It recently produced two outstanding volumes: *Measuring Health Care* (OECD, 1985) and *Financing and Delivering Health Care* (OECD, 1987). Much of the statistical content of this paper is based on these.

Efficiency concerns the relation of health care inputs to outputs. In the rest of this section we therefore look at international evidence on inputs and outputs and their interaction. For exposition purposes the UK will, where appropriate, be compared with the USA or an average of developed countries or both. Few data of comparable quality exist for the rest of the world, so the interesting and important problems of LDCs and the socialist countries must be neglected here.

In discussing outputs and inputs in any sector of the economy, there are three main practical problems: measurement, data collection, and interpretation. These apply equally to health services. Unfortunately, there is a prior problem with health service output, namely defining it. Not only is it important, as usual, to distinguish output from throughput (for example, the number of patient consultations), but also to realize that any output measure is likely to be indirect.

(a) *What is Output of the Health Sector?*

It is often said that the purpose of health care is to produce improvements in health, and these are the ultimate output of health services. If the assumptions of consumer sovereignty were met in health care markets, we could measure output in value terms by means of expenditures. Since this is not the case, improvements in health must be measured directly, but this is easier said than done.

One problem is that health care is not a homogeneous activity. Traditionally, there is a distinction drawn between curing and caring. Both can be measured in terms of throughput, but the effect of caring activities on health status is less easy to measure than curing. Indeed, its output could be thought of as general 'welfare' rather than health status as such. Finer distinctions can be drawn which make this problem even more complicated, for example including preventive activities (of many different types) whose effect on health may not be apparent until many years after they have been carried out. This leads to problems for international comparisons, since health services vary greatly in the mix of services provided. Analyses of efficiency are therefore hampered by comparing countries which produce essentially different 'products'.

Of course, it would be desirable to use a proper health status indicator for comparisons, but no indicator useful for such a purpose yet exists. Indirect measures are the best that we have, but even these are partial and not always available everywhere. The most common and therefore widely used of these measures are mortality rates. Obviously these can only approximate a true health indicator, and will be unlikely to pick up the effects of some caring activities.[1]

---

[1] Terminal care is an extreme example.

There is anyway a problem in attributing differences in health to health care. Suppose that North Americans are found to be more healthy than the rest of the world: is this because they have better health care, or because they have a better environment, a better diet, and advantages in other factors associated with good health? On the other hand, if they are less healthy, is this because their poor environment and diet offset their highly effective and efficient health care system?

Furthermore, there is always a problem when average levels of health are used, as they often are. If North Americans on average have poor health, is this because their health care is ineffective and inefficient, or because not all get it? Perhaps rich, even ordinary North Americans have excellent health due to good health care, but those with poor health do not have access to such care, and drag down the average.

Turning to the available evidence, many have attempted to discover whether or not expenditures are effective in altering health at the aggregate level, and most have failed to find any such effect. As suggested, this is not surprising given the lack of a health status indicator suitable for testing this. However, many researchers have used death rates as a proxy, and attempted to correlate this with expenditure per person.

The infant mortality rate (IMR) is often taken as a good indicator of a country's general health status, and in the sample reported by the OECD (1987) this was negatively related to health expenditure per person. However, this does not necessarily imply anything about the effectiveness of care to the whole population, and indeed infant health is unusual in that it may be possible to buy improvements in the IMR by using expensive neonatal care facilities. There is also an alternative explanation in that, as discussed below, higher health expenditure is associated with a higher national income. So it could simply be that rich countries have other advantages such as better nutrition, a cleaner water supply, better and more extensive public health services, and so on which improve their health, rather than large amounts of effective health care.

For adult women (but not men) life expectancy was positively related (and similarly death rates are negatively related) to health expenditures. Unfortunately there exists the same problem of disentangling more health expenditure from general availability of resources.

Other work using different time periods and data sets has in general not corroborated even these weak findings. Neither Maxwell (1981) nor Leu (1986) found that expenditure was related to mortality rates. Wolfe (1986) presented the best evidence in favour of a positive link between health status and medical expenditures, but the evidence is as yet thin. In the absence of any well-defined relationship between proxies for the ultimate output of health services and the volume of resources devoted to them, the prospects for analysing efficiency using aggregate data do not look promising.

(b) *Throughput Measures*

Throughput measures can never be as useful as output measures in assessing efficiency. Apart from ambiguities in their interpretation, it is very rarely that factors important in interpreting them, such as the quality of health care, are measured. However, many throughput indicators exist which do give useful information despite their distance from true output.

The OECD (1987) reported various throughput measures for hospitals. There are many problems in comparing these even within countries, and these are compounded when international comparisons are made. Hospitals differ in type—for example, chronic or acute, short stay or long stay—and therefore will have very different cost structures, lengths of stay, etc. Since countries tend, for historic and cultural reasons, to have different mixes of hospital types, overall comparisons are full of dangers. Similarly, there are differences in the extent to which outpatient care is provided in and by hospitals rather than in clinics or doctors' surgeries, which obviously also have cost and throughput implications.

Much is made in the literature of aggregate expenditure on various services. Analysing hospital expenditures has special problems—how much outpatient care hospitals carry out, and, for example whether or not hospital-based physicians are included in their accounts. They can be expressed in different ways: the OECD (1987) recorded, for fourteen countries where data are available, expenditures per person, per bed, per day, and per admission. All may be affected by differences between countries in definitions, conventions for recording figures, the mix of cases seen, and the mix of treatments given. As a result, what is left to be attributed to efficiency differences is debatable. For what it is worth, the UK's figures for all of these measures are below those of the average and of the USA. However, differences between countries in the different measures do not in general have a consistent pattern.

The OECD's findings on other hospital throughput measures may be summarized as follows. The UK has more in-patient days per person than the USA but slightly fewer than the average. It is impossible to tell whether this is good or bad, reflecting the level of met need or the underlying level of illness, let alone what it implies about efficiency. UK occupancy rates are above average and above those of the USA. This may or may not reflect more efficient use of available capacity. For overall admission rates (a measure of turnover) the UK is below both the average and the USA. This could reflect poor access to hospital services, or perhaps more illness being dealt with outside the hospital service. Average UK lengths of stay are slightly above average, but well above those in the USA. Unless a short length of stay reflects poor medical practice, this could well result from a more efficient service. However, very little can be made of this average because it is crucially affected by factors such as case mix. When lengths of stay for different diagnoses are looked at, there are vast variations between countries that defy simple interpretation.

In-patient medical care beds per person and bed days per person were strongly positively related, suggesting that there is an availability effect—a built bed is a filled bed. This is reinforced by the finding that occupancy rates are also positively related to number of beds per person. It seems that greater capacity leads to less rather than more slack. However, the average length of stay is also positively related to beds per person, implying that not all extra occupancy is by extra patients. That low lengths of stay do not necessarily imply efficient use of beds is suggested by the fact that these are not associated with low costs per case.

There is also information on out-patient care. The main finding for our purposes is that the UK has slightly fewer out-patient consultations per person than the USA, but is well below the average. This could reflect different institutional arrangements, levels of illness, or geographical factors (amongst other things), and even efficiency if out-patient management of disease differs in cost or effectiveness from in-patient management.

(c) *Physical Resources and Personnel*

Physical resources are not well-documented. This is not surprising for small items of equipment, and it is not really meaningful to compare amounts of large resources, such as hospitals, since these are scarcely comparable in size or function. Fragmented information is quite common for large-scale capital equipment such as CT scanners.

The OECD produced figures on in-patient medical care beds per person. The UK has more than the USA, but fewer than the average. It also gave a crude indicator of the amount of ambulatory care—the number of physicians per person. The UK has fewer than both the USA and the average.

Better information is available on the numbers of health care personnel in a country, although with the usual caveats about differing definitions and incomplete data. One issue is the mix of health care personnel between countries. Table 7.1 shows total numbers of nurses and midwives, physicians, dentists, and pharmacists in seventeen OECD countries in 1980, expressed as a percentage of the sum of these occupations. Obviously, some of the differences apparent can be explained by definitional problems, but they are so wide that it seems likely that the type of health care provided is very different between countries.

Parkin *et al.* (1987) compared different types of personnel per 100,000 population with GDP per person. The results (which are consistent with other studies, e.g. Leu, 1986) were that a high GDP per person is related to large numbers of dentists and nurses per person, but not to physicians or pharmacists per person. In so far as doctors provide cure and nurses care, this may show that rich countries emphasize care more, but there are many other equally plausible explanations.

Table 7.1
Personnel Mix : Percentage of Total Accounted for by
Categories Shown, 1980

	Doctors	Dentists	Nurses	Pharmacists
Australia	20.4	4.0	71.5	4.0
Belgium	53.4	9.5	16.1	21.1
Canada	16.5	4.2	73.2	6.2
Denmark	20.7	8.9	66.5	3.9
Finland	19.9	8.7	62.7	8.7
France	24.9	7.1	59.3	8.7
F R Germany	34.9	8.3	49.6	7.2
Greece	39.2	12.8	39.4	8.6
Iceland	22.2	8.1	62.8	7.0
Japan	19.4	6.9	68.9	4.8
New Zealand	17.8	4.2	69.8	8.3
Norway	18.4	7.7	67.6	6.2
Portugal	36.2	1.8	44.2	17.8
Spain	36.1	1.7	52.5	9.8
Sweden	20.1	11.4	64.2	4.3
Switzerland	16.3	4.8	76.8	2.1
USA	22.9	6.3	63.6	7.2
Average	25.8	6.8	59.3	8.0

Source: Figures calculated from OECD (1985).

(d) *Organizational Factors*

There are many different systems for financing and organizing health care, but they fall into distinct types. It is useful for analysis to place countries into groups defined by system type, to abstract from particular circumstances.   It is also instructive to study variations within types.   Various classification systems have been devised, for example Maxwell (1974) categorized health services using two dimensions—the source of finance and organizer of the service—stressing the extent of government involvement.   Even more complex classifications have been devised, but a simple scheme is often adopted, dividing them into social insurance (The Western European model), private finance (The American model), and state provision (The Eastern European model).

Since some of the stimulus for international comparisons comes from the desire to study organizational factors, such classifications are a potentially useful tool.[2] Unfortunately there are dangers. Although systems do fall into recognizable types, they have notable differences. The problem is that each can be recognized as unique, which is in a sense correct but is useless for analysis. An extreme example of this is the use by Leu (1986) in an analysis of health expenditures of a variable representing 'direct democracy', that is whether or not a country votes directly on tax increases. This seems a reasonable factor to look at, but there was only one country—Switzerland—in his sample which does this. It could therefore be a proxy for almost anything Swiss!

Leu found that some organizational factors did have more definable effects. He found that health expenditures are greater, the more government involvement in health care. The OECD (1987) found the opposite, that total expenditure is negatively related to the percentage spent publicly. Leu also found that centralized systems such as the NHS have lower expenditures, but this has the same problem as the direct democracy variable—only two countries had such systems. Leu also looked at the effect of organizational factors on mortality rates, the major finding being that the more uninsured people there are, the worse the neonatal mortality rate.

A frequent claim by NHS critics is that it is bureaucratic—leading to large administration costs—and has no market stimuli—leading to high production costs. By contrast, NHS supporters often argue that without the need to advertize and have billing systems, administration costs will actually be lower, and a centralized system with fairly rigorous budgetary control will have lower production costs than a decentralized system in which market forces are in reality extremely weak.

Maxwell (1981) found that public insurance as a percentage of total health expenditure is positively correlated with administrative expenditure. European-type social insurance systems therefore appear to have higher administration costs, but this is not the whole story since both NHS-type systems and private systems have small amounts of public insurance. Looking at the USA, however, shows their administrative costs to be far higher than those of NHS-type systems. Here it should be stressed that the data are not exact, there is debate about what constitutes an administration cost, and countries are inconsistent about what is included under this heading. Nevertheless, the evidence does not support the view that the NHS is inefficient in terms of transaction costs.

(e) *Can International Comparisons be Used to Judge Efficiency?*

This simple recitation of findings seems to show that very little can be said on the basis of them about efficiency, or indeed much else! Ambiguities abound, and the choice of interpretation is largely a matter of taste rather than judgement.

---

[2] Yule and Parkin (1986) used crude system types in analyses of a number of issues in the provision and finance of dental care in Europe, and found them to be useful and instructive.

Although the material presented above is obviously only a selection from a large amount, I do not believe that it misrepresents or caricatures the state of the art.

Not only are there problems in the data, there is no really useful framework for analysing them. Aggregate data are ill-suited to answering the essentially microeconomic questions which are those most commonly asked about health policy. Unfortunately, the theory of aggregate behaviour, which presumably the data might illuminate, is rather undeveloped. It is therefore prone to *ad hoc* procedures such as those described in the use of system types and organizational factors.

We will return to these themes and further underline the problems by examining the issue for which the best data are available, and on which the most sophisticated analyses have been carried out.

3. The Link Between Health Expenditures and National Income

The interpretation of high or low levels of spending by a country differs between commentators according to their purpose. Does low expenditure imply a low volume of health care or simply low levels of cost? Are high-spending countries buying more health care or do they simply have an inefficient system? It is extraordinary that the same measure is used for so many different purposes.

As suggested, UK expenditure is in absolute and relative terms lower than many other developed countries. But it has been pointed out that such countries are richer than the UK and can therefore afford to spend more. In general, high-spending countries are richer than low-spending countries. There have been many studies of the relationship between a country's health expenditure and its national income, but the major conclusions drawn from them have been challenged by Parkin *et al.* (1987) and Gerdtham *et al.* (1988).

Much work has been devoted to the collection of comparable health expenditure data over the last twenty years. Usually, only industrialized countries are covered because their statistical collection systems are more developed. Nevertheless, although figures probably suffice for rough comparisons, they should not be regarded as very accurate. Even in the UK, where most expenditure is dealt with by one agency, the figures are only estimates and guesses, and where there are many sources of funding, data collection problems are even greater.

In order to make them comparable, national expenditure levels are usually expressed as an amount per person. However, this ignores the distributions of expenditures within countries across their populations. Similarly, national income per person is not really a measure of average income, and does not take account of its distribution within countries.

Most such studies used exchange rates to convert them into a common currency (usually US$). The correlation between the figures obtained is always close: for example, Parkin *et al.* (1987) analysed figures for eighteen OECD countries in 1980, showing that differences in GDP per person accounted for 86 per cent of differences in national expenditures per person. The relationship between the sets of data has been quantified by using regression analysis, producing the result that around 8 cents out of an increase of $1 in GDP is spent on health. The average income elasticity calculated from this is typically around 1.25, and is always greater than one. Since such results have been repeatedly replicated, it has been concluded that this is a remarkably stable and scientifically verified relationship.

One criticism of this which we shall look at in greater detail is the use of exchange rates as a currency converter. Of course, some have recognized that exchange rates may distort the analysis, and have got round this by calculating the percentage of GDP spent on health care, which requires no currency conversion. Again, regression analysis has been used to compare this with GDP. Although the correlation is lower, there is always a finding that the higher income is, the greater is the proportion of it spent on health care. This strengthens the finding that the income elasticity is greater than one.

Many strong assertions have been drawn from this work, and we will look at three:

(1)   Because so much of the variation in expenditures is explained by it, only national income is important in determining them. Needs, disease prevalence, the efficiency and equity of the health system, its organization and sources of funding, ways of paying professionals, the extent of patient charges, and so on are all irrelevant. Various plausible explanations have been given for this. For example, Newhouse (1977) argued that health care prices are not important in determining expenditures, because in most countries rationing of health care is mainly by non-market means, and the role of prices is muted.

(2)   Health care is not a necessity (for which expenditures will not rise very much as incomes rise), but a luxury good bought in increasing amounts by the rich. Newhouse (1977) argued that this is because additional amounts of health care bought by richer countries do not produce improvements in physiological health, and contribute more to 'caring' for the sick than to 'curing' them.

(3)   Income *should* determine health expenditures. For example, the UK's expenditure is, in both absolute and relative terms, below that which would be predicted by the regression. It has been concluded that the UK government does not spend enough considering how rich the UK is. Presumably, this also implies that countries which spend more than predicted, for example the USA and Ireland, spend too much.

This work can easily be criticized on technical, theoretical, and methodological grounds. Not only is the logic of these conclusions questionable, the data and methods underlying them are suspect. It has also been shown that the analysis is very fragile, such that a small change in methods and assumptions collapses much of the evidence. We will now look at some of these issues, and conclude with some ways in which this work might be taken forward.

(a) *Choice of an Appropriate Analytical Framework*

The way in which the analysis of the relationship between expenditures and income is presented is immediately familiar to economists. It is an application of some of the simplest and most basic devices of microeconomic demand theory. The relationship itself is familiar as an 'Engel curve', although this terminology is rarely used. Well-known terminology such as income elasticity is invoked, and the traditional classification of goods into luxuries, necessities, and inferior goods is employed.

However, there are problems in interpreting a relationship between aggregates of expenditure and income over an aggregate economy using the same methods applicable to the individual (or household) consumer, which is the unit that Engel-curve analysis is designed to study. When Engel curves for other goods and services have been estimated, the data are cross-sectional within a country, based on household budgets. A relationship based on international data can only be interpreted as an Engel curve if the analysis is seen as a very highly aggregated econometric model of individual consumer (or household) behaviour. Unless this is done, it is not legitimate to use the terminology of luxuries and necessities.

Deaton and Muellbauer (1980) emphasized that macroeconomic relations often do not replicate their microeconomic foundations. The assumptions necessary to derive microeconomic implications from macroeconomic studies are highly restrictive, and seem particularly implausible for health care. For example, it must be assumed that there are no distributional effects. Such evidence as exists suggests that not only do income elasticities for health care vary over income groups, society finds inequality less tolerable for goods and services such as health care than for income, and may attempt to compensate for this. Another assumption is that there is a homogeneity of tastes for health care over consumers, which is especially implausible in the context of whole countries.

An obvious question to be asked, therefore, is why micro data have not been regarded as the appropriate way of looking at these microeconomic issues. When this is done, the estimated income elasticities have been low, and almost always less than one (e.g. Andersen and Benham, 1970).

Another way of looking at the aggregate relationship is as a macro-economic concept analogous to a consumption function. Here, the aggregates are variables in their own right, and need not behave in the same way as the components that make them up, or be influenced to the same degree by the same factors. As suggested, such a macroeconomic theory of behaviour in the health sector is not well-developed, and so it is difficult to interpret any results which are obtained.

One candidate for such a theory would be a public-choice model. Leu (1986) explicitly based his analysis on 'some well-known results in the public choice literature' but admitted that he had 'no stringent theoretical model' and that his choice of hypotheses was *ad hoc*. Such an approach cannot really be justified since it becomes very difficult then to interpret any findings, but it did at least attempt to look at important factors such as organization.

As an example of a perhaps more appropriate specification of a macroeconomic relationship, Dunne *et al.* (1984) modelled the allocation of public consumption between different types of expenditure. Essentially, the model employs the Treasury as the appropriate decision-maker, attempting to maximize the unobserved outputs of public services subject to an overall constraint on public expenditure. Outputs are produced by expenditures on services acting on needs for them, subject to lags caused by the long-term commitment involved in some expenditures. Such a model is a far clearer specification of the macroeconomic model, although it is not directly transferable to the international context. However, it is worth noting that, as with the micro evidence, the results of this analysis reveal an income elasticity for health care less than one. If this analysis is to be believed, the Treasury appears to agree with the general public that health care is a necessity.

(b) *Some Technical Problems*

Much of the empirical work carried out on this issue has a number of technical problems which rather undermine the reliability of its findings. These are discussed in detail by Parkin *et al.* (1987) and Gerdtham *et al.* (1988). It is not appropriate to look at these in detail here, but the following are the most important. There are two main econometric problems:

(1)   An econometric model linking a dependent variable to one independent variable is likely to be underspecified whether the underlying model is macro- or microeconomic. Moreover, misspecification of a microeconomic model will have its greatest effects when using highly aggregated data.

(2)   An important issue in estimating any relationship is its functional form. Conventional Engel-curve analyses use various forms, aiming to apply that which is the most appropriate for a good believed *a priori* to be a luxury or necessity. However, using regression analyses to test whether or not health care is a luxury is not legitimate, because the results of the

test could depend on the functional form chosen, as Parkin *et al.* (1987) show.

There are also technical problems concerning the theoretical assumptions underlying Engel-curve analysis:

(1)   Strictly speaking, Engel-curve analysis applies to a relationship between income and the demand for a good, at least if terms such as luxuries and necessities are to be used. Expenditures can be used as a proxy for demand, but only if the assumption is made that prices do not vary with income. This is not really tenable in the context of international comparisons, and we will look at this in more detail below.

(2)   Another assumption is that health care is a homogeneous good. This is not true even within countries, but it is also not true that the mix of health care delivered is exactly the same in every country. Parkin *et al.* (1987) found enormous differences in the relative shares of particular items of expenditure in aggregate expenditures across countries. It is extremely unlikely that data problems (which admittedly distort the picture somewhat) explain all of these.

(c) *Some Problems of Interpretation*

The suggestion that health care is not a necessity seems at first sight to be opposite to conventional views. Newhouse suggested that these are based on a presumption that the 'marginal unit of medical care' produces an improvement in physiological health. This led to the further argument that this marginal unit in fact probably produces more caring than curing.

There are a number of problems in using such an interpretation. First, there is the question of whether or not the 'marginal unit of medical care' has any meaning, especially in the aggregate. Since we are dealing with a heterogeneous good used in very different quantities by people, the marginal unit is difficult to identify conceptually, let alone in practice. On a more technical note, Lancaster (1969) has pointed out that terms such as luxury and necessity are usually and incorrectly attached to goods, but in aggregate Engel-curve analyses they really only refer to patterns of preferences. Income elasticities differ between people, and the overall income elasticity reflects only the average response. So even if the marginal unit of health care was the same for every consumer, their preferences for that unit might differ.

Secondly, it is arguable that in the industrialized countries used in the various analyses, medical expenditures do not involve the acquisition of marginal units of medical care, but rather of health insurance (private or social). If anything, it is insurance that should be labelled a luxury or necessity, and any inferences will concern what the marginal unit of insurance purchases. It is unlikely that these will reflect simply the marginal unit of medical care itself.

Thirdly, it is important not to confuse technical and everyday definitions of luxuries and necessities. It cannot seriously be argued that an income elasticity greater than one implies anything about physiological health, that the economic term 'necessity' is the same as that used to describe the effects of health care or that necessities and luxuries can be equated with curing and caring. As discussed earlier, it may be true that medical expenditures are ineffective in altering health, but this cannot be inferred from the size of an aggregate income elasticity.

(d) *Making Expenditures Comparable*

Parkin *et al.* (1987) pointed out that use of exchange rates is particularly suspect in this context. It is well-known that these are poor conversion factors for comparing expenditures between countries. They are determined by international currency markets and affected by the state of international trade, currency speculation, and other factors which are largely irrelevant to the size of domestic expenditure. They do not necessarily measure the comparative purchasing power of currencies, take no account of non-traded commodities, and are not specific to particular commodities. In addition, they are often not stable, leading to apparent fluctuations over time in calculations which use them which are entirely spurious.

Research has long been undertaken to obtain stable conversion factors which make currencies comparable in terms of what can be bought with them. Known as purchasing power parities (PPPs), these have become respectable mainly because of the work of the United Nations Statistical Office, Eurostat, and the OECD.[3] Following the famous publication by Kravis *et al.* (1978) of real GDP for many countries, the OECD has done much work to ensure that reliable PPPs are now regularly published for member countries. They produce PPPs which apply to the overall amount of goods and services produced, and others relevant to particular goods and services (Ward, 1985).

Unlike exchange rates, which are quoted prices, PPPs are not 'accurate' because of many problems involved in calculating them. In the past, their use was open to criticism as they were too speculative to be useful. However, they are now more finely calculated, and it is probably less justifiable to use exchange rates than to use PPPs for comparisons between OECD countries. It is better to use an inaccurate measure of the correct concept than an accurate measure of a concept known to be wrong. However, it is still true that PPPs for specific commodities are much less reliable than GDP PPPs, especially for services like health care whose typical product is difficult to define.

---

[3] Note that these PPPs are statistical constructs, and should not be confused with purchasing power parity theory, which seeks to explain exchange rates by reference to the relative purchasing power of currencies.

Health expenditure can be converted using either its own PPP or that for GDP, but the results must be interpreted in different ways. Using GDP PPPs, the calculated expenditure shows the cost to the economy as a whole of health care, allowing for different levels of general prices between countries. Using health care PPPs, it shows the volume of services provided, allowing for different levels of health care prices between countries. Table 7.2 shows figures for 1980,[4] with GDP per person for comparison, and the results of using exchange rates upon which the regression analyses described earlier were based.

In the context in which the data were being used, Parkin *et al.* (1987) argued that we should use GDP parities for GDP and health care parities for health care expenditure. Nevertheless, it is quite legitimate to use GDP parities for converting health care expenditures, which measures correctly the proportion of a country's resources devoted to health care.   Since this is little more than a rescaling of the data, it is not surprising that the relationship between GDP and health expenditures is largely unchanged. The size of the effect changes a little, but the explanatory power of the relationship and the finding that health care is a 'luxury' do not. Later studies by Culyer (1988a) and Gerdtham *et al.* (1988) confirm this finding.

However, very different figures are obtained by using health care parities. These measure the volume of resources that a country devotes to health.   Clearly, the proportion spent on health using this method of conversion has no meaning outside a comparison between countries: it depends upon which set of relative prices are used, which is an arbitrary choice. For example, using the same OECD figures the UK's proportion would be measured as 5.8 per cent using its own relative price structure, but 10.8 per cent using that of the USA.

This method of conversion is only really justifiable when it is desired to use cross-country comparisons to determine the pure effect of income.   For this, it is necessary to ensure that everything remains equal—in particular, prices. The use of health care PPPs for health expenditures ensures that all are converted to a common price structure.   If income and expenditure figures are recalculated using overall PPPs and health care PPPs respectively, they measure what expenditures and income would be if relative prices were the same in each country.

Analysing the resulting data produces very different results to those where the price structure is allowed to vary. The results of regression analysis seem at first sight similar to those given above. However, there are some important differences which affect the three earlier conclusions:

---

[4] This year is chosen because the OECD calculates PPPs properly only at five-year intervals, and 1985 health expenditure figures comparable to those in *Measuring Health Care* are not yet published.

Table 7.2
Health Expenditures and GDP per Person for 18 OECD Countries,
converted by Exchange Rates and Purchasing Power Parities (US$, 1980)

Country	Expenditure on health based on			Gross domestic product based on	
	ER[1]	GP[2]	MP[3]	ER[1]	PPP[2]
Austria	722	607	1119	10243	8612
Belgium	747	596	906	11877	9486
Canada	788	853	890	10792	11692
Denmark	880	668	894	12932	9816
Finland	684	564	1157	10800	8912
France	1040	839	1267	12188	9839
F R Germany	1065	818	1108	13221	10152
Greece	175	211	388	4163	5010
Ireland	480	510	684	5507	5854
Italy	479	541	854	7011	7911
Japan	569	537	1118	9101	8598
Luxembourg	836	707	1070	12703	10738
Netherlands	988	777	1168	11959	9406
Norway	964	773	1440	14118	11322
Portugal	150	237	502	2483	3925
Spain	334	376	544	5665	6381
UK	548	484	907	9482	8372
USA	1089	1089	1089	11446	11446

Notes: [1] ER = exchange rates
            [2] GP = GDP PPPs
            [3] MP = medical care PPPs
Source: Figures calculated from OECD (1985) and Ward (1985).

(1)   The relationship has a much lower explanatory power, 60 per cent in this sample. This considerably weakens the empirical base of the argument that other factors are irrelevant.[5]

(2)   There is little correlation between income and the proportion spent on health, but if anything it is negative. Health care appears to be (if anything) a necessity, not a luxury.

(3)   The UK apparently spends approximately what its income would predict that it should spend. It spends about the 'right' amount for its income but

[5] There is anyway little justification for interpreting the statistic of explanatory power (R^2) in such a way, in fact we might expect this to be large because of the highly aggregated data used.

pays less than average for it. Ireland, which apparently 'overspent' when exchange rate comparisons were used, also seems to spend the 'right' amount. Amongst other examples, the USA moves from 'overspending' to 'underspending', Canada from the 'right' amount to substantial 'underspending', and Japan from 'underspending' to substantial 'overspending'.

Using health care PPPs has some drawbacks—as suggested, they are far less reliable than GDP PPPs, for example. The main problem from a policy perspective is in interpreting the results they produce, since it may not be relevant to assume that relative prices will remain constant! Indeed, there is reason to believe that they will not—in fact, that there is a systematic relationship between relative prices and GDP. This may account to some extent for the different results arising from the different methods of calculation.

The ratio between GDP and health care parities gives us a measure of the relative price structure in a country compared to a base country.[6] For example, using the 1980 figures, the UK's ratio relative to a US ratio of one was 0.53—health care prices relative to all prices are a little over one-half that of the US. This has a significant correlation with real GDP, although the correlation at 0.48 is not high. So, although this is not the whole story, it appears that the higher the GDP the higher the relative price of health care. Countries with higher GDPs not only buy more health care, they have higher unit costs for it. In other words, some of their increased expenditure is due to their paying higher health care prices.

(e) Why are Health Care Prices Related to National Income?

What theory do we have that might explain this? Health care is a labour intensive service industry, and it is well-known that such industries have relatively low prices in poorer countries, particularly those that are very poor. Kravis et al. (1982) noted that 'services are much cheaper in the relative price structure of a typical poor country than in that of a rich country'. Their empirical evidence suggests a good positive relationship between the relative price of services and real GDP per person in countries.

They explained this in terms of the productivity of industries producing tradeable and non-tradeable goods: tradeable goods have large productivity differences between countries, whilst non-tradeable goods, such as services, do not. Given similar prices between countries in traded goods, wages in tradeable goods industries are determined by productivity, and are therefore low in low-productivity countries. These wages determine wages in non-tradeable goods industries, which in turn determine prices in them. So if productivity in service

---

[6] However, Hill (1984) has emphasized that PPPs have problems if used to make price comparisons, and are less valid for this than for converting expenditure.

industries is similar in all countries, wages—and therefore prices—will be relatively low in poor countries.

Bhagwati (1984) suggested that this explanation is unsatisfactory for a number of reasons. For example, there is no real evidence that non-traded sectors do have productivity parity, or that traded sectors are truly technologically inferior in poorer countries. (A further point is that full price parity in traded goods relies upon an assumption of free trade.) Bhagwati suggested an alternative, which does not have these problems and has another advantage in not requiring a definition of services according to whether or not they are traded.

It assumes that countries have the same production functions for all goods, but have different endowments of capital and labour. Poorer countries have relatively less capital than richer countries, so the rewards to capital are relatively large: the scarcity of capital raises its price. Looked at another way, the relative abundance of labour in poorer countries means that the price of labour relative to that of capital is lower. Consequently, goods produced by labour intensive industries are relatively cheaper.

Bhagwati's hypothesis is backed up by estimates of countries' capital/labour ratios. However, as with the Kravis *et al.* evidence on the relative cost of services, these relate to groups of countries banded together by income group. What these researchers have in mind is an explanation applying to countries having large differences in GDP: between 'rich' and 'poor', or LDCs and others. There is no reason, however, why it should not also apply to countries closer together in income. The question then is: are there differences in labour costs of health care between the kind of countries that we have been looking at which would explain our findings?

Sadly, international data on labour costs in health care are, if anything, harder to come by than expenditure figures, which makes it difficult to pursue the question. The OECD (1985) published useful figures on the average annual earnings of medical care professionals (including nurses, doctors, dentists, and pharmacists), but these are very incomplete and do not include ancillary workers. There are, however, just sufficient data on doctors' earnings to conduct some analyses.

Table 7.3 shows doctors' earnings and their relationship to GDP per person for eleven countries, calculated from the OECD figures. Two fairly uncontroversial matters from this table are that everywhere doctors' incomes exceed GDP per person, and that these incomes are higher where GDP is higher—in this sample there is a high correlation (0.70) between earnings and GDP per person.[7] Doctors, as highly trained professionals, would be expected to have greater than

---

[7] GDP per person is not really a proper measure of average incomes. However, similar figures relating doctors' incomes to average employees' incomes show the same patterns. See OECD (1987) and Reinhardt (1988a).

Table 7.3
Doctors' Earnings Relative to Gross Domestic Product per Person in 11 OECD Countries (US$ Converted by GDP PPPs, 1980)

Country (ranked by GDP per person)	GDP per person	Doctors' earnings	
		Value in US$	As multiple of GDP per person
Canada	11692	65185	5.58
USA	11446	80900	7.07
Norway	11322	26910	2.38
F R Germany	10152	76311	7.52
Denmark	9816	38358	3.91
Belgium	9486	34842	3.67
Finland	8912	23195	2.60
Japan	8598	28274	3.29
UK	8372	30813	3.68
Italy	7911	16979	2.15
Ireland	5854	16970	2.90

Source: Figures calculated from OECD (1985) and Ward (1985).

average incomes and it would also be likely that their incomes would grow along with that of the rest of the population.

However, it also seems that their incomes grow faster. From these figures, an increase of 10 per cent in GDP leads to a 22 per cent increase in doctors' earnings. So for at least one group there is support for the idea of increasing unit labour costs in health care with increasing national income. It is unfortunate that data limitations prevent analyses of this kind for other personnel.

It therefore seems quite possible that differences in labour costs account for some of the differences in the results using exchange rates and PPPs. Because health care is very labour intensive, differences between countries in the average incomes of health service personnel will produce differences in the price paid overall for health care. These income differences may be similar to those affecting other services in a country, but could also be caused by differences in methods of organization and funding of health services.[8]

Relatively low incomes of National Health Service personnel may account for some of the apparent UK underspending (although it could also reflect fewer real

[8] Ireland's 'overspending' shows another possible factor at work, namely the easy mobility of labour between Ireland and the UK. Wage rates in Irish hospitals must be relatively high to prevent a large flow to the UK of personnel, nurses in particular.

resources), whilst the apparently large expenditures of the USA reflect higher costs as much as greater resources. Of course, none of these figures tell us anything about the quality of health care, only its quantity.

4. Conclusions

This paper has outlined the considerable analytical difficulies which have been confronted by the various attempts to interpret international comparisons of health care expenditures. Problems with data and methodology have under-mined many of the more ambitious analyses of the relationship between national income and health expenditure. Nevertheless, it remains the case that interna-tional comparisons have considerable potential in analysing whole system issues. It is not always necessary to use sophisticated statistical and economic analysis to obtain insights into the comparative economics of health care in different countries.

Two examples will show this. First, there is plenty of existing evidence which is not at all supportive of the view that the NHS is at an aggregate level an inefficient system of delivering health care. The findings reviewed here are, in fact, more consistent with the opposite. Secondly, the figures in Table 7.3 could be highly suggestive to those seeking to control costs. What factors enable Norway and Canada to keep doctors' incomes so low? What features of the health care systems of the USA and the FRG enable their doctors to earn so much?

However, without the more complex analyses it is difficult to look more deeply into specific efficiency issues of concern to many countries. The way forward here lies in developing the conceptual and analytical models by which the data can be interpreted. Health economists cannot be content with the use of analytical constructs which do not fit at all well with their subject-matter and the data available on it. In the absence of such developments, their prospects of illuminating any policy debates in this area will be poor.

8

Post-war American Health Care:
The Many Costs of Market Failure

LOIS QUAM*

1. Introduction

American health care in the post-war era aptly illustrates the way in which the institutional provision of medical care can evolve in response to instances of both market and non-market failure. Three major periods are discernible. The first, from 1945 to the mid-1970s, was one of expansion in financial access to medical care through the passage of Medicare and Medicaid and expanded private insurance coverage as a benefit of employment. This increased demand created considerable profit opportunities for the suppliers. New entrants rushed to join the market. These new entrants did not compete on the basis of price. The ensuing steep rise in medical care expenditure prompted a shift in strategy from expanding access to cost containment.

Thus the second period, from the mid-1970s to the present, began with an emphasis on regulatory control mechanisms, but was dominated by a competitive market strategy for cost containment. The federal regulatory approach ended with the Carter administration in 1980. The Reagan administration looked to the market to control costs and quality (Stockman, 1981). This strategy took the form of a consolidation of health care purchasers' economic power through a restructuring of the health insurance industry and the adoption of prospective hospital payments by Medicare.

Despite the focus on cost containment, medical care inflation was unrestrained. Indeed, the increase in the annual rate of medical care expenditure was higher in the 1980s than during the 1970s (Long and Welch, 1988). Consequently, a new period in care is now being signalled by supporters of the competitive strategy (Roper *et al.*, 1988; Ellwood, 1988) and others. It is characterized by two factors. First, in an effort to redress information asymmetry

* Director, Research and Development, United HealthCare Corporation.

in the market for medical care, with public and private bodies introducing stronger regulatory mechanisms to monitor and control clinical practice. At the same time, financial access to medical care is again a visible issue. There is an increasing number of calls for national health insurance (*New York Times* leader, 1988; Caper, 1988; Fuchs, 1988; Dickman *et al.*, 1987; Frumkin and Taylor, 1988). In the meantime, the private sector is shifting more costs of medical care back on to patients.

2. The Period of Expansion

Private medical insurance, as a benefit of employment, grew in the post-war period. The federal government entered to fill gaps in private coverage with the passage of Medicare and Medicaid in 1965. As a result nearly 85 per cent of Americans were insured to some degree against medical expense.

This increased demand for health care created significant profit opportunities for its providers. The expansion in supply was swift and substantial. Along with fuelling demand for medical care through Medicare and Medicaid, the federal government also sponsored the increase in supply through grants and tax subsidies for new hospital building. The supply of physicians grew at an unprecedented rate. More of these newly trained physicians were specialists or sub-specialists rather than general practitioners. They were eager to use the wealth of newly available capital-intensive technologies and pharmaceutical treatments.

3. The Period of Cost Containment

This expansion drove health care expenditure up dramatically. Between 1965 and 1987, the cost of health care rose from 4 per cent to 11.1 per cent of the gross national product. The average price for family health insurance coverage to a private employer increased by nearly 50 per cent between 1981 and 1985, according to Bureau of Labour statistics (Jensen and Gabel, 1988). Premiums were expected to increase 20 to 30 per cent during 1989 (*Washington Post*, 1988).

Observers argued that the regulatory approach was ineffective largely because hospitals, the most expensive component of health care provision, were merely altering their billing practices in response to the increased regulation (Morrissey *et al.*, 1984). This argument was widely accepted by the Reagan administration, despite some later evidence to the contrary (Robinson and Luft, 1988). An alternative was proposed in the form of competition between health maintenance organizations (HMOs) which integrated health care financing and delivery (Ellwood *et al.*, 1971).

HMOs grew at an annual average rate of 14.2 per cent between 1970 and 1987. By the beginning of 1988, roughly 28.8 million Americans belonged to one (Interstudy, 1987). During the 1980s, HMOs and traditional indemnity insurers joined forces to form preferred provider organizations (PPOs). PPOs had enrolled over 17 million persons by 1988. PPOs encourage economic competition by negotiating discounted prices with a subset of providers in a given area.

In a market-place where physicians and hospitals were reimbursed at cost on a fee for each service rendered, HMOs served several functions. First, HMOs manage resource allocation in medical care. In other words, HMOs introduced the concept of marginal cost to a market, where the fee-for-service system of cost reimbursement had rendered it notably absent. Traditional insurers simply pay for care whereas HMOs adopt global budgets, central planning, and other measures to manage resource allocation. To meet these budgets, HMOs must encourage physicians to practise cost-effective medicine through financial incentives, utilization review, consensus panels, and the feedback of medical practice data.

Second, unlike the fee-for-service system, HMOs discourage costly and at times harmful overtreatment. The term 'health maintenance organization' was coined, because HMOs gave physicians financial incentives to maintain their patients' health rather than increase the volume of services. Moreover, HMOs place physicians at financial risk through capitation or other risk-bearing arrangements. To encourage preventive care further, HMOs, unlike the fee-for-service insurance system, initially did not charge co-payments or deductibles for medical services.

Third, HMOs increase economic competition between physicians and hospitals by bargaining on employers' behalf. Through HMOs, health insurers became price setters rather than price takers. Providers, who were accustomed to receiving reimbursement at cost, were forced to bid against each other. HMOs promised employers that their bargaining skill and management expertise would lower medical-care costs.

The Reagan administration actively supported the competitive strategy through the passage of prospective payment legislation for Medicare in 1983. The diagnosis-related groups (DRG) legislation paid hospitals prospectively on a per case basis rather than reimbursement for costs. The impact was substantial because Medicare revenues comprise roughly 40 per cent of all hospital revenues. Prospective payment for out-patient services is the focus of current federal government research.

4. The Failure of the Competitive Strategy to Control Costs and Ensure Quality

Arguing that the fee-for-service sector encouraged overtreatment, the competitive strategy sought to reduce the total volume of medical care. This objective was dramatically achieved in the in-patient arena. From 1980 to 1985 the hospital admissions rate fell 7.5 per cent (American Hospital Association, 1987).

But despite a return to 1960s hospital admission rates, health care expenditure in the 1980s, whether measured as a proportion of gross national product, constant dollars, or current dollars, continued to rise sharply (Anderson and Erickson, 1987). For example, in the north region of Colorado, total in-patient expenditures increased by 10 per cent during the period 1983 to 1985, despite a drop in the total number of in-patient days by 19 per cent (Reinhardt, 1987).

There are three main reasons for this continued rise in expenditure. First, administrative costs increased in the 1980s as competition resulted in a rise in the number and complexity of transfers. Second, the federal government, insurers, and employers attempted to redress the information asymmetry in medical care by monitoring the appropriateness of medical care. These attempts to detect inappropriate medical care proved very costly. Third, despite competition, health care providers maintained their incomes by increasing service volume, by competing on the non-price grounds of patient amenities and prestigious medical services, and by organizing effective bargaining units.

Cost containment has not reduced total expenditure or the incomes of health care investors, providers, or institutions. None the less, significant reductions have occurred in the provision of health care services to particular patients, for example the uninsured. As well as increasing cost, the 1980s has been a decade of declining quality of care as measured by several indicators, including the percentage of the population with health insurance, the infant mortality rate, and the childhood vaccination rate.

Increased quality of care was an intended outcome of the competitive strategy (Enthoven, 1978). However, increased competition exacerbated the financial access problem in the US. Health plans profit more readily from enrolling healthy patients than effectively managing medical care resource allocation. Furthermore, hospitals and physicians gripped in competitive manoeuvres are less willing to provide uncompensated care to uninsured patients. These events operate within an American health care environment in which over- and under-treatment based on a patient's insurance status has long been endemic.

5. Problems in Containing Costs in American Health Care

(a) *Rising Administrative Costs*

Administrative expenses are the fastest growing of all components of expenditure. Between 1981 and 1986 they increased by 160 per cent (Reinhardt, 1988b). In 1986 they accounted for 22 per cent of every health care dollar (Himmelstein and Woolhandler, 1986). It is also the case that the American health insurance industry's incomes and profits are buoyant (Waldo *et al.*, 1986).

The sheer number of independent agencies for financing medical care each with different eligibility requirements and benefits adds considerably to costs. The aggregation of federal programmes, separate state programmes for the poor, mentally ill, disabled, pregnant women, and young children, tax subsidies, veterans' programmes, military programmes, patient out-of-pocket payments, and over 1,000 private insurance companies is the financial mechanism for American health care. Every programme duplicates the costs of premium collection, billing, actuarial rate-setting, and financial management. Every health care facility must administer a billing and cost accounting apparatus to link each charge and service incurred to an individual patient. Every workplace must administer a benefits department to evaluate insurers' bids, forecast costs, and collect the premium.

The process of competition itself has increased costs. Hospital spending on advertising increased fivefold from 1984 to 1987 (Lewin, 1987). Expenditure by HMOs in Minneapolis, the most competitive HMO market in the nation, on radio, television, and direct mail advertising increased by 50 per cent, to $15 million, between 1984 and 1985 at the height of market competition (Kenney, 1985). To a British audience, advertising health care like fast food seems absurd. In the US, hospitals advertise on motorway billboards, television, and radio. The American College of Surgeons advertises in weekly news magazines, such as *Newsweek*, on the value of surgery.

(b) *The High Cost of Redressing Information Asymmetries*

Information transactions in the market for medical care are costly. The competitive strategy depends on HMOs' ability to act as informed demand agents on the consumer's behalf. In the United States, the problems of obtaining, analysing, and applying information have proved intractable. Evans (1986) hypothesized that the post-1983 medical care expenditure increase, as a share of GNP, reflects at least in part the costs of increased effort to control hospital utilization through data analysis and utilization review.

The distribution of information in the clinical transaction between physicians and patient is highly inequitable. Patients depend heavily on physicians because of the complexity of clinical information; the multiplicity of treatment choices;

the lack of a scientific basis for considering the effects of treatments on outcomes; and the patient's distressed state. To monitor the quality or efficiency of a physician's practice, insurers and employers have attempted to redress this information asymmetry. The costs of such monitoring have been substantial. In particular, the costs of duplicated efforts are not trivial. Utilization review, database development, and analysis are conducted independently by insurers, employers, and the government.

Both insurers and HMOs adopted utilization review programmes to monitor medical care provision. These review programmes certify prospective hospital admissions for medical appropriateness, obtain second medical opinions, and concurrently review hospital stays to schedule a patient's discharge. Duplication is rampant. Each insurer operates its own utilization review programme. The average urban hospital has forty separate such programmes (Reinhardt, 1988b).

A study by Paul Feldstein (1988) and colleagues at the University of California–Irvine estimated that utilization review cost an employer $1.58 per employee for an annual health care cost of $18,960 for 1,000 employees. Employers have also invested significantly in investigating their employees' medical expenditure. Disappointed by persistently high costs, employers consolidated into national and local coalitions to bargain with insurance companies.

(c) Providers' Monopoly Position

Despite the rapid expansion of HMOs, the income flow to health care providers has increased. In the 1980s, the difference between physicians' fee inflation and the consumer price index was 2.75 per cent as compared to 1.0 to 1.5 per cent for the whole post-war period (Evans, 1986).

This increase enhances already high incomes. American doctors earn far more than their British counterparts. The OECD (1987) study found that American doctors earn 5.1 times the national average wage in the United States, while British doctors earn 2.4 times the national average wage. US health care providers have maintained their incomes and profits by increasing the volume and intensity of services, engaging in non-price competition, and organizing into effective bargaining units.

(d) Increases in Volume to Recoup Unit Price Reductions

From 1975 to 1987 the number of physicians increased by 45 per cent, but the anticipated effect of the physicians' glut failed to materialize as the profession increased and differentiated their services to maintain their incomes (Luft and Arno, 1986). Indeed, the increasing supply of physicians was one of the factors which increased costs. An increase in the surgeon/population rate has been demonstrated to result in increases in *per capita* utilization and physician fees (Cromwell and Mitchell, 1986).

Several US studies provide strong evidence of supplier-induced demand through increases in the volume and intensity of services. In Colorado a 1 per cent drop in payment rates was found to be accompanied by a 0.61 per cent increase in the intensity of medical services, a 0.15 per cent increase in the intensity of surgeries, and a 0.52 per cent increase in laboratory tests (Rice, 1983). During the 1971 price freeze under the Economics Stabilization Program, the number of medical services provided in California increased, especially for office visits and laboratory and X-ray services. The result was greater total expenditure than prior to the price freeze (Holahan and Scanlon, 1979). Similarly, an increase in expenditure was recorded for Medicare during the freeze on physician fees from June 1984 to March 1986 (Anderson and Erickson, 1987).

(e) *Non-Price Competition*

As well as increasing the volume and intensity of services, hospitals and physicians have maintained their incomes by competing on non-price grounds. Non-price competition, by adding value to services as a means of attracting patients, increases total expenditure and is particularly powerful in medical care where information costs are so high that price is frequently a proxy for quality. Hospitals compete with each other by refurbishing hospital wards with fashionable colour-co-ordinated décor and providing video recorders, gourmet meals, and valet parking.

In the US, competitive markets have been demonstrated to have higher costs (Robinson and Luft, 1988), more duplication of services (Robinson and Luft, 1985), longer length of stays (Robinson *et al.*, 1988), and higher staff ratios (Robinson, 1988) than non-competitive markets. Luft and his colleagues (1986) wrote:

We found that the presence of nearby institutions and services increases the availability of most of these services (mammography, emergency services, cobalt therapy, heart surgery, and cardiac catherization) in neighboring hospitals. This supports the hypothesis that the competition among hospitals within an open-ended reimbursement environment takes the form of non-price competition for community based physicians through the acquisition of expensive clinical facilities.

Notably the provision of expensive, prestigious technologies grew rapidly during this period (Russell, 1979). These services are duplicated far beyond medical demand with resulting high cost. Robinson estimated the increase in cost associated with such effects to be 27.5 per cent in 1982 and 23 per cent in 1986 (Robinson and Luft, 1988).

There is no evidence, as yet, that competition between HMOs or PPOs has affected long-term utilization trends or medical inflation (Evans, 1986). Early research suggests that HMOs are unsuccessful in encouraging price-based competition between hospitals (Luft *et al.*, 1986). There appears to be no statistically significant relationship between HMO market share and hospital expenses *per capita* (McLaughlin *et al.*, 1984) or total hospital expenditure (McLaughlin, 1988a). The major HMO effect on hospital expenses may be a once-for-all drop in in-patient utilization, resulting in a brief fall in expenditure, until hospitals adjust and recoup their incomes by increasing intensity or price per unit.

(f) *Consolidation of Providers into Economic Bargaining Units*

Hospitals and physicians have both formed bargaining units to counter the bargaining power of HMOs. Hospitals joined for-profit corporations or non-profit associations. Physicians formed bargaining associations or used their clinic groups to counteract HMOs' efforts to force competition. The effectiveness of these physicians' bargaining units has resulted in close scrutiny by the US Department of Justice's antitrust division. The Department announced a stiffer enforcement policy 'to ensure that society's decision to rely on competition to hold down health care costs will not be frustrated by a handful of greedy individuals' (Gold, 1988).

6. Problems in the Quality of American Health Care

(a) *Lack of a Market for Universal Insurance Coverage*

The problem of adverse selection renders the provision of universal health care insurance impossible in a competitive market (Arrow, 1963). Enthoven (1986) and other proponents of the competitive strategy assumed that mechanisms would be developed to counteract insurers' incentives to enrol only healthy patients. Without statutory universal access, inequitable income distribution renders this assumption untenable. After the 1965 expansion of insurance coverage through Medicare and Medicaid, federal legislative efforts to expand coverage have been unsuccessful.

More than 37 million Americans (roughly 17 per cent of the total population) lack health insurance (Wilensky, 1988). In 1986, roughly 7 out of 10 uninsured persons lived in families with incomes exceeding the federal poverty threshold (Congressional Research Service, 1988). The number of uninsured Americans has increased approximately 40 per cent since the Reagan administration took office in 1980 because of cuts in general health care funding and tightening of existing programmes' means tests (Mundinger, 1985).

There are three major groups unable to gain access to the private insurance market and ineligible for government support—adults (and their children) working in low-paid jobs without health insurance benefits, persons with disabilities or chronic illnesses, and the unemployed. Medicaid provides little respite. Fewer than half of Americans with incomes below the official poverty line meet Medicaid eligibility standards (Newacheck, 1988). Insurance companies are allowed to enquire or use diagnostic tests to determine if candidates for health insurance have existing disabilities or serious illness, such as AIDS (Office of Technology Assessment, 1988). Roughly 65 per cent of the 12 million US workers affected by layoffs from 1979 to 1983 lacked health insurance (Podgursky and Swaim, 1987).

Perversely, families with catastrophic health expenditure (defined as over 5 per cent of the families' income) have been found to have worse insurance coverage than average families (Wyszewianski, 1986), largely because of the interaction of low income, poor insurance, and poor health. The Robert Wood Johnson (1983) study found that a chronic illness of a family member posed grave difficulties for the family. It caused an uninsured family to make a 'major change in job, housing or living arrangements' twice as often as an insured family. The study found that one million families in 1982 had at least one member refused care for financial reasons. Twenty-three per cent of the uninsured population did not have a general practitioner.

The effects of the above are considerable. Hayward (1988) and colleagues found: 'Among those with medical problems, the uninsured were 1.9 times as likely to have needed supportive medical care, medications, or supplies but not to have obtained them. They were 2.3 times as likely as insured respondents to have had their illness result in a major financial problem.' Newacheck (1988) found that uninsured children receive 50 per cent less ambulatory physician services.

Relative to other industrialized nations, the United States has performed poorly on standard health indicators, such as infant mortality and child mortality due to diarrhoeal diseases (Ho *et al.*, 1988). Between 1980 and 1985, the percentage of all US pre-school children adequately immunized against the seven major childhood diseases declined significantly. In 1985 20 per cent of all infants, and 40 per cent of non-white infants, were not adequately immunized against polio (Children's Defense Fund, 1987).

In the 1980s increasing competition has reduced access by diminishing cross-subsidization between insured and uninsured populations. Previously hospitals recovered the incremental cost of treating non-paying patients by inflating the bills of privately insured patients. Pockets of poor geographical access in urban and rural areas have emerged. In a stark example, the centre city Los Angeles California Medical Center closed its doors to emergency ambulances on 1 August 1988 because the institution lacked funds to treat uninsured patients. Roughly one-third of patients presenting at the emergency room were uninsured. Over the last two years fourteen other hospitals in Los Angeles have closed or downgraded their emergency rooms (Reinhold, 1988). This closure leaves the vast central area of Los Angeles without an emergency room.

(b) *Overtreatment of Insured Populations*

While undertreatment of some individuals is the most serious health care problem in the US, the long-standing problem of overtreatment of others, particularly in surgery, first identified by Wennberg and colleagues (Wennberg and Gittelsohn, 1977) persists. A study by Allan Greenspan (1988) and colleagues at the Albert Einstein Medical Center depicts the magnitude of the problem. Greenspan found high rates of pacemaker implantation without medical indication. One in 500 Americans has a permanent pacemaker and new implants are estimated to exceed 120,000 annually.

We found that 168 implants (44%) were definitely indicated, 137 (36%) were possibly indicated, and 77 (20%) not indicated. We conclude that in a large medical population in 1983, the indications for a considerable number of permanent pacemakers were inadequate or incompletely documented.

With an average cost per implant of $12,000, annual expenditures for these implants probably approach $2 billion.

The effect of overtreatment on the quality of health care may be considerable. New research at the RAND Corporation found high rates of inappropriate coronary artery bypass surgery (Winslow, 1988a), gastrointestinal endoscopy (Kahn *et al.*, 1988) and carotid endarectomy (Winslow, 1988b). The carotid endarectomy study examined the medical charts of a random sample of 1,302 Medicare patients in three geographical areas who had the procedure in 1981. On review by a physician panel, the study found that 32 per cent of the procedures were performed for equivocal reasons and 32 per cent for inappropriate reasons. The study found that after the procedure, 9.8 per cent of patients had a major complication defined as stroke with residual deficit at the time of hospital discharge or death within 30 days of surgery.

7. The Future

The high health care cost and diminished quality in the United States has forced a change in strategy. This change has two foci. First, government, private insurers, and employers increasingly seek to regulate clinical practice through close monitoring and audit of physicians' decisions. This scrutiny is dependent on research and the development of tools to enable external agents to assess the clinical encounter. In other words, this new period in American health care is focused on redressing the information asymmetry in the market for medical care.

Second, the gaps in insurance coverage, depicted in bold relief by the limits of insurability for AIDS (Hammond and Shapiro, 1986), increases the call for national health insurance or a national health service. In the intermission, however, employers, providers, and insurers are best able simultaneously to protect their incomes and profits by shifting the costs of care on to patients.

(a) *Strengthening of Public and Private Regulatory Controls*

The free marketeers are turning into public and private regulators of medical practice (Roper *et al.*, 1988). This regulatory approach assumes that decision-making in an arena of scarce resources is better made by external medical audit supported by empirical research than through independent decision-making by physicians.

The federal government is sponsoring research to develop external audit capabilities. The Medicare Trust Fund supports two major research projects with the objective of 'integrating and analysing existing data to determine the outcomes and costs of alternative (medical care) practice patterns . . . develop and test feasible and acceptable methods for reducing inappropriate variations' (National Center for Health Services Research, 1988).

Private insurers are undertaking major investments in the research and development of tools to screen insurance claims for medical appropriateness. More aggressive utilization review programmes, which audit physicians' treatment decisions before diagnoses and treatment, are underway. A major industry of private clinical audit firms, software developers, and the ubiquitous American consultant has developed to support and profit from these efforts.

This aggressive regulatory approach will have two ramifications on medical practice. First, American physicians will experience a decline in their clinical autonomy as insurers repeatedly audit medical care before and during its delivery. Physicians' treatment decisions will be increasingly questioned. This trend is not new. American physicians have repeatedly protected their incomes at the cost of declining clinical autonomy (Reinhardt, 1987). Second, medical care costs will increase with the costs of regulating millions of unique and complex clinical encounters.

(b) *Calls for a National Health Programme*

The worsening of the access problem under the Reagan administration has led to renewed calls for a national health programme which would be less costly and more equitable than the current arrangement. A national health programme is argued to be a more effective means of containing costs than the existing competition strategy or piecemeal reform (Himmelstein and Woolhandler, 1986). Legislation for both a national health service and national health insurance has been introduced in Congress.

Several states enacted interim solutions by mandating employers to provide private insurance coverage and by expanding Medicaid coverage. Hawaii has mandated insurance coverage as a benefit of employment since 1974. Massachusetts passed legislation in 1988. Ten states have legislative studies or pilots underway.

(c) *Shifting the Costs of Health Care to Patients*

In the current American medical care environment, the only means for health care providers, insurers, and employers to reap profits simultaneously is a strategy of shifting costs on to patients. The first transfer of medical expense back to patients in the post-war period is underway. Patients are bearing increased expense in four ways: additional co-payments and deductibles; decline in benefits covered; changes in insurance practice; and a shift from institutional to home care.

Many corporations have successfully negotiated reduced health care for their employees by adding large co-payments and deductibles (Ginzberg, 1987). United States Government Bureau of Labor Statistics reported an increase in the average annual deductible from 1981 to 1985 from \$88.67 to \$124.47 for an individual and \$206.01 to \$293.90 for a family. A steep increase in the proportion of employees with co-payments or deductibles has occurred. Some employers now subject all expenses to a deductible and thereby negate any limits on a patient's liability for medical cost (Jensen and Gabel, 1988). The Bureau of Labor Statistics reported a steep drop from 83 to 64 per cent between 1981 and 1985 in the percentage of employees with insurance for hospital care.

According to the RAND research, these charges are likely to reduce patient use of physician services particularly in preventive care (Shapiro *et al.*, 1986; Manning *et al.*, 1987). Low-income Americans will be the hardest hit, as found in the RAND study (Lohr *et al.*, 1986) and in Beck's (1973) finding that co-payment was associated with an 18 per cent reduction in utilization by the poor in 1968. Co-payments and deductibles, in interaction with the fee-for-service insurance system and information asymmetries in the market, appear to create perverse incentives for medical care consumption. Patients are deterred from seeking preventive and symptomatic care, while physicians are encouraged to increase the frequency and intensity of follow-up services (Dutton, 1987).

Changes in insurer practices exacerbate this problem by decreasing access to insurance amongst employed persons. Insurers increasingly avoid or fail to renew contracts with employers whose employees represent poor insurance risks. Each small employer group is quoted premium rates which reflect its own group's experience only. As a result, the consumer receives little benefit from insurance risk pooling. A small employer with one very ill patient may face extremely high annual premium-rate hikes or a cancelled contract at year end. In effect, costs are shifted back on to patients in denied insurance coverage or increased premium costs.

Health care insurers have also sought to shift patients from the hospital to home care as rapidly as possible. Home care appears less costly only because family members' inputs are not borne by the insurance company or employer (Ancona-Berk and Chalmers, 1986).

8. Summary

American health care remains in transition. Current research and development efforts to resolve the information deficiencies in monitoring the quality of medical care will make a substantial contribution to health economics and clinical research. These efforts, however, are unlikely to resolve the problem of spiralling cost. To some extent, they will contribute to it. Thus, the stress on financial access to health care in the US can be expected to continue to rise in the 1990s as more individuals lack health insurance and the real value of such insurance declines. At some point this coincidence of high cost and worsening health may be more damaging in political and economic terms than governmental action to limit provider monopoly power through a national health programme.

9

Health Care Financing Reform in the United States During the 1980s: Lessons for Great Britain

RICHARD M. SCHEFFLER AND ERIC NAUENBERG*

1. Introduction

In broad terms, the US health care system can be viewed as one that has increased the use of market forces in the 1980s. This last decade produced rapid and dramatic shifts in the organization and financing of health care. These changes followed a decade or more of intense government regulation and various attempts to use local health planning to direct resources, control health care expenditures, and provide an equitably acceptable distribution of medical services.

The shift to more competition in health care is best viewed as part of an overall philosophical change in the US to less government regulation and more reliance on the private sector. Although the pattern was not consistent in this regard, political forces led to the deregulation of the airline industry, the lifting of some federal regulations in the banking industry, and the placing of stricter limitations on price supports in agriculture. This climate of deregulation along with a rapidly expanding health care sector led to the increasing reliance on market forces to allocate health care resources.

This chapter reviews the major changes in the 1980s that have led to more reliance on the market for health care in the US. We focus on the major regulatory changes, lifting of legal barriers on market forces, and changes in organization and financing of health care. The paper points out some lessons that the United Kingdom could learn from the US experience with a more competitive health system which may be useful if the British government's White Paper reforms are implemented as planned.

* University of California, Berkeley. The authors would like gratefully to acknowledge the assistance of Elizabeth Slavin in researching this paper.

We begin with a brief overview of major trends in the US health care system during the 1980s. This is followed by a review of three major experiments with contracting out publicly financed health care services to the private sector. These experiments are all different, and they provide some notion of how internal markets under the NHS reforms might behave.

Competition in health care in the US has been stimulated by significant regulatory changes. We review the recent evidence on the importance of prospective payment (i.e. diagnosis-related groups—DRGs) in hospitals, and the very recent changes in Medicare policy toward a system of paying physicians based on a relative value scale (RVS). These rate-setting and administered price systems provide financial incentives for efficiency which are politically—rather than market—determined. There are, of course, market-driven forces taken into account in each of these systems.

Finally, we review the experience in the US with alternative delivery systems such as HMOs (health maintenance organizations) and PPOs (preferred provider organizations). In theory these systems of health care delivery have the potential to control health care costs in competitive markets. Their experiences, to date, in achieving these ends are examined.

It is well recognized that the US and UK systems of health care delivery are at this point very different. They are formed by the different governmental, historical, and cultural patterns in each country. Due partly to the conscription of medical personnel during the Second World War, Britain had a naturally smooth post-war transition to a nationalized health care system which centrally controlled the flow of expenditures. Some might argue that the NHS has been successful at controlling expenditures by underfunding certain programmes and through restricting salaries and the number of consultant positions. In the United States, on the other hand, consultants (known as specialists) have successfully maintained high incomes, but with heavy use of expensive medical technology.

Therefore, lessons derived from observations on one system should be viewed by the other system with interest and caution. It is safe to say that health care competition in the US may be very different to that which will be experienced in the United Kingdom. Nevertheless, the same errors in design committed in American programmes may produce similar results on the other side of the Atlantic. We are hopeful that this chapter will help prevent this from happening. The first step is to provide an overview of the changes which have transformed the American health care sector over the last decade.

2. Trends in the US Health Care System in the 1980s

The 1980s saw a new era in American health policy. While the 1970s was the age of regulation and health planning, the 1980s brought experimentation with deregulation and competition. These changes, designed partly to stem the rise in costs, have not produced the intended results. In constant 1982 dollars, national health care spending in the United Stated has risen from $333,470 million in 1980 to over $385,740 million in 1987. This represents about a 16 per cent real increase in health care costs since the beginning of the decade and a rate of increase higher than that experienced in the 1970s (Letsch et al., 1988). A part of this increase was due to burgeoning administrative expenses which increased by 186 per cent from $9,200 million to $24,500 million in just the first six years of the decade (Reinhardt, 1988c). Increases in malpractice and administrative costs mean that the total costs of a physician's practice now consume approximately half of his practice income; this figure contrasts with 36 per cent in Canada and 29 per cent in the United Kingdom (Maynard, 1975). Further increases in cost can be attributed to the proliferation of expensive new technologies and other capital expenditures which rose as much as five times the annual rate of labour expenditures (e.g. 1.1 per cent as compared to 5.5 per cent in 1986) in the first six years of the decade (Cromwell and Pope, 1989).

In viewing the American experience during the 1980s, it is important to realize that the institution of more competition into the health care sector depended on six major trends:

(1)   First, the supply of physicians increased dramatically throughout the 1970s and early 1980s. This has produced an estimated oversupply of over 26,500 physicians (or 5 per cent of the total demanded) which has undermined the ability of physicians to ignore the forces of competition (Singer, 1989). Moreover, the surplus[1] is projected to increase to 150,000 by the year 2000 (GMENAC, 1981). Greater numbers of women and minority groups entering the medical profession have diversified interests making it more difficult for physicians to remain united on any single issue.

(2)   Competition was enhanced by the liberalization of laws concerning advertising in the health care sector. Beginning in 1976 with the Supreme Court case Bates v. State Bar of Arizona (433 US 350), the Federal Trade Commission has issued less stringent regulation regarding hospitals and physicians advertising their services. Unlike 10–15 years ago, it is now possible to find many hospitals, physicians, and even pharmaceuticals advertising directly to patients. Such mediums as the yellow pages in telephone directories and newspapers are now filled with advertisements about services available. Television advertisements are also becoming quite common.

[1] Surplus of physicians is defined as the difference between year-specific demand for physicians and the year-specific supply of full-time-equivalent physicians in patient care.

(3)   The health care sector has experienced widespread deregulation since the beginning of the decade. Both the Federal and State governments have started to contract with the private sector to provide services to the poor and elderly under public programmes. Relying heavily on contracting, different levels of government are trying to shift the financial risk of caring for patients to the private sector. With greater risk now being incurred by the private sector, there is greater sensitivity to prices and overall costs of care.

(4)   There has been a proliferation of expensive new technologies and treatments. The increasing use and availability of such technologies as magnetic resonance imaging (MRI) has made both providers and payers much more conscious of costs. This effect has been compounded by the development of expensive treatments for combating AIDS like AZT and Oral Pentamadine.

(5)   The end of the artificially high rates of growth that American industry experienced after the Second World War finally came with the completion of the reconstruction era in both Japan and West Germany. Now American products are forced to compete at a level to which they are unaccustomed. As a result, business people have been searching for sources of large cost differences between their own products and those produced overseas. One of the largest differences they are discovering is in health care costs for employees, and they have taken large steps like self-insuring and contracting with selected providers in order to reduce this gap.

(6)   There were also significant changes in demography during the decade which, along with uninterrupted economic growth, have placed increased demands on the health care sector. The United States has experienced a significant aging of its population as more people are living into their eighties and nineties, and as the birthrate has declined since the mid-1960s. The population of 'the oldest old', citizens over 85, has grown since 1966 at an average annual rate of 4.6 per cent, more than double the rate of the rest of the elderly and much higher than the general population (Mariano, 1989). Since the most elderly citizens are the heaviest users of services, the implication of these figures is that ever greater percentages of people are requesting heavy use of technology. Given the expense, there was a great need to devise methods to contain utilization and costs at reasonable levels without sacrificing quality of care.

These factors provided the impetus to transform the health care system into one that relied more heavily on market forces. In analysing the National Health Service, we find a very different situation. Rather than facing an oversupply,

Britain is currently facing a shortage of physicians, especially consultants, and there are plans to increase this number (HMSO, 1989). In other words, the British are faced with underspending rather than overspending; to solve this problem, they see competition as a way of increasing output within broad, existing expenditure levels. This stands in contrast to the US experience where competition was aimed in part at reducing expenditures. Secondly, there currently is no pressure from the British business community to hold costs down since health care is largely funded through tax revenues rather than private insurance premiums paid by an employer. Even with efforts to encourage increased usage of private insurance, the US experience suggests that decades are necessary to increase enrolment in employer-sponsored plans from about 10 per cent of the populace to over 50 per cent—a level where insurance expenses may be of concern to the business community. Given continued low *per capita* health expenditures relative to other Western nations, Britain should not experience relatively high insurance premium costs which would diminish the price-competitiveness of British products. Lastly, Britain has not experienced the proliferation of expensive technologies as has the United States. With MRI and expensive transplants still relatively rare in Britain, the increased financial risk posed by such 'big ticket' items will not be incurred to the same degree as in the United States. However, even with these differences in mind, nothing precludes the possibility that the 'British System' might behave more competitively if the NHS White Paper reforms are instituted. In such a case, the lessons learned from the American experience should still be quite valuable.

(a) *Selective Contracting*

If implemented, the NHS reforms will widen the scope of contractual arrangements within both the NHS and the private sector through a bidding process known as competitive tendering. Designed to go beyond the non-clinical support services currently under contract, the NHS expects to engage in the 'wholesale "buying in" of treatments for patients from private sector hospitals and clinics' (HMSO, 1989). In addition, certain general practitioners will be assigned practice budgets under which they will be required to contract with hospitals for patient services while managing a fixed budget. Both kinds of arrangements have pervaded the American scene for the last decade. A number of states and the federal government have participated in processes that have either placed certain services open for competitive bid, or have negotiated contracts with specific providers. Several poignant examples help to illustrate this experience.

Arizona Health Care Cost Containment System (AHCCCS)

Beginning in 1982, the State of Arizona began an experiment in financing its joint federal–state programme—known as Medicaid—designed to care for its indigent population. In response to federal legislation passed in 1981, which both encouraged use of alternative financing mechanisms and waived requirements that Medicaid recipients should have free choice of provider, the state revamped its entire system. Rather than pay physicians according to the rule of 'customary, prevailing, and reasonable' (CPR) charges,[2] the state began a competitive bidding process between groups of providers. The idea was to provide a complete acute-care delivery system for the state's indigent population while providing cost control through capitated reimbursement—a standard per beneficiary payment made irrespective of service use. Other contracting techniques had been tried elsewhere, but never before had a state placed its entire system up for bid.

In opening up this sector for competitive bid, the state was actively encouraging certain kinds of organizations amenable to capitated budgets known as health maintenance organizations (HMOs). Essentially a form of pre-paid medical care, HMOs combine a financing mechanism based on capitation with group practice. The organization not only provides care, but it also assumes the financial risk of providing such care. Although there are several models of such organizations, their main feature long popular with economists has been a built-in incentive to contain costs since the organization retains any savings. Another structural feature of particular interest to the British is the 'gatekeeper' role assigned to primary care physicians and nurses who were given responsibility for channelling patients to the most cost-effective care available. Known as case managers, these health professionals were given the task of finding care at a competitive price as opposed to those who medically manage a case ensuring that the proper referrals are made. This splitting of physicians into these two groups was considered key to containing costs without adversely affecting care. This novel approach to care was viewed with much optimism, and in a short time, HMOs became the primary providers of care for a large portion of the state's Medicaid eligibles.

The record of AHCCCS has been mixed. Initially thought to be successful, the programme's costs increased drastically after a first year which did result in reduced costs. Funding in the fiscal year 1983 amounted to $115.2 million, of which the state paid $22.0 million; for the fiscal year 1984, these figures rose dramatically to $192 million and $41.3 million respectively. This amounted to an 88 per cent increase over the fiscal year 1983 (Brecher, 1984). However, to be fair, some of these increases should have been expected, and it might be possible to explain that such increases were due to an expansion of benefits rather than a rise in the cost of caring for such patients. For example, the programme was only operational for nine months of its first year, and new benefits, such as preventive services were added at the end of this period. In

---

[2] This is, in broad terms, a fee-for-service system which follows government regulations on how fees are set.

addition, enrolment levels increased significantly beyond expectations in the second year of operation (Brecher, 1984).

Nevertheless, the programme never functioned smoothly. The private firm hired to manage the AHCCCS programme had substantial difficulties maintaining an accurate and current eligibility file, paying providers in a timely fashion, and keeping overheads low. In addition, there were several accounts of conflict of interest (Brecher, 1984). As a result, administration of the programme was returned to public control under the aegis of the Arizona Department of Health and then to an AHCCCS administration created by the state legislature. Once control was placed back in the public sector, one of the first actions was to increase staff and alter the channels of authority (Schaller et al., 1986).

Case managers also performed poorly partly because they never fully understood their roles. They were unable effectively to direct patients to services that were appropriate while containing costs. Very few general practitioners were experienced in co-ordinating all aspects of a patient's care, and many showed a lack of interest in doing so. Large studies designed to ascertain the performance of case management programmes give legitimacy to Arizona's experiences and provide no clear conclusions regarding the efficacy of such programmes. One major study indicated that the administrative costs of such programmes are high but they at least produce short-term savings and generally enhance quality of life and care delivered (Henderson et al., 1987). In contrast, another study found higher utilization and costs in case-managed patients without producing a significant increase in quality of life (Franklin et al., 1987). There still is no consensus among researchers regarding the cost-effectiveness of such programmes.

One of the major lessons learned from the Arizona experience is that multiple rounds of bidding produce some adverse results. Because first-year bids exceeded anticipated levels, the state requested voluntary reductions from a number of those who won contracts in that year. And in the following year, a second round of bidding was instituted. Such actions distorted the incentives of a purely competitive process because when organizations are able to renegotiate and/or rebid, they are less likely to submit their lowest price during the initial round as they hope to leave some room to submit lower bids in succeeding rounds. Thus, initial bids are offered at prices significantly above average costs, raising costs to the government in the long run. As Gardner and Scheffler point out:

For truly effective price competition, the state would have had to provide sufficient funds to cover the costs of accepting initial bids of the providers with the lowest prices, even if this meant initially exceeding expected expenditures for the sake of long-term savings. Arizona's covering of initial bids would have indicated to providers bidding in subsequent years that to win contracts they needed to submit their most competitive bids from the outset. (Gardner and Scheffler, 1988)

California Medi-Cal Selective Contracting Programme

With a joint-federal programme similar to that in Arizona, California was the next state to propose innovative designs. Beginning in 1982, the state legislature authorized both the Medi-Cal programme (the name for Medicaid in California) and private insurers to engage in selective contracting with hospitals and physicians.   The programme solicited bids on standard *per diem* rates for in-patient care which served as a basis for further negotiations with individual hospitals. This stands in stark contrast to the AHCCCS programme which sought pre-paid capitated rates for comprehensive care rather than in-patient care only. The other interesting difference between the California and Arizona programmes is that in the former, the competitive bids only served as a gauge by which to negotiate with providers rather than as a binding offer; however, the state did not make known its intentions to negotiate *a priori* as in the Arizona programme (Brown *et al.*, 1985).

The results at the end of the first year (fiscal year 1982) were very impressive. Expenditures were $165 million below expected with 'little documented harm to beneficiaries' (Johns *et al.*, 1985a).   As of June 1983, 67 per cent of the state's hospitals had been awarded contracts and a large majority of them had agreed to rates below that which they had been paid the year before (Johns *et al.*, 1985a). The second year results were equally favourable with only 18 per cent of the original contracts awarded rate increases. Patient access has remained good throughout the programme and it has produced little dislocation of patients given that less than one out of six discharges in the year before contracting began were from hospitals that were not subsequently awarded a contract (Johns *et al.*, 1985b). The most recent evaluation of the programme confirms that, over the period 1982–6, selective contracting under Medi-Cal reduced the inflation rate for in-patient care. The results showed that selective contracting produced an overall savings of $836 million or 7.6 per cent of projected hospital expenditures without the introduction of selective contracting (Robinson and Phibbs, 1989). Yet, there are a number of caveats concerning generic problems of contracting which require consideration before suggesting that such results can be duplicated elsewhere.[3]

One of the reasons why California's programme was such a success has been attributed to the work of a special negotiator appointed by the state governor. Given wide latitude in deciding how the programme would work, the special negotiator showed solid resolve to achieve reform.   One account has it that he

[3] There were several instances of corruption and embezzlement in the 1970s stemming from contracts with HMOs to care for elderly recipients of Medicare, a universal public insurance programme for those over 65. Any time an organization deals with infirm or vulnerable elements of the population, the incentive to cheat on contract provisions is always present. As in other states, there are notable examples of reneging on the terms of a contract where the population served is infirm or unable to coalesce into an effective interest group.

was willing to 'walk away from the table with even the largest Medi-Cal provider in the State' (Johns *et al.*, 1987).

Large Medi-Cal hospitals did not believe the state would refuse to contract with them, but bids from three of the major Medi-Cal providers in San Francisco were initially rejected as too high. The rejection surprised the hospital community and generated a response: rejected hospitals sued the state, while hospitals in other areas of the state contacted [the negotiator's office] to lower their bids. (Bachman *et al.*, 1987)

Such resolve and leadership were not present in the Arizona AHCCCS programme which had a total of three directors in just the first year of operation (Bachman *et al.*, 1987).

Texas Purchased Health Services

Under the terms of the Texas Purchased Health Services (PHS) insurance programme, the Texas Department of Human Services makes a monthly premium payment to a private insurance underwriter designated for each Medicaid beneficiary. The contractor then assumes full financial risk for all covered Medicaid claims. Initially, any amount left over at the end of the year was channelled back into a Medicaid reserve designed to be used against future claims. Thus, there was no incentive for contractors to minimize costs beyond breaking even for a given year. This reserve was eliminated in 1983 when a new contract was awarded which stipulated an arrangement where the State and the contractor would share some of the risk and the returns from containing costs (Feldman and Gerteis, 1987). These new provisions allowed the insurer to gain or lose 15 per cent of the difference between claims and premiums provided that the total difference did not exceed 9 per cent of the latter. Under this arrangement, the contractor's liability is subject to a limit of ± 1.35 per cent (i.e. 15 per cent of 9 per cent) of premiums received. As a result of this risk-sharing plan, the premiums paid by the state no longer reflect an added charge for the full risk incurred by the contractor and thus are substantially lower than before (Feldman and Gerteis, 1987).

The results of the Texas programme are also mixed. On the one hand, there were political benefits from having a programme which incorporates the private sector to manage expenses. There is a popular belief among most Americans that the private sector is more efficient than the government in administering programmes and should therefore have lower overheads. In the health care sector and, in particular, regarding the Texas programme, this belief does not appear to be well grounded in factual information. Data gathered throughout the 1970s and early 1980s suggest that overheads have actually risen rather than fallen under the private contracting programme.

As the evidence in Table 9.1 shows, between 1973 and 1983 the administrative costs of the private arrangement grew by an average of 4.0 per cent annually

Table 9.1
PHS Administrative Overhead Charges Per Recipient Month, 1973–83
(1967 Constant Dollars)

Year	Contractor Overheads*	State Overheads (added premium to cover financial risk of contractor)	Total Overheads
1973	0.54	0.12	0.66
1974	0.47	0.06	0.53
1975	0.55	0.02	0.57
1976	0.57	0.02	0.59
1977**	0.55	0.24	0.79
1978	0.59	0.28	0.87
1979	0.56	0.28	0.84
1980	0.63	0.13	0.76
1981	0.65	0.32	0.97
1982	0.61	0.26	0.87
1983	0.71	0.27	0.98

Average annual % change (1973–83):

	+2.8%	+8.4%	+4.0%

Notes: * Includes utilization review costs incurred by the contractor between 1978 and 1983.

      ** There was a change of contractor in 1977 from Blue Cross/Blue Shield of Texas to National Heritage Insurance Company.

Sources: Texas Department of Human Resources, *Statistical Profile of the Texas Purchased Health Services Program, 1969–1980* .

       Penny H. Feldman and Margaret Gerteis, 'Private Insurance for Medicaid Recipients: The Texas Experience,' *Health Policy, Politics and Law*, **12**, 2, Summer 1987, pp. 271–98.

(data for the period after 1983 is not available). The more pertinent question, however, is how these administrative costs compare with those of states without privatized Medicaid programmes. Although exact comparisons are not possible due to different structures and programme aims, a general comparison between Texas and two other states—California and Michigan—has been made for the year 1982. In that year, both states had publicly run Medicaid programmes that reimbursed providers retrospectively Under these programmes, each state had total overheads for 1982 of $24–25 and $14–17 per Medicaid eligible respectively. These figures compare with total overheads of $35 per Medicaid eligible in the State of Texas which is more than twice as high as Michigan's overheads and 40 per cent higher than those of California (Feldman and Gerteis, 1987).

Not only was the Texas programme unable to contain administrative costs, but the total expenditures for care also rose, significantly outpacing the national average. In the period 1980–4, Medicaid acute and ambulatory expenditures per recipient rose from $429 to $680, going from below the national average of $464 in 1980 to above this average ($636) in 1984. While the US as a whole experienced a 8.2 per cent annual rise in expenditures, Texas's expenditures rose at a 12.2 per cent annual rate. This figure compares with only a 4.8 per cent and 5.5 per cent annual rise in California and Michigan respectively (US Department of Health and Human Services, 1980–1984)

The lesson learned from Texas is that perceptions do not always match reality. While some political benefit may be gained from supporting the widely held notion that the private sector is a source of fiscal austerity, the financial costs of such misconceptions are sometimes astounding. Only very mild cost-containment efforts were made by contractors partly because the terms of the contracts always left a large part of the financial risk with the State. Contractors were financially responsible for caring for people so long as expenses did not exceed some limit; so if they were over that limit, there was little incentive to reduce expenses. Any attempt to reduce expenses would be matched by a one-for-one reduction in State 'high-risk' funds down to the established limit.

In addition, changing contractors has not proved beneficial. Given start-up expenses and the general inability of the market to generate a true competitive spirit, a change of contract in 1977 produced no noticeable change in the upward spiral of costs. At best, the Texas experience suggests that there is no good evidence to support the contention that the private administration of a state programme is any more cost-effective than administration by a competent group of experienced public officials. In Texas, the programme served a widely diverse population in terms of both demographics and health status and had to contend with highly unpredictable costs given the availability of expensive technology to treat patients. Under these conditions, public sector management may have more flexibility and organizational capabilities than do private managers.

3. Rate Setting and Prospective Payment

The next big change experienced by the American health care system was a shift from retrospective to prospective payment for health care services. This shift happened in two steps: first, the reimbursement of hospitals was changed from a system tying reimbursements to cost-based charges to a prospective rate related to the illness category into which a patient fitted. Known as diagnosis-related groups (DRGs), the nearly five hundred categories serve as a framework for deciding how much to reimburse a hospital for a particular patient. Although initially applied only to the universal programme covering both elderly and disabled (Medicare), this system has been adopted by a variety of private payers in order to contain costs. Begun in 1983 and phased in over four years, this shift to prospective payment has been dramatic. The second change, legislated in late 1989, relates to the reimbursement of physicians under Medicare. Up to now, Medicare had traditionally agreed to pay physicians a fixed percentage of whatever charges were 'customary, prevailing, and reasonable' (CPR) in the market at any given time. In addition to a rapid escalation of fees across-the-board, this policy has led to an inequitable pattern of reimbursing physicians across specialties in which it was felt that primary care physicians were being under-reimbursed in comparison to some of the surgical specialties. To rectify this situation, Congress authorized the implementation of a relative value scale (RVS) which ties physician reimbursements to work effort, overheads, and malpractice insurance premiums. Like DRGs, RVS establishes a predetermined fee scale based on a series of weights which is determined centrally by the US Congress rather than in the market-place. However, while DRGs were designed to contain costs and increase efficiency, RVS was initially intended to be a budget neutral programme designed only to redistribute income amongst physicians; only later were cost-containment provisions added. The key point to remember with both systems is that rates are set centrally based upon analyses of cost data rather than through negotiation with individual hospitals or physicians. There was some concern that centrally establishing payments might undermine competition; however, the exact opposite has occurred. DRGs have encouraged hospitals to re-examine their uses of resources in order to improve efficiency, and while the physician payment reforms have only just been implemented, similar effects should occur with regard to physician services. Thus, although it appears to be an oxymoron, the notion of centralized pricing with local or institutional competition has had some success in changing economic incentives.

Both DRGs and RVS were a response to structural weaknesses in the original design of the Medicare programme. The payments systems were constructed so as to appease various interest groups; therefore, the programme was originally structured only to be a fiscal intermediary paying whatever was charged with minimal government interference. It was a self-fulfilling prophecy: the higher the charges in one period, the higher the costs in the next period. The result is illustrated in Table 9.1.

As illustrated, costs rose from about four billion dollars in 1967 to $58.9 billion in 1983 or, in constant 1983 dollars, from $14.2 to $58.9 billion—a four-fold increase in just 15 years.[4] The rate of increase was low at first, but started to grow

[4] Real monetary figures calculated using the Medical Care Price Index published in the CPI Detailed Report, Bureau of Labor Statistics, US Department of Commerce.

Table 9.1
Medicare Programme Expenditures 1967–83 (in millions of dollars)

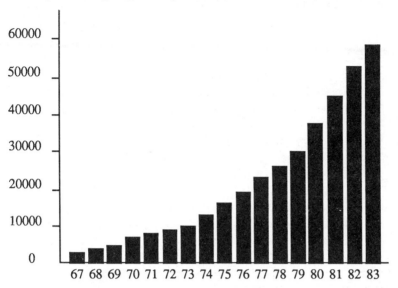

Sources: US Bureau of the Census, *Statistical Abstract of the United States*,
(110th and 102nd Editions), 1989 and 1981;
HCFA (1983), *The Medicare and Medicaid Data Book, 1983*, Tables
2.10 and 2.11, Washington DC.

exponentially, beginning in 1974 when the Nixon administration lifted wage-price controls on medical services which had been in effect for the past two years. Such actions may have precipitated the spiral upward in expenditures shown in the chart.

(a) *The Structure and Impact of Prospective Payment*

In response to concern over this escalation in costs, the federal government legislated strict limits on Medicare's reimbursements to hospitals beginning in 1982. These limits were only a temporary measure to allow for the development of permanent payment reform which was implemented beginning in October, 1983. This new system established prospective reimbursement rates for 467 diagnosis-related groups. These new prospective rates were developed from the historical costs associated with treating each condition with adjustments made for location of the hospital (urban or rural), wage level in a particular market, the level of teaching activity in a particular hospital, and, recently, for disproportionate shares of low-income patients. The DRG system used by Medicare classifies patients according to the patient's principal diagnosis, the principal surgical

Table 9.2
Selected Diagnosis-Related Groups

DRG number	Title	Fiscal 1988 Weight
10	Nervous system neoplasms with complications or comorbidities	1.2123
11	Nervous system neoplasms without complications or comorbidities	0.7729
106	Coronary bypass with cardiac catheterization	5.5415
107	Coronary bypass without cardiac catheterization	4.2858
127	Heart failure and shock	1.0222
176	Complicated peptic ulcer	0.9964
236	Fractures of hip and pelvis	0.9036
317	Admit for renal dialysis	0.3542

Source: Prospective Payment Assessment Commission (1988), *Adjustments to the Medicare Prospective Payment System: Report to the Congress*, Appendix C, Washington, November 1987.

Table 9.3
DRG Payments for a Fractured Femur at a Non-teaching Hospital with less than 15% Low-income Patients (Fiscal Year 1988)

Hospital location	DRG payment ($)
New York City	4,622
Chicago	4,099
Los Angeles	4,447
Baltimore	3,812
Bangor, Maine	3,442
Kokomo, Indiana	3,565
Ocala, Florida	3,242
Midland, Texas	3,904
Rural Alabama	2,504
Rural California	3,380

Source: Adapted from Table 2-2 in Louise Russell (1989), *Medicare's Prospective Payment System: Is it Working?* , Washington: The Brookings Institution.

procedure if one was performed, complications or comorbidities, and the conditions of discharge (e.g. discharge to skilled nursing facility) (ProPAC, 1985). Originally, advanced age (over 70 years) was used in several disease categories but was later dropped after research showed that complications were a more accurate determinant of extra costs (Chesney and Fleming, 1988). In addition, the system was to be phased in over four years so that, in the first year, only 25 per cent of charges would be paid prospectively, with 25 per cent increments every year thereafter until 100 per cent of payments were made prospectively. Progress was somewhat slower than planned, and, therefore, the system was not fully implemented until late 1987.

A sample of DRGs is included in Table 9.2 above, along with their assigned weights which reflect costs relative to the average Medicare in-patient.

Using this system of weights and adjustments for secondary factors, the following is an example of how a hospital payment was determined in 1983. In that year, the payment was a mixture of 75 per cent of the hospital specific rate (i.e. cost-based reimbursement) added to 25 per cent of the regional DRG rate. If the hospital specific rate = \$3,171 and the regional DRG rate = \$2,981.03 (region 1, urban) and the weighting factor for DRG 104 (cardiac valve procedure with pump and with cardiac catheter) = 6.8527 then the payment to the hospital will be calculated as follows (AMA, 1983):

$$(0.75 \times \$3,171) + (0.25 \times \$2,981.03) = \$3,123.51$$

then multiplying this by the weighting factor gives:

$$\$3,123.51 \times 6.8527 = \$21,404.48 = \text{hospital payment for this procedure.}$$

In order to get a sense of how these rates vary, Table 9.3 lists the DRG payment for a fractured femur at different locations throughout the United States.

Added to the deductibles (cost of one day in the hospital) and co-payments paid by beneficiaries, these rates were designed to meet the full costs of caring for a patient and were to be considered payment in full. Any extra savings hospitals could keep as profit while any losses would have to be absorbed by their budgets. With regard to this system of gains and losses the Congress had three goals (Russell, 1989):

(1)   First, and foremost, there was a desire to place government expenditures for this programme under controls which would limit their growth and make them more predictable from one year to the next. Given that in-patient expenditures account for approximately 70 per cent of total programme outlays, such a system could have a major impact on costs (Russell, 1989).

(2)   Next, Congress wanted to develop a mechanism for making hospitals more efficient. Given that it was widely believed that hospitals had become lackadaisical under the old payment system, many legislators felt that the same services might be produced more cheaply if hospitals were given the proper incentives to be innovative. It was hoped that a prospective payment system would provide the proper incentives.

(3)   Lastly, there was concern over maintaining quality standards. Given that there was the distinct possibility that hospitals might attempt to deny beneficial services to patients in order to reduce costs, Congress added a provision in the DRG legislation which led to the development of peer review organizations (PROs) to monitor quality. With the use of these monitoring organizations, it was hoped that hospitals would be more likely closely to examine any decision to forgo medical services.

The results of DRGs have generally been positive. First and foremost, they have been successful at controlling in-patient expenditures of Medicare beneficiaries. Comparing costs in 1980 dollars, outlays by Medicare's Hospital Insurance Trust Fund are now projected to be approximately $12 billion less in 1990 than was projected in 1984. At the expected price level in 1990, this figure translates to $18 billion dollars in savings from a projected outlay of 88.6 billion for that year alone (Russell and Manning, 1989). However, there is strong evidence that some physicians have circumvented the controls of the DRG system by doing surgery on an out-patient rather than in-patient basis (Fisher, 1987, 1988). Russell hypothesizes that the incentive for this switch came not from prospective payment but rather from the system's PROs which heavily scrutinized hospital admissions (Russell, 1989). Nevertheless, even with an increase in out-patient services, the net savings from the DRG system are expected still to amount to about 17 billion (1990 dollars) in the year 1990 (Russell, 1989).

Some private payers feared that the savings of the DRG system would come at their expense through a cost shift directed at them. The evidence suggests that this fear was unwarranted in the short run, and in fact, the system probably helped to reduce rather than increase their expenditures. Examining data on Blue Cross/ Blue Shield Plans[5] throughout the United States, Scheffler, Gibbs, and Gurnick found that prospective payment produced a decline in admissions beyond what would be expected, controlling for existing trends and other internal cost-containment programmes (Scheffler et al., 1988). This result was reinforced by another study examining total hospital revenues (Medicare and non-Medicare) which concluded that hospital revenues per patient were significantly reduced

---

[5] Blue Cross/Blue Shield Plans are private, non-profit insurers that cover about 30 per cent of the US population.

under prospective payment suggesting that savings achieved by prospective payment were not offset by higher charges for private payers (Sloan *et al.*, 1988). Given that Medicare provides hospitals with about 40 per cent of their revenues, it appears that DRGs have created a a standard for acceptable charges which has been universally adopted (Waldo *et al.*, 1986). Nevertheless, it is possible that the gradual phase-in period merely postponed cost-shifting until the last few years. In addition to limitations on the percentage of costs reimbursed based upon DRGs, this early period included very generous reimbursements which raised hospital profit margins in 1984 to record levels for most hospitals (Guterman *et. al.*, 1988). Since then, Congress has 'further tightened the bolts', reducing these margins and increasing the incentive to shift costs. However, private payers have also strengthened their cost-containment programmes making it more difficult to do so. Research on recently collected data should provide some answers as to whether cost-shifting among public and private payers will be of concern in the future.

Regarding the goals of efficiency, the DRG system has reduced admissions and in-patient length of stay which has produced excess capacity. Even though hospitals could have increased their revenues by continuing a trend of increased admission rates, it appears that the surveillance provided by the PROs helped reduce hospital admissions. Decreasing from 392 to 381 admissions per 1,000 Medicare beneficiaries in just the first year of prospective payment, the results on admissions were also mirrored by declines in average length of stay (9.7 days in 1983 to 8.8 days in 1988) and decreases in ancillary medical tests and procedures (admissions data: Bureau of the Census, 1984, 1985; length of stay: DesHarnais *et al.*, 1987a; Sloan, unpublished). Some suggest that the success of the PROs was assisted by technological innovations, such as new cataract surgeries, that permitted increased surgery on an out-patient basis. In any event, PROs hastened this transition by mandating pre-admission review once the new procedure was available (Ruther and Black, 1987; DesHarnais *et al.*, 1987b) Also, PROs had an incentive to be successful because of their relationship to the federal government. Unlike predecessor review organizations which were publicly run, PROs were privately run through contracts won under competitive bid to perform certain services; therefore, they had financial incentives to achieve results in order to renew their contracts.

On the issue of quality the PROs claim that quality has been maintained during prospective payment; nevertheless, problems with comparative data have produced disagreement within the research community. One study commissioned by the federal government found that 6.6 per cent of the Medicare patients examined between October 1984 and March 1985 received substandard care while the PROs only reported a figure of 0.8 per cent (Office of the Inspector General, 1989; Health Data Institute, 1987). Often it is unclear which services are responsible for producing which outcomes; therefore, more work on medical outcomes is required before making definitive assessments of the effects of DRGs on quality of care received.

One of the major lessons learned from the US experience with DRGs is that rate-setting has actually helped to make the hospital market-place more competitive. With in-patient occupancy rates declining from 75 per cent to 65 per cent since the advent of prospective payment, hospitals are engaging in more aggressive behaviour to attract patients in order to generate revenue (Melnick and Zwanziger, 1988). By constraining the amount of health dollars available, DRGs have created a market-place that emulates a zero-sum game: one hospital's gain is another's loss. Therefore, hospitals are scrambling to keep their share of the market.

Even so, total health care costs have continued to rise. For-profit hospitals, sensing that profits were greater elsewhere, moved out of the acute-care market largely controlled by the DRG system and into psychiatric hospitals and other areas reimbursed under the older retrospective cost system (Dorwart and Schlesinger, 1988). It is these areas as well as the pharmaceutical market which have experienced escalating costs which have offset the savings created by DRGs. The White Paper reforms might experience similar results. Whether a hospital is a self-governing NHS hospital or a private one, their structures would be designed to maximize net reserves. Greater choice of provider and hospital control over which services to provide gives an incentive for large amounts of resources to shift to where cost-containment policies are weakest. As the private sector in Great Britain grows, the position of the NHS *vis-à-vis* the privates will be significantly weaker in the future suggesting that opportunities outside of the public sector will grow. The US experience suggests that private insurers in Great Britain may not initially experience cost shifting if the NHS sets rates at a level which allows hospitals to generate adequate net revenues. The concern is not with services partially controlled by rate setting, but rather with those areas without established controls. Joan Higgins has expressed concern in this area speculating that American hospital corporations see large profits in the British market-place partly because of a lack of regulations governing the private sector (Higgins, 1988). Therefore, if the United Kingdom expects to increase the availability of services without causing an explosion in health care expenditures, they should seriously consider cost-control policies that apply to all sectors of the health care system. The US experience with 'squeezing one end of the balloon only to find the other end puffed out' should be avoided. In order to be successful, cost-containment strategies need to apply to the whole health care system.

The Physician Side: Relative Value Scale (RVS)

One of the areas in which rate regulation is now being extended is physician services. Unlike DRGs, the major purpose of the relative value scale is to tie reimbursements more directly to the value of services provided. But there are cost-containment provisions built into the system. First, there is a target for physician expenditures as a whole; if physicians go over this target, then next year's fees are adjusted downwards to recoup the previous year's losses. On the other hand, if the target is not broached then physicians will receive higher reimbursements in the following fiscal year. Second, there is a limitation placed on balance billing which prevents physicians from circumventing the fee schedule by having patients pay more out-of-pocket. Beginning in 1991, physicians will be only able to charge 125 per cent of the RVS fee. Thereafter, this figure will decline to 120 per cent in 1992 and 115 per cent in 1993. The effect of both this limitation and the cap should be to control escalation in physician fees and to enforce close compliance with the fee schedule (Physician Payment Review Commission, 1989)

The RVS is made up of three components (Physician Payment Review Commission, 1989):

- a 'physician work' component that is to reflect the time and intensity involved in providing a service;

- a 'practice expense' (or overhead) component that excludes the cost of professional liability premiums;

- a 'malpractice component' reflecting professional liability premium expenses.

Each of these three components is then assigned a weight associated with each specialty which is multiplied by a universal average, and then adjustments are made for geographic differences.

The programme, to be phased in over five years beginning in 1992, has just been legislated. Studies investigating this system will probably not be available until the late 1990s. It is only possible, therefore, to speculate about its future success. At this time, such a problem does not confront the NHS; however, the White Paper reforms do introduce fee-for-service payments for selected under-produced services (e.g. children's diseases). An RVS system may also be of some value in calculating a capitation rate and setting independent practice budgets.

3. Alternative Delivery Systems

On the whole, American alternative delivery systems were designed to control both expenditure and utilization more effectively than traditional provision of care. Whereas previously the functions of caring for patients and financing their care were placed under separate organizations, these new alternative structures were set up so that these functions would be combined. These alternative organi-

zations as well as physicians working for them would collectively bear some of
the financial risk of providing services. The main idea was that if these
organizations were faced with funding care out of some fixed budget under their
control, then they would be forced to weigh the costs against the benefits of
performing any particular procedure. In order more effectively to control utilization and expenditures, many of these alternative systems emphasize limiting
a patient's choice of physician to those who share the view of the organization
about how services should be provided. Yet, many also emphasize providing
good quality care so as to minimize durations of illness and associated expenditures. In encouraging the development of these alternative systems, the US government expected that they would have incentives to provide good quality care
at the least possible cost.

(a) Health Maintenance Organizations

As a structure, Health Maintenance Organizations (HMOs) have proliferated
rapidly with enrolment in such organizations growing from 7.1 million in 1980
to 32.5 million in 1989, a 357 per cent increase (Interstudy, 1989). Many
employers providing health insurance benefits have found the incentive structure of HMOs appealing and have hoped that they would help to control the rise
in employee health insurance premiums. Instead of paying premiums to an
insurer who retrospectively finances whatever care is chosen, employers pay a
premium to the HMO which serves as a capitated budget to care for a particular
employee. As in the NHS proposal for self-governing hospital trusts, these
capitated budgets are supposed to encourage efficiency in providing care. As a
result, many large corporations have offered employees incentives to switch
from indemnity insurance to alternative coverage like HMOs. An ever increasing number of corporations are now assuming the risk of insuring employees
themselves by contracting directly with HMOs rather than through insurance
companies. Moreover, corporations are banding together to form health care
coalitions designed to lobby for legislation which will facilitate cost containment. All of these trends have encouraged the development of alternative delivery systems; however, the main question is whether they have accomplished the
goals for which they were designed. Before addressing that question, a brief
explanation of the development of HMOs and their structure may prove useful.

The history of HMOs goes back to 1965. In that year, Paul Ellwood, a
physician and executive director of the American Rehabilitation Foundation,
noticed a basic paradox in the practice of rehabilitative medicine. As a programme succeeded in improving the quality of its care, occupancy and utilization rates began to fall, lowering revenues needed to cover costs. Improved care
meant placing a patient on a therapy regimen best suited to the particular case,
which often was best handled on an out-patient basis. Such a situation was

currently being faced by the Sister Kenney Institute Rehabilitation Hospital, a facility under the auspices of Ellwood's organization. Dr Ellwood observed that this practice was at odds with the prevailing insurance policies which only allowed reimbursement for care provided as an in-patient. Ultimately, neither the patient nor the hospital would be able to afford a better quality programme at a lower overall cost. Ellwood's attempts to continue the progress in rehabilitative medicine without leading hospitals towards bankruptcy led him to question the way in which medical care was financed in general and to propose a new idea—the health maintenance organization (HMO) (Falkson, 1980).

By 1969 the federal government was willing to listen. Health care costs were skyrocketing, going from 5.9 per cent of GNP in 1965 to 6.7 per cent by 1969 (Klarman, 1977). The Nixon administration was searching for a new national health policy to control this rise, and the HMO concept, presented by Ellwood at a meeting with officials of the Public Health Service, provided the foundation (Falkson, 1980). The Nixon administration became committed to this programme, and by 1973 the President signed the first of several acts that set standards and provided money to help HMOs get started.

With health care costs in 1990 projected to be $647.3 billion representing approximately 11.5 per cent of GNP, the need for organizational structures with incentives to reduce costs is ever more pressing (HIAA, 1989) By virtue of their organizational structure designed to minimize overall costs, HMOs are a possible solution to this problem. The national growth in HMO membership has almost quintupled in just a decade and the latest figures indicate that about 20 per cent of those with private insurance were covered by HMOs and this number is continuing to rise quickly (Interstudy, 1989).

An HMO is structured around the following elements (Luft, 1981):

(1)   The organization assumes contractual responsibility to provide a set of health services which includes both ambulatory and in-patient hospital care.

(2)   The organization serves a population defined by its enrolment.

(3)   Subscriber enrolment is voluntary. This implies that the organization is under competition to meet its subscribers' demands for services.

(4)   Subscribers pay a fixed monthly or annual fee independent of the use of services (this does not exclude minor charges related to utilization).

(5)   The organization assumes at least part of the financial risk in the provision of services.

(6)   Case managers are often assigned to control the flow of patients and the utilization of resources.

Three important areas that are not covered in the definition which are important in determining the cost structure are:

(1)   the manner in which physicians are paid (either fee-for-service, capitation, or fixed salary, and the payment of performance-related bonuses);

(2)   how physicians provide services (either in a single group connected with one facility, or in a loosely defined group with each physician providing his/her own facility);

(3)   the limits on physician autonomy especially regarding the use of resources.

The result is that many different types of organizational structures are possible within the confines of the definition. Four major types have emerged. They are staff HMOs, pre-paid group practices (PGPs), individual practice associations (IPAs), and networks. The following is a brief explanation of the workings of each type (Fox and Heinen, 1987):

•   Staff HMOs
      Under this arrangement, physicians are salaried employees responsible for providing most out-patient services at the HMO's health care centres. These are closed-panel systems that have fixed staffs and tight controls on utilization of outside services.

•   Pre-paid group practice
      With this structure, a multi-specialty group practice contracts with the HMO for a fixed capitated fee. Physicians assume the financial risk for caring for patients including any charges for outside referrals. Any savings are retained by the individual physicians or specialty group.

•   Independent practice associations
      This type of HMO consists of an open panel of private physicians or single-specialty groups who are usually reimbursed on a fee-for-service basis. Only requiring that physicians affiliate themselves with the HMO rather than limit their practices solely to the HMOs practices, these organizations have managed to attract large panels of physicians.

•   Networks
      Networks closely resemble pre-paid group practices except that they contract with more than one multi-specialty group. Physicians receive capitated payments for both hospital and physician services rendered or they increasingly share financial risk with the HMO. Under this model, physicians generally continue to treat fee-for-service patients as well as HMO patients.

With regard to the performance of HMOs, there have been numerous studies regarding the efficiency and costs associated with such organizations. They generally agree on a limited number of points. First, HMOs tend to have lower hospital utilization rates than more traditional insurance plans (in the range of 25–40 per cent lower) (Goldberg and Greenberg, 1980; Manning and Leibowitz, 1984; McLaughlin, 1987). Second, closed-panel models of HMOs have been better able to control in-patient use and other expenses than open-panel models like independent practice associations (Luft, 1985). However, these lessons can not be translated to mean that HMOs are more productively efficient[6] than current arrangements or are able to procure lower prices for services. Recent studies seem to indicate that rather than engaging in classical cost-containing competition based upon price, newly created HMOs are engaging in cost-increasing rivalry (McLaughlin, 1988b). Promoting actual or perceived product differentiation, some HMOs are wooing new members with amenities rather than better care. Results from two studies concluding that HMOs had lower in-patient utilization than fee-for-service plans could find no correlation between HMO growth and in-patient expenses *per capita* (Hay and Leahy, 1984). McLaughlin suggests that this provides indirect evidence that prices are not lower in markets with HMOs (McLaughlin, 1988b). Nevertheless, there is evidence suggesting that in some markets where multiple HMOs are competing, like in Minneapolis, Minnesota, HMOs do compete on the basis of price (Feldman *et al.*, 1989). But at this point, there are very few markets which are this developed competitively.

The evidence on HMOs and cost containment is incomplete. In analyzing the effects of different policy changes on hospital expenses, Hadley and Swartz found that an increase in HMO enrolment from 4.0 per cent to 7.1 per cent of the population between 1980 and 1984 reduced hospital expenses by only 0.9 per cent in comparison to a 12.5 per cent reduction due to prospective payment (Hadley and Swartz, 1989). However, this result may reflect that HMOs still had not enrolled a large proportion of the population in those years and that they tend to attract people who are younger and healthier than average (Hellinger, 1987). More studies on recent data need to be conducted before any definitive conclusions can be reached on this matter.

With regard specifically to the British system, Allain Enthoven has explored the possibility of incorporating HMO-like structures into the NHS. Favouring a plan creating actively competing health districts, he proposes that each district be permitted to purchase and sell medical services to other districts (Rayner, 1988). By emphasizing the comparative advantages of each district, only the comparatively efficient services will be provided in each district. Duplicated services will be removed and more services for the same cost will be produced.

---

[6] Productive efficiency is achieved when the costs of producing a given level of care is minimized.

One problem with this approach is that inevitably certain services and certain patients will be favoured over others. Those services with relatively predictable costs and patients who are relatively healthy will be favoured across-the-board. This concern over selection bias is a serious limitation of this approach (Scheffler, 1989). Although most health districts contain enough residents to absorb the impact of adverse selection, there will still be incentives to avoid this problem by restricting the supply of those procedures utilized by high-cost patients. There may also be incentives to compete for healthy patients in other districts as well.

In addition, setting up competing health districts brings up a problem of local natural monopolies. While the plan of competing DHAs works in large urban centres like London or Manchester where districts are relatively small and competing services are geographically close to one another, the same is not true of more rural areas. Large numbers of people have only one source of a particular medical service (e.g, specialized cardiac care) within a reasonable distance from their home. If a competitive system were established, that sole source could set monopoly prices for services rendered. Under such a system, some rural districts might be forced to pay more for the same level of services. It is always important to ensure that there are enough parties to allow competitive forces to connect; otherwise, regulation might be a better solution to existing distributional problems.

A lesson for the United Kingdom is that HMOs may be more productively efficient in theory. However, their efficiency varies in actual practice. HMOs still do not cover large proportions of the population in most areas of the United States and often there are only one or two HMOs from which to choose. These are not the conditions under which price competition will thrive under the HMO model. In comparison to HMOs which have administrative overheads of between 12.6 per cent and 25.8 per cent of total revenues, the Family Practitioner Committees currently serving the United Kingdom have average overheads of only 2 per cent (Rayner, 1988). Consequently, the United Kingdom should be cautious about adopting an HMO model either through competing self-governing hospital trusts or DHAs. American experience with such a system suggests that its potential for greater allocative and productive efficiency may only be realized where there are several competing units providing a large percentage of the region's care. To date, few areas in the United States have met such preconditions. If the United Kingdom does decide to adopt such a model, it should consider only instituting it in certain areas of the country where the potential for competition can reasonably be met. The NHS should then expect greater short-term expenses until competition has established itself.

(b) *Preferred Provider Organizations*

Preferred provider organizations (PPOs) are another alternative delivery system that has grown during the 1980s. Increasing from 1.3 million people eligible to use such services in 1984 to 17 million in 1989, such organizations have become a viable alternative for many people seeking coverage (AAPPO, 1989). Currently, over 11 per cent of employees are in PPOs mostly concentrated in the western United States (Rice *et al.*, 1989) PPOs can be sponsored through insurance companies or by an employer, with the former being the prevalent form. Like HMOs, PPOs are structured to contain costs by encouraging efficiency. Their main strategy is to use financial incentives to direct people to the community's most cost-effective providers (hospitals and/or physicians). In PPOs, providers and payers agree to a contract in which providers agree to provide care for a discount in exchange for a guaranteed volume of patients.

To reimburse hospitals, 41 per cent of insurer-sponsored PPOs use *per diem* payment, and about the same percentage use discounted charges. Approximately one out of six pays hospitals on the basis of DRGs. For physician reimbursement, 57 per cent use a pre-established fee schedule. Other methods include charge formulas (21 per cent) and percentage discounts off usual charges (Gabel *et al.*, 1987). A typical PPO contracts for an average discount 16 per cent lower for hospital services and 12 per cent lower for physician services than other patients must pay (Gabel *et al.*, 1987). By using such negotiated contracts along with a strong utilization review programme, PPOs hope to reduce hospitalization and contain costs. However, unlike HMOs, the preferred provider organizations allow patients the choice of whether to use providers not contracted with the PPO. As long as they agree to pay more out-of-pocket in order to see another provider, patients are free to do so. Also unlike HMOs, physicians in PPOs generally do not face any financial risk from excessive use of specialist and hospital services.

Most successful at controlling costs have been large insurer-sponsored PPOs. Because of their size, they are able to employ sophisticated methods for selecting cost-effective providers which are unavailable to other smaller organizations. In one survey, while 86 per cent of PPO executives indicated that they analyzed cost data generated by either insurer claims, state-mandated hospital reports, and/or Medicare cost reports, fewer than half of PPOs sponsored by non-insurers claimed that they analyzed costs in selecting preferred hospitals (Gabel, 1986). On the physician side, PPOs have not been as stringent in selecting physicians, but insurer-sponsored PPOs have still been more stringent than their non-insurance sponsored counterparts with 41 per cent using cost data in contrast to less than 10 per cent for the other group (Gabel, 1986).

With large numbers of American hospitals experiencing excess capacity and an oversupply of physicians in the US, large insurance-sponsored PPOs hold relatively more power in the negotiating process. With larger numbers of potential bidders unable to generate sufficient business, it is relatively easy to negotiate significant discounts. Where the dynamic changes—as in Britain, where there is an undersupply of consultants—it may be relatively difficult for an organization like the District Health Authorities to negotiate discounts since these physicians already have sufficient business. On the other hand, general practitioners who are granted practice budgets might be able to negotiate effectively with hospitals to obtain discounts, especially if the practice is large, much like insurer-sponsored PPOs. With lower densities of physicians and hospitals relative to the US, British providers are in a stronger negotiating position *vis-à-vis* fiscal intermediaries. This should be acknowledged and policies should be designed to take advantage of this situation.

In terms of performance, PPOs have provided mild cost savings over conventional insurance plans while maintaining a high level of satisfaction with services provided. In a survey conducted in 1987 of 16,000 employers, it was found that, when controlling for levels of coverage, median costs of a PPO policy covering a family was lower than that for either a conventional indemnity plan or an HMO. In comparison to $226 per month—spring, 1987—for the conventional plan and $222 per month for the HMO, the same coverage available under a PPO cost just $209 (Rice *et al.*, 1989). Moreover, these figures do not show that PPO coverage, is on average, much more comprehensive than conventional plans. Thus, the real bargain of PPOs may be even greater than the cost savings suggests. Since the evidence also indicated that PPO beneficiaries were not significantly healthier than average, the surveyors postulate that PPOs do have a minor cost-savings potential (Rice *et al.*, 1989).

The preferred provider organization is the American organization which may be useful to those who will have to implement the proposed NHS reforms. Many of the mechanisms designed to improve availability of services are contractual arrangements similar in many respects to the type of contracts negotiated with PPOs. However, one must be careful in applying the analogy too closely; American PPOs were created to contain costs unlike the British proposals which are mainly designed to improve access to care. In other words, American PPOs were designed to improve productive efficiency—minimize cost of a given level of care—while the British are more concerned with improving technical efficiency—maximizing availability of care from a given set of resources. Therefore, all of the analysis of PPO performance based on the ability to contain costs may not be of interest to the United Kingdom where performance would have a different meaning.

4. Conclusion

In the 1980s, the US health care reforms designed to make greater use of market forces have not reduced the overall increase in health care costs. While the system has become more expensive during the past decade, the portion of uninsured Americans has increased from 30 million to over 37 million (Swartz,

1989). If such trends continue, the pressure for universal coverage will surely lead to further changes in the US system.

Our review of the experience with contracting out to the private sector and competitive bidding under the aegis of 'privatization' has produced mixed results. We do find examples in which efficiencies are achieved, but they seem to depend a lot on the proper implementation and administration of the contracting process. This element may be more important than the actual method of contracting used. Our experience suggests that, contrary to popular belief, good public management of health care programmes can be as efficient as private management.

Making hospitals sensitive to costs through the use of administered prices appears to promote efficiencies. PROs have demonstrated that health care institutions and providers can and will respond quickly to economic incentives. Patterns of resource allocations in hospitals can be altered dramatically by a system of prices whether they are competitively set or administered by the government. Hospital competition in the US functions with a system of administered prices (DRGs) and hospital contracts to private as well as other governmental (Medicaid) payers. The key lesson is that the switch from reimbursing hospitals based upon costs to pre-established prices is the source of most efficiency gains. Yet, experience suggests that economic pressures have led some hospitals to circumvent the regulatory controls of the DRG system somewhat by recoding patients into higher reimbursement categories. Such actions have tended to mitigate the cost-minimizing forces of fixed-price systems. But such problems do not warrant abandoning such a system. It is only recommended that future programmes of centrally-administered prices have better systems of monitoring payments and more clearly defined payment categories.

Competition between systems of delivery, such as HMOs and PPOs, is a useful idea to pursue. In the US, selection among a limited set of alternative systems by patients is seen as a method of stimulating competition. There is evidence that in heavily competitive areas, price competition between such organizations does exist. However, concerns over adverse selection in competitive systems should be clearly recognized. Unprofitable treatments and patients will be avoided by systems that compete on price alone. Adjustments for adverse selection are possible but are often difficult to administer. In addition, non-price competition has been observed in many American markets. For example, advertisements emphasize amenities rather than cost-effectiveness in order to attract more subscribers. And even if market research has shown that this maximizes returns on advertising dollars, it does not produce price competition and lower costs. The inability of most people to distinguish amenities from health care quality is the key source of trouble in these markets. If the British expect to adopt an HMO model for the DHAs and/or self-governing hospitals, they will need to overcome these information asymmetries—through regulation or professional standards of conduct—if they expect competition to produce quality care at minimum cost.

The structural weaknesses in some HMO and PPO markets have led to the development of large administrative bureaucracies. While new entrants into the market were intended as a catalyst for price competition, the proliferation of smaller systems has led to the growth of administrative bodies and duplication of services. As Lois Quam writes in this volume, 'Every programme duplicates the costs of premium collection, billing, actuarial rate-setting, and financial management [and] every health care facility must administer a billing and cost accounting apparatus to link each charge and service incurred to an individual patient'. Little attention was given to economies of scale in the rush to encourage new entrants, and each of these organizations followed the path of least resistance in trying to generate profits. As in the case of DRGs, these alternative delivery systems often found circumventing competitive forces easier than minimizing costs. Competing DHAs and hospitals could also experience the same results. The lesson is that instituting competition does not guarantee competitive outcomes unless 'the path of least resistance' and economic incentives lead organizations in this direction.

Lastly, the NHS should be wary of the tendency of providers to unify behind organizations designed to fight the emergence of competition. During the 1980s, American hospitals and physicians have formed interest groups designed to counter the bargaining power of HMOs. Some of these organizations have been sufficiently effective in preventing competition to warrant investigations by the US Department of Justice's antitrust division (Quam, this volume). However, producing an effective case against these organizations will be very difficult especially given the current *laissez-faire* attitude. The British should be aware that hospitals and providers may feel threatened by the advent of competition and may try to produce a counterforce to attempt to stop it.

The lessons learned must be viewed with caution. There are many differences between the United States and Great Britain which even transcend structural differences in their health care systems. Cultural differences in terms of respect for authority and general attitudes toward the proper function of the State can make great differences in terms of performance of different proposals. There is nevertheless a common thread across nations that allows learning from others' experiences. It is only hoped that the lessons of the competitive era in American health care will help the British Government design a competitive system that avoids these pitfalls.

10

A Mixed Economy of Health Care:
Britain's Health Service Sector in the Inter-war Period

ALASTAIR M. GRAY*

1. Introduction

Britain's health care arrangements before the advent of the National Health Service in 1948 have attracted little attention from economists. However, the publication of the 1989 White Paper 'Working for Patients' (HMSO, 1989) may heighten interest in inter-war health services, and for a number of reasons. First, some proponents of radical reform have claimed that pre-war health care had certain desirable features that were destroyed by the NHS and which should be re-introduced. Green (1985a, 1985b), for example, has claimed that inter-war competition in the supply of health care helped to contain prices, reduced the monopoly power of the medical profession, and stimulated innovation. Second, critics of the White Paper proposals have claimed that if implemented they would reproduce the failings of pre-war health care that the NHS was designed to rectify. Speaking in Parliament in April 1989, former Secretary of State for Social Services David Owen argued that the proposals would eventually create a two-tier system of mainly private health care for those who could afford it and a publicly funded lower quality health care safety net for those who could not: 'There is nothing new about such a system—it operated in this country in the 1920s and 1930s. It was rejected by the people when the National Health service was created in 1948, and many of us are determined that it should not be reintroduced through either the front or the back door' (Owen, 1989, col. 210).

Many of the reforms proposed in the 1989 White Paper do have clear echoes in the pre-NHS arrangements. In particular, the inter-war health services offered a mix of private and public involvement in both finance and delivery; many hospitals were of independent or self-governing status and relied for their

* Centre for Socio-Legal Studies, Wolfson College, Oxford. I would like to thank Peter Bartrip, Paul Fenn, Ali McGuire, and, especially, Charles Webster for helpful comments on an earlier draft of this paper, and Paul Weindling for an opportunity to present and discuss aspects of it at a graduate seminar at the Wellcome Institute for the History of Medicine, Oxford. I retain the usual liabilities.

continued existence on their ability to attract patients; a high proportion of the public remuneration of general practitioners was derived from capitation fees, with freedom of choice for patients between providers of primary care; a significant volume of services was funded through insurance schemes operated by competing agencies; the involvement of the voluntary and charitable sector in raising finance and providing services was encouraged; and an elaborate regulatory apparatus was developed.

It is unlikely that any organizational features of pre-NHS health care will or indeed could be replicated, and so reference to the past in order directly to inform policy debate is bound to be misleading. But it is possible that something can be learnt by looking at economic characteristics of this system which the NHS replaced, describing some of the difficulties—in terms of efficiency and equity—to which these characteristics gave rise, and considering some of the policy implications of these difficulties. The structure and trends of health care expenditure in the inter-war period are examined in section 2 of this paper. Section 3 considers the National Health Insurance scheme and section 4 the hospital sector, and some conclusions are drawn in section 5.

2. Inter-war Health Expenditure

Health services in the inter-war period were elaborately diverse in both funding and provision, and estimating expenditure on health care during this period carries risks of double-counting or omission. There are essentially four main components to any estimate: (1) the publicly funded system of hospital and other services, largely originating in the Poor Law workhouses but after 1929 increasingly in the hands of local authorities;(2) the voluntary hospitals, mainly dating from the late eighteenth century onwards but some much older, which had been raised on charitable and philanthropic foundations; (3) the compulsory National Health Insurance scheme, which had been introduced in 1911 to provide the working population with a limited range of sickness-related cash benefits, and with medical care from general practitioners; and (4) personal out-of-pocket expenditure on health care goods and services.

A variety of estimates of the relative importance of each of these components in relation to total health care expenditure towards the end of the interwar period are summarized in Table 10.1, and their broad consistency is reassuring. They indicate that the publicly funded hospital services accounted for around 30 per cent and the voluntary hospitals for approximately 12 per cent of total expenditure; another 10 per cent of total spending went on the National Health Insurance scheme; and most of the remainder—around 40 to 50 per cent—could be attributed to personal expenditure on doctors' and dentists' fees and on self-medication. Thus in comparison with the post-war period, out-of-pocket ex-

Table 10.1
The Funding of Pre-War Health Services in Britain

Service	Percentage of total expenditure			
	A	B	C	D
Local authority hospitals	16	10	12	
				} 19
Poor law hospitals	5	5	6	
Mental hospitals	9	9	10	10
Other local authority services	1	8	9	4
NHI doctors' fees	7	7	6	7
NHI medicines	3	2	4	2
Voluntary hospitals	13	10	13	12
Doctors' and dentists' fees	32	31	27	32
Self-medication	14	17	14	16
All sources (%)	100	100	100	100
Total expenditure (in £ millions)	140	149	140	126

Notes: A: Hilliard and McNae (1941), pp. 11–15.
             B: P.E.P. (1937), pp. 388–92.
             C: Medical Planning Research (1942).
             D: HMSO (1944), White Paper (Cmnd 6502), p. 53.
Source: Derived from Webster (1988), p. 13.

penses were high, the claims of doctors and dentists on total spending were high, and the proportion spent on hospitals was low.

Family budget surveys from the 1930s provide another way of examining expenditure on private medical services, and data from these are summarized in Table 10.2. Ignoring contributions to the public health services through taxation and rates, the table none the less shows that a significant proportion of total family expenditure was being committed to medical care: around 4 per cent amongst middle-class families, compared with around 3 per cent amongst working-class families. Analysis of these budget surveys by Prais and Houthakker (1955) provided expenditure elasticities for all budget items, and those relating to medical services are also presented in Table 10.2: these indicate that the proportion of household expenditure devoted to doctors' fees etc. showed a very high propensity to increase as income rose, and for the middle classes was equalled only by the propensity to increase expenditure on travel, leisure, and household furnishings.

Table 10.2

Household Expenditure on Medical Services, 1937–8

Household	Total average weekly expenditure (pence per person)	Average weekly medical expenditure (pence per person)	Of which (pence per person)				Medical expenditures as % of total household expenditure
			Fees to doctor, dentist, nurse, optician	Purchase of medicines, drugs, and midwife, etc.	Hospital funds and fees appliances	NHI contributions	
Middle-class, head of household earning (£ p.a.):							
250–350	228	8.4	5.5	1.8	1.0	0.1	3.7
350–500	256	11.0	8.1	1.8	0.9	0.1	4.3
500–700	320	12.5	8.9	2.1	1.4	0.1	3.9
700+	404	15.7	12.4	2.6	0.7	0.0	3.9
all	263	10.4	7.4	1.8	0.9	0.1	3.9
Agricultural working-class:	76	2.3	0.8	0.5	0.3	0.7	3.0
Industrial working-class:	114	3.1	1.2	0.7	0.4	0.9	2.7

Expenditure elasticities (and standard errors)

	Fees to doctor, dentist, nurse, optician, midwife	Purchase of medicines, drugs, and appliances	Hospital funds and contributions
Working-class	1.62 (0.17)	1.35 (0.09)	1.08 (0.09)
Middle-class	1.58 (0.18)	0.85 (0.07)	1.16 (0.15)

Note: NHI contributions calculated by multiplying standard weekly contribution in 1937 (4.5 pence) by the number of wage-earners in the household (for middle-class households wage-earners other than the head of the household) and dividing by average size of household.

Source: Middle-class data derived from Massey (1942), Tables VI, XIX, and XXII. Agricultural working-class data from Ministry of Labour (1941), pp. 7–9. Industrial working-class data from Ministry of Labour (1940), pp. 300–5. Expenditure elasticities from Prais and Houthakker (1955), Table 20, pp. 106–7.

In absolute amounts, expenditure per person on medical services amongst middle-class families was roughly three to four times that in working-class families. Middle-class wage-earners were generally above the earnings limit for membership of the NHI scheme, and the bulk of family medical expenditure was incurred on fees to health professionals. Such fees were also the largest single item of health care expenditure amongst working-class families.

What is known of the trend of total health expenditure in the inter-war period, and its relation to gross national product? An estimate can be made by combining separate series on private and public spending. Table 10.3, adapted from Peacock and Wiseman's work on UK public expenditure, shows that between 1920 and 1938 local and central government expenditure on health services more than doubled in current prices whilst social service expenditure as a whole expanded by less than half that amount and total public expenditure in current prices was for most of the period falling or static. In relation to GNP, public expenditure on health care expanded steadily from 0.8 per cent in 1920 to 1.6 per cent by 1930, reached 1.9 per cent by 1932 as nominal GNP contracted sharply, but by 1938 retained a 1.9 per cent share despite the recovery in GNP from 1932 onwards.

Information on the trend of private health care expenditure is presented in Table 10.4. This indicates that in current prices expenditure rose by around one-third from £57 million in 1920 to over £75 million by 1938, and that health expenditure took a constantly rising share of total consumer expenditure. In relation to GNP, private health care expenditure rose from 0.93 per cent in 1920 to a peak of almost 1.5 per cent by 1932, and thereafter remained fairly level.

Private and public health care expenditures are combined in Table 10.5, which shows that the proportion of GNP devoted to health services approximately doubled in less than 20 years, to reach 3.3 per cent by 1938. The shares of private and public expenditure in the total were fairly even, but with a drift towards the public sector over time. As Figure 10.1 makes clear, most of the expansion took place in the period 1920–32, after which health expenditure's share of GNP reached a plateau, but with signs towards the late 1930s of an upward trend reasserting itself.

Some features of this expansion are discussed in more detail below, but it should be noted that rising relative prices and an increasing quantity of services both played a part. The price index for private health expenditure (Figure 10.2), taken from Stone and Rowe (1966), remained consistently and substantially above the index for all goods and services throughout the period. There is at present no reliable price deflator for public health expenditure: the deflator used by Peacock and Wiseman for public health expenditure—like their deflator for government current expenditure in total—was simply the index for all goods and services shown in Figure 10.2. Quantity changes in public and private health services are discussed in more detail below, but the trend is revealed in a wide

Table 10.3
Inter-war UK Public Expenditure Trends

Year	Government expenditure in current prices on:			GNP	Index, 1920=100			Shares of GNP		
	Health	All social services	Total all programmes		Health	All social services	Total all programmes	Health	All social services	Total all programmes
1920	48.8	411.8	1,592.1	6,070	100	100	100	0.8	6.8	26.2
1921	55.8	490.7	1,429.5	4,860	114	119	90	1.1	10.1	29.4
1922	54.1	423.2	1,177.3	4,230	111	103	74	1.3	10.0	27.8
1923	52.2	358.7	1,025.2	4,230	107	87	64	1.2	8.5	24.2
1924	54.0	365.0	1,027.0	4,332	111	89	65	1.2	8.4	23.7
1925	56.7	389.3	1,071.9	4,435	116	95	67	1.3	8.8	24.2
1926	62.4	424.4	1,106.3	4,303	128	103	69	1.5	9.9	25.7
1927	67.1	436.0	1,105.8	4,594	138	106	69	1.5	9.5	24.1
1928	66.4	434.3	1,094.7	4,523	136	105	69	1.5	9.6	24.2
1929	69.0	438.0	1,107.2	4,628	141	106	70	1.5	9.5	23.9
1930	71.9	484.7	1,144.8	4,386	147	118	72	1.6	11.1	26.1
1931	74.3	516.8	1,173.5	4,074	152	125	74	1.8	12.7	28.8
1932	64.5	511.1	1,138.0	3,973	153	124	71	1.9	12.9	28.6
1933	75.2	497.2	1,066.0	4,141	154	121	67	1.8	12.0	25.7
1934	75.7	498.3	1,060.9	4,326	155	121	67	1.7	11.5	24.5
1935	78.8	519.2	1,117.4	4,587	161	126	70	1.7	11.3	24.4
1936	83.3	532.7	1,186.8	4,804	171	129	75	1.7	11.1	24.7
1937	90.1	554.5	1,303.5	5,064	185	135	82	1.8	10.9	25.7
1938	98.9	596.3	1,587.0	5,294	203	145	100	1.9	11.3	30.0

Source: Adapted from Peacock and Wiseman (1967), Tables 10, A-2, A-5.

Table 10.4
Inter-war UK Private Expenditure Trends

Year	Personal expenditure on health services (current prices: £m)	Total UK consumer expenditure (current prices: £m)	% of total consumer expenditure on health	GNP (current prices: £m)	Personal expenditure on health services (% of GNP)
1920	56.6	5,087.2	1.11	6,070	0.93
1921	53.3	4,393.8	1.21	4,860	1.10
1922	52.2	3,905.7	1.34	4,230	1.23
1923	51.6	3,771.3	1.37	4,230	1.22
1924	51.5	3,845.9	1.34	4,332	1.19
1925	52.5	3,939.4	1.33	4,435	1.18
1926	53.2	3,892.1	1.37	4,303	1.24
1927	52.2	3,946.8	1.32	4,594	1.14
1928	53.8	4,000.4	1.34	4,523	1.19
1929	54.9	4,042.9	1.36	4,628	1.19
1930	54.8	3,989.7	1.37	4,386	1.25
1931	56.3	3,859.8	1.46	4,074	1.38
1932	58.4	3,744.6	1.56	3,973	1.47
1933	60.6	3,752.9	1.61	4,141	1.46
1934	61.7	3,861.7	1.60	4,326	1.43
1935	65.1	3,994.5	1.63	4,587	1.42
1936	68.1	4,141.2	1.64	4,804	1.42
1937	71.9	4,345.5	1.65	5,064	1.42
1938	75.3	4,456.7	1.69	5,294	1.42

Source: Derived from Stone and Rowe (1966), Table 21, minus hairdressing expenditure, and Table 45. GNP from Peacock and Wiseman (1967), Table A-2.

range of summary statistics: the number of doctors and dentists rose in the private sector by 38 per cent between 1920 and 1938, and in the public sector by 37 per cent (Stone and Rowe, 1966, p. 49); the number of hospital beds rose in the private sector by 54 per cent between 1921 and 1938, in the public sector by 2 per cent, and in total by 17 per cent (Pinker, 1966, Tables 1 and 4); data on nursing numbers are more scrappy, but it appears that the number of paid nurses in voluntary hospitals increased three-fold between 1901 and 1938, and in public hospitals increased eight-fold (as public sector bed numbers remained virtually static, this represented a substantial improvement in staff–bed ratios); between 1933 and 1937 alone there was an increase of over 13 per cent in total hospital nurses: 12 per cent in the voluntaries, 18 per cent in the municipal hospitals, and 6 per cent in the mental hospitals (Abel-Smith, 1960, pp. 120–1, 270).

Table 10.5
Inter-war UK Health Expenditure as a Percentage of GNP

Year	Expenditure on health services (% of GNP)			Private/public mix (% of total)	
	Personal	Public	Total	Private	Public
1920	0.93	0.80	1.74	54	46
1921	1.10	1.15	2.24	49	51
1922	1.23	1.28	2.51	49	51
1923	1.22	1.23	2.45	50	50
1924	1.19	1.25	2.44	49	51
1925	1.18	1.28	2.46	48	52
1926	1.24	1.45	2.69	46	54
1927	1.14	1.46	2.60	44	56
1928	1.19	1.47	2.66	45	55
1929	1.19	1.49	2.68	44	56
1930	1.25	1.64	2.89	43	57
1931	1.38	1.82	3.21	43	57
1932	1.47	1.88	3.35	44	56
1933	1.46	1.82	3.28	45	55
1934	1.43	1.75	3.18	45	55
1935	1.42	1.72	3.14	45	55
1936	1.42	1.73	3.15	45	55
1937	1.42	1.78	3.20	44	56
1938	1.42	1.87	3.29	43	57

Sources: Stone and Rowe, 1966, Tables 21 and 45; Peacock and Wiseman, 1967, Tables 10, A-2, A-5.

Figure 10.1
UK Health Expenditure as a Percentage of GNP

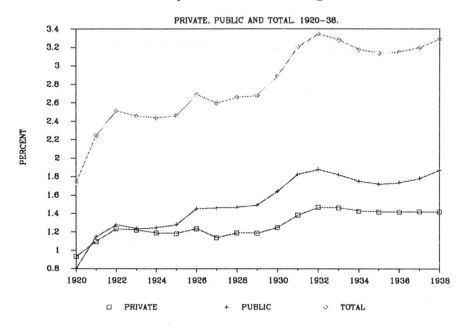

PRIVATE, PUBLIC AND TOTAL, 1920–38.

□ PRIVATE   + PUBLIC   ◇ TOTAL

Figure 10.2
Price Indexes for Private Health Care

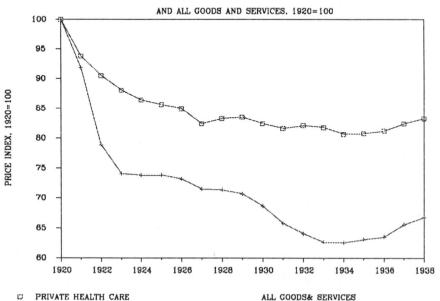

AND ALL GOODS AND SERVICES, 1920=100

□ PRIVATE HEALTH CARE   ALL GOODS& SERVICES

In summary, therefore, inter-war health care expenditure showed fairly vigorous signs of growth, partly as a consequence of rising relative prices and partly due to the increased quantities of services being supplied: public spending on health services grew more rapidly than on most other items of public expenditure, and private health care spending increased significantly in relation to average spending on all consumer goods and services.

3. National Health Insurance

The National Health Insurance scheme was a compulsory system of contributory insurance which was introduced in 1911 and which was restricted by and large to the manual workforce. From the scheme's inception membership increased from 11.5 million people (27.4 per cent of the population) to 20.3 million people (43 per cent of the population) by 1938. (Levy, 1944; Eder, 1982; Gilbert, 1970). This expanded coverage was due partly to modest increases in the earnings limit governing admittance to the scheme, which was set at a maximum of £160 in 1911, raised to £250 in 1920, and to £420 in 1942.

(a) *Structure*

NHI was administered through existing friendly societies, which were mutual benefit organizations already involved in providing medical benefits, and the industrial insurance companies, which had 70,000 door-to-door agents strategically placed to collect contributions and pay benefits (Carpenter, 1984, p. 75). These organizations became approved societies, which received the relevant proportion of contribution from the state, made arrangements to collect the remainder from the worker or his employer, and had the responsibility of paying benefits. About 14,000 separate financial units were approved to administer the scheme in 1912, but amalgamations and closures caused the number to fall to approximately 7,000 by 1937 (Levy, 1944, p. 222).

To preserve some semblance of a voluntary principle, and to provide the approved societies with some incentive towards managerial efficiency, they each received the same flat-rate contributions but were allowed to distribute to their members discretionary benefits above the minimum set of cash and medical benefits. This gave rise to wide variations between insurers, some examples of which are given in Table 10.6.

The friendly societies had traditionally employed or nominated doctors to regulate benefit payments on their behalf. However, this was vigorously opposed by the BMA, who wanted a system where (1) every physician had a right to provide medical treatment to insured persons; (2) every insured person had a free choice of physician, and (3) remuneration depended upon the number of

Table 10.6
Variations in Additional Benefits from NHI Approved Societes, 1942

Benefit	Type of society			
	Trade union (skilled) 24,900 members	Trade union (sedentary) 7,000 members	Local friendly 10,300 members	Collecting 387,000 members
Sickness increase	nil	25p	20p	30p
Dental	nil	75% of cost	50% of cost	50% of cost
Hospital	nil	≤ 3 guineas per week	nil	nil
Medical/surgical appliances	nil	full cost	nil	100% of expenses to £1; 50% of expenses to £2.20
Nursing	nil	full cost	nil	full cost

Source: Clarke (1943), p. 105

persons using the physician's services.[1] Bowing to this pressure, the government devised a scheme which gave insured persons the right to choose between a 'panel' of local doctors who had opted to participate in the scheme. So separation of insurer and provider and a capitation-based remuneration system became part of the fabric of the scheme. The number of doctors participating in the scheme rose from 13,700 in 1920 to 19,060 by 1938—around 90 per cent of active general practitioners. This increase was in line with the expanded membership of the scheme, and so the average number of panel patients per doctor remained fairly constant between approximately 920 and 990 (Digby and Bosanquet, 1988, p. 76).

(b) *Problems*

Economic analysis routinely identifies a number of consistent market failures in health care insurance (McGuire *et al.*, this volume):

(1)   High risk groups such as the chronic sick find it hard to be accepted by insurers because the likelihood that they will require the insurable event—health care—is close to certain. These are the people most in need of health care.

---

[1] There is thus a striking contrast between the BMA's advocacy of a capitation-based system then and hostility to it now.

(2)   Contagious or infectious diseases create externalities, making risks inter-
       dependent and causing insurance failures.

(3)   Information is not equally shared between the parties to the insurance
       contract. This makes it difficult for the insurer to discriminate between
       risks, which tends to lead to equalized premiums, with a *de facto*
       redistribution of wealth from low-risk to high-risk groups. This in turn
       makes it more likely that high-risk individuals will seek insurance cover,
       and that low-risk individuals will opt-out: a phenomenon known as
       adverse selection. Consumers of insurance may in turn be incompetent
       because of lack of information in relation to the relative costs and benefits
       of contracts offered by competing insurers.

(4)   Increasing returns to scale amongst insurance providers, particularly
       relating to transaction costs, may encourage the development of monop-
       oly provision.

(5)   Moral hazard is likely to be present, and may take the form of producer's
       moral hazard—or supplier-induced demand—if producers have incen-
       tives to provide patients with more medical care than they would in the
       absence of these incentives; or consumer's moral hazard, where the
       existence of insurance encourages the insured to maximize consumption
       of services (Culyer, this volume).

All these problems were present to some degree under National Health Insurance.

Approved societies claimed the right to exclude eligible persons if they had a
record of chronic ill health or disability that was likely to be abnormally
burdensome on the funds. This tended to include, for example, sufferers from
goitre, duodenal ulcers, and asthma. Provision was made for this category of
persons by setting up a Deposit Insurance Contributors Fund. However, persons
in this scheme were entitled only to the statutory benefits and not to any
additional benefits. About a quarter of a million people were in this situation
within a few years of NHI beginning (Clarke, 1943, p. 100), and in 1938 256,000
people were still non-insured with an approved society for reasons of inferior
health or expulsion (Levy, 1944, p. 212).

Additional benefits could be paid out by any society which was found to have
a 'disposable surplus' at the statutory five-yearly valuation. As additional
payments tended over time to bring prestige and hence new members to
societies, they had an incentive to economize on statutory benefits (Clarke, 1943,
p. 102). However, societies with a high average age and a high rate of sickness
tended to incur more statutory benefits and have smaller surpluses. In effect, the
societies whose members most needed additional benefits were least likely to be

able to give them (Clarke, 1943, p. 102). Switch of membership was meanwhile discouraged: benefit was not transferable and there was normally a two-year qualification period for additional treatment benefits and a four-year period for additional cash benefits. Thus '. . . individuals who happen to join a society with a large number of bad risks are differentiated against' (Cohen, 1924, pp. 35–6).

The imposition of flat-rate contributions and variable benefits above certain minima was defended on the grounds that it created incentives for efficiency in administration and management. However, the inevitable consequence was that very little account could be taken of risk-proneness: 'The society . . . takes its insurable persons wherever it can get them; . . . the result is that where a society happens to draw its members from occupational groups with particularly heavy sickness risks its financial status becomes more endangered than would otherwise be the case' (Levy, 1944, p. 246). Larger societies consequently were placed at an advantage, as much by their ability to pool risk and avoid financial difficulty as by the economies of scale they could realize in their administration.

The inequalities in benefit that riddled the system were considered by the Royal Commission on National Health Insurance, which sat between 1924 and 1926, but the majority report took the view that inequalities in benefit, and even in the security of benefits, was simply an aspect of consumer choice:

Under the present system an insured person is free to choose the Society to which he shall belong, and if he selects a Society which proves to be relatively unsuccessful, and, as a consequence, unable to provide substantial benefits, he is, to some extent, responsible for the unfortunate position in which he finds himself. (Para. 251)

This view was formed despite the fact that the Commission itself had had to appoint a supporting committee of actuarial and financial specialists to guide it through the complexities of the system (Levy, 1944, p. 26).

Evidence given to the Royal Commission made clear that the NHI system contained some inherent tendencies towards concentration: 'the *per capita* expense is large in small units by reason of overhead charges', whilst the amalgamation of separate branches into large units '. . . had on the whole resulted in more efficient administration' (Evidence, QQ 618-9, 21, 405, quoted in Levy, 1943, p. 249). These economies of scale, plus the great variations between societies in the provision of additional benefits, inevitably resulted in the membership declining in societies in deficit or paying no additional benefits and growing in those which had disposable surpluses, especially the larger industrial assurance and collecting societies. These membership changes came about primarily by means of exits (deaths) and entrances (new members), transfers being discouraged by devices noted above. Thus expanding membership meant a lower average age of membership, a lower death rate, and therefore more additional funds for dispersion to members, whilst in the trade union and branch societies the inverse occurred. Commentators suggested that 'The tendency to concentration, once begun, will go on cumulatively' (Clarke, 1943, p. 110), and the data presented in Table 10.7 seem to bear out the trend.

Evidence of moral hazard is never easy to obtain. Under the panel system there was a rapid increase in the rates of surgery attendances and home visits. The government actuary's working assumption in 1911 of 1.7 items of service per patient per year compared with an actual figure of 3.8 items in 1924, rising to 5.1 items by 1936 (Digby and Bosanquet, 1988, pp. 86–7), and part of this increase was attributed to moral hazard, with complaints of patients bringing 'trifling ailments' to the doctor because of the 1911 Act (Cox , 1921, p. 1397). This is hard to separate, however, from other factors such as rising demand stimulated by scientific developments which were perceived to have increased the effectiveness of some interventions, and certainly the evidence referred to earlier indicates that expenditure elasticities for some medical items were high.

The economic incentives which capitation-based remuneration for NHI panel patients created for general practitioners were crude and powerful: cost minimization, restricted quality of service, and high throughput. Evidence that GPs responded to these incentives is plentiful (Digby and Bosanquet, 1988). An early strategy of some GPs was to recruit as many panel patients as possible on to their list, and complaints by patients and approved societies of poor standards of treatment forced the Ministry of Health to introduce a maximum limit of 3,000 patients in 1920; in 1924 the limit was reduced to 2,500. Most GPs, already well within these limits, followed the strategy of keeping consultation times with panel patients as short as possible, thus maximizing the time available to develop

Table 10.7
Composition of Approved Societies in NHI Scheme, 1931

	Rate of growth of membership 1926–31 (%)	Modal age-group of membership	Death rate per 1,000 members
Friendly societies with branches	+0.4	25–35	7
Friendly societies without branches	+7.4	16–25	7
Industrial assurance & collecting societies	+6.0	16–25	7
Trade unions	−3.5	45–55	10
Employers funds	−0.9	45–55	8

Source: Clarke, 1943, p. 109.

private practice with patients excluded from the NHI scheme. In 1924 the BMA and Ministry of Health agreed that on average a panel doctor would obtain half his total net income from panel work but would spend just two-sevenths of his time with panel patients (Digby and Bosanquet, 1988, p. 82). The structure of incentives led to chronic under-investment in consulting surgeries, and the P.E.P. report in 1937 concluded that 'the panel doctor. . . often has neither the facilities nor the equipment which, as precise diagnosis becomes daily more possible, are necessary to provide an adequate service' (P.E.P., 1937, p. 162). Complaints by panel patients and other observers of the quality of care were widespread, and official action was eventually taken to debar GPs from several treatment areas, notably the treatment of fractures (Honigsbaum, 1979, p. 159).

By responding to these economic incentives, however, GPs in the inter-war period were able to improve substantially their earnings. Private practice, supported and in effect cross-subsidized by panel work, grew from 50 per cent of GPs' total net income in 1922 to 66 per cent by 1936–8 (Digby and Bosanquet, 1988, p. 80). The earnings of medical practitioners rose markedly against the average for all men, from around four times the average in 1913–14 to almost 6 times the average by 1935–37, and also outstripped the performance of others in the higher professional class: between 1922–4 and 1936–8 the average earnings of GPs increased by 36 per cent, compared with an average increase of 9 per cent for the higher professional class as a whole, and of 4 per cent for all occupations

Figure 10.3
Changes in British Medical Earnings

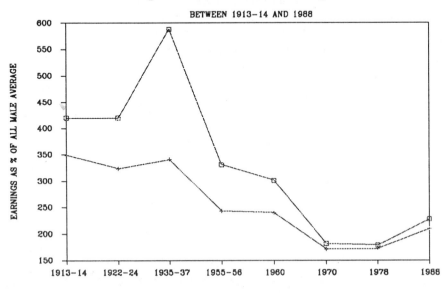

BETWEEN 1913–14 AND 1988

□ MED. PRACTITIONERS   +   ALL HIGHER PROFs.

(Digby and Bosanquet, 1988, p. 77). Figure 10.3 shows clearly how well medical earnings performed during this period.

Estimates of the costs of administering NHI varied, but the minimum calculation in 1938 was that approximately 13 per cent of total receipts were required for administration of the system, three-quarters of this being incurred by the approved societies themselves, and the remainder by the central departments and local insurance committees. As a percentage of benefits paid out, this was equivalent to 17 per cent, which compared unfavourably with other systems, although none had impressively low administrative costs: 16 per cent in Austria, 13 per cent in Japan, 12 per cent in Germany, 10 per cent each in Sweden and Switzerland, and 7 per cent in France (ILO, 1938). The reason lay partly in the intrinsic bureaucracy of an insurance-based system, and partly in the large number of insurers involved in the NHI system. Even this comparison flattered the British scheme, insofar as it benefited from voluntary and charitable support, and unlike the continental systems was not involved at all in administering complex medical benefits such as hospital and specialist care.

(c) *Regulation*

Part of the reason for the high costs of administering NHI was the growth of an elaborate regulatory framework. The need for governmental control generated a substantial legislative burden, '. . . almost an annual series from 1913 to 1945' (Carpenter, 1984, p. 79). By means of these wide-reaching administrative controls, the delivery of sickness insurance by the approved societies was '. . . thoroughly fenced against maladministration and abuse' (Levy 1944, p. 214), but the grosser structural inefficiencies were untouched. Central regulation was extensive in its process, but very restricted in its objectives.

A key area of conflict between providers and insurers was the issuing of certificates of incapacity to insured members by GPs. Approved societies employed 'sick visitors' to visit and check on workers who had been given certificates and were therefore presumably ill in their homes. Larger societies employed full-time workers in this job, who visited 'assiduously' (Clarke, 1943, p. 95), whose objective was to prevent malingering and fraudulent claims, and who were greatly resented by doctors and patients alike.

Approved societies and doctors in conflict over particular patients could refer the patients for examination to regional medical officers, who were full-time salaried officers employed by the Ministry of Health. This surveillance of panel doctors increased greatly during the 1920s, as rising unemployment created fears that the NHI scheme might become insolvent, and the proportion of panel patients referred in England and Wales went up from 0.6 per cent in 1921 to 4.3 per cent by 1931 (Digby and Bosanquet, 1988, pp. 85–6). An idea of the scale of this regulatory activity is given by the fact that in 1938 421,660 references were made, 420,010 from approved societies and only 1,650 from insurance doctors.

Only 38 per cent of those referred for examination turned up and were found to be incapable for work, illustrating the economic incentives bearing upon doctors to issue certificates of incapacity rather than run the risk of losing their patients (Clarke, 1943, pp. 95–6). The regulators also advanced on this problem by erecting barriers which made it difficult for patients to circumvent the rationing activity or clinical judgement of doctors by moving from one panel doctor to another. By 1927 it was established that a fortnight's notice was required, and in 1931 the period had increased to one month (Digby and Bosanquet, 1988, p. 85). This did not seem to lessen the ease with which patients could obtain certificates of incapacity.

Another constant regulatory issue was the volume of prescribing by doctors in the NHI scheme. This grew from 38 million items in 1920 to about 62 million items in 1932, and from an annual cost of £1.2 million to £2.1 million over the same period (Hicks, 1938, p. 55). An elaborate government-sponsored monitoring system was devised to contain this: pricing bureaux calculated the price of every ingredient in every prescription issued by insurance doctors, partly for accounting reasons, but partly to forward statistics to the central departments. This did not contain the problem, however: insurance committees were instructed under regulations framed in 1928 to uncover excessive costs arising from prescribing, 'having regard to such standard of comparison as is available to the committees—which is normally the average cost in their area' (Harris, 1946, p. 161). This approach neglected the wide variations between areas: for example, 4.8 prescriptions per person in Rochdale, and 7 per person in Salford.

The deepest flaws in these regulatory apparatuses were that they contained only the coarsest measures of performance, with little or no concern with quality of care. The overall objective tended to be the limitation of aggregate expenditure. 'Nowhere in the [NHI] Act nor in its administration', commented a contemporary analyst, 'is there any provision for the encouragement of positively good practice. Each doctor sets his own standards, and his only index of efficiency is the number of his patients.'(Clarke, 1943, p. 93). But whichever objective the regulatory apparatuses are judged against, the evidence that they were successful is meagre.

4. The Hospital Sector

(a) *Structure*

The numerical structure of pre-NHS hospital provision is summarized in Table 10.8. Voluntary hospitals provided around one-third of total beds, public hospitals approximately two-thirds. (The discussion in this section refers exclusively to hospitals for the physically ill; the large number of mental hospital beds was almost entirely provided by the public sector, but reliable information on their

Table 10.8
Pre-NHS Hospital Bed Provision

	1891	1911	1921	1938
Number of beds in:				
voluntary hospitals	29,520	43,221	56,550	87,235
public hospitals	83,230	154,273	172,006	175,868
all hospitals	112,750	197,494	225,556	263,103
Beds per 1,000 population:				
voluntary hospitals	1.02	1.20	1.49	2.12
public hospitals	2.87	4.28	4.54	4.29
all hospitals	3.89	5.48	6.03	6.41

Average annual % growth of bed numbers:	(1891–1911)	(1911–21)	(1921–38)
voluntary hospitals	1.92	2.72	2.58
public hospitals	3.13	1.09	0.13
all hospitals	2.84	1.34	0.91

Note: Hospitals for physically ill only.
Source: Derived from Pinker, 1966, Tables 1 and 4.

numbers, cost, or staffing is very hard to obtain. Including them would have accentuated the overall preponderance of public bed provision). Between 1911 and 1938 the total number of beds increased by 65,000, and two-thirds of this increase was in the voluntary sector. The more rapid rate of growth in the voluntary sector was especially apparent in the period from 1921 to 1938, when the number of voluntary beds grew at an annual rate of 2.6 per cent, compared to a growth rate of just 0.1 per cent in the public sector.

The types of hospital care provided by the voluntary and public sectors differed greatly, as Table 10.9 illustrates. Voluntary hospitals had no legal obligation to accept all classes of patient, and 'had long discriminated against chronic and other uneconomic cases' (Eckstein, 1964, p. 93). In consequence, around 84 per cent of beds in the voluntary sector in 1938 were in teaching, general, and specialist hospitals, while the provision of in-patient care for infectious, T.B., and chronic patients was left largely to the public sector, which provided over 90 per cent of such beds.

Hospital services were not covered by the NHI scheme, but the incentive structure operating within the NHI's capitation system encouraged doctors to pass patients quickly on to hospital, while patients not covered by NHI had

Table 10.9
Scale and Type of Inter-War Hospitals

	Number of hospitals		Number of beds		Average size of hospitals	
	1911	1938	1911	1938	1911	1938
Teaching:						
voluntary	24	25	8,284	12,610	345	504
General:						
voluntary	530	671	21,651	45,397	41	68
public	76	133	40,927	52,974	539	398
Maternity:						
voluntary	9	235	311	3,587	39	15
public	0	176	0	6,442	–	37
Other specialist:						
voluntary	121	175	6,495	15,114	54	86
public	0	18	0	5,572	–	310
Infectious, T.B., and chronic:						
voluntary	101	149	6,480	10,527	64	71
public	1,328	1,555	112,046	110,880	84	71
Total:						
voluntary	783	1,255	43,221	87,235	55	70
public	1,404	1,882	154,273	175,868	110	93
all	2,187	3,137	197,494	263,103	90	84

Source: Derived from Pinker, 1966, Tables 7 and 9.

reason to go straight to out-patient departments for medical attention. Observers have thus generally concluded that NHI led to greater demand for hospital services (Abel-Smith, 1964, p. 247). Technical and therapeutic innovations which expanded the range and safety of hospital-based treatment were another reason for increased demand.

The ability of the voluntary hospitals to meet rising demand was endangered not least because their main source of income, charitable gifts and donations, had been reduced by the fiscal innovations of surtax and death duties (Hicks, 1954, p. 44). In these circumstances, the voluntary hospitals made the classic response of attempting to integrate provision with insurance: they encouraged the formation and spread of pre-insurance schemes, by which in return for a weekly payment contributors received general hospital care without further payments or means tests. By 1931 at least 132 contributory schemes were being run by the voluntary hospitals themselves, and at least 80 by other organizations. By 1938, 418 contributory schemes were listed in the Hospitals Year Book (Abel-Smith, 1964, p. 390). The largest was the Hospital Savings Association, which grew very rapidly from 62,000 members in 1924 to 650,000 by 1929 and 1,650,000 by 1936. By then, a minimum of 5,241,000 subscribers were making weekly contributions to contributory schemes, giving coverage to approximately 10 million persons (PEP, 1937, p. 235).

Figure 10.4 shows the way in which the share of income from gifts and investments fell whilst these contributory schemes, alongside other payments from patients (casual payments assessed on a fairly *ad hoc* basis by the hospital almoners, and medical fees levied from private patients), came to account for a rapidly rising proportion of the voluntary hospitals' income: 16 per cent in 1911, 38 per cent by 1921 and 52 per cent by 1938. The inescapable conclusion was that '... charity, as the Victorians understood the term, had long ceased to be the main financial mainstay of the voluntary movement. Payments, either in cash or from insurance contributions, were the principal source of revenue' (Pinker, 1966, p. 154). The hospital contributory schemes were watched with concern by the BMA, and by posing the question whether members of the pre-insurance schemes had a right of access to hospitals, they exacerbated the conflicts between general practitioners and the voluntary hospitals (Abel-Smith, 1964, pp. 390–91).

Figure 10.4
Voluntary Hospitals: Sources of Income

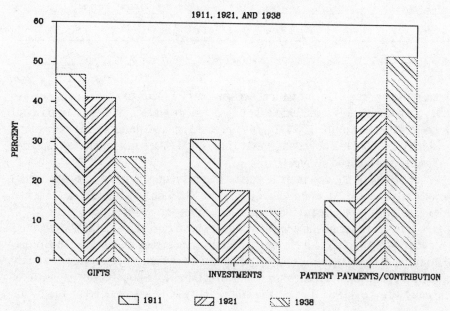

Within the public sector hospitals, as Table 10.8 indicated, the number of beds barely increased in the period from 1921 to 1938, the main area of new provision being in maternity care (this followed the 1918 Maternity and Child Welfare Act, which empowered local authorities to take steps to improve provision for expectant mothers). However, the static overall numbers disguise a number of changes, notably a transfer of ownership of many hospitals from Poor Law to local authorities.

The proportion of all non-mental beds in local authority control was just 17 per cent in 1911, but rose to 23 per cent by 1921 and 47 per cent by 1938 (Pinker, 1966, Table IX): this growth was mainly attributable to the transfer of Poor Law institutions following the Local Government Act of 1929, although some new hospitals were also built. In addition, local authorities were the principal providers of services for the mentally ill and mentally deficient, with an estimated 143,000 asylum beds in Britain and over 20,000 beds for mental defectives (PEP, 1937, pp. 275–9). By 1938 local authorities were the foremost providers of hospital services. Funding of these services, as with other local authority services, was 50 per cent central-government-aided, and although in theory authorities were expected to levy means-related charges from patients for services used, in practice charges were often low: the proportion of hospital running costs met from patient payments was around 10 per cent in general hospitals (PEP, 1937, p. 252).

The transfer of many hospitals to ownership by local authorities was followed in many instances by steps to improve the quality of care. In place of mixed wards and hospitals there was more patient segregation, and the acute sick were gathered into the better buildings. Consultant staff were hired in increasing numbers on a part-time basis from the voluntary hospitals (Abel-Smith, 1964, pp. 374–7). The rate of expansion of nursing staff exceeded that in the voluntary hospitals, and recruitment of nurses was assisted by hours of work and rates of pay that were better than those prevailing in voluntary hospitals (Abel-Smith, 1960, p.122).

(b) *Problems*

The inter-war hospital sector was beset by a number of problems that were frequently identified but never adequately solved. Four in particular were: the financial insecurity of voluntary hospitals; the uneven geographical distribution of hospital services and lack of co-operation between voluntary and public sectors; difficulties in the recruitment and retention of staff, especially nurses; and concern over the quality of care.

The development of patient payment through pre-insurance schemes temporarily eased the financial plight of the voluntary hospital sector, although many individual hospitals remained in difficulty (in 1935 293—that is, over 30 per cent—of the 960 British voluntary hospitals making returns to the Central Bureau of Hospital Information were in deficit (PEP, 1937, p. 232)). Between 1938 and 1947, however, a decline in patient payments and a further fall in gift income pushed the voluntary hospitals into deep trouble. They were rescued by direct contributions out of public funds, which in the example of the London voluntary hospitals grew from 8 per cent of income in 1938 to 46 per cent of income by 1947. Even then, '. . . the [voluntary] system could function only by neglecting the most vital expenditures, and for this reason even the steep rise in payments by public authorities does not entirely reflect the public bill which the voluntary system . . . was rapidly incurring' (Eckstein, 1964, p. 75).

The development of hospital pre-insurance schemes had the effect of increasing demand for hospital services, and there was a substantial supply response measured by voluntary bed numbers, as noted earlier. But it was uneven, and geographical variations in supply attracted particular attention. Differences between London and the rest of the country were marked, and whilst in aggregate terms the disparity in terms of beds per 1,000 population narrowed, from a ratio of 1.63:1 in London's favour in 1911 to 1.32:1 in 1921 and 1.17:1 by 1938, there remained a heavy preponderance of teaching and specialist facilities in the capital (Pinker, 1966, p. 84). This pattern was reinforced rather than countered by the public sector: estimates of public beds per 1,000 population give a ratio of 3.52:1 in London's favour in 1911, falling to 2.23:1 by 1938, and notwithstanding the sketchiness of these estimates '. . . it seems clear that London was far better served with public hospital provision than the provinces' (Pinker, 1966, p. 90).

Outside London, there were wide variations in bed provision between cities, between districts, and between regions. Again, these occurred in the private and the public sectors. A careful comparison of total provision in four cities conducted by the Ministry of Health in 1933 gave beds per 1,000 population of 6.18 in Birmingham, 8.04 in Glasgow, 8.72 in Manchester, and 9.84 in Liverpool (PEP, 1937, p. 258). A more comprehensive picture of provision in 1938 is obtainable from a series of ten hospital surveys conducted in 1945 for the Ministry of Health. They indicated that, for example, total provision varied from 5.1 per 1,000 population in Sheffield and the East Midlands to 5.4 in the North East, 6.2 in the Eastern region, 6.6 in Yorkshire, 6.8 in South Western, and 7.9 in the West Midlands. Within regions the variations were of course wider still: in Yorkshire, provision varied from 4.9 beds per 1000 in York to 10.8 in Halifax and 12.3 in Dewsbury; in Plymouth and West Cornwall there were 5.5 beds per 1,000, in Bath and Wiltshire 8.8 (Ministry of Health, 1945).

In the public sector the provision of hospitals was partly related to the attitudes of local councillors, and partly to the ability of local authorities to generate revenues from rates, so that health services were more difficult to support in depressed areas than in prosperous parts of the country (Webster, 1985; 1988, p.

8). In the voluntary sector the location of hospitals depended on the particular 'parochial allegiance' of charitable founders (Eckstein, 1964, p. 63). In neither sector did the basic unit of decision-making normally correspond with patient catchment areas. Variations in provision often resulted in large variations in occupancy rates, and, especially in small towns and rural areas, cottage hospitals were often operating with very large excesses of capacity.

The nature of the inter-war hospital system also ensured that most hospitals that were built were very small. As Table 10.9 shows, the average hospital size in 1911 was 90 beds, falling to 84 by 1938. The average size of the almost 230 maternity hospitals built by the voluntary sector over this period was 15 beds, while the average general hospital in the voluntary sector in 1938 had just 68 beds. Again, the problem could be related to generally small administrative units in the public sector, and to the amount of charity that any individual philanthropist could normally bequeath to the voluntary sector. Whatever the reasons, the consequence was '. . . somewhat depressing by economic and possibly also medical criteria. It is very likely that the prevalence of small institutions for the physically ill was a burden on running costs which limited the equipment and amenities available to patients and staff' (Pinker, 1966, p. 59).

However, the voluntary hospitals were independently constituted and financed, and it proved difficult for them to articulate a common interest, far less any social interest, even when it was to their advantage to do so. It was not until 1935—fourteen years after the Cave Report—that the British Hospitals Association eventually commissioned a report (the Sankey Report) on the problems that had arisen through lack of planning or regulation of capital investment. The report, published in 1937, painted a picture of

. . . congestion in some hospitals with empty beds in others, the building of new minor hospitals without due regard to the requirements of the region as a whole, the attempt of each minor hospital to do the work of a General Hospital in miniature and to waste money in equipping itself for work it should not attempt, and the consequent employment of staffs of consulting and general practitioner grades indifferently on whatever cases may happen to arise in the immediate vicinity. (British Hospitals Association, 1937, Para 52)

Although the voluntary and public hospitals were able to expand their nursing staffs considerably during the inter-war period, they faced constant difficulties in obtaining trained nurses, and the nursing 'shortages' were the subject of several enquiries (Lancet, 1932; Ministry of Health, Board of Education, 1939). Part of the problem could again be traced to the surfeit of small hospitals that characterized in particular the voluntary sector. A statutory register of qualified nurses, supervised by the General Nursing Council, had been introduced in 1921, and professional nursing opinion held that small hospitals were less able to give satisfactory training to probationers than larger hospitals. The small hospitals at first opposed registration, then resisted the powers of the GNC to approve hospitals for training purposes, but were increasingly unable to recruit trained or in-training nurses and had to increase their reliance on unqualified staff (Abel-Smith, 1960, pp. 115–29).

Another factor contributing to the nursing 'shortage' was hospital finance. In the public sector, as noted above, local authorities were able to improve the pay and conditions of nursing staff to aid recruitment so long as rate revenues allowed. The precarious finances of the voluntary sector generally did not allow such a solution, although it had become clear that the recruitment of nurses could not be increased without major improvements in their pay and conditions. When the government-appointed Athlone Committee submitted an interim report in 1939 recommending the introduction of higher and nationally regulated nursing salaries, improved hours and holiday entitlements, and better accommodation and conditions of work in order to increase recruitment, it concluded that the voluntary hospitals would be bankrupted by the proposals unless they were paid for out of public funds (Ministry of Health, Board of Education, 1939, p. 70). The proposals were shelved, but during the war were retrieved and implemented.

Clinical standards in the voluntary and public hospitals cannot easily be assessed, but during the 1930s an increasing number of areas were identified in which performance seemed poor. For example, a BMA Committee on Fractures reporting in 1935 revealed a '. . . total inadequacy of the provision of organised clinics' (PEP, 1937, p. 77). Following this report, an Inter-Departmental Committee on the Rehabilitation of Persons Injured by Accidents was established, and reported in 1937. It revealed that over 200,000 fracture cases were treated annually in British hospitals, but only a quarter of those in hospitals with fracture clinics. Permanent incapacity resulted in only 1 per cent of cases treated in clinics, but in 37 per cent of those cases treated elsewhere. The disability period for an ankle fracture was 11 weeks in a clinic case, but almost 38 weeks in a non-clinic case (PEP, 1937, p. 259). In similar vein, a report by the Radium Commission in 1937 estimated that only one in five of the 40,000 cancer patients who might benefit from radiation treatment was in fact obtaining treatment (PEP, 1937, p. 297).

The main areas of deficiency were exposed thoroughly when central government made preparations through the Emergency Hospital Service to deal with wartime casualties. Surgical facilities were especially inadequate, and almost 1,000 operating theatres had to be installed almost as soon as the Emergency Medical Service commenced. Many items of hospital equipment and supplies, including basics such as bandages and dressings, forceps, and clamps, were found to be in short supply and had to be supplied in large quantities (Titmuss, 1950, p. 83). It was apparent that 'the huge demands for equipment made on the Emergency Scheme were clearly the result of more than emergency requirements. They also indicated a long accumulated financial hunger and the lack of fitness of many hospitals for modern general hospital work' (Eckstein, 1964, p.

90). In summary, the evidence suggested that 'Britain's performance in the health field was steadily declining by comparison with other English-speaking countries and Scandinavia. Lack of co-ordinated services for cancer, orthopaedics, gynaecology, etc, underlined the failure of the hospital service to adapt to growing problems of ill-health' (Webster, 1988, p. 14).

(c) *Regulation*

A central problem of the hospital services was the lack of co-operation within and between the voluntary and public hospital sectors, and a series of regulatory strategies were devised in the inter-war period to try to improve matters.

The first attempt to encourage co-operation between hospital providers was made by the Cave Committee (Ministry of Health, 1921), which drew attention to the diseconomies arising from lack of co-ordination between the voluntary and public sectors. The 1929 Local Government Act took up this issue, by placing a duty on local authorities to consult with the governing bodies and the medical and surgical staffs of voluntary hospitals in their areas when making provision for hospital accommodation. Partnership did develop in a number of areas, including maternity care, tuberculosis services, and services for the mentally and physically handicapped (Webster, 1988, p. 4). In isolated instances full co-operative planning of services took place (Liverpool, Oxford, and Manchester were examples), but generally this duty was ignored and 'on the whole local authorities expanded their hospital services independently, or in competition or emulation' (Webster, 1988, p. 20).

The 1929 Act was also an attempt to tackle waste and inefficiency within the public hospital sector by transferring the functions of Poor Law authorities to local government, thereby reducing areas of overlap, confusion, and duplication. Even so, some problems remained: instead of co-operating, Leicestershire County Council and Nottinghamshire County Borough built brand new sanatoria within five miles of each other; a county maternity home at Cleethorpes was located within three miles of a municipal maternity home in Grimsby (Ministry of Health 1945, p. 7); in Liverpool residents of suburbs such as Huyton were excluded from city hospitals because they were beyond the city boundaries, while residents of Bootle had access because they lived within the boundaries of the former Poor Law Union which had originally built the hospitals (PEP, 1937, p. 255). By 1937 local authorities across England and Wales had formed 97 joint hospital boards to make co-ordination easier, but these did not overcome the basic problem that local authority areas did not normally coincide with what might be considered logical hospital areas (Eckstein, 1964, p. 70).

The general stance of the Ministry of Health towards the internal affairs of the voluntary hospital sector was non-interventionist, and public supervision of the voluntary hospitals fell to agencies such as the Charity Commission, who often had powers to examine but not to audit voluntary hospital accounts. As in the public hospital sector, no formal system existed through which standards of care could be exercised (PEP, 1937, pp 29–30, 32).

The voluntary hospital movement generally resisted any calls for co-operation to be enforced, and placed reliance on self-regulation. The mechanism of self-regulation that was most frequently held up for emulation was the King Edward's Hospital Fund in London, which had been established in 1897. It was able with the consent of the voluntary hospitals in the area (an 11-mile radius from St Paul's) to act as a central collecting and clearing agency for legacies and donations, and by thus distributing up to 10 per cent of their income could thereby encourage planned development and co-ordination.

Even in London, however, the King's Fund was not notably successful in moving facilities out of the centre of the metropolis, and the Westminster and Middlesex hospitals were both rebuilt on central sites during the interwar period. Elsewhere the inability to transcend local sentiment and the separatist tendencies of the more specialist—especially the teaching—hospitals normally ensured that there was more rivalry than co-operation between voluntary hospitals.

In 1937 the Sankey Report, commissioned by the weakly representative British Hospitals Association to consider the future interests of the voluntary hospitals, proposed the adoption of regional councils which would pool and distribute income on the lines of the King's Fund, with hospitals graded and organized into more efficient groupings. The proposals aroused the enmity of the many special hospitals, whose interests were most threatened by the proposals, and little progress had been made when events were overtaken by the Emergency Hospital Service. Thus the voluntary hospitals' failure to evolve a self-regulatory apparatus resulted in a continuing failure to meet either the demands of the market or even some clinical consensus on medical need.

5. Conclusions: The Transition to a National Health Service

During the 1930s a widening circle of opinion held that Britain's existing health services were deeply flawed, and that structural alterations rather than new regulatory mechanisms were required to deal with the problems identified above. Full exposure of prevailing health and health care conditions during the wartime emergency strengthened the calls for root and branch reform.

The objectives and nature of the NHS derived in part from the limitations and problems of the prewar system: the complexity and administrative cost of NHI set opinion firmly against insurance-based funding; the lack of co-ordination or co-operation between voluntary and public hospital sectors pointed in the direction of regional planning and unified provision; the maldistribution of services could be addressed by machinery gradually to reallocate resources.

There have been occasional attempts by economists to evaluate the performance of the NHS in light of these objectives. For example, Cooper and Culyer's
survey of progress towards territorial justice concluded that in the period up to
the mid-1960s there had been an improvement in the geographical distribution
of general practitioners, but little progress in the distribution of hospital consultants or other types of manpower or expenditure (Cooper and Culyer, 1971).
However, two areas in which the NHS had most striking effect were not explicit
objectives at all: aggregate expenditure control, and the use of monopsony power
in bargaining with professional groups, especially doctors.

Central control on health service expenditure after 1948 had the effect of
holding the proportion of GNP devoted to the NHS at or perhaps below the level
of the 1930s. From 3.75 per cent of GNP in 1949–50, the cost of the NHS
declined to 3.24 per cent by 1953–4 (Abel-Smith and Titmuss, 1956, p. 60).
Central control proved particularly successful—perhaps far too successful—in
restricting the level of health service capital expenditure. By the late 1930s, it
appears that hospital capital expenditure was running at a level equivalent to 19.6
per cent of hospital current expenditure, reflecting the steady expansion in bed
numbers during the inter-war period. Comparable figures for other countries are
hard to come by, but in 1951 the comparable ratio of capital to current hospital
expenditure in the United States was not dissimilar at 23.4 per cent. However,
stringent financial controls on NHS capital expenditure were introduced in 1948
and progressively tightened in following years, so that by 1952–3 the ratio of
capital to current expenditure in the hospital sector had slumped to 4.1 per cent.
This was less than a third of the pre-war volume of capital expenditure measured
in 1952–3 prices, and implied a bed replacement period of 220 years (Abel-
Smith and Titmuss, 1956, pp. 48–57, 137–8). The squeeze continued for 12
years, until the Hospital Plan of 1960 laid out a long-term capital programme.

The rise in medical earnings during the inter-war period was discussed earlier,
and shown in Figure 10.3. Perception of the performance of doctors' earnings
within the NHS has tended to be coloured by Bevan's often quoted remark that
he had quieted the hospital doctors by stuffing their mouths with gold. However,
between 1948–9 and 1953–4 medical salaries were static, while the price index
for nurses rose by 31 per cent and for other staff by 25 per cent (Abel-Smith and
Titmuss, 1956, p. 96). By 1955–6, as Figure 10.3 makes clear, the relative
earnings of medical practitioners had been pulled back sharply, while during the
1960s doctors and dentists did 'much worse than the average for all men' (Routh,
1980, p. 164), so that by the 1970s medical earnings were very much in line with
the higher professional group as a whole, for the first time this century.

A version of this might be, that in order to obtain consent from the medical
practitioners to get involved in the NHS, substantial pay concessions were
required, but once inside the system the government was able to exercise its
power as a monopsonistic purchaser to limit provider monopoly power, and

thenceforth proved much more able to contain medical earnings than had the many providers in the pre-war system.

The organizational features of inter-war health services are unlikely to be replicated in any future reforms, no matter the number of parallels that could be drawn with current proposals for reform. However, many of the problems which arose, and many of the regulatory responses, can be related to structural rather than organizational features of the inter-war services. To that extent it is valid to examine current proposals in the light of the inter-war experience as well as against the subsequent performance of the NHS.

Bibliography

AAPPO (American Association of Preferred Provider Organizations) (1989), Data collected over the telephone, 12 December 1989.

Abel-Smith, B. (1960), *A History of the Nursing Profession*, London: Heinemann.

— (1964), *The Hospitals 1800–1948: A Study in Social Administration in England and Wales*, Cambridge: Cambridge University Press.

— (1967), *An International Study of Health Expenditure*, Geneva: World Health Organization.

— (1984), *Cost-Containment in Health Care*, London: Bedford Square Press.

— and Maynard, A. (1979), *The Organisation of Financing and Cost of Health Care in the European Community*, Brussels: Commission of the European Communities.

— and Titmuss, R. M. (1956), *The Cost of the National Health Service in England and Wales*, Cambridge: Cambridge University Press.

Akerlof, G. A. (1970), 'The market for lemons; quality uncertainty and the market mechanism', *Quarterly Journal of Economics*, **84**, 488–500.

AMA (American Medical Association) (1983), *DRGs and the Prospective Payment System: A Guide for Physicians*, Appendix A.

American Hospital Association (1987), *Economic Trends*, **3**, 1.

Ancona-Berk, V. A. and Chalmers, T. C. (1986), 'An analysis of the costs of ambulatory and inpatient care', *American Journal of Public Health*, **76**, 1102–4.

Andersen, R. and Bentham, L. (1970), 'Factors affecting the relationship between family income and medical care consumption', in H. Klarman (ed.), *Empirical Studies in Health Economics*, Baltimore: Johns Hopkins Press.

Anderson, G. F. and Erickson, J. E. (1987), 'National medical care spending', *Health Affairs*, Fall, 96–104.

Arrow, K. J. (1963), 'Uncertainty and the welfare economics of medical care', *American Economic Review*, **53**, 941–73.

— (1964), 'The role of securities in the optimal allocation of risk-bearing', *Review of Economic Studies*, **31**, 91–6.

— (1968), 'The economics of moral hazard: further comment', *American Economic Review*, **57**, 537–9.

— (1969), 'The organisation of economic activity', in *The Analysis and Evaluation of Public Expenditure; the PPB System*, Washington: Joint Economic Committee of the US Congress.

Atkinson, A. B. (1987), 'Economics of the welfare state: introductory comments', *European Economic Review*, **31**, 177–81.

Auster, R. D. and Oaxaca, R. L. (1981), 'Identification of supplier induced demand in the health care sector', *Journal of Human Resources*, 16, 327–42.

Bachman, S. S., Beatrice, D. F., and Altman, S. H. (1987), 'Implementing change: lessons from medicaid reformers', *Journal of Health Politics, Policy, and Law*, 12, 2, 243.

Barr, N. (1987), *The Economics of the Welfare State*, London: Weidenfeld and Nicholson.

Beauchamp, T. L. and Childress, J. F. (1983), *Principles of Biomedical Ethics*, Oxford: Oxford University Press.

Beck, R. G. (1973), 'The effects of co-payments on the poor', *Journal of Human Resources*, 9, 129–42.

Becker, G. (1965), 'A theory of allocation of time', *Economic Journal*, 75, 493–517.

Beckerman, W. (1986), 'How large a public sector?', *Oxford Review of Economic Policy*, 2, 7–24.

Bergner, M. *et al.* (1976), 'The sickness impact profile: conceptual formulation and methodology for the development of a health status measure', *International Journal of Health Services*, 6, 3, 393–415.

Bergson, A. (1938), 'A reformulation of certain aspects of welfare economics', *Quarterly Journal of Economics*, 52, 310–34.

Berwick, D. M. and Weinstein, M. C. (1985), 'What do patients value? Willingness to pay for ultrasound in normal pregnancy', *Medical Care*, 23, 881–93.

Besley, T. J. (1988a), 'A simple argument for merit good arguments', *Journal of Public Economics*, 35.

— (1988b), 'Optimal reimbursement health insurance and the theory of Ramsey taxation', *Journal of Health Economics*.

— (1989), '*Ex ante* evaluation of health states and the provision for ill health', *Economic Journal*, 99, 132–46.

Bhagwati, J. N. (1984), 'Why are services cheaper in the poor countries?', *Economic Journal*, 94, 279–86.

Bloom, B. S. and Jacobs, J. (1985), 'Cost effects of restricting cost-effective therapy', *Medical Care*, 23, 7, 872–80.

Böhm-Bawerk, E. von (1888), *The Positive Theory of Capital*, trans. W. Smart, G. E. Stechert and Co., 1891.

Bombardier, C., Wolfson, A. D., Sinclair, A. J., and McGreer, A. (1982), 'Comparison of three preference measurement methodologies in the evaluation of a functional stratus index', in R. Deber and G. Thompson (eds.), *Choices in Health Care: Decision Making and Evaluation of Effectiveness*, Toronto: University of Toronto Press.

— Ware, J., Russell, I. J., *et al.* (1986), 'Auranofin therapy and quality of life in patients with rheumatoid arthritis', *The American Journal of Medicine*, 81, 4, 564–78.

Boyle, M. H., Torrance, G. W., Sinclair, J. C., and Harwood, S. P. (1983), 'Economic evaluation of neonatal intensive care of very-low-birth-weight infants', *New England Journal of Medicine*, 308, 1330–7.

Brecher, C. (1984), 'Medicaid comes to Arizona: a first-year report on AHCCCS', *Journal of Health Politics, Policy, and Law*, 9, Fall, 411–25.

British Hospitals Association (1937), *Report of the Voluntary Hospitals Commission (Sankey Report)*, London.

Broome, J. (1978), 'Trying to value a life', *Journal of Public Economics*, **9**, 91–100.

— (1985), 'The economic value of life', *Economica*, **52**, 281–94.

Brown, E. R., Price, W. T., and Cousineau, M. R. (1985), 'Medi-Cal hospital contracting—did it achieve its legislative objectives?', *Western Journal of Medicine*, **143**, 118–24.

Buchanan, J. (1965), 'The inconsistencies of the National Health Service', Institute of Economic Affairs, *Occasional Paper No. 7*, London.

— and Stubblebine, W. G. (1962), 'Externality', *Econometrica*, 371–84.

Bureau of the Census (1984, 1985), *Statistical Abstract of the United States*, 386 and 372 respectively.

Buxton, M. J. (1987), 'Problems in the economic appraisal of new health technology: the evaluation of heart transplants in the UK', in M. F. Drummond (ed.), *Economic Appraisal of Health Technology in the European Community*, Oxford: Oxford University Press.

— et al. (1985), *Costs and Benefits of the Heart Transplant Programme at Harefield and Papworth Hospitals*, London: HMSO.

— Ashby, J., and O'Hanlon, M. (1986), 'Valuation of health states using the time trade-off approach: report of a pilot study relating to health states one year after treatment for breast cancer', *HERG Discussion Paper No. 2*, London: Brunel University.

Calabresi, G. and Melamed, A. D. (1972), 'Property rules, liability rules and inalienability: one view of the cathedral', *Harvard Law Review*, **85**, 1089–125.

Caper, P. (1988), 'Solving the medical care dilemma', *New England Journal of Medicine*, **318**, 1535–6.

Carpenter, G. (1984), 'National Health Insurance: a case study in the use of private non-profit making organisations in the provision of welfare benefits', *Public Administration*, **62**, Spring, 71–89.

Central Statistical Office (1982), 'The effects of taxes and benefits on household income 1981', *Economic Trends*, **350**, 94–125.

— (1987), 'The effects of taxes and benefits on household income 1985', *Economic Trends*, **405**, 100–17.

Chambers, L. W., Sackett, D. L., Goldsmith, C. H. et al. (1976), 'Development and application of an index of social function', *Health Services Research*, **11**, 430–41.

Chandler, A. (1962), *Strategy and Structure*, New York: Anchor Books.

Chesney, J. D. and Fleming, S. T. (1988), 'Should DRG assignment be based on age?', *Medical Care*, **26**, February, 124–31.

Children's Defense Fund (1987), *Whose Watching Our Children's Health: Immunization Status of American Children*, Washington, D.C.: Children's Defense Fund.

Clarke, J. S. (1943), 'National health insurance', in W. A. Robson (ed.), *Social Security*, London: Allen and Unwin.

Cohen, J. L. (1924), *Social Insurance Unified*, London.

Collard, D. (1978), *Altruism and Economy. A Study in Non-Selfish Economics*, Oxford: Martin Robertson.

Collins, E. and Klein, R. (1980), 'Equity and the NHS: self-reported morbidity, access and primary care', *British Medical Journal*, **281**, 1111–5.

Congressional Research Service (1988), *Health Insurance and the Uninsured: Background Data and Analysis*, Washington, DC: Congressional Research Service.

Cooper, M. H. and Culyer, A. J. (1971), 'An economic survey of the nature and intent of the British National Health Service', *Social Science and Medicine*, **5**, 1–13.

Cox, A. (1921), 'Seven years of national health insurance in England: a retrospect', *Journal of the American Medical Association*, **76**, 1397–403.

Cromwell, J. and Mitchell, J. B. (1986), 'Physician-induced demand for surgery', *Journal of Health Economics*, **5**, 293–313.

— and Pope, G. C. (1989), 'Trends in hospital labor and total factor productivity, 1981–1986', *Health Care Financing Review*, **10**, 4, Table 3.

Cullis, J. G. and West, P. A. (1979), *The Economics of Health: An Introduction*, Oxford: Martin Robertson.

Culyer, A. J. (1971a), 'Merit goods and the welfare economics of coercion', *Public Finance*, **26**, 546–71.

— (1971b), 'Medical care and the economics of giving', *Economica*, **151**, 295–303.

— (1971c), 'The nature of the commodity "health care" and its efficient allocation', *Oxford Economic Papers*, **23**, 189–211.

— (ed.) (1974), *Economic Policies and Social Goals: Aspects of Public Choice*, London: Martin Robertson.

— (1976), *Need and the National Health Service*, Oxford: Martin Robinson.

— (1978a), 'Needs, values and health status measurement', in Culyer and Wright (1978).

— (1978b), *Measuring Health: Lessons for Ontario*, Toronto: University of Toronto Press.

— (1979), *Expenditure on Real Services: Health*, Milton Keynes: Open University Press.

— (1980), *The Political Economy of Social Policy*, Oxford: Martin Robertson.

— (ed.) (1983), *Health Indicators: an International Study for the European Science Foundation*, London: Martin Robertson.

— (1986), 'The scope and limits of health economics', *Jahrestagung des Vereins fuer Socialpolitik Gesellschaft fuer Wirtschafts- und Soczialwissenschaften*, Berlin: Duncker and Humblot.

— (1987), 'The future of health economics in the UK', in G. Teeling Smith (ed.), *Health Economics: Prospects for the Future*, London: Croom Helm.

— (1988a), *Health Care Expenditures in Canada: Myth and Reality; Past and Future*, Toronto: Canadian Tax Foundation.

— (1988b), 'The radical reforms the NHS needs—and doesn't', in *Minutes of Evidence Taken Before the Social Services Committee*, London: HMSO.

— (1989), 'Commodities, characteristics of commodities, characteristics of people, utilities and the quality of life', in S. Baldwin, C. Godfrey, and C. Propper (eds.), *The Quality of Life: Perspectives and Policies*, London: Routledge.

— Brazier, J. E., and O'Donnell, O. (1988), *Organising Health Service Provision: Drawing on Experience*, London: Institute of Health Services Management.

— Donaldson, C., and Gerard, K. (1988), *Financial Aspects of Health Services: Drawing on Experience*, London: Institute of Health Services Management.

Culyer, A. J. and Jönsson, B. (eds.) (1986), *Public and Private Health Services*, Oxford: Basil Blackwell.

— Lavers, R., and Williams, A. (1971), 'Social indicators: health', *Social Trends, 2*, 31–42.

— Maynard, A., and Williams, A. (1981), 'Alternative systems of health care provision: an essay on motes and beams', in M. Olsen (ed.), *A New Approach to the Economics of Health Care*, Washington, DC: American Enterprise Institute.

— and Wright, K. G. (eds.) (1978), *Economic Aspects of Health Services*, London: Martin Robertson.

Danzon, P. M. (1985), *Medical Malpractice: Theory, Evidence and Public Policy*, Cambridge, Massachusetts: Harvard University Press.

Dasgupta, P. (1986), 'Positive freedom, markets and the welfare state', *Oxford Review of Economic Policy*, **2**, 25–36.

Davis, C. K. and Rhodes, D. J. (1988), 'The impact of DRGs on the cost and quality of health care in the United States', *Health Policy, 9*, 117–31.

Deaton, A. S. and Muellbauer, J. N. J. (1980), *Economics and Consumer Behaviour*, Cambridge: Cambridge University Press.

Debreu, G. (1959), 'Theory of value', *Cowles Foundation Monograph*, Yale.

DesHarnais, S. *et al.* (1987a), 'The early effects of the prospective payment system on inpatient utilization and the quality of care', *Inquiry*, **24**, Spring, Table 2.

— (1987b), 'The impact of the prospective payment on hospital utilization and the quality of care: trends and regional variations in the first two years', paper presented at the October 1987 meeting of the American Public Health Association.

DHSS (1976), *Sharing Resources for Health in England*, London: HMSO.

— (1980), *Inequalities in Health*, London: HMSO.

— (1986), 'Resource management (management budgeting) in health authorities', HN(86)34.

Diamond, P. A. (1967), 'The role of the stockmarket in a general equilibrium model with technological uncertainty', *American Economic Review, 57*, 759–76.

Dickman, R. L., Ford, A. B., Liebman, J., *et al.* (1987), 'An end to patchwork reform of health care', *New England Journal of Medicine*, **317**, 1086–9.

Digby, A. and Bosanquet, N. (1988), 'Doctors and patients in an era of national health insurance and private practice, 1913–1938', *Economic History Review*, 2nd ser. XLI, I, 74–94.

Dingwall, R. and Fenn, P. (1987), '"A reasonable profession"? Sociological and economic perspectives on the regulation of professional services', *International Review of Law and Economics*, **7**, 51–64.

Donaldson, C. and Gerard, K. (1989), 'Paying general practitioners: shedding light on the review of health services', *Journal of the Royal College of General Practitioners*, **39**, 114–7.

Dorwart, R. A. and Schesinger, M. (1988), 'Privatization of psychiatric services', *American Journal of Psychiatry*, **145**, 5, 543–53.

Dowie, J. (1988), *Professional Judgment*, Introductory Text 8, Milton Keynes: Open University.

— (1989), *Professional Judgment*, Text 5, Milton Keynes: Open University.

Drummond, M. F. (1987), 'Resource allocation decisions in health care: a role for quality of life assessments', *Journal of Chronic Diseases*, **40**, 6, 605–16.

— Stoddard, G. L., and Torrance, G. W. (1987), *Methods for the Economic Evaluation of Health Care Programmes*, Oxford: Oxford University Press.

Dunne, J. P., Pashardes, P., and Smith, R. P. (1984), 'Needs, costs and bureaucracy: the allocation of public consumption in the UK', *Economic Journal*, **94**, 1–15.

Dutton, D. B. (1987), 'Patterns of ambulatory health care in five different delivery systems', *Medical Care*, **XVII**, 221–41.

Dyer, J. S. and Sarin, R. K. (1982), 'Relative risk aversion', *Management Science*, **28**, 8, 875–86.

Eckstein, H. (1964), *The English Health Service: Its Origins, Structure and Achievements*, Cambridge, Massachusetts: Harvard University Press.

Eder, N. R. (1982), *National Health Insurance and the Medical Profession in Britain 1913–39*, London: Garland Publishing Inc.

Ellwood, P. M. (1988), 'Outcome management: a technology of patient experience', *New England Journal of Medicine*, **318**, 1549–56.

— Anderson, N., Billings, J., *et al.* (1971), 'Health maintenance strategy', *Medical Care*, **291**, 250–6.

Enthoven, A. (1978), 'Shattuck Lecture: Cutting cost without cutting the quality of care', *New England Journal of Medicine*, **298**, 1229–38.

— (1986), 'Managed competition in health care and the unfinished agenda', *Health Care Financing Review*, Annual Supplement, 105–19.

— (1987), 'The US health care economy; from guild to market in ten years', *Health Policy*, **7**, 2, 241–51.

Evans, R. G. (1974), 'Supplier-induced demand—some empirical evidence and implications', in M. Perlman (ed.), *The Economics of Health and Medical Care*, London: Macmillan.

— (1976), 'Modelling the objectives of the physician', in R. D. Fraser (ed.), *Health Economics Symposium*, Kingston: Queen's University Industrial Relations Centre.

— (1981), 'Incomplete vertical integration: the distinctive structure of the health-care industry', in J. van der Gaag and M. Perlman (eds.), *Health, Economics, and Health Economics*, Amsterdam: North-Holland.

— (1983), 'The welfare economics of public health insurance: theory and Canadian practice', in L. Soederstroem (ed.), *Social Insurance*, Amsterdam: North-Holland.

— (1984), *Strained Mercy: the Economics of Canadian Medical Care*, Toronto: Butterworths.

— (1986), 'Finding the levers, finding the courage: lessons from cost containment in North America', *Journal of Health Politics and Law*, **11**, 4, 58–615.

— (1987), 'Public health insurance; the collective purchase of individual care', *Health Policy*, **7**, 115–34.

— and Wolfson, A. D. (1980), 'Faith, hope and charity: health care in the utility function', mimeo, Vancouver: Department of Economics, UBC.

Falkson, J. L. (1980), *HMOs and the Politics of Health Service Reform*, Chicago: American Hospital Association.

Farley, P. J. (1985), 'Who are the underinsured?', *Milbank Memorial Fund Quarterly*, **63**, 476–503.

Feeny, D. H. and Torrance, G. W. (1989), 'Incorporating utility-based quality-of-life assessment measures in clinical trials: two examples', *Medical Care, Supplement*, **27**, 3, 190–204.

Feldman, P. H. and Gerteis, M. (1987), 'Private insurance for Medicaid recipients: the Texas experience', *Journal of Health Politics, Policy, and Law*, **12**, 2, 271–98.

Feldman, R., Kralewski, J., and Dowd, B. (1989), 'Health maintenance organizations: the beginning or the end?', *Health Services Research*, **24**, 2, 196.

Feldstein, M. S. (1967), *Economic Analysis for Health Service Efficiency*, Amsterdam: North-Holland.

— (1973), 'The welfare loss of excess health insurance', *Journal of Political Economy*, **81**, 251–80.

— (1980), *Hospital Costs and Health Insurance*, Boston: Harvard University Press.

— Wicker, R. M., and Wheeler, J. R. C. (1988), 'Private cost containment', *New England Journal of Medicine*, **318**, 1310–4.

Ferguson, B. A., Buxton, M. J., and Drummond, M. (1987), 'Measuring and valuing states relating to visual impairment: a review of literature, concepts and methods', *HERG Discussion Paper No. 3*, London: Brunel University.

Fisher, C. R. (1987), 'Impact of the prospective payment system on physician charges under Medicare', *Health Care Financing Review*, **8**.

— (1988), 'Trends in Medicare enrollee use of physician and supplier services, 1983–1986', *Health Care Financing Review*, **10**.

Fox, P. D. and Heinen, L. (1987), *Determinants of HMO Success*, Ann Arbor: Health Administration Press.

Franklin, J. L., Solovitz, B., Mason, M., Clemons, J. R., and Miller, G. E. (1987), 'An evaluation of case management', *American Journal of Public Health*, **6**, 674–8.

Frumkin, H. and Taylor, I. (1988), 'National health care: proposed cure for medicine's ills', *Massachusetts Medicine*, May/June, 13–4.

Fuchs, V. (1978), 'The supply of surgeons and the demand for surgical operations', *Journal of Human Resources*, **13**, 35–56.

— (1982), 'Time preference and health: an exploratory study' in V. R. Fuchs (ed.) *Economic Aspects of Health*, Chicago: University of Chicago Press.

— (1987), 'The counter revolution in health care financing', *New England Journal of Medicine*, **316**, 18, 1154–6.

— (1988), 'The competition revolution in health care', *Health Affairs*, **7**, 5–24.

Fuller, M. F. and Lury, D. A. (1977), *Statistics Workbook for Social Science Students*, Oxford: Philip Allan.

Gabel, J. (1986), Comments made at conference 'Swing beds, experience and future directions', 24 February, Washington DC: Brookings Institution.

— Jajich-Toth, C., Williams, K. *et al.* (1987), 'The commercial health insurance industry in transition', *Health Affairs*, Fall.

Gafni, A. and Torrance, G. W. (1984), 'Risk attitude and time preference in health', *Management Science*, **30**, 4.

Gardner, L. B. and Scheffler, R. M. (1988), 'Privatization in health care: shifting the risk', *Medical Care Review*, **45**, 2, 215–53.

Gerdtham, U., Andersson, F., Sögaard, J., and Jönsson, B. (1988), *Econometric Analysis of Health Care Expenditures: a Cross-section Study of the OECD Countries*, Linköping: Centre for Medical Technology Assessment.

Gilbert, B. B. (1970), *British Social Policy 1914–39*, London: Batsford.

Ginzberg, E. (1987), 'A hard look at cost containment', *New England Journal of Medicine*, **316**, 18, 1151–4.

GMENAC (1981), 'Report of the Graduate Medical Education National Advisory Committee (GMENAC) to the Secretary, Department of Health and Human Services, Vol. 1', *GMENAC Summary Report*, Washington DC: Government Printing Office.

Gold, A. R. (1988), 'Competitive squeeze seen leading to more medical antitrust cases', *New York Times*, 8 December.

Goldberg, L. G. and Greenberg, W. (1980), 'The competitive response of Blue Cross to the health maintenance organizations', *Economic Inquiry*, **18**.

Goodin, R. E. and Le Grand, J. (1987), 'Introduction', in R. E. Goodin and J. Le Grand (eds.), *Not Only the Poor: The Middle Classes and the Welfare State*, London: Allen and Unwin.

Gorman, W. M. (1959/1980), 'A possible procedure for analysing quality differentials in the egg market', *Review of Economic Studies*, **47**, 843–56.

Gorovitz, S. (1982), *Doctor's Dilemmas*, New York: Oxford University Press.

Gottschalk, P., Wolfe, B., and Haveman, R. (1986), 'Health care financing in the US, UK and the Netherlands: distributional consequences', paper presented to 42nd Congress of the International Institution of Public Finance, Athens.

Green, D. G. (1985a), *Which Doctor? A Critical Analysis of the Professional Barriers to Competition in Health Care*, IEA Research Monograph No. 40, London: IEA.

— (1985b), *Working Class Patients and the Medical Establishment*, London: Temple Smith.

Green, J. R. (1978), 'Physician-induced demand for medical care', *Journal of Human Resources*, **13**, 21–34.

Greenspan, A. M. *et al.* (1988), 'Incidence of unwarranted implantation of permanent cardiac pacemakers in a large medical population', *New England Journal of Medicine*, **318**, 158–63.

Greenwald, B. and Stiglitz, J. E. (1986), 'Externalities in economies with imperfect information and incomplete markets', *Quarterly Journal of Economics*, **101**, 229–84.

Grogono, A. W. and Woodgate, D. J. (1971), 'Index for measuring health', *Lancet*, 1024–6.

Grossman, M. (1972a), *The Demand for Health: a theoretical and empirical investigation*, New York: National Bureau of Economic Research.

— (1972b) 'On the concept of health capital and the demand for health', *Journal of Political Economy*, **80**, 233–55.

Guterman, S. *et al.* (1988), 'The first 3 years of Medicare prospective payment: an overview', *Health Care Financing Review*, **9**, 1, 67–77.

Guyatt, G. H., Berman, L. B., Townsend, M., *et al.*, (1987), 'A measure of quality of life for clinical trials in chronic lung disease', *Thorax*, **42**, 773–8.

Hadley, J. and Swartz, K. (1989), 'The impacts on hospital costs between 1980 and 1984 of hospital rate regulation, competition, and changes in health insurance coverage', *Inquiry*, **26**, 35–47.

Ham, C. (ed.) (1988), *Health Care Variations: Assessing the Evidence*, London: King's Fund Institute.

Hammond, J. D. and Shapiro, A. F. (1986), 'AIDS and the limits of insurability', *The Milbank Memorial Fund Quarterly*, **64**, 143–67.

Harris, A. I., Cox, C., Smith, C. R. W., and Buckle, J. R. (1971), *Handicapped and Impaired in Great Britain*, London: HMSO.

Harris, J. (1977), 'The internal organisation of hospitals; some economic implications', *Bell Journal of Economics*, **8**, 467–82.

— (1987), 'QALYfying the value of life', *Journal of Medical Ethics*, **13**, 117–23.

Harris, R. W. (1946), *National Health Insurance in Great Britain 1911–1946*, London: Allen and Unwin.

Harsanyi, J. C. (1955), 'Cardinal welfare, individualistic ethics, and interpersonal comparisons of utility', *Journal of Political Economy*, **63**, 309–21.

Hay, J. W. and Leahy, J. J. (1984) 'Competition among health plans. Some preliminary evidence', *Southern Economic Journal*, **11**, 831–46.

Hayward, R. A. *et al.* (1988), 'Inequities in health services among insured Americans', *New England Journal of Medicine*, **318**, 1507–12.

Health Data Institute (1987), 'National DRG Validation Study, report prepared for the Office of Inspector General, Department of Health and Human Services', Lexington, Massachusetts.

Hellinger, F. J. (1987), 'Selection bias in health maintenance organizations', *Health Care Financing Review*, **9**, 2.

— (1989), 'Expected utility theory and risky choices with health outcomes', *Medical Care*, **27**, 3, 273–9.

Helm, D. (1986), 'The assessment: the economic borders of the state', *Oxford Review of Economic Policy*, **2**, 2, i–xxiv.

Henderson, M., Bergman, A., Collard, A., Souder, B., and Wallack, S. (1987), 'Private sector medical case management for high cost illness', paper presented at the conference 'Private Sector Involvement in Health Care: Implication for Access, Cost, and Quality', 9 April, Menlo Park, California: SRI International.

Hey, J. D. (1979), *Uncertainty in Microeconomics*, Oxford: Martin Robertson.

HIAA (Health Insurance Association of America) (1989), *Source Book of Health Insurance Data*.

Hicks, U. (1938), *The Finance of British Government 1920–1936*, Oxford: Oxford University Press.

— (1954), *British Public Finances: Their Structure and Development 1880–1952*, Oxford: Oxford University Press.

Higgins, J. (1988), *The Business of Medicine*, London: Macmillan Education Ltd.

Hill, T. P. (1984), 'Introduction: the special conference on purchasing power parities', *Review of Income and Wealth*, **30**, 125–33.

Hilliard, L. T. and McNae, C. J. (1941), 'If the medical services are free', *Medicine Today and Tomorrow*, March, 11–15.

Himmelstein, D. U. and Woolhandler, S. J. (1986), 'Cost without benefit: administrative waste in US health care', *New England Journal of Medicine*, **314**, 441–5.

HMSO (1944), *A National Health Service*, Cmnd. 6502, London: HMSO.

—— (1956), *Report of the Committee of Enquiry into the Cost of the National Health Service*, Cmnd. 9663 (the Guillebaud Report), London: HMSO.

—— (1979), *The Royal Commission on the National Health Service*, Cmnd. 7615 (the Merrison Report), London: HMSO.

—— (1980), *Inequalities in Health*, (the Black Report), London: HMSO.

—— (1983), *The NHS Management Inquiry* (the Griffiths Report), London: HMSO.

—— (1989), *Working for Patients: The Health Service. Caring for the 1990s*, Cm. 555, London: HMSO.

Ho, M-S., Glass, R. I., and Pinsky, P. F. (1988), 'Diarrheal deaths in American children', *Journal of the American Medical Association*, **260**, 22, 3281–5.

Hochman, H. M. and Rodgers, J. D. (1969), 'Pareto optimal redistribution', *American Economic Review*, **59**, 542–57.

Holahan, J. and Scanlon, W. (1979), 'Physician pricing in California: price controls, physician fees, and physician incomes from Medicare and Medicaid', *Health Care Financing Grant and Contracts Report*, HCFA Publication No. 03006.

Honigsbaum, F. (1979), *The Division in British Medicine*, London: Kogan Page.

Hunt, S. M., McEwen, J., and McKenna, S. P. (1986), *Measuring Health Status*, London: Croom Helm.

Hurst, J. (1985), *Financing Health Care in the US, Canada and Britain*, London: King's Fund.

Illsley, R. and Le Grand, J. (1987), 'The measurement of inequality in health', in A. Williams (ed.), *Health and Economics*, London: Macmillan.

ILO (International Labour Organization) (1938), *Economical Administration of Health Insurance*, Geneva: ILO.

Interstudy (1987), *Interstudy Edge*, Excelsior, Minnesota: Interstudy.

—— (1989), Data gathered over the telephone, December 12.

Italian Ministry of Justice (1978), 'Legge 833: Istitutizione del Servizio Sanitario', Supplement to *Gazzetta Ufficiale*, December 28 1978.

Jensen, G. A. and Gabel, J. R. (1988), 'The erosion of purchased health insurance', *Inquiry*, **25**, 328–43.

Jewkes, J., Jewkes, S., Lees, D. S., and Kemp, A. (1963), 'Ethics and economics of medical care—discussion', *Medical Care*, **1**, 234–44.

Johns, L., Anderson, M. D., and Derzon, M. A. (1985a), 'Selective contracting in California: early effects and policy implication', *Inquiry*, **22**, 24–32.

—— —— —— (1985b), 'Selective contracting in California: experience in the second year', *Inquiry*, **22**, 335–47.

—— —— —— (1987), *Selective Contracting for Health Services in California: First Report*, Washington DC: National Governors Association, Center for Policy Research.

Kahn, K. L., Kosecoff, J., Chassin, M. R. *et al.* (1988), 'The use and misuse of upper gastrointestinal endoscopy', *Annals of Internal Medicine*, **109**, 664–70,

Kahneman, D. and Tversky, A. (1979), 'Prospect theory: an analysis of decision under risk', *Econometrica*, **47**, 2, 263–91.

Kakwani, N. C. (1977), 'Measurement of tax progressivity: an international comparison', *Economic Journal*, **87**, 71–80.

— and Podder, N. (1976), 'Efficient estimation of the Lorenz curve and associated inequality measures from grouped observations', *Econometrica*, **44**, 137–48.

Kant, I. (1930), *Lectures on Ethics*, London: Macmurray.

Kaplan, R. M., Bush, J. W., and Berry, C. C. (1976), 'Health status: types and validity and the index of well-being', *Health Services Research*, **11**, 478–507.

Karnofsky, D. A. and Burchenal, J. H. (1949), 'The clinical evaluation of chemotherapeutic agents in cancer', in C. M. MacLeod (ed.), *Evaluation of Chemotherapeutic Agents*, New York: Columbia University Press.

Keeler, E. B., Newhouse, J. P., and Phelps, C. E. (1977), 'Deductibles and the demand for medical services: the theory of a consumer facing a variable price schedule under uncertainty', *Econometrica*, **45**, 641–55.

— and Cretin, S. (1983), 'Discounting of life-saving and other non-monetary effects', *Management Science*, **29**, 3.

Kenney, J. B. (1985), 'Using competition to develop a buyer driven market', *Business and Health*, **3**, 39–42.

Kind, P., Rosser, R. M., and Williams, A. H., (1982), 'Valuation of quality of life: some psychometric evidence', in M. W. Jones-Lee (ed.), *The Value of Life and Safety*, Amsterdam: Elsevier/North-Holland.

Klarman, H. E. (1963), 'The distinctive economic characteristics of health services', *Journal of Health and Human Behaviour*, **4**, 44–9.

— (1965), 'The case for public intervention in financing health and medical services', *Medical Care*, **3**, 59–62.

Klarman, R. E. (1977), 'The Financing of Care', *Daedalus*, **106**, 1.

Kravis, I., Heston, A., and Summers, R. (1978), 'Real GDP *per capita* for more than one hundred countries', *Economic Journal*, **88**, 215–42.

Lambert, P. J. (1985), 'Tax progressivity: a survey of the literature', Working Paper No. 56, London: Institute for Fiscal Studies.

— and Pfahler, W. (1988), 'On aggregate measures of the net redistributive impact of taxation and government expenditure', *Public Finance Quarterly*, **16**, 178–202.

Lancaster, K. (1969), *Introduction to Modern Microeconomics*, Chicago: Rand McNally.

Lancet (1932), *The Lancet Commission on Nursing*, London.

Langlois, R. N. (1986), *Economics as a Process, Essays in the New Institution Economics*, Cambridge: Cambridge University Press.

Lee, M. L. (1971), 'A conspicuous production theory of hospital behaviour', *Southern Economic Journal*, **38**, 48–58.

Lees, D. S. (1960), 'The economics of health services', *Lloyds Bank Review*, **56**, 26–40.

— (1962), 'The logic of the British national health service', *Journal of Law and Economics*, **5**, 111–8.

— (1967), 'Efficiency in government spending: Social services: Health', *Public Finance*, **22**, 176–89.

Le Grand, J. (1978), 'The distribution of public expenditure: the case of health care', *Economica*, **45**, 125–42.

— (1982), *The Strategy of Equality*, London: Allen and Unwin.

— (1984), 'Equity as an economic objective', *Journal of Applied Philosophy*, **1**, 39–51.

Le Grand, J. (1987a), 'Inequalities in health: some international comparisons', *European Economic Review*, **31**, 182–91.

— (1987b), 'Equity, health and health care', forthcoming in *Social Justice Research*.

— and Rabin, M. (1986), 'Trends in British health inequality, 1931–83', in A. J. Culyer and B. Jönsson (eds.), *Public and Private Health Services*, Oxford: Basil Blackwell.

— and Robinson, R. (1984), *The Economics of Social Problems*, London: Macmillan.

Letsch, S. W., Levit, K. R., and Waldo, D. R. (1988), 'National health expenditures, 1987', *Health Care Financing Review*, **10**, 2, 109–29 (figures were deflated using the medical care consumer price index from the US Department of Commerce. Nominal figures were $248,100 million and $500,300 million in 1980 and 1987 respectively).

Leu, R. E. (1986), 'The public–private mix and international health care costs', in A. J. Culyer and B. Jönsson (eds.) (1986).

— and Frey, R. L. (1985), 'Budget incidence, demographic change and health policy in Switzerland', in A. J. Culyer and G. Terny (eds.), *Public Finance and Social Policy*, Detroit: Wayne State University Press.

Levy, H. (1944), *National Health Insurance: A Critical Study*, Cambridge: Cambridge University Press.

Lewin, T. (1987), 'Hospitals pitch harder for patients', *New York Times*.

Lindsay, C. M. (1969), 'Medical care and the economics of sharing', *Economica*, **144**, 351–62.

— (1973), 'Real returns to medical education', *Journal of Human Resources*, **8**, 331–48.

Lipscomb, J. (1989), 'Time preference for health in cost-effectiveness analysis', *Medical Care, Supplement*, **27**, 3, 233–53.

Llewellyn-Thomas, H., Sutherland, H. J., Tibshirani, R., Ciampi, A., Till, J. E., and Boyd, N. F. (1984), 'Describing health states: methodological issues in obtaining values for health states', *Medical Care*, **22**, 543–52.

Lohr, K. N., Brook, R. H., Kamberg, C. J., Goldberg, G. A., Leibowitz, A., *et al.* (1986), 'Use of medical care in the Rand health insurance experiment: diagnosis and service-specific analyses in a randomized controlled trial', *Medical Care*, **24**, Supplement.

Long, S. H. and Welch, W. P. (1988), 'Are we containing costs or pushing on a balloon?', *Health Affairs*, Fall, 113–7.

Loomes, G. (1988), 'Disparities between health state measures: an explanation and some implications', paper presented to the UK HESG meeting, Brunel.

— and McKenzie, L. (1988), 'The scope and limitations of QALY measures', *Social Science and Medicine*, **27**.

— — (1989), 'The use of QALYs in health care decision making', *Social Science and Medicine*, **28**, 299–308.

— and Sugden, R. (1982), 'Regret theory: an alternative theory of rational choice under uncertainty, *Economic Journal*, **92**, 805–24.

Luft, H. S. (1981), *Health Maintenance Organizations: Dimensions of Performance*, New York: John Wiley & Sons.

— (1985), 'Competition and regulation', *Medical Care*, **23**, 5, 383–99.

Luft, H. S. and Arno, P. (1986), 'Impact of increasing physician supply', *Health Affairs*, **5**, 31–6.

— Robinson, J. C., Garnick, D. W., *et al.* (1986), 'The role of specialized clinical services in competition among hospitals', *Inquiry*, **23**, 83–94.

McGuire, A. J. (1986), 'Ethics and resource allocation; an economist's view', *Social Science and Medicine*, **22**, 1167–74.

— (1987), 'The measurement of hospital efficiency', *Social Science and Medicine*, **24**, 719–24.

— Henderson, J. B., and Mooney, G. H. (1988), *The Economics of Health Care*, London: Routledge and Kegan Paul.

McLachlan, G. and Maynard, A. (1982), 'The public/private mix in health care: the emerging lessons', in G. McLachlan and A. Maynard (eds.), *The Public/Private Mix in Health Care: The Relevance and Effects of Change*, London: Nuffield Provincial Hospitals Trust.

McLaughlin, C. G. (1987), 'HMO growth and hospital expenses and use: a simultaneous-equation approach', *Health Services Research*, **22**, 183–206.

— (1988a), 'The effect of HMOs on overall hospital expenses: is anything left after correcting for simultaneity and selectivity?', *Health Service Research*, **23**, 421–41.

— (1988b), 'Market responses to HMOs: price competition or rivalry?', *Inquiry*, **25**, 207–18.

— Merrill, J. C., and Freed, A. J. (1984), 'The impact of HMO growth on hospitals and costs utilization', in Schleffer, R. M. and Rossiter, L. F. (eds.), *Advances in Health Economics and Health Services Research*, **5**, Greenwich, Connecticut: JAI Press.

McNeil, B. J., Weichselbaum, R., and Pauker, S. G. (1978), 'Fallacy of the five year survival in lung cancer', *New England Journal of Medicine*, **299**, 1397–401.

— — — (1981), 'Tradeoffs between quality and quantity of life in laryngeal cancer', *New England Journal of Medicine*, **305**, 982–7.

McPherson, K., Strong, P. M., Epstein, A., and Jones, L. (1981), 'Regional variations in the use of common surgical procedures: within and between England and Wales, Canada and the USA', *Social Science and Medicine*, **15A**, 273–88.

Malinvaud, E. (1972), 'The allocation of individual risks in large markets', *Journal of Economic Theory*, **4**, 312–28.

Manning, W. G., Leibowitz, A., *et al.* (1984), 'A controlled trial of the effect of prepaid group practice on use of services', *New England Journal of Medicine*, **310**, 23.

— Newhouse, J. P., Duan, N., Keeler, E. B., Liebowitz, A., and Marquis, M. S. (1987), 'Health insurance and the demand for health care; evidence from a randomised experiment', *American Economic Review*, **77**, 251–77.

Margolis, H. (1982), *Selfishness, Altruism and Rationality*, Cambridge: Cambridge University Press.

Mariano, A. L. (1989), 'Growth of the Medicare population', *Health Care Financing Review*, **10**, 3, Table 2.

Massey, P. (1942), 'The expenditure of 1360 British middle-class households in 1938–9', *Journal of the Royal Statistical Society*, **CV**, 159–85.

Maxwell, R. J. (1974), *Health Care: the Growing Dilemma*, New York: McKinsey and Co.

Maxwell, R. J. (1981), *Health and Wealth: An International Study of Health Care Spending*, Lexington, Massachusetts: Lexington.

Maynard, A. (1975), *Health Care in the European Community*, London: Croom Helm.

— and Williams, A. (1984), 'Privatisation and the National Health Service', in J. Le Grand and R. Robinson (eds.), *Privatisation and the Welfare State*, London: Allen and Unwin.

Meade, J. E. (1973), *The Theory of Economic Externalities*, Leiden: Sijthoff.

Medical Planning Research (1942), 'Interim general report', *The Lancet*, **ii**, 609.

Mehrez, A. and Gafni, A. (1987), 'An empirical evaluation of two assessment methods for utility measurements for life years', *Socio Economic Planning Science*, **21**, 6, 371–5.

— — (1989), 'Quality-adjusted life-years, utility theory and healthy years equivalents', *Medical Decision Making*, **9**, 142–9.

Melnick, G. and Zwanziger, J. (1988), 'Hospital behavior under competition and cost-containment policies: the California experience, 1980–1985', *Journal of the American Medical Association*, **260**, 18, 2669–75.

Mill, J. S. (1979), *Utilitarianism, On Liberty, and Essay on Bentham*, New York: New American Library.

Ministry of Health (1921), *Voluntary Hospitals Committee (Cave Committee) Final Report*, London: Ministry of Health.

— (1939), Board of Education, *Inter-Departmental Committee on Nursing Services, Interim Report (The Athlone Report)*, London: HMSO.

— (1945), Parsons, L. G., Clayton Fryers, S., and Godber, G. E., *Hospital Survey: The Hospital Services of Sheffield and East Midlands Area*, London: HMSO.

Ministry of Labour (1940), 'Weekly expenditure of working-class households in the UK in 1937–38, I: industrial etc. workers', *Ministry of Labour Gazette*, December, 300–5.

— (1941), 'Weekly expenditure of working-class households in the UK in 1937–38, II: households of agricultural workers', *Ministry of Labour Gazette*, January, 7–11.

Mirrlees, J. A. (1971), 'An exploration in the theory of the the optimal income tax', *Review of Economic Studies*, **38**, 175–208.

Mooney, G. H., (1983), 'Equity in health care: confronting the confusion', *Effective Health Care*, **1**, 179–85.

— (1986), *Economics, Medicine and Health Care*, Brighton: Wheatsheaf.

— (1987), 'What does equity in health mean?', *World Health Statistics Quarterly*, **40**, 296–303.

— (1988), *QALYs: Some Qualifications*, paper presented at the Nordic HESG, Oslo, September.

— and McGuire, A. (1987), 'Distributive justice with special reference to geographical inequality and health care', in A. Williams (ed.), *Health and Economics*, London: Macmillan.

Morris, C. N. and Preston, I. (1986), 'Taxes, benefits and the distribution of income: 1968–83', *Fiscal Studies*, **7**, 18–27.

Morrissey, M., Conrad, D., Shortell, S., *et al* (1984), 'Hospital rate review: a theory and an empirical review', *Journal of Health Economics*, **3**, 25–47.

Mueller, D. C. (1979), *Public Choice*, Cambridge: Cambridge University Press.

Mulley, A. G. (1989), 'Assessing patients' utilities: can the ends justify the means?', *Medical Care, Supplement*, **27**, 3, S269–81.

Mundinger, M. O. (1985), 'Health service funding cuts and the declining health of the poor', *New England Journal of Medicine*, **313**, 44–7.

Musgrave, R. A. (1959), *The Economics of Public Finance*, New York: McGraw Hill.

National Center for Health Services Research (1988), *Patient Outcome Research*, September, Washington, DC: US Department of Health and Human Services.

Newacheck, P. W. (1988), 'Access to ambulatory care for poor persons', *Health Services Research*, **23**, 401–19.

Newhouse, J. P. (1977), 'Medical care expenditure: a cross-national survey', *Journal of Human Resources*, **12**, 115–25.

— and Phelps, C. E. (1976), 'New estimates of price and income elasticities of medical services', in R. N. Rosette (ed.), *The Role of Health Insurance in the Health Service Sector*, New York: National Bureau of Economic Research.

New York Times Leader (1988), 'For rational, national health care', *New York Times*, 9 August, 22.

Nord, E. (1988), 'Prioriteringer i helsevesenet ut fra nyttevurderinger', Avd. for helsetjeneste-forskning, Oslo: SIFF.

O'Brien, B., Buxton, M. J., and Ferguson, B. (1986), 'Measuring the effectiveness of heart transplant programmes: quality of life data and their relationship to survival analysis', mimeo, London: Health Economics Research Group, Brunel University.

O'Donnell, O. (1987), 'An examination of the distribution of health care across income groups in Britain', MSc Dissertation, University of York, Department of Economics.

OECD (1977), *Public Expenditure on Health*, Paris: OECD.

— (1985), *Measuring Health Care*, Paris: OECD.

— (1987), *Financing and Delivering Health Care*, Paris: OECD.

Office of Technology Assessment (1988), *Medical Testing and Health Insurance*, OTA-H-384, Washington, DC: United States Government Printing Office.

Office of the Inspector General (1989), Office of Analysis and Inspections, 'National DRG validation study: quality of patient care in hospitals', Washington DC: Department of Health and Human Services.

Owen, D., (1976), *In Sickness and in Health*, London: Quartet Books.

— (1989), *Parliamentary Debates* (Hansard), **151**, 87, Tuesday 18 April 1989, Column 210, London: HMSO.

— McGuire, A., and Yule, B. (1987), 'Aggregate health care expenditures and national income: is health care a luxury good?', *Journal of Health Economics*, **6**, 109–28.

Paterson, M. (1988), 'Assessment of treatment in rheumatoid arthritis', in G. Teeling Smith (ed.), (1988).

Pattanaik, P. K. (1968), 'Risk, impersonality and the social welfare function', *Journal of Political Economy*, **76**, 6, 1152–69.

Pauker, S. G. and McNeil, B. J. (1981), 'Impact of patients' preferences on the selection of therapy', *Journal of Chronic Diseases*, **34**, 77–86.

Pauly, M. V. (1968), 'The economic and moral hazard: a comment', *American Economic Review*, **51**, 531–7.

— (1970), 'Efficiency in the provision of consumption subsidies', *Kyklos*, **23**, 33–55.

Pauly, M. V. (1971), *Medical Care at Public Expense*, New York: Praeger.
— (1974), 'Overinsurance in the public provision of insurance', *Quarterly Journal of Economics*, **88**, 44–62.
— (1980), *Doctors and their Workshops*, Chicago: University of Chicago Press.
— (1986), 'Taxation, health insurance and market failure in the medical economy', *Journal of Economic Literature*, **24**, 629–75.
Peacock, A. T. and Wiseman, J. (1967), *The Growth of Public Expenditure in the UK*, London: Unwin.
Pechman, J. (1985), *Who Paid the Taxes, 1966–1985?*, Washington: Brookings Institution.
PEP (Political and Economic Planning) (1937), *Report on the British Health Services: A Survey of the Existing Health Services in Great Britain with Proposals for Future Development*, London: PEP.
Phelps, C. E. (1986), 'Induced demand—can we ever know its extent?', *Journal of Health Economics*, **5**, 355–66.
— and Newhouse, J. P. (1974), *Co-insurance and the Demand for Medical Services*, Santa Monica: Rand Corporation.
Physician Payment Review Commission (1989), 'Physician payment reform: summary of provisions of H.R. 3299, Omnibus Budget Reconciliation Act of 1989'.
Pinker, R. (1966), *English Hospital Statistics*, London: Heinemann.
Pliskin, J. S., Shepard, D. S., and Weinstein, M. C. (1980), 'Utility functions for life years and health status', *Operations Research*, **28**, 1, 206–24.
Podgursky, M. and Swaim, P. (1987), 'Health insurance loss: the case of the displaced worker', *Monthly Labor Review*, **110**, 30–3.
Prais, S. J. and Houthakker, H. S. (1955), *The Analysis of Family Budgets*, Cambridge: Cambridge University Press.
ProPAC (Prospective Payment Assessment Commission) (1985), *Technical Appendixes to the Report and Recommendations to the Secretary*, Washington DC: US Department of Health and Human Services.
Public Accounts Committee (1980/81), Seventeenth Report, HC255, London: HMSO.
— (1983/84), Sixteenth Report, HC213, London: HMSO.
Puffer, F. (1986), 'Access to primary care: a comparison of the US and the UK', *Journal of Social Policy*, **15**, 293–313.
Raffel, M. W. (1984), *Comparative Health Systems*, Pennsylvania: Pennsylvania State University Press.
Rawls, J. (1972), *A Theory of Justice*, Oxford: Clarendon Press.
Rayner, G. (1988), 'HMOs in the USA and Britain: a new prospect for health care?', *Social Science and Medicine*, **27**, 4, 305–20.
Read, J. L., Quinn, R. J., Berwick, D. M., Fineberg, H. V., and Weinstein, M. C. (1984), 'Preferences for health outcomes: comparison of assessment methods', *Medical Decision Making*, **4**, 315–9.
Reinhardt, U. E. (1987), 'Resource allocation in health care: the allocation of lifestyles to providers', *The Milbank Quarterly*, **65**, 153–76.
— (1988a), 'The resource transfer from patients to providers of health services', in T. B. Binns and M. Firth (eds.) *Health Care Provision under Financial Constriant*, London: Royal Society of Medicine.

Reinhardt, U. E. (1988b), *Presentation to the Carondolet Life Care Corporation*, Minneapolis, Minnesota, 27 October.

— (1988c), 'The medical B-factor: bureaucracy in action',*WashingtonPost*, 9 August.

Reinhold, R. (1988), 'Crisis in emergency rooms: more symptom than cures', *New York Times*, 28 July, 1.

Reynolds, M. and Smolensky E. (1977), *Public Expenditures, Taxes, and the Distribution of Income: the United States, 1950, 1961, 1970*, New York: Academic Press.

Rice, T. H. (1983), 'The impact of changing Medicare reimbursement rates on physician induced demand', *Medical Care*, **21**, 803–15.

— (1987), 'Comment on "Induced demand—Can we ever know its extent?" by Charles E. Phelps', *Journal of Health Economics*, **6**, 375–6.

— Gabel, L., and de Lissovoy, G. (1989), 'PPOs: the employer perspective', *Journal of Health Policy, Politics, and Law*, **14**, 2, 367–82.

Richardson, J., Hall, J., and Salkeld, G. (1989), 'Cost utility analysis: the compatibility of measurement techniques and the measurement of utility through time', paper presented to the 11th Annual Conference of the Australian Health Economists' Group, ANU, 7–8 September.

Robbins, L. (1938), 'Interpersonal comparisons of utility', *Economic Journal*, **48.**

Robert Wood Johnson Foundation (1983), *The Updated Report on Access to Health Care for American People*, Princeton, NJ: Robert Wood Johnson Foundation.

Robinson, J. C. and Luft, H. S. (1985), 'The impact of hospital market structure on patient volume, average length of stay, and the cost of care', *Journal of Health Economics*, **4**, 347–53.

— — (1988), 'Competition and the cost of hospital care, 1972 to 1982', *Journal of the American Medical Association*, **259**, 696–700.

— — McPhee, S. J., and Hunt, S .S. (1988), 'Hospital competition and surgical length of stay', *Journal of the American Medical Association*, **259**, 696–700.

Robinson, J. D. and Phibbs, C. (1989), 'An evaluation of Medicaid selective contracting in California', *Journal of Health Economics*, **8.**

Roper, W. L., Winkenwerder, W., Hackbarth, G. M., and Krackauer, H. (1988), 'Effectiveness in health care: an initiative to evaluate and improve medical practice', *New England Journal of Medicine*, **319**, 1197–1202.

Rosser, R. (1983), 'Issues of measurement in the design of health indicators; a review', in A. J. Culyer (ed.), *Health Indicators*, Oxford: Martin Robertson.

Routh, G. (1980), *Occupation and Pay in Great Britain, 1906–1975*, London: Macmillan.

Royal College of Radiologists (1981), 'Costs and benefits of skull radiography for head injury', *Lancet*, **ii**, 791–5.

Russell, L. B. (1979), *Technology in Hospitals: Medical Advances and their Diffusion*, Washington, DC: Brookings Institution.

— (1989), *Medicare's New Hospital Payment System: Is it Working?*, Washington DC: Brookings Institution.

— and Manning, C. L. (1989), 'The effect of prospective payment on Medicare expenditures', *New England Journal of Medicine*, **320**, 441.

Ruther, M. and Black, C. (1987), 'Medicare use and cost of short-stay hospital services by enrollees with cataract, 1984', *Health Care Financing Review*, **9**, 91–9.

Rutten, F. and Janssen, R. (1987), 'An economic view of inequality in health care', in Scientific Council for Government Policy (ed.), *The Unequal Distribution of Health Care*, The Hague (in Dutch).

Saltman, R. B. and Von Otter, C. (1987), 'Revitalizing public health care systems: a proposal for public competition in Sweden', *Health Policy*, **7**, 21–40.

Schaller, D. F., Bostrom, A. W., and Rafferty, J. (1986), 'Quality of care review: recent experience in Arizona', *Health Care Financing Review*, annual supplement, 65–74.

Scheffler, R. M., (1989), 'Adverse selection: the Achilles heel of the NHS reforms', *The Lancet*, April 29, 950–2.

— Gibbs, J. O., and Gurnick, D. A. (1988), 'The impact of Medicare's prospective payment system and private sector initiatives: the Blue Cross experience, 1980–1986', report prepared by the Blue Cross and Blue Shield Association with the Research Program in Health Economics, University of California, Berkeley.

Schoemaker, P. J. H. (1982), 'The expected utility model: its variants, purposes, evidence and limitations', *Journal of Economic Literature*, **xx**, June, 529–63.

Sen, A. (1977), 'Social choice theory: a re-examination', *Econometrica*, **45**, 53–90.

— (1979), 'Personal utilities and public judgments: or what's wrong with welfare economics?', *Economic Journal*, **589**, 537–58.

— (1980), 'Equality of what?', in *The Tanner Lectures on Human Values*, Cambridge: Cambridge University Press.

— (1986), *Commodities and Capabilities*, Amsterdam: North-Holland.

Shapiro, M., Ware, J., and Sherborne, C. D. (1986), 'Effects of cost sharing on seeking care for serious and minor symptoms', *Annals of Internal Medicine*.

Shavell, S. (1977), 'Theoretical issues in medical malpractice', in R. Helms (ed.), *The Economics of Medical Malpractice*, Washington, DC: American Enterprise Institute.

Simon, H. A. (1955), 'A behavioral model of rational choice', *Quarterly Journal of Economics*, **69**, 174–83.

— (1961), *Administrative Behavior*, New York: Macmillan.

Singer, A. M. (1989), 'Projections of physician supply and demand: a summary of HRSA and AMA studies', *Academic Medicine*, May 1989, Table 3.

Sloan, F. A. (unpublished), 'Medicare prospective payment and the use of medical technologies'.

— and Feldman, R. (1978), 'Competition among physicians', in W. Greenberg, (ed.), *Competition in the Health Care Sector: Past, Present, and Future*, Germantown: Aspen Systems.

— Morrisey, M. A., and Valvona, J. (1988), 'Effects of the Medicare prospective payment system on hospital cost containment: an early appraisal', *Millbank Quarterly*, **66**, 191–220.

Smeeding, T. M., Schmauss, G., and Allegreza, S. (1985), 'An introduction to LIS—the Luxembourg income study', Working Paper No. 1, Luxembourg Income Study, Walferdange, Luxembourg.

Smith, A. (1987), 'Qualms about QALYs', *Lancet*, (i), 1134–6.

Spitzer, W. O., Dobson, A. J., Hall, J., *et al.*, (1981), 'Measuring the quality of life of cancer patients: a concise QL-index for use by physicians', *Journal of Chronic Diseases*, **34**, 585–97.

Stiglitz, J. E. (1982), 'The inefficiency of stock market equilibrium', *Review of Economic Studies*, **49**, 241–61.

Stockman, D. A. (1981), 'Premises for a medical market-place: a new conservative's view of how to transform the health system', *Health Affairs*, **11**, 5–18.

Stone, J. R. N. and Rowe, D. A. (1966), *The Measurement of Consumer Expenditure and Behaviour 1920–1938*, Cambridge: Cambridge University Press.

Sugden, R. (1980), 'Altruism, duty and the welfare state', in N. Timms (ed.), *Social Welfare: Why and How?*, London: Routledge and Kegan Paul.

—— (1982), 'On the economics of philanthropy', *Economic Journal*, **92**, 341–50.

—— (1983), 'Who cares? an economic and ethical analysis of private charity and the welfare state', IEA Occasional Paper No. 67, London: Institute for Economic Affairs.

—— and Williams, A. (1978), *The Principles of Practical Cost-Benefit Analysis*, Oxford: Oxford University Press.

Sutherland, H. J., Llewellyn-Thomas, H., Boyd, N. F., and Till, J. E. (1982), 'Attitudes towards quality of survival—the concept of "maximal endurable time"', *Medical Decision Making*, **2**, 3, 299–309.

Swartz, K. (1989), *The Medically Uninsured: Special Focus on Workers*, Washington DC: The Urban Institute.

Teeling Smith, G. (ed.) (1988), *Measuring Health: A Practical Approach*, Chichester: John Wiley & Sons.

Thompson, M. S., Read, L. J., Hutchings, G., *et al.* (1988), 'The cost effectiveness of auranofin: results of a randomized clinical trial', *Journal of Rheumatology*, **15**, 35–42.

Titmuss, R. M. (1950), *Problems of Social Policy*, London: HMSO.

—— (1970), *The Gift Relationship*, London: Allen and Unwin.

Tobin, J. (1970), 'On limiting the domain of inequality', *Journal of Law and Economics*, **13**, 263–77.

Torrance, G. W. (1976), 'Social preferences for health states, an empirical evaluation of three measurement techniques', *Socio-Economic Planning Science*, **10**, 129–36.

—— (1982), 'Preferences of health states: a review of measurement methods', *Operations Research*, **30**, 6, 1043–69.

—— (1986), 'Measurement for health state utilities for economic appraisal, *Journal of Health Economics*, **5**, 1–30.

—— (1987), 'Utility approach to measuring health-related quality of life', *Journal of Chronic Diseases*, **40**, 593–600.

—— Thomas, W. H., and Sackett, D. L. (1972), 'A utility maximisation model for evaluation of health care programs', *Health Services Research*, **7**, 2, 118–33.

Trebilcock, M. J., Tuohy, C. J., and Wolfson, A. D. (1979), *Professional Regulation*, Toronto: Ministry of the Attorney General.

US Department of Health and Human Services (1980–84), Health Care Financing Administration, Bureau of Program Operations, 2082 data.

Van de Ven, W. P. M. (1983), 'The effects of cost-sharing in health care', *Effective Health Care*, **1**, 47–8.

Vayda, E., Mindell, W. R., and Rutkow, I. M. (1982), 'A decade of surgery in Canada, England, and Wales, and the US', *Archives of Surgery*, **117**, 846–53.

Von Neumann, J. and Morgenstern, O. (1944), *Theory of Games and Economic Behavior*, New York: Wiley.

— — (1953), *Theory of Games and Economic Behaviour*, New York: Wiley.

Wagstaff, A. (1986), 'The demand for health: some new empirical evidence', *Journal of Health Economics*, **5**, 195–233.

Waldo, D. R., Levit, K. R., and Lazenby, H. (1986), 'National health expenditures', *Health Care Financing Review*, **1**, 1–22.

Walker, S. R. and Rosser, R. M. (eds.) (1988), *Quality of Life: Assessment and Application*, Lancaster: MTP Press.

Ward, M. (1985), *Purchasing Power Parities and Real Expenditures in the OECD*, Paris: OECD.

Washington Post Leader (1988), 'Health and insurance', *The Washington Post*, 8 November.

Webster, C. (1985), 'Health, welfare and unemployment during the depression', *Past and Present*, **109**, 204–30.

— (1988), *Peacetime History—The Health Services Since The War. Volume I: Problems of Health Care: The National Health Service Before 1957*, London: HMSO.

Weinstein, M. C. (1977), 'Foundations of cost-effectiveness analysis for health and medical practices', *New England Journal of Medicine*, **296**, 31, 716–21.

— and Stason, W. B. (1976), *Hypertension; A Policy Perspective*, Cambridge, Massachusetts: Harvard University Press.

Weisbrod, B. A. (1961), *The Economics of Public Health*, Philadelphia: University of Pennsylvania Press.

— (1978), 'Comment on Pauly', in W. Greenberg (ed.), *Competition in the Health Care Sector*, proceedings of a conference sponsored by the Bureau of Economics, Federal Trade Commission, Germanstown: Aspen Systems.

Weitzman, M. L. (1977), 'Is the price system or rationing more effective in getting a commodity to those who need it most?' *Bell Journal of Economics*, **8**, 517–24.

Wennberg, J. and Gittelsohn, A. (1977), 'On the incidence of tonsillectomy and other common surgical procedures', in J. P. Bunker, B. A. Barnes, and F. Mosteller (eds.), *Costs, Risks and Benefits of Surgery*, New York: Oxford University Press.

West, P. A. (1981), 'Theoretical and practical equity in the National Health Service in England', *Social Science and Medicine*, **15c**, 117–22.

Wickings, H. I. and Coles, J. (1985), 'The ethical imperative of clinical budgeting', *Nuffield/York Portfolios No. 10*, London: Nuffield Provincial Hospitals Trust.

Wiggins, D. and Dirmen, S. (1987), 'Needs, need, needing', *Journal of Medical Ethics*, **13**, 63–8.

Wilensky, G. R. (1988), 'Filling the gaps in health insurance', *Health Affairs*, **7**, 133–49.

Williams, A. (1972), 'Cost–benefit analysis: bastard science or insidious poison in the body politick?', *Journal of Public Economics*, **1**, 199–216.

— (1974), 'Need as a demand concept (with special reference to health)', in Culyer (1974).

— (1978), 'Need: An Economic Exegesis', in A. J. Culyer and K. G. Wright (eds.) (1978).

Williams, A. (1985), 'Economics of coronary artery bypass grafting', *British Medical Journal*, **291**, 326–9.

— (1986), 'The cost–benefit approach to the evaluation of intensive care units', in D. R. Miranda and D. Langrehr (eds.), *The ICU—a Cost–Benefit Analysis*, Elsevier.

— (1987a), 'Quality-adjusted life-years', *Lancet*, (i), 1327.

— (1987b), 'Response [to Harris]: QALYfying the value of life', *Journal of Medical Ethics*, **13**, 123.

— (1987c), 'Measuring quality of life' in G. Teeling Smith (ed.), *Health Economics: Prospects for the Future*, London: Croom Helm.

— (1988a), 'Ethics and efficiency in the provision of health care', in J. M. Bell and S. Mendus (eds.), *Philosophy and Medical Welfare*, Cambridge: Cambridge University Press.

— (1988b), 'Priority setting in public and private health care. A guide through the ideological jungle', *Journal of Health Economics*, **7**, 173–83.

Williamson, O. E. (1973), 'Markets and hierarchies: some elementary considerations', *American Economic Review*, **63**, 316–25.

— (1975), *Markets and Hierarchies Analysis and Antitrust Implications*, New York: Free Press.

Winslow, C. M. *et al.* (1988a) 'The appropriateness of performing coronary artery bypass surgery', *Journal of the American Medical Association*, **260**, 505–9.

— (1988b), 'The appropriateness of carotid endarectomy', *New England Journal of Medicine*, **318**, 721–6.

Wolfe, B. L. (91986), 'Health status and medical expenditures: is there a link?', *Social Science and Medicine*, **22**, 993–9.

Wright, R. A. (1987), *Human Values in Health Care*, New York: McGraw Hill.

Wyszewianski, L. (1986), 'Families with catastrophic health care expenditures', *Health Service Research*, **21**, 5, 617–34.

Yule, B. and Parkin, D. (1986), *Financing of Dental Care in Europe (Part 1)*, Copenhagen: World Health Organization.

Index